EDUCATION AND JOBS

The Center for Urban Education is a private, nonprofit corporation supported in part as a regional educational laboratory by funds from the United States Office of Education, Department of Health, Education, and Welfare. The opinions expressed do not necessarily reflect the position or policy of the Office of Education, and no official endorsement by the Office of Education should be inferred. The Center for Urban Education is located at 105 Madison Avenue, New York, N.Y. 10016.

EDUCATION AND JOBS:
THE
GREAT
TRAINING
ROBBERY

by IVAR BERG

with the assistance
of Sherry Gorelick

Foreword by Eli Ginzberg

Published for the
CENTER FOR URBAN EDUCATION
by PRAEGER PUBLISHERS
New York • Washington • London

PRAEGER PUBLISHERS
111 Fourth Avenue, New York, N.Y. 10003, U.S.A.
5, Cromwell Place, London S.W.7, England

Published in the United States of America in 1970
by Praeger Publishers, Inc.

Portions of this publication result from work performed
under a contract with the United States
Department of Health, Education, and Welfare,
Office of Education.

Library of Congress Catalog Card Number: 74-99815

Printed in the United States of America

To Alex Inkeles

Contents

Foreword
by Eli Ginzberg

This foreword has several objectives. First, it will seek to relate Professor Berg's inquiry into the educational requirements for employment to antecedent and current work carried on by the Conservation of Human Resources Project of Columbia University.

Second, it will abstract some of the key findings and policy recommendations of a research investigation that has been under way since 1966, under a subcontract from the Center for Urban Education in New York City, one of the Regional Laboratories of the Office of Education of the United States Department of Health, Education and Welfare. The relations between the Conservation Project and the Center for Urban Education have been cooperative and constructive, and for this we are in debt to Dr. Robert Dentler and Mr. Lawrence Perkins, respectively the Director and the Associate Director for Administration of the Center.

A third objective is to consider a few of the difficult questions that have been precipitated by Professor Berg's investigation and illuminated by his data and theories, but to which he has been unable to present definitive answers. As in every good research undertaking, the problems that are opened up may be even more important than those that are closed out.

During the past decade, much of the effort of the Conservation Project has been focused, not on the disadvantaged, but on the educated and the talented. From these studies we concluded that, while education often provides access to better jobs and better incomes, it offers no guarantee of either. Our investigations also called attention to difficulties that may arise for both the employee and the employer if a man's work requires far less performance than his educational level and his potential would permit. We had earlier concluded that too little education is a disadvantage; apparently, the proposition must be entertained that under certain conditions too much education also can create difficulty.

The studies referred to above were person-centered. They sought to illuminate various aspects of group behavior by analyzing the characteristics and performance of groups. In addition, during the past several years the Conservation Project has carried on a series of investigations into the economic and social institutions that constitute the framework within which people can earn their living:

The Pluralistic Economy (1964)*
Electronic Data Processing in New York City (1966)
Manpower and the Growth of Producer Services (1967)
Manpower Strategy for the Metropolis (1968)
The Process of Work Establishment (1969)
The Peripheral Worker (1969)
Allied Health Manpower: Trends and Prospects (1969)
The Hard-to-Employ in Western Europe: Policies and Programs (1970)

The thrust of these investigations was to emphasize the extent to which the American economy is being transformed in focus from the production of goods to the production of services, and the ever-larger role of the not-for-profit sector (government and nonprofit institutions); the wide range in

* Published by McGraw-Hill. All the other books listed are published by the Columbia University Press.

the educational and other characteristics of people employed
in the service sector; the extent to which new industries are
able and willing to tap sources of labor supply irrespective
of formal qualifications; the subtle and not-so-subtle competition for jobs between white women and Negroes; the way in
which employer practices in hiring, assignment, and promotion help to shape the labor market; and the striking differences between the United States and Western Europe in
making room for the disadvantaged, including the poorly educated.

While these several investigations of the Conservation
Project were under way, directed toward deepening our understanding of the workings of the labor market so that we
would no longer have to rely on a model at once too simple
and too rigid, public leaders and academic economists were
giving birth to a new ideology. They proclaimed that the key
to economic development is liberal expenditures for education, which, by improving the quality of labor, are the heart
of productivity increases. From the President down, the leadership proclaimed throughout the land: "Education pays; stay
in school." The economists calculated to a fraction of a per
cent the extent to which education pays.

Professor Berg, by temperament a skeptic, by training a
sociologist, and by choice a student of manpower, found the
new orthodoxy neither intellectually compelling nor emo-
tionally satisfying. He therefore set out to study the relations
of education to employment, in part by collecting new data,
in part by critically reviewing the principal empirical studies
that had earlier been concerned with this theme.

Here are some of the important findings that emerge from
his study. Professor Berg begins by stressing the bias inherent
in American life and thought that makes us look at a mal-
functioning of the labor market in terms of the personal failings of workers in search of jobs. What is more reasonable
than to postulate that if only these workers had more educa-

tion and training they would not be unemployed or under-employed?

Reasonable, yes—but not necessarily right. Among his incisive analyses is Professor Berg's critique of the conventional wisdom of researchers who have elaborated the "human capital" approach. These academics have adduced evidence suggesting that the return on investment in people is greater than the average return on other forms of investment. But Professor Berg correctly cautions that one must not be caught in circular reasoning. The critical point is not whether men and women who complete high school or college are able subsequently to earn more than those who don't, but whether their higher earnings are a reflection of better performance as a result of more education or training or of factors other than the diplomas and degrees they have acquired.

In Professor Berg's terms, perhaps the key to the puzzle is not what education contributes to an individual's productivity but how it helps him to get a better-paying job in the first place. He is careful not to challenge the "human capital" economists on the narrow ground that their calculations are faulty or that they fail to support their conclusion that "education pays"; rather, he focuses on the reality that underlies their tenet. To prove their case, Professor Berg argues, they would have to study education in relation to the intervening variable of productivity rather than jump over it and deal only with income. To bring the point home sharply, I have often asked my students at Columbia's Graduate School of Business why a leading company is willing to pay them, when they graduate, $11,000 to $12,000 annually to sell soap or breakfast foods. Why do large companies offer such handsome salaries to beginners, even those with M.A.'s? The trouble with the argument offered by "human capital" theorists may be that it is a rational explanation of behavior that is largely irrational.

One of the interesting statistical exercises in which Professor

Berg engaged was to recalculate with care the large body of data assembled by the United States Department of Labor about workers' characteristics and employers' requirements, to determine the nature and extent of changes in skills required over time in comparison with changes in the educational preparation of the American working population. His most critical finding is that with the passage of time there has been a tendency for a larger group of persons to be in jobs that utilize less education than they have. If this is a valid conclusion from the admittedly rough data, it suggests the need for caution in propagating the nostrum that more education is the answer to the nation's problems.

Educational requirements for employment continue to rise. Employers are convinced that, by raising their demands, they will be more likely to recruit an ambitious, disciplined work force that will be more productive than workers who have terminated their schooling earlier. Professor Berg's principal analyses are directed to this central line. His conclusions fail to support employer practices and convictions. First, he re-emphasizes the point made by many students about the wide range in education and other characteristics of workers in the same job category—that is, workers who do the same work and earn the same wages. Next, he finds that in certain areas, such as the selling of insurance, workers with less education but more experience perform better and earn more. This is hardly surprising, since the skill involved is modest and education is irrelevant beyond a qualifying level. Nevertheless, the enthusiasts of education continue to press for higher qualifications without reference to the task to be performed or the environment in which the work is to be carried out.

Many employers seek to justify their high educational demands by reference to the need for promoting workers into higher ranks, where their education *will* be needed. But Professor Berg makes two telling points. In many companies only a small percentage of those who are hired are ever promoted

to such positions. Further, the more highly qualified are often
no longer in the company when the opportunity for promotion arises. Their frustration with work that does not fully
utilize their educational background leads them to seek jobs
elsewhere.

Professor Berg demonstrates, by reference to the ways in
which schoolteachers receive higher compensation, the illogic
of the "education craze." Teachers who take additional
courses in order to earn salary increments eventually catapult
themselves out of the teaching arena, since they finally are
"overeducated" for classroom work.

Among the largest and most revealing bodies of data that
Professor Berg selects to review critically are those that he
obtained from the armed services and the federal civil service.
His findings are unequivocal. In every instance, the data prove
overwhelmingly that the critical determinants of performance
are not increased educational achievement but other personality characteristics and environmental conditions.

On the policy front, Professor Berg is cautious and constrained despite his devastating attack on the errors in contemporary thought and action which hold that education is
the open sesame to economic wellbeing. Specifically, he argues
in favor of upgrading many of the "overeducated" who now
fill positions in the middle ranks into the less crowded upper-
level jobs and at the same time upgrading those at the bottom
so that they could advance into middle-level positions. The
hard-to-employ could then be fitted into the lower-level jobs.
This is directly in line with the recommendations made early
in 1968 by the National Manpower Advisory Committee to
the Secretaries of Labor and HEW Manpower Programs.

The final implication of Professor Berg's analysis is for
policy-makers to focus much more on actions aimed at increasing the demand for labor. If there is a shortfall in demand—
and the federal estimate places about 11 million persons in
subemployment categories—then indeed, changing the char-

acteristics of workers by adding to their schooling cannot be *the* answer.

But trenchant as is Professor Berg's treatment of the conventional wisdom, he has had to leave certain critical issues in suspense. They should, however, be briefly noted.

The question of how enlarged efforts on the educational front are specifically connected to increasing productivity of the economy finds no answer in his book—or in the books of the many economists who have addressed themselves specifically to this issue. No one doubts that a linkage exists, but its nature remains obscure. Will economic expansion best be speeded by reducing the proportion of illiterates, improving graduate training, making certain that women are educated to their full potential, raising the level of vocational education? All these questions suggest more education, but it remains to be demonstrated just how doing more on one or all of these fronts is related to accelerating economic growth.

Another subject that has yet to be confronted sharply and clearly is the relation of education to employment from the vantage point of qualifying rather than optimal considerations. Again, few students would deny that minimal levels of educational achievement have distinct relevance, although the concept of the optimum remains to be delineated.

A third tantalizing subject, with which the author deals in passing, relates to the place of education in selection for the entrance job versus its role as a screening factor for career progression. Failure to consider future positions in initial screening is an error matched only by neglect of the consequences of having a surplus of "overqualified" persons on the staff, all waiting for advancement.

Other problems that are touched upon but not considered in depth include the relative return on investment in educational effort before and after a man enters employment. In what fields of endeavor is the level of education likely to be of determining importance in performance, and in what fields is it likely to be only indirectly related to output? How can the circularity of current "rate of return" analyses be broken into so that more meaningful findings can emerge about the relations of education, productivity, and earnings? To what extent is education a surrogate for other qualities that are predictive of a higher level of eventual performance? What are the dangers of gearing wage increments to educational accomplishments?

A book that helps to illuminate a large number of important issues, even while forced to bypass others, provides the reader with rich fare. In addition, Professor Berg has opened up important new questions and has cast serious doubts upon accepted answers to old questions that most Americans had long believed were beyond discussion. In attacking the hallowed beliefs of statesmen, employers, economists, and educators, he has let in new light where light has long been needed. And he has done so with scholarly acumen, stylistic grace, and a saving sense of humor—qualities all too rare in academe.

Preface and Acknowledgments

It gives an educator no pleasure to present the materials in this volume. As they stand, these materials will discourage both those with lofty conceptions of what education could be and those of a more practical bent who see no fundamental inconsistency between a highly principled and a highly pragmatic stance concerning education in America.

The researcher, of course, has some obligation to comment on his findings, and I have done so in selecting the book's subtitle and in the concluding chapter. It has saddened me that the data adumbrated in the research process did not inspire a more optimistic reaction; the times are sufficiently out of joint without adding the independent weight of the scientist's tables and statistics to the gloom prevailing among thoughtful Americans. It is particularly distressing to appear to launch what some will construe, mistakenly, to be an "attack" on education in its present beleaguered state. Surely there is a distinction between an effort to confront widespread and rather uncritical ideas about education with relevant data, on the one hand, and an anti-intellectual attack, on the other. The careful reader will, meanwhile, forgive a measure of despondency in an author whose science is tempered by an occasional self-indulgent expression of his feelings.

My feelings toward the research enterprise as such are less complex. It enabled me to work with many people, and, if the results of that work are distressing, the work itself was an unqualified pleasure. Sherry Gorelick, now a doctoral candidate in Columbia University's Department of Sociology, has been a creative and stimulating colleague from the outset. She more than repaid my confidence in her innumerable capabilities. Marcia K. Freedman was a constant benefactor, and it is a pleasure to acknowledge the fact in general terms. Her specific contributions are noted in appropriate contexts, but these do no justice to her role as collaborator in the best sense of the word. Gretchen Maclachlan helped at all stages of the study and inventively adapted esoteric data-processing techniques to a number of the blocks of data.

Several distinguished colleagues have read drafts of the manuscript and given abundantly of their very limited time. Among them are Professors Giulio Pontecorvo, James W. Kuhn, and Maurice Wilkinson, of Columbia University's Graduate School of Business. These gentlemen made detailed comments and gave much helpful technical advice. Professor S. M. Miller, of New York University, also gave generously of advice and, in a way, helped to bring about the research effort by his encouragement before the formal study ever began. Edward Robie, of the Equitable Life Assurance Company, was most generous in offering comments after a close reading of the document. Professor David Rogers, of New York University, read a very early draft and made many valuable suggestions, as did Professor Robert Dreeben, of the University of Chicago. None of these readers bear any responsibility, however, for the formulations or interpretations contained in the report.

I am especially pleased to acknowledge the thoughtful comments of Louis Hacker, Emeritus Professor of History at Columbia. This indefatigable scholar, with endless patience and extraordinary erudition, is a model intellectual. I am richer for having made his acquaintance and will recall this enterprise as the happy excuse that brought us together.

Robert Dentler, Director of the Center for Urban Education, and his staff have been helpful at all points. Professor

Dentler's generous views toward the original project and the Center's support facilitated my work to a most significant degree. The fact that he never once sought to influence the study in any way speaks more than a little for this scholar's sensitivity to the nature of research. In the same context, I am happy to acknowledge the support of the Faculty Research Review Committee of the Columbia Business School; its members were more than tolerant.

I am grateful, too, for a sabbatical leave from Columbia during the academic year 1966–67; Deans Courtney Brown and Garland C. Owens, with the then Provost of the University, Jacques Barzun, arranged for the details of my association with the Center for Urban Education to be appropriately folded into my Columbia University obligations during that valuable year.

Thanks must also go to many students and colleagues who patiently listened to me during the long period in which I was "fixated" on my work. I must have bored them often indeed, but they never acknowledged that.

Finally, it is a pleasure to acknowledge the valuable help rendered by Ruth Szold Ginzberg in her thorough review of the final draft of the book; she facilitated the movement from typescript to book by her careful and graceful work. At the final stage I am the beneficiary of Gladys Topkis, of Praeger, whose enthusiastic guidance has made my relationship with my publisher a most agreeable one.

It is impossible to properly acknowledge Eli Ginzberg's many important roles in my life as colleague and friend. He has been a constant source of delight and support. It is similarly impossible to express my gratitude to my wife; among other things, she saw me through a series of personal tragedies at the study's outset and, thereby, made so many things possible.

The dedication to Alex Inkeles, of Harvard University, reflects, in part, the fact that I had trouble with a question he raised in 1957; psychologists refer to the phenomenon as the Ziegarnik Effect. It required an entire book to be liberated from the enduring sense of "task incompletion."

IVAR BERG

New York City
November, 1969

EDUCATION AND JOBS

I Educational Commitments: An Overview

Few other topics enjoy the favored place accorded education on the contemporary American agenda of public concerns—a reflection of the "academocracy" we have become. There are almost as many people attending school full time in America as there are working in full-time occupations. Today 99 per cent of all eligible preteen children are in school; as recently as 1910 there were nearly two million employed youngsters aged 7–13.

No matter what statistics are charted to measure America's educational commitments, the direction is up and the magnitudes are increasing. In 1950, 59 per cent of all persons 17 years or older had graduated from high school; by 1964 the figure was 76.3 per cent. Americans spent $9 billion on education in 1950, $29 billion in 1963, and nearly $49 billion in 1966–67. In 1956, some 309,000 Americans earned college degrees, compared to 500,000 in 1964. And whereas slightly more than 20 per cent of the students who completed fifth grade in 1944 went on to college, more than 40 per cent of fifth-graders in 1957 eventually entered college, a remarkably high "school retention" figure.

The public has become education-conscious to an extraordinary degree, a fact that helps to explain the considerable rise in the educational attainments of the work force and the boom in what has been termed, somewhat infelicitously, the knowledge or education industry. The well-publicized concern of parents, young people, and a variety of social commentators with education and academic performance is more than matched by the concern of researchers, educators, government policy-makers, and businessmen. Thus we note a phenomenal increase in interest in education—that is, in schooling and related training programs—among economists, manpower experts, foreign-aid officials, marketing specialists, publishers, and even investment analysts in the nation's financial centers. In each of these circles, education, generally equated with years of formal schooling, is seen as a major factor affecting productivity, economic growth, income shares, and the array of other phenomena that corporations consider in decisions regarding plant location, advertising, and production planning. But the possibility that there may *not* be a considerable disparity between the educational achievements of the American work force and the educational requirements for a significant proportion of jobs—a possibility explored in this book—has been ignored.

Sociologists, of course, have traditionally regarded education as among the crucial influences affecting the rates of everything from social mobility to social pathology. In a task-force report of the President's Crime Commission, two sociologists mobilized data suggesting that juvenile delinquency is linked to school failure and to shortcomings in the response of the educational establishment to the challenge that such failure poses.[1]

The "education craze" in America has resulted from a number of overlapping though distinguishable sets of forces. Although it is not possible to assign weights or even precise chronological priorities to these forces, they deserve mention here since many of them have helped to shape the correlates

[1] Walter E. Schafer and Kenneth Polk, "Delinquency and the Schools," *Juvenile Delinquency and Youth Crime* (Washington: President's Commission on Law Enforcement and Administration of Justice, 1957), pp. 222–27.

that this study undertakes to identify and examine; they have helped to generate the commitments regularly translated into massive expenditures for education and into the increasing educational achievements of the American people.[2]

Our commitment to education is, in historical perspective, well established. America has no feudal tradition, a fact that Karl Marx counted as significant in appraising the character of social classes in America; for example, there has been no systematic effort on the part of the "haves" in this country to counter the interests of other citizens in developing a public school system.

The support given the school system by particular groups, of course, has not been entirely free of class and class-related values; the content of public (as well as private) education that benefits from the political and financial backing of a pluralistic society understandably reflects the many bends and twists in the ideologies of the groups of which this pluralism is composed. Although class politics cannot be divorced from American education in its development, such politics did not have a simple negative effect; rather, it helps to explain both our commitment to education in general and the disparities among the components of our educational system.[3] Our class structure has thus been part of the pluralistic system in which ethnic, racial, religious, and other affiliations have shaped people's and groups' wishes and choices in such ways that the politics of status has cut across the politics of class.

The nineteenth-century frontier, with some of the "safety valve" effects imputed to it by the historian Frederick Jack-

[2] For present purposes "educational achievement" refers to years of formal schooling completed. Educational achievement in other places and times will be explored later in this chapter.
[3] For an overview, see Lawrence A. Cremin, *The Transformation of the School* (New York: Random House, Vintage Books, 1964). The best picture of present-day commitments to American education can be found in Solon T. Kimball and James E. McClellan, Jr., *Education and the New America* (New York: Random House, 1962).

son Turner, reduced the pressures on the population to see education as the one means to economic wellbeing. At the same time, it helped to reduce the potential for conflict among classes that were more clearly delineated than they were before the turn of that century. As a consequence of ethnic, regional, and other differences, debates over education were often of a different order than would have been predictable in a society of elites contending with a volatile population constrained in their economic circumstances by limited educational opportunities.[4]

The predominant reaction of Americans to the Great Depression of the 1930's provides another clue to evolving conceptions of education in America. The reports of such sensitive scholars as E. Wight Bakke, of Yale University, brought home the fact that Americans had learned well the importance of education in a society that had become highly industrialized. Bakke documented what many suspected; namely, that, by and large, unemployed Americans were more likely to blame themselves than the "system" for their unhappy circumstances in those bitter years.

Among the causes of misery regularly identified by Bakke's respondents were their shortsighted decisions to seek income over educational achievement during the boom of the '20's. Many of them stated that they were more likely to have had depression-proof jobs had they been willing to defer the gratifications that they expected to achieve by entering the labor force in favor of continuing or completing their education.[5] No one can estimate how much of the educational achievement of the population aged 40–50 today is attributable to the economic pressures generated in the "dirty

[4] For an interesting analysis of splits within a large Norwegian-American group over the common school, religious instruction, and language training, see Nicholas Tavuchis, *Pastors and Immigrants* (The Hague: Martinus Nijhoff, 1963).

[5] E. Wight Bakke, *The Unemployed Worker* and *Citizens Without Work* (New Haven: Yale University Press, 1940).

thirties" and perceived directly by them or transmitted to them by their parents.

Laws of the late depression period restricting the labor-force participation of youths gave added impetus to the role of education; almost by default, education assumed an increasingly important place as a result of the new limitation on young people's working established in child-labor legislation. In a bizarre manifestation of Parkinson's Law, education expanded to fill the time of many youths whose social roles had been redesigned by the several state legislatures, with diminished opposition from the courts, and by the 1938 Fair Labor Standards Act.[6]

Historical commitments, depression-born experiences, and the discontinuities in traditional social arrangements decreed by lawmakers thus provided a necessary cultural base for the emergence of new popular attitudes toward education. The needs of the World War II period subsequently drove home additional lessons about the significance and potential of education, as America adapted institutions and attitudes to the exigencies of international conflict.

Wartime productivity gains in the domestic economy and the successes of our military forces were, to a considerable degree, related reflections of the capacity of Americans to train and educate large masses of people in a relatively short time. That the members of a "civilian" Army (and Navy) should be rewarded for their sacrifices by subsidized educational and training opportunities (the "G.I. Bill") reflected the nation's implicit acknowledgment of the importance of education and training even as it sought a way to express its gratitude to returning servicemen and women. Screening programs, con-

---

[6] A federal child-labor law, the Keating-Owen Act, was passed by Congress in 1916 but was declared unconstitutional in 1918. A similar act of 1919 was declared unconstitutional in 1922. The Child Labor Amendment to the Constitution was submitted to the states for ratification in 1924; by 1950, only 26 of the necessary 36 states had ratified it.

ducted in connection with the needs of the War Department during World War I, had already indicated some of the manpower losses that accrue to a society through inadequacies in its educational programs. Such losses, reconfirmed by the rejection figures of the Selective Service System in the '50's and '60's, have strengthened arguments that a great deal of training must be undertaken to satisfy America's defense requirements, even if there were no substantial benefits to individuals or to the economy to be derived from public policies to "upgrade" the intellectual-educational achievements of "disadvantaged" Americans.

Education and the Postwar Years

The Employment Act of 1946 spelled out the federal government's responsibility for economic planning and research and virtually guaranteed education a place in the forefront of public-policy concerns. Despite events during the worst years of the Cold War and the tight labor market of the postwar era, interest in education continued to grow; after all, during the early postwar years the population move to the nation's suburbs took on boom proportions. This movement was caught up almost immediately with concerns about the educational dollar. The facts of population growth, technological changes, and the upgrading of job requirements also guaranteed continuing cumulative commitments favoring education.

The place of education in popular thinking was nowhere better illustrated than in the apparent indifference and therefore approval with which the American people responded to the policy that gave large numbers of college students deferments from military service during the Korean War. With almost no opposition, defense manpower planners Anna Rosenberg and John Hannah, the latter a college president, were able to encumber a democracy with the strange idea that "brainpower" must be liberated from the military obligations facing the many thousands of World War II veterans who were recalled as reservists to fight in Korea and the hundreds of thousands of younger men for whom college was not a likely prospect. This concept, which has enjoyed Congressional support, has continued to inform Selective Service policy during the war in Vietnam.

The launching of Sputnik in 1957 and the attendant successes of the Soviet scientific establishment spotlighted education in America as never before. Critics of American education capitalized on this highly sophisticated scientific achievement of a rival power to stir deep American anxieties about the state of education. Admiral Rickover's battles with those of his fellow officers who had been notably unenthusiastic about the role of nuclear technology in the United States Navy were featured in news columns, and comparisons were drawn between Soviet and American educational programs, to the disadvantage of the latter. Indeed, an obscure Harvard graduate student who had written a book on Soviet professional education a year before Sputnik[7] became a national figure overnight when he interrupted his doctoral studies for a televised interview with the late Edward R. Murrow, in which these comparisons were reviewed. Although it is nonsensical to believe that Sputnik "caused" the current excitement, it does seem that the orbiting packages of Soviet scientific and technological achievements, together with East-West tensions, provided the necessary impetus to move a host of issues surrounding American education to stage center. Most knowledgeable observers, for example, would credit the National Defense Education Act of 1958 to Sputnik.

A revolution with respect to research and development in

[7] Nicholas DeWitt, *Soviet Professional Manpower: Its Education, Training and Supply* (Washington: National Science Foundation, 1955).

America, of course, was already under way before the advent of Sputnik; reports had appeared with increasing frequency concerning alleged shortages of engineering and scientific personnel. Business leaders, meanwhile, were paying technicians starting salaries of a magnitude that reflected manpower shortages in industry. The growth of defense industries, the beginning domestication of computer technology, and the enormous strides of the electronics industry had contributed significantly to the growing demands for "educated manpower."

In the period after the Korean War, before we became parties to a space race, it was already apparent that the outcome of our contest with the Soviet Union would not be unrelated to developments in the American economy. Recognition of this fact, during a time when the economy was sluggish, generated a prolonged debate about the conditions necessary for increasing the rate of economic growth. Although this problem had interested professional social scientists concerned with European recovery and, later, those concerned with the "developing nations" of Africa, Latin America, and Asia, the role of education in national economies had not been considered systematically before the mid-1950's.

It was perhaps in connection with this problem of growth that education received its biggest boost since Sputnik. This boost, inevitably, was reflected in the work of economists. In a widely heralded effort to delineate the contribution of various factors to economic growth, Edward Denison, of the Brookings Institution, reported his estimates that education accounted for 23 per cent of the growth in total national income and 42 per cent of the growth in per capita income in the United States from 1929 to 1957.[8] His figures were remarkably close to those in the landmark study published in

[8] Edward F. Denison, *The Sources of Economic Growth in the United States and the Alternatives Before Us* (New York: Committee on Economic Development, 1962).

the same year by Theodore Schultz, of the University of Chicago.[9]

These studies and others by Schultz and Denison, together with studies of the "rate of return" on investments in "human capital" by Gary Becker (1962 and 1965), Jacob Mincer (1962), Fritz Machlup (1962), and related investigations by Weisbrod, Hansen, and others[10] have almost persuaded economists to consider "improvements in the quality of human resources as one of the major sources of economic growth."[11] These conclusions, which are examined in Chapter II, confirm the assumption of most sociologists that education is one of the most significant characteristics of American social structure.

Since students in these two disciplines assigned such enormous weight to education in their studies of economic growth and social mobility, it is hardly surprising that their views found expression in the policies of a government responsive to intellectuals in general and social scientists in particular. President Kennedy's design for his war on poverty especially gave considerable weight to programs calculated to remedy the individual and personal deficiencies of the poor and unemployed. These deficiencies were defined, in large part, as shortcomings in the educational backgrounds of low-income groups, shortcomings that had to be eliminated in order that the "other America" might find work in an economy that by 1962 was beginning to quicken its pace.

The idea fell on willing ears in a society that accepted a mechanistic interpretation of the relationship between education and employment. If jobs require increasing educational

---

[9] Theodore W. Schultz, "Reflections on Investment in Man," Supplement, Oct., 1962, "Investment in Human Beings," *Journal of Political Economy*, LXX, Part 2 (1962), 1-8.

[10] See Mary Jean Bowman, "The Human Investment Revolution in Economic Thought," *Sociology of Education*, XXXIX (1966), 111-37, for a convenient summary and detailed citations.

[11] Schultz, *op. cit.*, p. 3.

achievements, and if the society provides opportunities for education, then, according to the sapient orthodoxy, the burden falls upon the individual to achieve the education necessary for employment.

On the face of it, such logic is not vulnerable to much criticism. Difficulties arise, however, if "educational opportunities" are not truly available, without restriction, to all. Difficulties also arise if the quality of education is not uniform and if, as a consequence of variations, some groups encounter education in a way that diminishes rather than reinforces the urge to pursue academic achievement.

For all its advantages, the war on poverty in its first years has had little impact on urban schools in low-income areas, where young people have dismal encounters with the learning enterprise. Nor has the "war" substantially affected the distribution of American wealth in ways that facilitate the formation of positive attitudes among low-income people toward their children's schools or educational experiences. Nevertheless, it has become accepted doctrine that education is an important answer to many of the questions that emerged when the "other America" was discovered on the "new frontier" by the builders of the "great society."

The emphasis on education in the war against poverty was not entirely naive, as the preceding paragraph might imply, nor was it entirely misplaced. Changes in the occupational structure of the American economy cannot be gainsaid by pointing to the oversimplifications in programs that do not create jobs in proportion to population increases, or that fail to educate large numbers of urban youths. Thus, while America fools many of its young by linking job opportunities to diplomas and degrees from schools that provide sometimes pitifully inadequate—indeed, appalling—experiences, the demand for a better-educated work force has grown in relation to changes in the mix of occupations accompanying technological and other changes in American industry.

These changes, which are considered in Chapter III, undoubtedly help to account for the changing educational requirements for jobs. Employers, particularly in the private sector, are generally committed to the position that it is entirely sensible to keep raising their educational requirements. By so doing they have contributed significantly to the concerns about education already discussed. The fact that education has also become a profitable area for business enterprise both reflects and feeds the surges of interest embodied in popular debate and public policy concerning education.

Education, in fine, has become a big issue. The events, problems, and assessments of the post-World War II era have seemingly confirmed the relevance of education in a society in which education was, early, a valued component of its cultural base. Our democratic commitments give ideological support to the proposition that an educated population is an informed population, better equipped to govern itself through judicious appraisals of public issues. Our commitments to cultural traditions, such as they are, give additional impetus to the expansion of facilities in which creativity and sensitivity are nurtured. Our commitment to pragmatism assures a place for education as the instrument by which utilitarian values are most rationally transmitted. Our concern—at least the concern of most Americans—that Americans share a political ethos guarantees schools a sanctified place in the hierarchy of institutions in which the imperatives of citizenship and other tribal values may be transmitted.

The Present Research Problem

In most assessments of the benefits and "returns" accruing to America and its citizens from education, there has been a distinct bias in favor of the assumptions, logic, and methods of the economist. However, although a method that employs dollar values may reveal some of the elements in the story, it does not make room for other correlates of education to which pecuniary value are not easily attached. The present investigation was undertaken specifically to identify some of these correlates.

As was noted earlier, employers are among the groups contributing to the current emphasis on education, and, since job opportunities are so intimately linked with the wellbeing of our citizens, employers' use of educational requirements in the labor market becomes strategically important. It is their behavior and the consequences of their behavior upon which the present research focuses.

Analyses which examine the benefits of education tend to consider only income and related returns and to define costs in narrow terms. Employers have been inclined to accept a parallel logic without much question in the administration of wages and salaries, believing in general that better-educated employees will be better for their organizations. According to managers in private enterprise, educational achievements have been taken as evidence of self-discipline and potential for promotion. Moreover, trainability is presumed to correlate with educational achievement, as are productivity, personality —important in many jobs— and adaptability.

When employers' assessments are combined with the careful accounting calculations of economists and the findings of sociologists that increased education is associated with "better" social values and child-rearing practices, the case for education seems buttressed indeed. However, the bearing of education upon the numerous problems that perturb employers and, when given publicity, other interested observers has not been examined.

In this study such problems as turnover, productivity, and worker dissatisfaction are considered in conjunction with the educational achievements of workers in a large number of occupations, at the upper as well as the lower end of the skill hierarchy, in a broad array of organizations, both public and private.

It is not easy to put a price tag on worker dissatisfaction, nor is it easy to evaluate quantitatively the net gains and losses to employers and to the "system" that accrue from worker turnover and other aspects of personnel policy. Nevertheless, the case for investments in education[12] and for upgrading educational requirements in personnel-selection procedures is not complete until a broader analysis of costs in the world of work has been developed and applied. Aggregated data on productivity and income in their relation to education tell us little of the "effects" of education in a given occupational setting and in the attitudes of workers. Moreover, the assumptions of employers concerning the alleged superiorities of better-educated employees are no substitutes for data demonstrating their validity.

To broaden the concept of costs and returns and to give a fuller picture than can be drawn with the economist's mathematical reconstructions, it is necessary to back away from gross data on earnings and consider other aspects of employee performance, including productivity. To test the assumptions of employers, it is necessary to examine both the data they collect about their employees and relevant data collected from representative samples of workers outside their employ.

The specific steps undertaken in the research will be explained in the chapters that follow, but the main lines of the investigation can be outlined here:

The argument presented by proponents of the general increase in educational requirements rests in part on the assumption that jobs themselves have changed in such a way that

---

[12] We are leaving aside the "consumption" value of education to individuals and society; in this study our goal is more modest—to extend the lines of analysis staked out by economists in this area and join them in begging the interesting question bearing on the cultural, political, and psychological benefits associated with education.

they require workers with higher educational achievements than were required of workers who performed similar jobs in an earlier time period. In this argument, of course, technological changes that have contributed to this state of affairs are singled out in support. However, it is not easy to assess the effects of technological change.[13] An attempt to survey the changes in "actual" educational requirements between 1936 and 1966, based on careful job studies by field representatives of the United States Employment Service, proved impossible to complete because of discontinuities in sampling procedures from 1936 to 1957. Had such longitudinal analysis been possible, the effects of the size of the labor market and of technological changes could have been examined with some degree of confidence, since these job descriptions are highly detailed, and since data on employment rates over time do capture changes fairly well, however inadequate they may be to describe a given period.

It *was* possible, however, to examine the educational requirements for about 4,000 jobs whose "constituent parts" had been examined systematically in 1957 *and* in 1965, and for which educational and training requirements were meaningfully estimated for both periods. These data, adjusted so that they could be used in conjunction with census reports on the educational achievements of the work force by occupation, have made it possible to estimate the relationship of "real" educational requirements for jobs to the educational achievements of the American labor force.[14] In Chapter III the mechanics of this laborious enterprise are reported, together with the conclusion that since "achievements" appear to have exceeded requirements in most job categories, it cannot be argued helpfully that technological and related changes attending most

<hr>

[13] For a brief, lucid, and relevant discussion, see Robert M. Solow, "Technology and Unemployment," *The Public Interest*, No. 1 (1965), 17–26.

[14] Such an analysis was first attempted in 1962, by R. S. Eckaus, of the Massachusetts Institute of Technology. See Chapter II, below.

jobs account for the pattern whereby better-educated personnel are "required" and utilized by managers.

In the face of these findings, we will examine in detail the reasons managers give in defense of educational requirements for employee selection, with special reference to job categories for which educational requirements have been raised in recent years. In Chapter IV these reasons are reported as they were gleaned from interviews with employers in the packaging, steel, rubber, textile, and other industries. In most industries the employers sought to justify the decision to use education as a "screening device" by claiming that educational achievement is evidence of an ability to get along with others and to make the most of opportunities. They also made reference to the greater potential of better-educated workers for promotion to higher-paying, more skilled and responsible jobs.

However, when efforts were made to pinpoint the ways in which "better-educated" workers prove to be superior to those with less formal education, it was discovered that business firms typically do not collect data that would make such comparisons possible. Where relevant data are available—for example, on such matters as grievance patterns, turnover, productivity, absenteeism, and worker attitudes—they are rarely analyzed as a means of discovering the validity of *any* selection procedure or screening device. The argument of employers that "information costs are high" must be weighed against the facts that computer technology has made personnel studies increasingly easy and that manpower costs are among the largest expenses facing most enterprises.

Assessment of the data in the next three chapters suggests the need for consolidating from other sources the parts of the puzzle they help to define. Chapters V–VIII accordingly report our efforts to specify the relationships between educational achievement and workers' performance on the basis of (1) published materials that typically deal with the work performance of employees in middle- and low-level occupations;

(2) a secondary analysis of data on white-collar workers in each of several firms; and (3) original studies of a variety of employees in an insurance company, a large metropolitan bank, a national news magazine, the eight branch plants of a Southern textile company, and a paper-manufacturing company.

The conclusions do not give much comfort to those who argue that educational requirements serve managers well as a screening device with respect to either potential or actual performance.

Since managers frequently point to the importance of hiring "promotable" employees, it is useful and relevant to consider whether employees in diverse employment settings go up the ladder of occupational success more rapidly as they are better educated. The results of an examination of employees' careers in a large urban telephone company, an urban power company, six electrical manufacturing companies, and at the middle levels of a large company in the electronics field indicate that organizational careers are a function of loyalty, longevity, and a certain managerial capacity to splinter the skills of others into diverse vertical categories that exhibit nominal rather than real differences. Except at higher levels (engineers and scientists), educational differences tend to wash out among employees at any organizational level. These findings, reported in Chapter V, illuminate those reported in a later chapter, that frequency of turnover is positively related to education.

Since better-educated workers have higher turnover rates, an organization is often obliged to promote substantial numbers of employees regardless of their educational achievements and regardless of the employer's "bias" in favor of education as a screening device. Sometimes managers are surprised to learn of the relationships between education and turnover, as in one company in which managers reported that the better-educated technicians in their employ were the "best" technicians. As the data from his company will show, the less educated technicians received higher evaluations from supervisors and had longer service than technicians with higher educational achievements in comparable jobs; the managers, however, assumed that these "better" employees had completed more years of schooling!

An assessment of education in its relation to worker attitudes is a risky enterprise, for we do not know what mixture of favorable and unfavorable work attitudes is optimal for the firm, for the individual or for our industrial society. It is hard to believe that worker discontent necessarily detracts from ambition or that satisfaction contributes to productivity. The literature in this realm of sociological interest could be selectively cited to prove almost anything.[15]

In general, however, managers spend considerable sums of money on worker surveys, personnel programs, sensitivity training for leaders, work benefits, and other efforts to improve employee morale. The relevant question, therefore, may well be whether these practices are not in large measure designed to undo the demoralizing effects of hiring policies that stress education. In light of the current concern with employee "morale," it was logical to re-examine published studies of worker satisfaction and to undertake secondary analyses of studies in which available data pertaining to the attitudinal correlates of education had not been exploited.

The data from both types of analysis reveal that education is more often than not an important factor accounting for dissatisfaction among workers in many occupational categories and is related to dissatisfaction in a considerable variety of work experiences and employer policies. Chapters VI and VII, which present the relevant results, support the conclusion that managers who raise educational requirements are likely to

---

[15] See the widely cited discussion of this problem in Harold L. Wilensky, "Human Relations in the Workplace: An Appraisal of Some Recent Research," in Conrad Arensberg et al., eds., Research in Industrial Human Relations (New York: Harper, 1957), pp. 25-50.

purchase for themselves some, if not all, of the very dissatisfactions that their expensive personnel practices are calculated
to reduce.

The increasing numbers of employees in the public sector
make it most desirable to consider data from this population
as well. Data on the career experiences of a 5-per-cent sample
of nearly 200,000 federal civil servants, which were only partially exploited before the present investigation, are examined
in Chapter VIII, as are relevant data on the Federal Aviation
Agency; they seem to reveal somewhat more judicious recruiting and assignment practices than obtain in the private sector.
Data on the performance of military personel in technical and
other schools support the assertion that there are better predictors of the learning and "trainability" capabilities of personnel than formal educational achievement. There is scarcely
a single program in the Armed Forces for which discrete measures of aptitudes, weak as they may be, are not *much* better
predictors of performance than educational achievement.

Methodology is better examined in each of the separate
contexts in which specific methodological options were ex-
ercised. Our research moved on a broad front in the interest of
detecting the direction of the effects of education in juxtaposition with other "variables." The cumulative weight of the
evidence, together with the diverse character of the data collected, seems to support the position that we in America ought
not to accept education as an unqualified good, without taking
account of its negative correlates. Moreover, we must recognize the possibility that the positive effects of increasing educational achievement reported in some analyses, especially
those by economists, include a number that have been inferred
from somewhat spurious correlations.

II Education in Economic Perspective

Faithful adherence to tribal values requires that a discussion of education begin with the recognition that it is a good thing in itself. Unlike Oscar Wilde's cynic, who knew the price of everything and the value of nothing, Americans are eager to acknowledge the liberating and otherwise personally gratifying effects of time spent in the house of intellect. In PTA manuals, commencement speeches, and college catalogues, zealous defenders of culture and learning express paeans to the "well-rounded man." And few doubt the benefits to a democratic society of a citizenry whose constructive participation in the process of self-government is enhanced by the "decent respect for the opinions of mankind" that can best be learned as part of the educational experience.

These widely held and entrenched beliefs have caused economists to be wary in their studies of expenditures for education, although they have long known that people, or their productive capacities, are an important part of what Adam Smith called the wealth of nations. While a few economists in recent years have sought to pursue the implications of the fact that people "invest" large sums in themselves, others have objected that the mere thought of investment in human beings is offensive. In a discussion of the point, one of the leading economists at work in this field has written:

> Our values and beliefs inhibit us from looking upon human beings as capital goods, except in slavery, and this we abhor. We

are not unaffected by the long struggle to rid society of indentured service and to evolve political and legal institutions to keep men free from bondage. These are achievements that we prize highly. Hence, to treat human beings as wealth that can be augmented by investment runs counter to deeply held values. It seems to reduce man once again to a mere material component, to something akin to property. And for man to look upon himself as a capital good, even if it did not impair his freedom, may seem to debase him.[1]

Accordingly, a colleague, from his position of leadership in an important professional society, has charged that the economics profession is demeaned by analyses which indiscriminately draw analogies between physical capital and the "human capital" that is "formed" by education; the calculation of rates of return on education, he argues, represents a form of misplaced empiricism. For him and others, the most significant benefits of education, including the critical faculties of educated men and women that lead them to change society, are not amenable to quantitative techniques.[2] Faith, at least as much as reason, should guide our worship at the shrine of knowledge.

In their daily living, however, few Americans see any conflict between education as an end in itself and education as a means to other, "lesser" ends. A bizarre expression of this attitude is observable among some of the students who have recently upset university campuses and who have demanded that courses be offered, with academic credit, in methods of campus revolt.

Social scientists presumably pervert education no more

[1] Theodore W. Schultz, "Investment in Human Capital," *American Economic Review*, LI (1961), 1–17, reprinted in Marc Blaug, ed., *Economics of Education*, I (Baltimore: Penguin Books, 1969), p. 14.

[2] Neil Chamberlain, "Second Thoughts on the Concept of Human Capital," Presidential address, Industrial Relations Research Association, 1967, reprinted in *The Development and Use of Manpower: Proceedings of the Twentieth Annual Winter Meeting* (Madison, Wisc.: 1968), pp. 1–13.

than academic purists when they seek to identify the rather large "residual" secular benefits that remain after appropriate expression has been given to education's loftier meanings.[3] One need not contest or even gainsay the highminded view of education held by the critics of the "human capital" school, as Professor Schultz has pointed out. "There is nothing in the concept of human wealth contrary to [J. S. Mill's] idea that [wealth] exists only for the advantage of people; by investing in themselves, people can enlarge the range of choice available to them. It is one way free men can enhance their welfare."[4]

Nor is it helpful to disregard the real world surrounding teachers, classrooms, and students in the service of a narrow, highly principled position on the qualitative significance of education to men in society. The fact is that education costs money; as an object of expenditures, public and personal, it will and must, therefore, be compared with other objects for which scarce resources are to be allocated by individuals and by the nation, since there are both individual and social costs to consider. It is also a fact that the educational credentials of people typically have a determinate effect, not only on the types of opportunities they will have in American society, but on whether they will have any opportunities at all.

These facts and the implications that immediately arise from them make sensitivity to the economics of education mandatory, even at the risk of taking off the emperor's robes. Surely, the most idealistic would take comfort from any evidence that their intentions concerning education are at the very least *consistent* with a modicum of social efficiency and a maximum of social equity.

---

[3] Whether the system of education in fact produces well-rounded Americans rather than cultural doughnuts is a question we typically leave to professionals in the nation's schools of education. The trained incapacities of some of these investigators may combine with their vested interests to protect us all, purists included, from the risk that any of the arguments concerning the merits of education will be much shaken by skillful and imaginative research.

[4] Schultz, *op. cit.*, p. 14.

The materials considered in this and the following chapter bear upon questions generated by the fact of education's cost and the fact of our legitimate concern with efficiency in America. For it is often implied by policy, when indeed it is not made explicit in the rhetoric of those who justify the *status quo*, that our investments in education are a factor in efficiency; that they are "needed" or "required," speaking in economic terms. It is therefore useful to identify the contributions of education to the commonwealth in socioeconomic as well as in purely cultural and intellectual terms. Does the commonwealth benefit from investments in education as much as, more, or less than the people who are educated? How do social and individual costs differ? Are there technical or, better, "functional" requirements for capabilities linked to formal education in the workaday economy, and, if there are, do they exceed in the aggregate or do they fall below the achievements of the "work force"? What methodological problems lie in the way of answers to questions pertaining to the operation of the market in which the supply and demand for education are alleged to operate?

In a society in which the market is supposed to allocate resources and, in the process, to punish inefficiency, in which full employment is a statutory objective, and in which material wellbeing is often regarded as a prerequisite to a stable and responsive political system, we wonder whether on balance there is reason or prejudice in the short-run decision-making processes that link education to the work opportunities and welfare of citizens. To put this in another way, the market imperfections in the supply and demand of education may be more important for some policy purposes than the actual definition of long-run equilibrium.

Americans who value work, individualism, and material progress often view with equanimity the disadvantages of those who stand outside their system of production. Their assumption that the education-employment nexus is rationally defined—*i.e.*, that the market is operating—squares with the judgment that those without credentials simply do not qualify for jobs and that these wretches have largely themselves to blame for their lot. The same logic can be (and often is) applied in connection with occupational mobility and income among the employed members of the American community as well: if the educational requirements for better jobs are real —that is, "functionally" necessary—and if educational opportunities are available, then the individual knows almost precisely "where it's at."

The Economic Criteria for Education and the Development of "Human Capital"

The economics of education developed relatively recently in response to "the puzzle confronting economists . . . that the rate of growth in the output that was being observed has been much larger than the rate of increase in the principal resources that were being measured."[5] On closer inspection, the "puzzle" turned out to be a problem created by economists themselves; in studies of increases in national product, they had been using such narrowly defined and refined estimates of capital and labor that they had excluded qualitative improvements in both these resources.

The remedy was a number of studies pointing to improvements in the quality of labor as one of the major sources of economic growth. These efforts were in many cases informed by the idea that investments in "human capital" could be treated, with minor modifications in conventional theories of investment, in the same manner as investments in physical capital.

[5] Theodore W. Schultz, "Reflections on Investment in Man," Supplement, Oct., 1962, "Investment in Human Beings," *Journal of Political Economy*, LXX, Part 2 (1962), 3.

Reviews of the statistical association between educational investments and growth rates provided sharp presumptive evidence that the educational achievements of a nation's work force was a significant factor in improving the "quality" of labor as a "factor of production." Two facts, however, alerted economists to the likelihood that such cross-cultural data deserved more careful interpretation. First, as Bowen points out,[6] there was considerable dispersion in the correlations between school-enrollment ratios and GNP per capita among countries, particularly in the middle range. Second, it is clear that there can be problems in countries that educate a stratum of the population whose occupational expectations are well beyond the opportunities the economy may provide in the short or even the long run.

Even allowing that the quality and distribution of investments in education are of greater moment than the quantity alone, education, it is commonly argued, makes three direct and fundamental contributions to economic development.[7] First, new techniques and ideas flow from higher education and research establishments, and these new techniques can be embodied in physical capital, which in turn determines the rate at which an economy can advance. Second, the more rapidly new skills can be given to members of the work force, "the more easily they are able to make use of production techniques, and the more likely they are to initiate changes in methods of production and methods of organization."[8] A

6 William G. Bowen, "Assessing the Economic Contribution of Education: An Appraisal of Alternative Approaches," in Seymour Harris, ed., *Economic Aspects of Higher Education* (Paris: Organization for Economic Cooperation and Development, 1964), pp. 177–200.

7 John Vaizey, *Education in the Modern World* (London: World University, 1967), pp. 52–53.

8 *Ibid.*, p. 53. This process is identified as an outcome of formal education. It is worth noting that there is evidence pointing to the increasing role of schooling over on-the-job training in America. See Jacob Mincer, "On-the-Job Training: Costs, Returns and Some Implications," in "Investment in Human Beings," *Journal of Political Economy*, LXX, Part 2 (1962), 50–73.

third but less tangible aspect of education's role inheres in the "underlying complex of relationships and attitudes which link consumers and workers and management."[9]

These are reasonable statements as they stand, and they will upset few since they assert no specific ideas about magnitudes and weights. Economists, however, like other scientists, are not typically satisfied with broad qualitative statements, and a number of them have attempted to give specificity to their theoretical formulations. Among the most interesting of these attempts are those that seek to identify the personal and social rates of return on investments in education, and those that seek to identify the contribution of education to the portion of economic growth that remains after the contributions of other factors of production have been considered.

Despite differences in the detailed calculations as well as in the scope of these attempts to quantify education as an "economic good," they may for present purposes be considered together.[10] These studies have a number of revealing similarities that are more relevant in the present context than their differences in methodological tactics or over-all strategic purposes.

They measure the nation's formal educational "input" in years of schooling of the employed labor force. Apart from distinguishing in some instances among levels of schooling, they do not usually differentiate education by type or quality —that is, professional *versus* vocational education, or education in prosperous suburban schools compared with that in the schools of poverty-ridden inner-city areas. With a few exceptions, definitions of education used in the most widely cited studies, including those cited in this chapter, tend to

[9] Vaizey, *op. cit.*, p. 53.

[10] Bowen, *op. cit.*; Bruce Wilkinson, *Studies in the Economics of Education* (Ottawa: The Queen's Printer, 1965), Chapter I; Seymour Harris, "General Problems of Education and Manpower," in Harris, ed., *op. cit.*, pp. 11–95; Mary Jean Bowman, "The Human Investment Revolution in Economic Thought," *Sociology of Education*, XXXIX (1966), 111–37; and Schultz, *op. cit.*

homogenize what on even perfunctory inspection is a hetero-
geneous variable.

Education is often presumed also to be a continuous variable; approximately the same marginal differences in the
economic values are assumed to exist between, say, any two
successive years of high school. And researchers assume this
despite the recurrent finding that diplomas and degrees command a price in the labor market that goes well beyond the
marginal increment of learning that may be achieved between
the third and fourth year of high school or college.[11] An
extreme example: A number of law schools have recently be-
gun awarding a doctorate to their graduates in place of the
traditional Bachelor of Laws degree. As a result, these graduates *automatically* start at higher civil-service classifications
if they go to work for the federal government, even though
their preparation has not changed.

In some studies, on-the-job training is not broken out for
separate analysis and so it becomes a tricky matter to draw
conclusions about the distinctive role of formal schooling. As
one economist has noted, "what schooling contributes [to
national product] depends upon the factors with which human skills are combined in production and the opportunities
for on-the-job learning and training, which are in turn functions of the pace of change."[12]

The cross-sectional data on age cohorts that are typically
used in studies of the economic returns to education pose
problems as well, for they present only approximations of
lifetime earnings. This fact makes it difficult to draw accurate
inferences about the actual "returns" on education, and the
results vary a good deal depending on whether average or

[11] Once again there are exceptions; most current research on the economics of education focuses precisely on "the different marginalities at
different age levels."

[12] Bowman, *op. cit.*, p. 119. For an estimate of the degree of the depend-
ence to which Professor Bowman refers, see Mincer, *op. cit.*

median income figures are used for the categories of people whose incomes and achievements are compared and analyzed.[13]

The analysis of the costs of education, against which its benefits might be juxtaposed, is also fraught with difficulties, and economists have reached less than full agreement on its clarification.[14] Among the biggest bones of doctrinal contention is the manner in which best to handle the "incomes foregone" by people engaged in study. Those economists who are concerned with the workaday operations of the economy (who therefore have a strongly "institutionalist" orientation) worry about calculations of foregone earnings that assume the employability of school attenders; they argue that such assumptions are suspect in the presence of significant unemployment. Even freewheeling model-builders are a little restive about this issue, although some assume that working-age members of the population who are enrolled in school would earn not only as much as their fully employed, less educated peers but more, because they "are superior in intelligence, ambition, and dependability to those who would have better employment opportunities."[15] The reasoning, meanwhile, that

. . . the "sudden" appearance of some ten million young people on the labor market could not result in anything but wholesale unemployment . . . would be fallacious since there is no question of actual transfer, either sudden or gradual,

[13] See Harris, *op. cit.* Professor Gary Becker uses both average and median earnings in his analysis and argues that the former "are clearly more appropriate when calculating cohort gains; perhaps medians are better for other purposes" (*Human Capital*, New York: Columbia University Press, 1964, p. 76). Average incomes have an upward bias owing to the effect of a relatively small number of very high incomes.

[14] For a helpful and essentially nontechnical discussion, see M. Blaug, "The Rate of Return on Investment in Education," in Blaug, *op. cit.*, pp. 231–36, reprinted from *The Manchester School*, XXXIII (1965).

[15] Fritz Machlup, *The Production and Distribution of Knowledge in the United States* (Princeton: Princeton University Press, 1962). p. 95. Professor Machlup does not *commend* such an assumption; he merely says that this would be "another procedure" regarding opportunity costs in studies of education.

from school to the labor market. The comparison is between hypothetical systems, both long established and well functioning; hence no transition period, no adjusting with frictions, need be taken into account.[16]

"Hypothetical systems," of course, can always be made to be "well functioning." Such a statement by itself, however, provides a wondering critic with no reassurance concerning various estimates of earnings potentials of students-turned-employees. Imperfections in the market for labor make it difficult to accept the "marginalist" argument without reservation or qualification. Nevertheless, estimates of such earnings potentials are used in numerous studies reported in the economics literature when foregone earnings—as much as three fifths of the cost of education in some studies—are added to other educational costs. The argument tends to slip from assumption to policy recommendation rather too quickly in these studies to leave one entirely sanguine about the inadequacy of the logic or the possibility that the dislocation problem to which Professor Machlup refers is merely one of marginal significance and of short- *versus* long-run nature.

There are, after all, many steps on a scale between one "marginal" student who chooses work over study and "ten million" extra young people in the labor market, as an examination of the rewards to workers of different educational achievements makes clear. Thus the large numbers of young people with college-level abilities who do not attend college will not necessarily earn incomes substantially higher than others who enter the work force either after high school or during their high-school years. As Professor Becker points out in a summary at the end of his path-breaking analysis,

General observation indicates that college graduates tend to be more "able" than high-school graduates, apart from the effect

16 *Ibid.*, p. 94.

of college education. This is indicated also by information gathered on I.Q., rank in class, father's education or income, physical health, ability to communicate, and several other distinguishing characteristics. A few studies permit some assessment of the relative importance of ability and education in explaining earning differentials between college and high-school persons. By and large, it appears, ability explains only a relatively small part of the differentials, and college education explains the larger part. Apparently, moreover, the rate of return from college is positively related to the level of ability since there is evidence that *ability plays a larger part in determining the earnings of college than high-school persons.*[17]

It has also been established, in analyses of wage differentials between whites and nonwhites, that the latter will have lower earnings than whites *in each category of educational achievement*, a fact that underscores the considerable difficulties of dealing with the matter of foregone incomes in calculating private returns on educational investment. Indeed, these difficulties highlight the importance of employment levels and such related factors as "market and nonmarket discrimination." The average 1967 income among nonwhite men who had completed high school or had one year of college or more, and who were employed in March, 1968, was about three fourths the average of similarly situated white men.[18] These disparities occur no matter how the data are broken down; Dr. Waldman, an economist in the Bureau of Labor Statistics, points out:

> Even within an occupation group, nonwhite workers are more likely to be found in the less skilled, lower paying jobs. Among men employed as white-collar workers, there was little difference in 1968 in the median years of school completed—13.3 for white men and 13.0 for the nonwhites. Despite this, in every

[17] Becker, *op. cit.,* p. 154–55. Emphasis added.
[18] Elizabeth Waldman, "Educational Attainment of Workers," *Monthly Labor Review,* XCII (February, 1969), 14–22.

educational category, average nonwhite income was $2,000 to $2,500 lower than white income.

Better educated nonwhite men frequently have the same if not lower income as lesser educated white men in the same occupation. In white-collar work, the average income for white men who had completed elementary school or less ($5,900) was about the same as that for nonwhite men who had high school diplomas. In professional, technical, or related jobs, white high school graduates averaged about $8,550 in 1967 compared with $6,200 for nonwhite men with one to three years of college and $8.050 for nonwhite college graduates. White college graduates in professional and related occupations averaged $10,500. The same income relationships held true among blue-collar and service workers.[19]

The cumulative effect of marginal cases on the aggregated data do not, therefore, leave one entirely comfortable with the dichotomy implied in theoretical thinking on the subject of earnings, educational achievement, and employment.

Another issue that attends the marginalist argument has to do with the fact that a useful estimate of foregone earnings must take into account the alternative uses to which educational dollars might be put by the investor. Professor Bowen makes this technical point clearly in a classic survey of the published literature on the economics of education:

Since the monetary benefits of education accrue over time, it is necessary to use some discount factor to take account of the fact that a dollar earned tomorrow is less valuable than a dollar earned today, and computations of the present value of the future stream of benefits to be expected from education are, of course, very sensitive to the discount factor used. Houthakker has made some calculations (based on 1950 census data for the United States) which indicate that the capital value (present value) at age 14 of before-tax lifetime income associated with four or more years of college ranged from a figure of $280,989

19 *Ibid.*, p. 22.

if a zero discount rate is used to $106,269 at a 3-per-cent rate of discount to $47,546 at 6 per cent and to $30,085 at 8 per cent. Unfortunately, there is no simple answer to the question of what is the right discount factor, and this question has in fact been the subject of considerable debate.[20]

Income as a Measure of the Value of Education

Many of the issues generated in efforts to assess the personal or social costs of education are related to an even more fundamental problem than that of foregone earnings. In nearly all empirical studies of the economics of education, the income of population groups differentiated by education is considered a measure of their productivity—that is to say, of the contribution of each educational group to the economy. The logic involved in such formulations, which human-capital theory borrowed from earlier and more general economic thinking, has gained credibility from its widespread use in the study of education.

The result is that the problematical quality of assumptions linking productivity to income by using education as an "independent variable" is scarcely recognized in economic research that draws on human-capital studies. To cite a recent example, a high positive correlation between rates of change in output per worker and total labor compensation over ten industry groups suggests to the researcher that "differential trends in productivity have been associated with differential trends in labor quality."[21] In a footnote at this point, he adds:

[20] W. G. Bowen, "Assessing the Economic Contribution of Education: An Appraisal of Alternative Approaches," *Higher Education*, report of the Committee under the Chairmanship of Lord Robbins, 1961–63 (London, HMSO, 1963), Appendix IV, pp. 73–96, Comnd 2154-4. Reprinted in Blaug, *op. cit.*, pp. 67–100; citation from p. 90.

[21] Victor R. Fuchs, *The Service Economy* (New York: Columbia University Press, 1968), p. 60. "Labor quality" in this study includes age, sex,

"An alternative inference—that the differential trends in compensation are a result of the weakness of competitive forces and are unrelated to labor quality—seems less plausible but cannot be rejected *a priori*."[22] Here the matter drops from sight; no further attempt is made to explore the suggested alternative.

What makes it "less plausible" is the underlying assumption about the relationship of wages and productivity that informs neoclassical marginal analysis. The objections of economists who do not accept the proposition that earnings are an indicator either of productivity or of educational achievements embodied in productivity are not identical, but they are sufficiently similar to summarize together.

It has been argued that earnings reflect ability more than they do educational achievements, but this question has been clarified somewhat by studies purporting to show that educational achievement is a more powerful predictor of earnings than ability when ability is measured by I.Q. scores and class standing.[23] Such findings raise two different issues. First, they imply that the credentials are more important determinants than naked ability, or at least that the training component of educational experience has a more pronounced effect than general educational development.

Secondly, one might question the adequacy of measures of ability that rest largely on reading skills. The reader may ponder for himself the logic (and equity) of crediting with high intelligence those comfortable sons of the middle- and upper-income groups who have highly developed reading skills, extensive educational exposure, and high income while gain-

and color as well as education, but the logic is the same; the example was chosen for its explicitness.

[22] *Ibid.*

[23] See Edward F. Denison, "Appendix to Edward F. Denison's Reply," in Study Group in the Economics of Education, *The Residual Factor and Economic Growth* (Paris: Organization for Economic Cooperation and Development, 1964), pp. 86–100; and Becker, *op. cit.*, Part II.

saying the intelligence of less fortunate young people whose deplorable school experiences rarely facilitate performance on tests or in classrooms but whose survival gives abundant testimony that they are not fools.

Consider also that in our way of life there are abilities and abilities. It is by no means clear how one can defend a system of income distribution without falling back on a set of values. The economy rewards some abilities well and others not at all. As Paul Samuelson once pointed out, it is singularly easy to account in technical economic terms for the differences in wages between butchers and surgeons; a more complex logic might be needed, however, to explain why plastic surgeons typically earn more than cardiac surgeons.[24]

Perhaps it is sufficient to remind ourselves that a number of complex issues arise in the use of income data. The fact of the matter is that the use of data on earnings involves different problems depending on where one stands; the idea that "we are paid what we are worth" is more easily accepted by those who stand on any given rung when they look *down* than when they look *up* the income ladder. The idea that income reflects productivity leaves open the prior issue of the determinants of productivity, but whether these be ability or surrogates for ability, such as education, certain other problems remain that weaken the causal linkages.

One difficulty arises in the way in which the income of a nation is computed. By definition, the earnings of individuals represent their contribution to national income, which is, after all, simply the sum of individual incomes. The trouble is that there are some people, as everybody, including economists, knows—hard-working wives and mothers, for example— who contribute to social welfare even though they are not in the "labor force."

This omission, however, is not the only source of distortion.

[24] Paul Samuelson, *Economics: An Introductory Analysis*, 6th ed. (New York: McGraw Hill, 1964), p. 560.

The analysis of the contribution of education (or human capital, more broadly defined) to productivity and economic growth rests on the neoclassical concept of the production function, a (mathematical) function showing for a given state of technological knowledge the greatest output quantities that can be obtained from any quantitative combination of various input factors.[25] Of this method, Erik Lundberg has remarked:

> If the total income distribution from period to period is determined mainly, or at least substantially, by factors other than marginal productivity relations, then we cannot be so sure that an estimate of the relative contribution coming from the input-factors can be based on national income shares.[26]

When Lundberg points to "factors other than marginal productivity relations," he is implying that market imperfections may have more to do with income distribution than the maximizing behavior attributed to a firm under perfect competition. When economists cross their marginal cost and revenue curves, they are, of course, thinking about hypothetical firms. They do not allow for such distortions as employers with the market power to indulge their tastes; the tendency to create a corps of permanent workers in internal labor markets; the typically limited information of job-seekers; and

[25] Evidence that academics, including economists, do not fetter themselves with the detailed trappings of production functions may be found in the pages of the *Bulletin of the American Association of University Professors*, in which economists examine university pay scales. Most professors would have to acknowledge their gratitude to Professor Baumol for his imaginative efforts in his colleagues' behalf; some of them may even be glad that he foregoes a discussion of academics' productivity in these helpful and scholarly presentations.

[26] Erik Lundberg, "Comments on Mr. Edward F. Denison's Paper," in Study Group in the Economics of Education, *op. cit.*, p. 69. In this same context, Professor Lundberg points out (p. 68) that "the great explanatory importance that Denison can attribute to education, in fact, depends on the big share of labor income, 70–75 per cent. The low share of capital, 20–25 per cent, gives this factor its subordinate position and instead permits more room for the residual."

the growing importance of noncompetitive groups of workers where the distinctions among groups are not necessarily continuous increments of skill or education but roles, socially defined on the basis of such variables as age, sex, and color. Furthermore, when they talk about production functions, they are typically talking about long-run trends. The problem begins when we try to fit the experience of real people and real firms into econometric models; as Lord Keynes once reminded us, the economist's long run may be a man's whole lifetime.

In a strong statement on this matter, Lord Balogh argues that the attribution of sensational effects to education is based on calculations in which the larger social framework is utterly disregarded. Instead, human-capital studies

. . . derive a residue of growth rate—i.e., that part of the growth rate which, on the basis of their own particular assumptions and constructions, remains unexplained by the increase of other factors of production—a conclusion unproven and unprovable. They then assume, equally unwarrantably, that investment in education is not merely a cause (rather than the effect, or one of several conditions) but the sole and sufficient cause responsible for the whole, or a certain artificially selected portion, of this residual growth experienced in certain historical examples.[27]

They then reverse the roles of the historical conditions and the so-called input factors and make an "iron law of education."[28]

Although Lord Balogh imputes a stronger position to the marginalists and growth economists than they themselves claim—certainly they have formulated no "iron laws"—he nevertheless reminds us that the results of many economic studies of education are at least in significant degree an arti-

[27] Thomas Balogh, "Comments on the Paper of Messrs. Tinbergen and Bos," in *Study Group in the Economics of Education, op. cit.,* p. 183.
[28] *Ibid.*

fact of the assumptions that inform the work, including the "marginalist" assumptions concerning the relationship between wages and productivity.

Without passing judgment on the matters in dispute, we can state that, used with care, the results obtained in the studies referred to have heuristic value.[29] The problems in them, however, inevitably leave us uneasy about their usefulness in helping to establish the *economic* "rationality" of making further gigantic investments in education.

One may be satisfied in the abstract that the classical models are adequate for "understanding," but they clearly do not apply in much detail to the world we know, the world in which policy is made by employers, elected leaders, and others who administer and control the nation's resources. The reader, meanwhile, will find interminable and inconclusive discussions of these issues in the literature of economics, which will convince him that many of the contentious issues in regard to the meaning of wage rates and wage levels must ultimately be regarded as matters of faith.[30]

[29] For a straightforward and lucid discussion of the programmatic utilities of these approaches, see Wilkinson, *op. cit.*, Chapter I. The ultimate utility of these approaches will be a function, not only of the resolution of the issues discussed here, but of other issues that bear, particularly, on the social gains of education to society. This question is only opened up in the present discussion.

[30] For an empirical analysis of wage rates and wage levels, see Richard Lester and Joseph Shister, eds., *Insights into Labor Issues* (New York: Macmillan, 1948), pp. 197ff. See also John T. Dunlop, "The Task of Contemporary Wage Theory," in George W. Taylor and Frank C. Pierson, eds., *New Concepts of Wage Determination* (New York: McGraw-Hill, 1957), pp. 117–39; E. Robert Livernash, "The Internal Wage Structure," in Taylor and Pierson, eds., *op. cit.*, pp. 140–72. For theoretical discussions, see Fritz Machlup, "Theories of the Firm: Marginalist, Behavioral, Managerial." *American Economic Review*, LVII (1967), 1–33: and Dennis H. Robertson, "Wage Grumbles," in William Fellner and Bernard F. Haley, eds., *Readings in the Theory of Income Distribution* (London: Allen and Unwin, 1954), pp. 221–36.

It should be emphasized, as Barbara Wootton remarked in a related context, that

> Nothing that has been said must be construed as evidence that classical wage theory, within the limits of its own carefully defined assumptions, is actually wrong. Indeed, it is characteristic of this and other economic theories that they are cast in a shape in which it is impossible to prove them wrong.[31]

Our confidence in the economic criteria that might be used to help us make sense out of the implications of policy options would be enhanced if we could fall back on more direct methods of establishing the needs, narrowly speaking, for education in our complex economy than may be inferred from studies based on classical wage theory. The idea that rate-of-return analysis provided an insufficient basis for educational policy decisions was the impetus for a more direct type of research carried out by R. S. Eckaus in 1964[32] and subsequently by several others. Despite innumerable methodological difficulties, their procedures, with some revisions and appropriate updating, facilitate a discussion of the changing relationship between job "requirements" and the educational achievements of the working population. The next chapter presents the results of an extension of this earlier work.

[31] Barbara Wootton, *The Social Foundations of Wage Policy* (New York: Norton, 1955), p. 67.
[32] R. S. Eckaus. "Economic Criteria for Education and Training," *Review of Economics and Statistics*, XLIV (1964), 181-90.

III Job Requirements and Educational Achievement

Professor R. S. Eckaus, of the Massachusetts Institute of Technology, is one economist who has misgivings about the "human capital" approach to education when the term "capital" is used almost precisely as in analyses of physical capital. To him the term is permissible only when it is used in a loose way, to denote an idea, an analogy, without any implication that educated people should be handled as physical capital—in the national accounts, for example. He argues that prices, while useful in making estimates that may serve as a basis for policy decisions on the allocation of resources, "must reflect the relative scarcities of the factors involved."[1]

He argues, further, that wages and salaries are not "reasonably good prices in the markets for education and educated labor which can be used for valuing 'human capital' and its return," and he goes on to discuss market imperfections, the difficulties in identifying the benefits of education to the firm or the worker, and other problems in accounting and in estimating relevant dimensions of the supply of and demand for education and educated people.[2] "The existence of real economic requirements for education and training," he maintains, "is not contradicted by the presence of various obstacles to the use of market values in measuring the amount of productive

[1] R. S. Eckaus, "Economic Criteria for Education and Training," *Review of Economics and Statistics*, XLVI (1964), 181–90.
[2] *Ibid.*, p. 182.

education and the return on it. An alternative approach is to attempt to estimate these requirements directly."[3]

The approach in which the demand for particular categories of "educated" labor is compared with supply, as Eckaus has pointed out, is not a novel one. Professor Seymour Harris, in an earlier and more controversial study, used a less detailed set of calculations than those reported in the following pages or those presented by Eckaus. Professor Harris advised in 1949 that parents, policy makers, and students be mindful that America was producing more college graduates than could be absorbed into occupations they would "expect" to fill and at the relatively high salaries such occupations traditionally have commanded; his suggestion receives some support in the present study.[4]

The term "some support" is used advisedly, for the data are subject to manipulation in accordance with several sets of assumptions about the meaning of various levels of educational requirements for jobs, and about the relevance to actual behavior on the job of formal educational achievements that exceed the minimum functional requirements for adequate job performance.[5] On the last point, our efforts both help and

---

[3] *Ibid.*, p. 183.

[4] I gratefully acknowledge the collaboration of Marcia K. Freedman, of the Columbia University Conservation of Human Resources Project, in the preparation of this and the early sections of the following chapter. The job was an extensive and detailed one and was successfully completed only because she willingly bore its considerable burdens and because she has the necessary technical skills and imagination. We discovered together that, as Professor Parnes pointed out in a review of the manpower-forecasting approach, "despite the limitations, the approach [of Eckaus] is deserving of additional experimentation. However, the basic data required for the analysis would take considerable time to develop." See his "Relation of Occupation to Educational Qualification," reprinted in M. Blaug, ed. *Economics of Education, I* (Baltimore: Penguin Books, 1968), p. 284. We were assisted in the task by Gretchen Maclachlan, whose skills we gratefully exploited, and by Hugh Appet.

[5] Nomenclature is obviously a problem here and in the rest of the discussion. It is not easy to determine what portion of formal education is, more narrowly speaking, a part of pre-employment training. Ideally we would speak of "functional requirements" for adequate performance, some of

hinder us in attempting to clarify the degree to which educational achievements of people in an occupational category are the result of sensible employers' efforts to improve the "quality" of their work forces when loose labor markets permit them to raise educational requirements, or are simply a reflection of the "taste" (or prejudices) of employers.[6]

On the one hand, because the data are longitudinal in nature, our efforts help make it possible, with a few parsimonious assumptions, to discover whether job requirements are changing faster than the population's educational achievements or *vice versa*. On the other hand, they hinder clarification because they make no allowance for the contribution of "excess" education to employers and their firms, a matter considered in later chapters. The issue is a crucial one and requires that we go beyond standard economic approaches, both direct and indirect, in order to speculate intelligently about whether the "excess" education is a boon, a bane, or a matter of no moment to employers and their workers.

Job Requirements and Occupational Scales

Earlier research points strongly to the proposition that, with the exception of "professionals and ditchdiggers," with respect to single personal traits and characteristics, occupations

---

which are fulfilled by formal education. To the extent that employers screen applicants according to educational achievements, we may use the term "requirements" rather broadly.

[6] In this regard, both Professors M. W. Reder and Albert Rees, in their respective reviews of Gary Becker's work (cited earlier), suggest, for example, that the earnings advantages of college graduates are less a reflection of the greater productivity of better-educated workers than of the prejudices of employers. See M. W. Reder, "Gary Becker's *Human Capital:* A Review Article," *Journal of Human Resources,* II (Winter 1967), 103; and A. Rees (Book Review), *American Economic Review,* LV (1965), 950–60.

cannot be placed in a hierarchical order that corresponds to the income hierarchy of occupations; variations in the characteristics of people performing adequately *within* occupational groups have been found to be as great as variations *among* these groups.[7]

The review by Lawrence G. Thomas, the study by Thorndike, and the technical discussion of personnel-selection devices cited here all make it clear that job requirements must be conceived as complex *patterns* rather than in unidimensional terms. In the first two references, data on the civilian occupations and personal attributes of large samples of American military personnel during both world wars provide strong circumstantial evidence that Americans of diverse educational achievements perform productive functions adequately and perhaps well in all but a few professional occupations.

These studies also make it clear that it is not possible to construct an occupational scale according to the intellectual abilities required by diverse occupations. To be sure, some correspondence between job levels and test scores was revealed in a study of the Army General Classification Test scores of more than 81,000 men in 227 occupations. On the face of it, such test data would be encouraging if the prospect of a national scale of occupational differences depended only on the validity of the sample and the reliability of the measures used. The difficulty that plagues this approach, however, as Professor Thomas points out, is that there is

. . . striking *variation* in test scores made by members of any *one* occupation . . . . If we examine the variation in test scores

[7] Lawrence G. Thomas, *The Occupational Structure and Education* (Englewood Cliffs: Prentice-Hall, 1956); Robert L. Thorndike, "The Prediction of Vocational Success," in John T. Flynn and Herbert Garber, eds., *Assessing Behavior: Readings in Educational and Psychological Measurement* (Reading, Mass.: Addison-Wesley, 1967), pp. 240–55; and Marvin D. Dunnette, *Personnel Selection and Placement* (Belmont, Calif.: Wadsworth, 1966).

in only those 172 occupations from which at least fifty enlisted men were drawn (so that our samples will be large enough to show characteristic distributions), we find that men scoring 108.3 points [the mean, or average, of the median scores of all 227 occupations] would rank above the lowest quartile of *all but 26* of these 172 occupations, and would rank above the lowest 10 per cent in all but nine occupations.[8]

Such data obviously discourage us from translating occupational wage differences into ability differences and encourage us to find alternative ways of characterizing job requirements.

Professor Thomas himself commended the job classifications that were being developed by the United States Employment Service's Occupational Analysis Section at the time he conducted his examination of education and occupational structure. The classifications that resulted from the agency's efforts are those used by Eckaus, to whose work reference has been made, and by other investigators whose methods and results are related to the present use of these classifications.[9] These studies employed estimates of "general educational development" (GED) required for jobs, estimates that were constructed through the collaboration of personnel from the Division of Placement Methods, the Occupational Analysis Branch, and the Entry Occupations Sections, all of the Bureau of Employment Security (BES) of the United States Employment Service.

[8] Thomas, *op. cit.*, p. 265. The categories and classification systems used would not adequately account for these results. Emphasis in the original.

[9] The first of these anticipated the others; it used categories approximating those of the 1940 and 1950 censuses and was based upon the *minimum* amount of education demanded by employers of job applicants in 2,216 occupations in 18 industries. See H. M. Bell, *Matching Youth and Jobs* (Washington: American Council on Education, 1940). The others: Bruce Wilkinson, "Some Aspects of Education in Canada," unpublished doctoral dissertation, MIT, 1964; John G. Scoville, "Education and Training Requirements for Occupations," *Review of Economics and Statistics*, XLVIII (1966), 387–94.

Confidence in these estimates of education (and training)[10] requirements for jobs is obviously contingent upon the validity of the scale of GED requirements that was constructed from job descriptions. Since the findings of the studies, including this one, depend so heavily on the scale of GED requirements, it is appropriate to describe that scale here. A lengthy description of the procedure involved in making the estimates in the first (1956) analysis of jobs is available elsewhere.[11]

The GED scale embraces three types of development—reasoning, mathematical, and language. Each of these was estimated separately on a scale from 1 (low) to 7 (high), and the final estimate of the requirement of each job in the analysis was the highest of the three. For this reason, and also because of variation in the quality of schooling and the possibility of learning from other experience, the Bureau specifically eschewed any attempt to translate GED into levels of educational achievement.[12] Nevertheless, in previous studies, the

[10] The two sets of estimates, one in 1956 and the other in 1966, include estimates of required "specific vocational preparation" (SVP) as well as GED; these training requirements are not considered here.

[11] *Estimates of Worker Trait Requirements for 4,000 Jobs as Defined in the Dictionary of Occupational Titles*, Washington, D.C.: Bureau of Employment Security, U.S. Employment Service, U.S. Department of Labor, 1956, pp. iv–ix, and Appendix A, "Manual for Rating Training Time," pp. 111–20.

[12] "Ordinarily such education is obtained in elementary school, high school, or college. It also derives from experience and individual study." U.S. Department of Labor, Bureau of Employment Security, *Dictionary of Occupational Titles*, 3rd ed. (Washington: Government Printing Office, 1966), Vol. II, p. 651. In the 4,000-trait study already cited, the Bureau stated that "approximate school grade equivalents are provided on the inside of the covers of this volume as an aid in evaluating an applicant's General Educational Development." This passage was deleted, however, by an erratum notation in 1958 ("Correction List No. 1"), and, in fact, no such equivalents were ever placed inside the covers of the volume. The issue is an important one, as Dr. Sidney Fine, who was Chief of the Entry Occupations Section, has emphasized in a review of the weaknesses of studies based upon these trait estimates. See his "The Use of the *Dictionary of Occupational Titles* as a Source of Estimates of Educational and Training Requirements," *Journal of Human Resources*, III (1968), 363–75.

first step was to translate GED into "years of schooling," as follows:

GED	Years of Schooling
1	0
2	4
3	7
4	10
5	12
6	16
7	18

Requirements were then reported as years of schooling, and interpretations made accordingly.

The operational problem for the present research was to compare, through a series of gross estimates, the achieved education of the labor force with the educational requirements of the jobs held for the two census years, 1950 and 1960. Since only the 1956 Worker Traits Analysis was available to previous researchers, they perforce applied the same estimates of requirements to the occupational distributions of the different census years. The publication of the second Worker Traits Analysis in 1966[13] made it possible to include the effects of changes in estimated requirements as well as in the distribution of people among jobs.

To measure the changes in requirements, it was necessary to deal with the same sample of jobs. For this purpose, the 4,000 jobs included in the first analysis were extracted from the 14,000 of the second analysis.[14] Our findings are reported in

[13] *Dictionary of Occupational Titles*, 3rd Ed., *op. cit.*, Supplement, *Selected Characteristics of Occupations*.

[14] The task was complicated by the fact that the jobs in the first analysis were designated by the code used in the Second Edition of the *Dictionary of Occupational Titles* (DOT), while the second analysis used the altogether revised coding system of the Third Edition. It was possible, however, to make the translation by using the *Conversion Table of Code and Title Changes Between Second and Third Edition Dictionary of Occupational Titles*. This matching involved many operations, the details of which need

the terms of the second analysis, since we adjusted the seven-point GED scale of the first trait analysis to the second analysis, in which a six-point GED scale was used.

Our second major operation was to assign a GED level to each of 256 occupational groups in the census tables showing years of school completed by the experienced civilian labor force.[15] This was facilitated by work sheets prepared by the Bureau of Employment Security as a first approximation to converting DOT titles to census categories. Once this process was completed, the median GED for each group was weighted by the number of workers. The result was a distribution of educational requirements (GED) for all jobs. Finally, for purposes of comparison, the educational achievements (years of school) of the labor force were reproduced from the same census tables.

Factors Contributing to Changes in Requirements from 1950 to 1960

Table III-1 presents our basic findings—the distribution of the reported educational achievements of the labor force and our estimate (using the method described above) of the distribution of educational requirements for the jobs held by the

---

not detain us here. We are indebted to Frank Cassell, Leon Lewis, Jack Newman, Adeline Padgett, and many others at the U.S. Employment Service for their assistance in this enterprise. They provided cards containing the data from the two "trait" studies, and they gave abundantly of their time and expert advice. We hope we have come close to living within the guidelines they delineated for using the estimates. We are especially grateful to Mr. Lewis and Mr. Newman, who were nearly collaborators with us in our effort. They are, however, in no way responsible for the results and are, in particular, not responsible for the translations we have made.

[15] 1950 Census, *Occupational Characteristics* (Special Report P-E No. 1B), Table 10; 1960 Census, *Occupational Characteristics* (Subject Report PC(2) 7A), Table 9. The 256 groups represent some aggregation, but they cover the entire experienced civilian labor force.

Table III-1
Education and the Experienced Civilian Labor Force, by Sex, 1950 and 1960

	Education Achieved (in millions)			Education Required (Median GED) for Census Occupations (in millions)			Median GED
	Males	Females	Total	Males	Females	Total	
1950							
Less than 8 years	10.3	2.6	12.9	3.8	0.2	3.9	1
8 years	8.1	2.3	10.4	8.9	6.2	15.1	2
1–3 years high school	7.9	3.1	11.0	8.9	6.0	14.9	3
High-school graduate	8.4	4.9	13.3	15.7	1.9	17.7	4
1–3 years college	2.9	1.6	4.5	2.2	1.3	3.5	5
College graduate	2.8	1.2	4.1	0.9	0.2	1.1	6
1960							
Less than 8 years	7.9	2.5	10.4	—	—	—	1
8 years	6.9	2.6	9.5	6.8	2.0	8.8	2
1–3 years high school	9.7	4.7	14.4	14.8	10.6	15.4	3
High-school graduate	10.6	7.1	17.7	12.7	4.9	17.6	4
1–3 years college	4.2	2.4	6.5	8.0	3.3	11.3	5
College graduate	4.3	1.7	6.0	1.2	0.2	1.4	6

labor force. These data are considered in the analysis that follows, first in the disaggregated form of Table III-1, and subsequently in different juxtaposition. Before discussing the relationships between achievements and requirements, however, we must distinguish the factors that produced changes from 1950 to 1960 *within* these distributions.

On the achievement side, the answer is straightforward; the difference simply shows the increase in years of schooling undertaken by the larger labor force. On the requirements side, however, the change in the distributions from 1950 to 1960 is the result of two distinct factors in addition to population growth: (1) the reclassification of the GED required for the component jobs (an artifact of the BES method), and (2) the growth or decline in the numbers of people holding jobs at each level.[16] Of these sources of change, the shifts that are due to reclassification (the "upgrading" or "downgrading") of individual jobs are by far the more important component.

A comparison of the 1956 and 1966 Worker Traits Analyses shows that 54 per cent of the 4,000 jobs retained the same GED, but 31 per cent were rated higher and 15 per cent lower. The majority of shifts were among low-rated jobs, and this may suggest some of the reasons for the general upward trend. Jobs at the lower GED levels tend to be designated by many different titles and vary according to industry and even from firm to firm. Apparently in an effort to simply nomenclature, the BES, in preparing the Third Edition of the *Dictionary of Occupational Titles*, combined a number of titles in the Second Edition into a new single title. The effect of these consolidations on our own study was to reduce the 4,000 job titles in the first Worker Trait Analysis by approximately one third. It was reasonable to expect some consequent up-

---

[16] Whatever bias stems from our method of aggregation and the choice of medians to represent the occupational groups is consistent for the two census years.

TABLE III-2

PERCENTAGE CHANGE IN EDUCATION REQUIRED
FOR CENSUS OCCUPATIONS, 1950–60

Type of Change in GED for Aggregated Census Occupations, 1950–60	1950 Education Required (Median GED)					
	1	2	3	4	5	6
Males						
Reclassification of GED	−100	−30	62	−19	182	−5
Population change	0	7	4	0	78	33
Total change	−100	−23	66	−19	260	28
Females						
Reclassification of GED	−100	−79	35	100	82	−17
Population change	0	11	43	53	69	13
Total change	−100	−68	78	153	151	−4

ward bias, since the GED for the new title had to be high enough to encompass the highest of the old titles. It is possible that this consolidation reflects actual upgrading of a number of low-level jobs. We can speculate that employers, having access to better-educated workers, have in fact expanded the scope of some jobs.

Whatever the reasons for the higher GED requirements, these changes had far more weight than changes in the number of individuals at each level. Table III-2 compares these two types of change for males and females. The total for each column shows the percentage change from 1950 to 1960. Thus, the net decline in jobs for males requiring GED 2 from 1950 to 1960 was 23 per cent.[17]

[17] The reader can check this by the following calculation, which uses the appropriate data in Table III-1:

$$\frac{(\text{GED-2 males, 1950}) - (\text{GED-2 males, 1960})}{(\text{GED-2 males, 1950})} = \frac{8.9 - 6.8}{8.9} = 23\%$$

The components of this change were a decrease of 30 per cent in jobs *formerly* classified at this level (weighted by the populations of these groups) and the combined increases of (a) groups reclassified *into* this level and (b) groups that remained the same (7 per cent).

Inspection of each GED level for males and females separately shows only two cases in which the increase in number outweighs the effect of GED reclassification: in jobs for women requiring GED 3, and in jobs for men requiring GED 6. In all the rest, the general upward movement of GED requirements accounts for most of the difference.

Assuming that the requirements presented in Table III-1 represent the best available estimates, while somewhat exaggerating the differences between 1950 and 1960, we can now assess them in light of the achieved education of the experienced civilian labor force. The data in Table III-1 are presented in as many categories as the constraints of the census education classifications allow; nevertheless, a comparison of "required" with achieved education involves equating years of school with specific GED levels. In addition to the problems mentioned earlier in connection with the GED scale itself, there are other difficulties in making this kind of translation; for example, we must assume that education is a continuum measured in "years of school."

Even in the unaggregated data in Table III-1, there are problems of overlapping. It is difficult, for example, to distinguish between the conceptual skills of an eighth-grade graduate and those of a high-school dropout. A more serious problem arises at the upper levels of GED and achieved education. Since the 1950 census did not distinguish those with advanced degrees from other college graduates, our first approximation of a match for jobs requiring GED 6 had to lump *all* college graduates together. This left only college dropouts and two-year technical-school graduates to fill GED 5, in spite of the fact that this is a mixed group including the second-level professions (*e.g.*, musicians, airplane pilots, nurses). In making *any* kind of match, GED 5 is the most difficult; the findings are quite different depending on how this particular problem is solved.

TABLE III-3

FIVE VERSIONS OF THE MATCH BETWEEN EDUCATION ACHIEVED AND EDUCATION REQUIRED (MEDIAN GED): PERCENTAGE DIFFERENCES FOR THE EXPERIENCED CIVILIAN LABOR FORCE, BY SEX, 1950 AND 1960[a]

| Education Match | | % Difference Between Achieved and Required Education | | | | | |
| Achieved | Required | 1950 | | | 1960 | | |
		Males	Females	Total	Males	Females	Total
Version 1							
Less than 8 years	1	16.1	15.7	15.9	18.1	12.0	16.1
8 years	2	−2.0	−24.6	−8.2	0.2	3.0	1.1
1–3 years high school	3	−2.5	−18.2	−6.9	−11.8	−28.1	−17.1
High-school graduate	4	−18.0	18.9	−7.6	−4.9	10.3	0.1
1–3 years college	5	1.7	1.5	1.6	−8.7	−4.5	−7.4
College graduate	6	4.7	6.7	5.2	7.1	7.3	7.2
Version 2							
Less than high-school graduation	1–2	33.7	10.7	27.3	40.5	37.4	39.5
High-school graduate, some college	3–4	−32.9	−9.0	−26.2	−29.3	−29.0	−29.2
College graduate	5–6	−0.8	−1.7	−1.1	−11.2	−8.4	−10.3
Version 3							
Less than high-school graduation	1–3	11.6	−27.1	0.8	6.5	−13.1	0.1
High-school graduate, some college	4–5	−16.3	20.4	−6.0	−13.6	5.8	−7.3
College graduate	6	4.7	6.7	5.2	7.1	7.3	7.2
Version 4							
Less than high-school graduation	1–3	11.6	−27.1	0.8	6.5	−13.1	0.1
High-school graduate	4	−18.0	18.9	−7.6	−4.9	10.3	0.1
Some college	5–6	6.4	8.2	6.8	−1.6	2.8	−0.2
Version 5							
Less than high-school graduation	1–3	11.6	−27.1	0.8	6.5	−13.1	0.1
High-school graduate, some college	4,5—[b]	−13.1	27.4	−1.7	−9.0	13.3	−1.7
College graduate	5+,6[b]	1.5	−0.3	0.9	2.5	−0.2	1.6

a This table was constructed by calculating the per cents for the columns in Table III-1, aggregating the appropriate cells, and subtracting the required education from that achieved.

b Occupational groups requiring GED level 5 were divided into those with median educational achievement of less than 16 years (5—) and those with 16 or more years (5+). See text.

Comparing Requirements and Achievements

Although there is a finite number of ways in which the data can be arranged, nothing is fixed about the relationship of GED and years of schooling. Depending on different assumptions about their correspondence, that is, about the matching of "requirements" with "achievements," the "direct approach" to the economic criteria for education afforded by this method can yield extraordinarily diverse findings. Thus, for example, whether there is a shortage or an "excess" of college graduates depends on whether jobs requiring a GED of 5 are regarded as jobs for college graduates or as jobs that can be performed adequately by persons who have graduated from high school and have undergone some college training. The rest of this chapter is devoted to a discussion of five different versions of the data which illustrate the importance of the assumptions that inform this kind of research.

Table III-3 presents these versions. For each version, the "required" education for a given group of occupations was subtracted from the achieved education of given labor-force groups. These differences are discussed in the text.

Version 1

Version 1 (Table III-3) shows the percentage differences for the numerical data presented in Table III-1. It exhibits the following features:

1. The excess of individuals with less than an eighth-grade education over the number required for GED-1 jobs was about the same in 1960 as in 1950—about 16 per cent.

2. A comparison of eighth-grade graduates with those in jobs requiring GED 2 shows that the match improved from

1950 to 1960 because the number of these jobs decreased faster than the population of eighth-grade graduates decreased.

3. For GED 3, the match is reversed; the increase in these jobs was greater than the increase in the number of high-school dropouts presumably available to fill these jobs.

4. A comparison of jobs requiring GED 4 (the largest single category of jobs) with high-school graduates (the largest category on the achievement side) shows that the match improved from 1950 to 1960. The proportion of jobs declined and the number of high-school graduates increased; they matched almost perfectly.

5. The increase of jobs at GED level 5 converted an "oversupply" of achievers in this category (individuals with some college) in 1950 to a shortage in 1960.

6. For GED-6 jobs, the "oversupply" of college graduates was even more striking in 1960 than in 1950 (7 per cent compared to 5 per cent).

Version 2

In the second version, the first three achieved-education categories are grouped (non-high-school graduates) and compared with levels 1 and 2 of required education; the high-school graduates and those with some college are compared with levels 3 and 4; finally, the college-graduate group is aligned with levels 5 and 6. Matched in this way, the data support the conclusion that the demand for better-educated workers has far outrun the available supply, a position often taken in connection with policy proposals calculated to upgrade the labor force's educational achievements. Accordingly, there seems to be an enormous and growing shortage of both high-school and college graduates. Such a conclusion draws some support from their wage changes relative to those of the "lowest" educational achievers. Again, however, these wage changes may reflect the tastes, perhaps the prejudices, of employers and must be interpreted with caution.

The assumptions underlying such a construction of the basic data are extreme indeed; one premise would be that high school dropouts can fill only menial jobs. Furthermore, jobs in GED level 3 would have to be defined as requiring high school graduates. Finally, by this logic, jobs at GED levels 5 and 6 can be filled suitably only by college graduates. In this version, in short, all educational requirements are defined at a maximum, and the result approaches the selection practices of employers in periods in which labor markets are "loose."

To accept this set of definitions is to accept the apocalyptic conclusions of some in America who foresee employment in the future only for the highly educated. The fact is, however, that the vast majority of the workers represented in these data *are* employed, and if the match between the job requirements and the achievements were as poor as Version 2 suggests, one could only marvel at the continued progress of the economy and the society it supports. Some readers simply will not find it credible that *two thirds* of the jobs in the American economy required a high school diploma, or more, in 1950; it would be even more incredible if the equivalent requirements covered fully *86 per cent* of the jobs in the '60's.[18]

18 Eli Ginzberg and Neil Chamberlain have cautioned us to temper these words on the grounds that we can too easily consider only one side of the picture. Another colleague reminds us that we imply an excessively narrow conception of a job, and that more realistically we should recognize that if opportunity costs in terms of creativity are included, the "excess" education pays considerable returns. The economy, they argue, might function at even *higher* levels of performance if greater numbers in the work force were well educated, an issue touched on below and in later chapters. The questions they raise go to the heart of the present study and relate to the problem of determining how much more than minimun educational achievements the economy's jobs can absorb. One may at least be suspicious of the proposition that most jobs make much room for the inputs of workers that go beyond task performance, given the foreseeable trends in the managerial arts.

Version 3

In Version 3 most of the assumptions of the previous version are "stood on their head." Here, workers without high-school diplomas are assumed to be capable of filling jobs at GED levels 1, 2, and 3. Grouped in this way, the changes in both requirements and achievements from 1950 and 1960 wash out, leaving a good match at the lower levels of the occupational distribution. High school graduates and those with post-high-school education short of a college degree are matched against jobs at GED levels 4 and 5 combined, and college graduates against level 6 jobs. For both 1950 and 1960, the "surplus" of college graduates presumably filled jobs at levels 4 and 5.

The totals, however, obscure important differences between the utilization of men and women. For men, the "oversupply" of achievers at both the top and the bottom level presumably filled the gap at the middle level. The shift of low achievers to middle-level jobs, we hypothesized, is largely attributable to age; that is, older workers with low educational achievements can offer experience as a substitute. Furthermore, long-time incumbents of certain positions often pick up additional skills on the job that permit them to function effectively in organizational slots for which the actual requirements may go up.

Some evidence for this conclusion was obtained by analyzing the educational achievements of workers holding jobs at GED levels 4, 5, and 6.[19] At each of these levels, workers over 45 years of age were underrepresented among college graduates and overrepresented among those with less than a high-school education. For the population in GED 5, for example,

[19] This analysis was limited by the number of discrete groups for which both a median GED and a cross-tabulation from Census that includes age and education were available. The population for which such information was available represented 63 per cent of workers in groups with a GED median of 4, 54 per cent of the GED 5's, and 81 per cent of the GED 6's.

workers over 45 constituted somewhat less than half of the total but 65 per cent of the non-high-school graduates and 36 per cent of the college graduates.

Among women, the disparity between achievements and "requirements" was considerably reduced from 1950 to 1960, but the picture continued to show a general downward trend with considerable "underemployment," since the number of low-level jobs for women continued to exceed the supply of poorly educated women. The higher participation rates of better-educated women undoubtedly account for the disparity between achievements and "requirements" among women; these high rates conspire to reduce the number of lower-level jobs available for less educated women.

Viewing the data in this way points up one of the reasons that unemployment rates are highest for young female Negro high-school dropouts—they are competing unsuccessfully for lower-level jobs with an available, much better-educated population group. The fact that women, for a number of reasons, move in and out of the work force, meanwhile, probably limits their opportunities to obtain higher-level jobs that employers seek to fill with more regular workers.

In this version, as in the unaggregated data in Table III-1, GED level 6 is treated as a separate category consisting of the traditional professions, scientists, and academicians. According to this version, the increase in the proportion of the total labor force in these occupations between 1950 and 1960 was negligible, from 2.0 to 2.1 per cent. Meanwhile, the proportion of college graduates went up 30 per cent, leaving a theoretical "oversupply" of highly educated manpower.

Version 4

From 1950 to 1960, there was a marked increase in the proportion of jobs at GED level 5. It is reasonable to suppose that most of the "surplus" college graduates in Version 3 were in fact employed at level 5. It is therefore worthwhile to see how the match is affected if level-4 jobs are allocated to high-school graduates and levels 5 and 6 are combined and matched with the entire group of those who went to college, whether or not they received a degree. The results appear in Version 4, and here the changes from 1950 to 1960 seem to have brought supply and demand into perfect balance, at least with regard to the totals. This version lends enormous support to recent educational policy, since the increase in achievements in the decade (added to earlier increments) was sufficient to provide the personnel for the vast increase in level-5 jobs.

What would seem to be a highly desirable state of affairs is on closer inspection a somewhat problematical one. While men, according to this version, appear to be increasingly less underutilized,[20] women appear to be *more* underutilized than before.

An even more fundamental objection may be made to the assumption necessary in this version that all GED-5 jobs require college graduates. This large and growing category, as we noted earlier, is a mixture of lower-level professions and white-collar occupations that may be homogeneous with respect to the standards that inhere in the GED apparatus but that vary greatly in certification requirements. Although not all practicing engineers and teachers are college graduates, the trend is to require a baccalaureate degree for new entrants to these occupations. College graduates in these two fields who hold degrees appear in the statistics as having attended college for four or more years. Given their typical academic preparation, however, it might be argued that their time in academe has been spent largely in what the United States Employment

[20] Students of American social structure may see in this view of developments a factor of some significance; males with educational achievements that surpass those "required" for the jobs they hold, from one point of view, have been "upwardly mobile."

Service analysts call Specific Vocational Preparation (SVP) and that they have undertaken training rather than education.

Version 5

To avoid such tendentiousness we accepted the conventional definitions and sorted the GED 5's into two groups: those occupations that usually require a four-year college degree of any kind, and those that clearly do not. The criterion was the median years of schooling reported for each occupation: those with 16 years or more were placed in the "college" group. Weighted by population, the jobs requiring college degrees accounted for 68 per cent of the GED 5's in 1950 and 32 per cent in 1960. Actually, the GED-5 jobs usually associated with college graduates increased, but the shift of many "non-college" jobs up to this level (and their increase) was responsible for the decline in the proportion of "college" jobs between 1950 and 1960.

The issue here is decidedly important in light of the considerable growth in middle-level jobs in our economy, jobs that seem to require several elements of what sociologist Erving Goffman terms "the presentation of self in everyday life." Insurance adjusters, to take just one example, must present themselves in their workaday lives as middle-class archetypes, a requirement that, willy nilly, tends to be confounded with concepts of general educational development. The gloss is an important product of the educational process in America,[21] and in a transitional period these new and expanding occupations (especially in the so-called service sector), not surpris-

[21] The experience of one major insurance company, as we shall see in Chapter V, indicates that there is no significant correlation between the gloss of its salesman, thus conceived, and the dollar values of their sales.

ingly, are likely to be miscast in terms of their "true" educational requirements. In any case, Version 5 represents a final attempt to strike a balance between theory and practice by redistributing GED-5 jobs in two segments: the "non-college" segment is combined with the GED-4 level and the "college" segment with the GED 6's. (GED levels 1-3 remain matched with non-high-school graduates, as in the two previous versions.) Therefore, Version 5 represents a compromise among possible assumptions about the nature of job requirements. The totals indicate that there is a "surplus" of college graduates who presumably "drift down" to fill the deficit at the next lowest level, but this phenomenon seems confined to males. The near-perfect match between the supply and the demand for women college graduates seems to be due to the shift of teachers involved in the allocations of the GED 5's, a hypothesis that appears to square with relevant evidence. Among women, about three fourths of all GED-5 jobs defined in this fifth version as requiring college degrees were in teaching.

Otherwise, in this last version there is the same "move toward the middle" observed with respect to males in previous versions, while women are once again filling "deficits" in supply at the lowest level of jobs.

Conclusions

No one version of the data presented in this chapter is clearly superior to the others. In each case some assumptions are attractive and some are unacceptable. The problems in estimating the nature of the utilization of educated manpower in the United States by the "direct" approach are, at the very least, a good deal more complex than might be supposed from a reading of the earlier and ground-breaking studies, even allowing for their cautious stipulations concerning the adequacy of the data.

In the conceptually most attractive versions (3 and 5), there is a distinct drift of "better" educated people into "middle" level jobs and a reduction in the number of "less" educated people who move up into middle-level jobs in the decade covered by the data. The increase in educational requirements for middle-level jobs—which may not be gainsaid by reference to other versions that are concerned with whether the increases are "justified" by changes in the jobs themselves—may thus be taking place at some cost to a society that has historically prided itself on its mobility opportunities.

Of greater concern in the present context is the finding that it is not easier to locate useful estimates of "true" job requirements by the "direct" approach than by the more straightforward approaches considered in the previous chapter. The "direct" approach, however, does avoid the specific pitfalls encountered in efforts that are anchored in classical investment theory and leaves open a variety of ways for the consideration of employer "tastes," or prejudices. As we move between Versions 3 and 5, on the one hand, and the remaining versions, on the other, we can identify somewhat more clearly the nature of these tastes and, by making different assumptions, weigh their place in manpower equations. The questions that emerge from this exercise bear precisely upon this issue.

Granted that the USES estimates of trait requirements are reasonably good and that the *best* matches of supply and demand among the versions presented actually prevail in the economy, the next problem is to determine whether, if job requirements continue to change as they have in the past, educational achievements (supply) will in the *future* outdistance demand.

A related question is whether an "excess" of the supply over the demand in the economy for education will be absorbed to the advantage or disadvantage of the nation, the managers, and people of diverse educational backgrounds. If education is a formal credential of progressively less economic importance, a more serious question arises than whether the most educated people in our society are "utilized" in some economically meaningful way. For such a "credentialling" process isolates a significant population group—those with modest educational achievements—from the rest of American society. America, it may be argued (in either moral or economic terms), can afford such a development even less than it can afford to have disenchanted college graduates in its work force.

In the next chapter the problem of the absorption of educated manpower is considered briefly from a demographic point of view and then from the point of view of employers interviewed during the present study.

IV Demographic and
Managerial Requirements

The vague misgivings one may have about the inventive indirect or "human capital" approaches to the identification of economic criteria for education are not completely or even largely dissipated by the employment of more direct methods. Thus myriad conceptual and methodological problems attended the efforts, described in the preceding chapter, to compute actual job requirements from trait analyses.

Nevertheless, the fact that such efforts to examine the supply of and "actual" demand for different levels of educated manpower are longitudinal in character is a source of their strength. Because the data are descriptive of two time periods, it was possible to examine the trends, presented in five different versions, that represent more or less conservative conceptions of present-day manpower policies and practices in America. Even the versions that correspond most closely to the *status quo*, and thus support the "education craze," contain some hints that the rising demand for workers with more elaborate educational credentials, in the short run, is in response to available supply rather than to long-unsatisfied organization needs, and that developments on the educational and employment fronts cannot be viewed with total equanimity.

In this chapter it is therefore appropriate to present, first, such demographic data as will provide clues to developments in the near future and, second, the relevant views of employers.

Educational Achievements and the Demands for an Educated Work Force

In making estimates of future trends in education and employment, an important issue is whether the rate of change in educational achievements will outdistance the change in educational requirements. The data on changes in educational achievements of the experienced labor force (Table IV-1) give one reason for pause, even assuming that all of the shifts in the occupational structure are "real" and significant.[1]

The data in Table IV-1 are based on the experienced civilian labor force, 14 years old or over, in each of three census years. In 1940, however, they do not include about 2.5 million workers, or about 5 per cent of the total, who were on public emergency work. This omission may be responsible for the fact that the decline in the lowest education group was greater in the second decade considered (1950–60) than in the first (1940–50). The only other striking difference is the smaller increase in the high-school-graduate group in the second decade. One can only speculate that as high-school graduation became a norm, a large increase from 1940 to 1950 resulted from the backlog—the pent-up demand, so to speak—left over from the depression; after 1950, the increase was expectedly somewhat less.

[1] How real these shifts are, and the precise magnitude of real *versus* pseudo shifts, is not easily established, as the analysis in Chapter III perhaps makes clear. The fact that educational achievement is sometimes combined with income in efforts to locate Americans in the "occupational structure" confuses this particular issue. See, for example, the strategy employed in Peter Blau and Otis Dudley Duncan, *The American Occupational Structure* (New York: Wiley, 1967).

TABLE IV-1

PERCENTAGE CHANGE IN YEARS OF SCHOOL COMPLETED
BY THE EXPERIENCED CIVILIAN LABOR FORCE,
1940–50, 1950–60, 1940–60

Years of School Completed	Percentage change		
	1940[a]*–50*	*1950–60*	*1940*[a]*–60*
8 years or less	−9.3	−14.4	−22.4
1–3 years high school	27.8	30.4	66.7
High-school graduate	44.0	32.7	91.1
1–3 years college	49.5	46.2	118.6
College graduate	47.7	47.5	117.8
Total labor force	12.9	14.8	29.6

[a] The 1940 data exclude 5 per cent of the experienced civilian labor force, who were on public emergency work.

SOURCE: 1940 Census, *Occupational Characteristics*, Table 3; 1950 Census, *Occupational Characteristics* (Special Report P-E No. 1B), Table 10; 1960 Census, *Occupational Characteristics* (Subject Report PC[2]-7A), Table 9.

Another interesting feature presented by the table is the maintenance of parity in the growth of both parts of the college population, those with less than four years and those with four or more years of higher education. In each decade, each group increased by almost half. For the two decades, growth was about 118 per cent, compared to 91 per cent for high-school graduates.

If we consider the changing educational achievements of the total population in such a way that the cumulative effects on the base used in percentaging are eliminated by regarding equivalent but nonoverlapping subpopulations, the results are even more startling, as Table IV-2 shows.[2]

[2] The changes are still more dramatic when data for the civilian labor force rather than the total population are used as the basis for comparisons. Since labor-force participation rates are continually changing (upward), the total population is used here as the more relevant base for present purposes. It may be usefully noted, for example, that "about one third of the labor-force expansion between 1961 and 1968 was among women 25 years old and over, most of whom were married, and over half was made up of youth 16 to 24 years of age." U.S. Department of Labor, *Manpower Report of the President* (Washington: Government Printing Office, 1969), p. 50.

TABLE IV-2

Percentage Distribution of Population 18–24 Years of Age, by Years of School Completed, by Sex, 1940, 1950, and 1960

Years of School Completed	Males			Females			Total		
	1940	1950	1960	1940	1950	1960	1940	1950	1960
8 years or less	34.0	26.0	15.1	28.8	19.3	11.2	31.3	22.6	13.2
1–3 years high school	26.8	26.5	27.2	25.7	25.6	26.5	26.3	26.0	26.9
High-school graduate	28.0	30.3	36.5	34.9	40.3	44.3	31.5	35.4	40.4
1–3 years college	8.7	14.0	16.8	8.3	11.4	14.6	8.5	12.7	15.6
College graduate	2.5	3.2	4.4	2.3	3.4	3.4	2.4	3.3	3.9
Total	100.0	100.0	100.0	100.0	100.0	100.0	100.0	100.0	100.0
Number (in millions)	(8.1)	(7.5)	(7.6)	(8.4)	(7.9)	(7.9)	(16.5)	(15.4)	(15.5)

Source: 1960 Census, Vol. 1, *Characteristics of the Population*, Part 1, U.S. Summary, table 173; 1950 Census, Vol. II, *Characteristics of the Population*, Part 1, U.S. Summary, table 114; 1940 data from 1950 Census, *ibid*.

The important question for the future is whether the increase in college population will begin to level off (parallel to the observed trend for high-school graduates), or whether the growth will continue. The trends described in Tables IV-1 and 2 are not likely to be reversed. Indeed, they are likely to be intensified. The expansion of community colleges, the boom in junior colleges, and the college building efforts of recent years will add to other forces that contribute to an increase in the numbers of citizens who will, in the future, achieve higher educations.

That the growth has continued in the nine years since the last census is already clear. The effects of ever-increasing school enrollments among a larger school-age population indicate that by 1975, about 66 per cent of workers 25 years old or over will have had at least four years of high school, and 15 per cent will have graduated from college.[3]

> By 1975, the adult work force . . . will include as many college graduates as those with 8 years of schooling or less . . . in 1959, college graduates as a group in the work force were but one third the size of the other component.[4]

The Problem of a Growing Supply of Educated People

It is neither unreasonable nor irrelevant to ask, in light of the prospects these trends imply, whether education in the future might offer Americans at each level of educational achievement something less than the expectations engendered by educational experience. It was this issue that concerned Seymour

---

[3] Denis F. Johnston, "Education of Adult Workers in 1975," *Special Labor Force Report No. 95* (Washington: Government Printing Office, 1968), p. 12.
[4] *Ibid.*, p. 10.

Harris twenty years ago in the study to which reference was made earlier:

> . . . *in the light of our college graduates' vocational expectations the numbers are, and will be increasingly excessive* . . . a large proportion of the potential college students within the next twenty years are doomed to disappointment after graduation, as the number of coveted openings will be substantially less than the numbers seeking them.[5]

Professor Harris's gloom has often been cited as a classic case of the clouded crystal ball. It is conceivable that he was simply prematurely anxious; it is even more likely that, in the two decades since he wrote his book, large numbers of jobs have been "educationally upgraded."

Some support for this conclusion may be found in a recent monograph on education based on the 1960 census. The analysis, which is confined to white males aged 35 to 54 years, subdivided into nine major occupational groups commonly used in the census, shows that "the association of education and occupation has been moderate but is declining." (Gamma $= .52$ in 1940, $.50$ in 1950, and $.39$ in 1960).[6] The study then seeks to determine whether the demand for more-educated workers rose because the supply increased, or whether demand stimulated the growth of the supply. Subdividing the rise in educational attainment into a component due to increases in educational attainment within occupational groups shows that upgrading within groups is by far the more important:

> Overall, about 85 per cent of the rise in educational attainment may be attributed to increased educational levels *within* occu-

[5] Seymour Harris, *The Market for College Graduates* (Cambridge: Harvard University Press, 1949), p. 64. Emphasis in original.

[6] John K. Folger and Charles B. Nam, *Education of the American Population*, 1960 Census Monograph (Washington: Government Printing Office, 1967), p. 169.

pations, and only 15 per cent to shifts in the occupational structure from occupations requiring less education to occupations
requiring more. . . . .
Only at the extremes of the attainment distribution (that is,
for college graduates and for persons with no education) was
as much as one half the change in educational attainment attributable to shifts between occupations.[7]

Because the occupational categories were so broad, the authors, while supporting the view that "the educational levels
of workers in various occupations do change and reflect the
'supply' of persons as well as the occupational demand," conclude that "how much of the change reflects increased skill
requirements . . . and how much is due to the availability of
better-educated persons for the same jobs cannot be finally
determined from these data."[8]

It is clear, however, that recent increments of college graduates have spread out into the middle levels of the occupational structure. Between 1950 and 1960, the labor force
gained about a half-million *more* male college graduates than
were required to maintain 1950 educational attainment levels.
Only 12 per cent of these (a little over 100,000) were added
to the professions; about 225,000 went into managerial occupations, 100,000 into sales occupations, and the remainder
(75,000) were scattered through the other occupations. Most
of the additional males with a high-school diploma were concentrated in the craftsman and operative categories.[9]

If 1975 distributions for males remain the same as obtained
in 1960, "there will be about 3.1 million more high-school
graduates, 850,000 more persons with some college education,
and 3.3 million more college graduates than will be required. . . ."[10] Even if the upgrading trend continues within

[7] *Ibid.*, pp. 171–72. Emphasis added.
[8] *Ibid.*, p. 173.
[9] *Ibid.*, p. 175.
[10] *Ibid.*, p. 174.

occupational groups, the prospects for a greater rate of absorption of college graduates into the professions is unlikely (since the proportion is already high). The large projected increase, perforce, will have to be absorbed in "managerial, sales, clerical, and some craftsmen occupations."[11]

These data imply that we may be able to absorb more highly educated people by redefining the requirements for employment, if not the job itself, and thus, in the fashion of Humpty Dumpty, make the content of work what we say it is.[12] In effect, this was demonstrated in Chapter III in the presentation of five different versions of the "match" between job requirements and educational achievements. Those who take an optimistic view of the match, at present and for the near future, should pause long enough to examine some possible consequences:

1. The "unemployed college man" is probably a "spectre." Nevertheless, disequilibrium may set in. The College Placement Council estimated, for example, that from 1967 to 1968, the decline in the number of jobs offered youths leaving college was 2 per cent for graduates with a bachelor's degree, 19 per cent for those with a master's degree, and 12 per cent for Ph.D.'s.[13] It is not possible to determine whether this a cyclical or a secular phenomenon, but it does demonstrate that the demand curve may well take a direction other than up.

2. More serious is the possibility of increasing "underemployment" of college men—and women. There is a real question whether middle-level white-collar jobs, those that have shown the greatest proliferation, actually make suitable use of their incumbents' preparation. In setting the requirements for work, it is well to keep in mind that "people *normally* operate within the bounds of a great deal of intellectual

---

[11] *Ibid.*, p. 176.

[12] Humpty Dumpty also said, "When I make a word do a lot of work like that, I always pay it extra."

[13] College Placement Council, *Salary Survey, Final Report*, June, 1968 (Bethlehem, Pa.: The Council, 1968), p. 1.

slack" so that it is difficult to measure the effects of marginal increments of knowledge.[14] The noneconomic factors[15] of managerial policy and the organization of work play an important mediating role between input and output; while these may act to improve efficiency, they may also involve unanticipated costs, as we shall see in later chapters.

Apropos of such anticipated costs, Professor Harris's statement about expectations becomes a real-life issue. At a recent high-level conference concerned with the prospect of collective bargaining among scientific and technical employees and professionals, the conferees agreed that "automation and computerization are eating away at the decision-making powers of these workers," and that "as their numbers increase, the uniqueness of the individual and his talents will decrease."[16] The problem, then, has several parts—the potential for actual underutilization, the workers' perceptions of how the facts fulfill their expectations, and the costs to employers and workers alike.

3. The most serious consequence of the educational upgrading of work opportunities is already with us—the displacement of a significant population at the other end of the labor force, who must compete for jobs once held by people of modest educational achievement and with people whose educational achievements have gone up. Neither the "human capital" approach nor the approach whereby educational requirements are computed directly helps to determine where

[14] Harvey Leibenstein, "Allocative Efficiency vs. 'X-Efficiency'," *American Economic Review*, LVI (1966), p. 405.

[15] For a discussion of one aspect of this issue, see Armen A. Alchian and Reuben A. Kessel, "Competition, Monopoly and the Pursuit of Pecuniary Gain," in National Bureau of Economic Research, *Aspects of Labor Economics* (Princeton: Princeton University Press, 1962), pp. 157–75, in which the authors note managerial tastes for "prettier-than-usual" secretaries, for example, in place of profit maximization.

[16] Conference on "Collective Bargaining and Professional Responsibility," sponsored by the AFL-CIO and conducted by the University of Illinois Institute for Labor and Industrial Relations, *AFL-CIO News*, July 13, 1968.

narrow economic necessities with respect to education leave off in the production process and where the sociological advantages of educational requirements to organizations, individuals, and society begin. There *may* be sociopsychological benefits to people and organizations stemming from diplomas and degrees, but these benefits must be seen in a perspective that takes account of the consequences for the "uncredentialed."

Most programs designed to deal with this problem have been geared to helping unemployed workers compete in the labor market by improving their qualifications. In the meantime, we reward the highly educated with superior incomes on the grounds of their productive contribution. If a man cannot meet the educational standards, his work is, by the definition of his income, or lack of income, less productive. Like Petruchio, we have been willing to accord those at the bottom neither the beef of a living and steady wage nor the mustard of a share in the over-all gains of the economy. Petruchio, however, had only to tame a shrew; we have to deal with the question of equity for a whole society.

As the specific work activities of men are further and further removed from a discernible end product, it becomes more and more difficult to assign each one his fair share of the proceeds, and the decision is particularly complex at the middle skill levels. We have chosen to allocate income largely according to educational achievement. As a result, the version of the relationship between supply and demand that requires improvement in educational achievements and upgrading of jobs to move at the same rate is not without its price, even if we put aside the problem of "underutilized" college graduates.

There are, of course, those who see the matter differently, who see far many more advantages and benefits than costs accruing to a society in which the educational credentials for jobs are upgraded beyond those necessary for "adequate" performance. The "human capital" writers, for example, offer abundant arguments in favor of present trends. One economist, in enumerating a host of so-called external benefits of education that redound to individuals as well as to the nation, includes such "social benefits" as the simplifications in income-tax collection that an educated population makes possible![17] By lengthening the list, one can, with only a little imagination, make investments in education pay off handsomely indeed. According to such logic, *by definition* there can be no "excess" education with respect to society.

Another argument maintains that earning differentials confirm the benefits employers receive from the greater educational achievements of individual employees; the pressures of the marketplace will enjoin the employer to use his workers with maximum efficiency and to recruit the members of his work force with an eye to his revenues. In such a formulation, however, as we noted earlier in connection with efforts to identify economic criteria for education by rate of return analysis, there is considerable overlap between *explanans* and *explanandum*. The problem is formulated in such a way that antecedent assumptions affirm that which is to be proved.

If, in fact, excess education is obviated by assuming the economic rationality of wage differentials, it is sensible to look behind the troublesome methods, direct and indirect, that have so far been discussed, and to determine whether managers themselves can assure us that educational credentials are worth what economists say they are.

Economists do not deal with individual firms when they work with theoretical apparatuses constructed for purposes of examining the concomitant variations in aggregated economic data, and some have expressed reasonable doubts about the utility (*i.e.*, the marginal costs) of information gathered from

---

[17] Burton A. Weisbrod, *External Benefits of Public Education: An Economic Analysis* (Princeton: Industrial Relations Section, Department of Economics, Princeton University, 1964), pp. 24–26. It would be interesting to contemplate a series of tax reforms which, while making taxes more equitable, would also reduce the complexities facing taxpayers.

practicing businessmen for such analytical purposes.[18] An examination of business behavior, however, may give the theoretician precious little comfort. Indeed, one might wish, in light of a number of studies of policy-making in the nation's great enterprises, that the jump from theory to policy might be undertaken more gingerly than economists suggest.

Educational Credentials in Managerial Perspective

Interviews with highly placed executives responsible for personnel policies revealed the same bewildering behavior concerning educational credentials that has been endlessly recounted by social scientists who have patrolled the shops and offices of business and government ever since the days of the classic experiments at the Hawthorne works of the Western Electric Corporation. These discussions with managers evoked the same question-begging responses that were obtained in investigations of business decision-making, including pricing decisions and decisions to subcontract. Two of the author's colleagues reported that some of the companies they investigated make only rough cost calculations in "make-or-buy" decisions, while fully 40 per cent make no calculations whatever.[19] In fact, with a few obvious changes in wording, the following description by three Brookings Institution economists of pricing decisions in "a representative sample of large enterprises" could serve to describe the findings of our interviews with ten large employers.[20]

---

[18] See Fritz Machlup, "Theories of the Firm: Behavioral, Managerial and Marginalist," *American Economic Review*, LVII (1967), 1–33.

[19] Leonard Sayles and Margaret Chandler, *Contracting Out: A Study of Management Decision Making* (New York: Columbia University Graduate School of Business, 1959), pp. 36ff.

[20] The "sample" included three of the four largest rubber companies; one large bank; one hospital supply company; one packaging company; one of

It was evident that most of the executives with whom interviews were conducted did not ordinarily concern themselves with pricing details; instances appeared in which they were not intimately aware of how their products were priced. Even those who were quite familiar with company policy in the pricing area were among those who could not illustrate the policy by a detailed follow through of particular price decisions. The fact that in some of the companies there was a gulf between the top officials and the price makers is in itself significant.

Even where the people doing the pricing tended to have certain staff information placed before them while making up their minds, whether and just how the information was taken into consideration often remained obscure. . . . Repeatedly reference was made to the "art" or "feel" of pricing rather than observance of a formula.[21]

Personnel and manpower decisions are *made*, to be sure, but the histories of such decisions are little more than hazy and unsubstantiated recollections of the "it-seemed-like-a-good-idea" variety. Our sample of firms is as small as it is simply because the responses to probes were so drearily similar from firm to firm that there seemed to be no benefit to be gained from expanding the effort. Our effort at interviews was therefore terminated early in the research.

Considerable manpower planning was undertaken in these firms with respect to executive personnel: like most large companies, they have a variety of executive development programs, either in association with universities or within the company, or in combination of the two. These programs range from short "exposure" to prolonged residency, during which a host of issues and techniques bearing on "human rela-

the biggest textile companies; one of the "big five" steel companies; one large, diversified textile company, and two small textile manufacturers. While abundant notes were compiled, no effort was made to treat the responses as formal "survey research" data.

[21] Abraham D. H. Kaplan, Joel B. Dirlam, and Robert Lanzilotti, *Pricing in Big Business: A Case Approach* (Washington: Brookings Institution, 1958), p. 5.

tions" and macro-economic policy problems are covered, with excursions in between into "systems analysis" and "sensitivity training." The latter is designed to make managers more "interpersonally competent" and to modify their behavior so that their peers and subordinates will experience a heightened sense of "self-actualization."

Most executive development efforts are organized around the principle that participants are drawn from the ranks of the nation's college graduates, whose educational backgrounds prepare them for sophisticated efforts calculated to make them better leaders and decision makers. All the spokesmen made bold statements about the value to their firms of college-educated men, and even those with graduate degrees, although these firms all had highly placed personnel with more modest credentials. On the face of it, the claims make sense. There can be no gainsaying the fact that a large firm might suffer if its executives were politically naive, organizationally heavy-handed, or intellectually uninformed about the complexities of the American economy.

Efforts to obtain data comparing the performance of better- and less-educated executives, however, ended in failure. In an extended conversation with one personnel executive and his assistant, it developed that they had a series of profiles, including graphs, portraying the accomplishments of their executives with respect, for example, to promotions, sales records, bonuses, and the like. These profiles, a few of which we were privileged to examine, had not been systematically analyzed, however, and it was impossible to make any judgments about the relationships between the personal traits and the performance records of these men.

Since the profiles were neatly compiled and readily accessible, the two executives were asked about the value of educational credentials in selection. The answers did not appear to be based on even casual perusal of the available data. In the matter of the *number* of people to which the profiles and our conversation referred, the respondents made incredibly divergent estimates; one said 800 men, the other said 300! It was clear that *no* effort had been made to consider the issue of educational credentials and equally clear that the issues of people, work, and even efficiency were negligible in the minds of these executives.

In this and other companies, however, it was readily acknowledged that the turnover of young executives varies only slightly; there is an average loss of *half* of all college graduates within the first five years of employment. Manpower planning at this organizational level was "therefore" uniformly informed by this "fact of life," as it was called; twice as many college graduates were recruited as were "needed."

There was, of course, abundant testimony concerning the worth of college graduates, and in this testimony the unifying theme was the diligence and "stick-to-it-iveness" of a young man who can endure four years of college. The college degree was consistently taken as a badge of the holder's stability and was apparently a highly prized characteristic of young recruits. Most of the respondents made it perfectly plain that the content of a college program mattered a good deal less than the fact of successful completion of studies. The poise and self-assurance of college graduates received considerable attention as well.

One highly successful company is staffed at the junior executive level by a unique group of college graduates; its college recruiters select many candidates from among those who have worked in men's haberdasheries catering to collegiate customers, on or near campuses, in the belief that these young fellows combine a highly desirable set of appetites, skills, and styles. Recruiters from this company also look for vacant seats on airplanes next to well-appointed young men whose college background can be inferred from the rings they wear. These airborne campaigns, an executive assuringly pointed out, were highly productive, although consultations with a designer of occult psychological tests were the closest these executives came to scientific investigation.

When questioned about the high turnover rates of young college graduates, nearly all the respondents answered impressionistically, by outlining the reasons supplied in termination interviews and in occasional and rather crude "career follow-ups" by the personnel officers. Many, they said, left simply because they were unhappy with their locations, or because their families had made poor adjustments to their environments. But others left because they felt that they were not getting ahead and that their jobs, by their standards, were insufficiently challenging.

Such attitudes were typically written off, however, as the reactions of "kids who want too much" or who "think they are better than they are" or "who haven't yet learned the facts of life, that you have to bide your time." In only one company did the jobs to which college men were assigned during their early careers sound like responsible positions. This company, in the packaging industry, frequently assigns new graduate-business-school alumni to jobs as assistant plant managers or as highly placed supervisory personnel with major responsibilities for developing the marketing, financial, or other programs of a plant. Their turnover levels were appreciably lower than the 50-per-cent figure given by the other respondents.

Another company, mindful of the increasingly simplified nature of the production processes in their plants, had experimented with the recruitment of American Indians whose educational backgrounds were modest by any standard. The executive who recounted the story claimed, with justifiable pride, that the program had been successful but indicated that it would take a great deal of work, combing "dead" piece-rate payment files, to determine the benefits to production of his company's exciting venture in social experimentation.

One hopes that the effort was indeed a success; perhaps executives get their rewards in heaven when they thus walk on the side of the angels. The researcher, however, must wait for the evidence. An invitation to look at the raw data was coupled with intimations of the company's inconvenience, a forthright statement that race and ethnic data were privileged, and intimidating descriptions of the magnitude of the coding problem that would have to be surmounted. The same company, in the meantime, has computerized all nonpersonnel data, but personnel data were ignored in accordance with the pervasive logic (implicit in all the interviews) that one of the biggest cost areas—personnel—is amenable to neither study nor influence.

The other companies had also ignored the question of education and its economic benefits and had conducted very little experimentation in connection with hiring requirements, except where signs of good faith were needed for a local, regional, or national job or poverty campaign. One company, for example, in collaboration with researchers from the University of Notre Dame's Department of Sociology, was examining the benefits of hiring ex-convicts. Virtually all of the companies belonged to business associations that sought jobs for "hard-core" unemployed, but headquarters personnel, perhaps wisely, discussed these efforts rather elliptically. The public press, meanwhile, continues to suggest that these efforts have been fragmentary in nature and more often than not marginal to the concerns of the corporate manpower specialists in high places.[22]

In only one company were the educational characteristics of manpower—at all job levels—routinely reported to personnel and other company officials. In the East Chicago offices of

---

[22] The foregoing is intended not to detract from these undertakings but merely to imply that the problems are a good deal more serious than these efforts can handle. For encouraging information see Ivar Berg, "Help Wanted," *Columbia University Forum*, III (Fall, 1964), 10-15.

Inland Steel, manpower planners *apologized* for having data that were already one week old! And they were surprised to learn that other companies did not have equivalent computer print-out for planning purposes. In the other companies, educational data were filed away in personnel applications and employment forms, never to distract executives from their determined efforts to "improve the quality of our people." To a man, the respondents assured us that diplomas and degrees were a good thing, that they were used as screening devices by which undesirable employment applicants could be identified, and that the credentials sought were indicators of personal commitment to "good middle-class values," industriousness, and seriousness of purpose, as well as salutary personal habits and styles. One executive pointed out that with only two people conducting interviews of job applicants, "we needed something to cut the sheer numbers down to what the personnel office could handle." To the executive, this logic was self-evident.

The interviews produced a picture of the results of this logic; most (not all!) of the respondents were confounded by questions that cast any doubt on the managerial wisdom underlying the raising of educational requirements. Although his term was not employed, a version of Marx's notion of the surplus army of labor was regularly invoked in a favorable way, the idea being that unemployment, especially among younger job applicants, makes it possible to take advantage of the self-selection and social-selection processes that differentiate between the desirable and undesirable—*i.e.*, the better- and less-educated—additions to a work force. The "loose" labor market of the '50's, then, was considered a boon in the personnel offices of these companies.

Uneasy about logic that purports to be "self-evident," one pursues the issue even less productively in specific terms than in generalities. Thus it turned out that *none* of the companies had considered educational achievements in studies of turnover, absenteeism, productivity, grievance patterns, output "restriction," terminations "for cause," unionization interests, job satisfaction, supervisors' evaluations, or any other directly or indirectly relevant dimension of work behavior. This, of course, may be due in part to the fact that few companies had even undertaken studies of these problems, although all the companies admitted that they suffered organizationally from one or more of them.

Every company had instituted complex personnel benefit programs, morale-building programs, human-relations activities, or combinations of these efforts, to reduce costly problems and increase productivity. Despite this, most of the headquarters offices had relatively little knowledge of the personnel issues facing the local managers of plants and subsidiaries, or of the efforts undertaken, if any, to resolve them. "We are quite decentralized from that point of view," was not an unusual response to probes calculated to determine whether the variances in a problem area could in fact, as was implied, be attributed to "lower-quality" employees.

To be sure, people responsible for decisions to hire personnel gave reasons for raising educational requirements in companies that encouraged, ordered, or merely tolerated such practices: "Better-educated people are more promotable." Like college alumni, high-school graduates, by virtue of their staying in school rather than by virtue of their particular learning experiences or skills, were considered simply "better" and more likely, more able, and more intelligent prospects.

The promotability argument had an attractive ring—what teacher could fail to hope that he had made at least *that* contribution to the regiments of people that pass through his fumbling hands? Once again, however, the argument was unsupported by any evidence that better-educated people compare favorably with their less educated peers who started at some given point on the organization ladder. The fact that better-educated people in almost *any given job category* in these firms were *younger* than their peers suggests that the better-educated had started higher on the ladder when they joined the firm, and that any correlation of rank with education would probably be the substantially tautological results of recruiting and assignment strategies.

Job Requirements and Employer Practices

Discouraged by repeated confrontations with the self-fulfilling prophesies that appeared to be as rampant among employers as among the economists who accept the rates of return on education as a measure of its economic efficiency, we turned to published studies and to analyses of such raw data as were generously provided by the handful of employers who shared our suspicions about the wisdom of using educational credentials as a screening device.

The "quality" argument, in fine, had not been impressive; in the absence of data, neither were arguments that jobs were changing so fast in content as to require better-educated people. The trait study discussed in the previous chapter had already suggested that educational achievements were changing much more rapidly than jobs, however much concession is made to technological and other influences on work, a finding that induced cautious interpretations about the "automation revolution" to which respondents made reference.

Other data increased our suspicions that there may be a significant margin of education that goes beyond what employers need even for *good* plant and corporate performance. In this connection, the National Industrial Conference Board's exploratory study of job vacancies in New York's Monroe County (which includes Rochester) reports that educational requirements vary with the academic year and appear to be geared to semester endings and commencement exercises:

The proportion of vacancies which did not require high school graduation was much higher in August than in February or May [1965]. In August, about 3,900 openings, or 45 per cent of the total, required less than 12 years of schooling. The corresponding percentages in February and May were 37 and 35, respectively.

The relative importance of vacancies requiring exactly 12 years of schooling declined sharply from May to August, thus returning to a level similar to that existing in February.[23]

The National Industrial Conference Board, a not-unfriendly critic of business decision-making, is probably right when it concludes from its data that

. . . it seems reasonable to attribute these changes to recruiting in May for recent high-school graduates. Employers may have tailored their requirements to match the qualifications of this new supply of labor.[24]

A study based on the USES trait requirements, the same type of achievements-requirements analysis reported in Chapter III, further supports this somewhat skeptical view of corporate practices.[25] While the authors carefully eschewed *any* translation of general educational development into years of education, they did compare all the 1956 and 1966 trait requirements delineated by the USES (including GED) as

[23] "Measuring Job Vacancies: The Third Survey," *The Conference Board Record* (New York: NICB, November, 1965), p. 31.

[24] *Ibid.*, pp. 31–32. The summary study in this series shows essentially the same results but the authors do not comment on the meaning of the calendar shifts in demand for better-educated workers. See John G. Myers and Daniel Creamer, *Measuring Job Vacancies: Studies in Business Economics*, No. 97 (New York: NICB, 1967), pp. 49–51.

[25] Morris A. Horowitz and Irwin L. Herrnstadt, "Changes in the Skill Requirements of Occupations in Selected Industries," in "The Employment Impact of Technological Change," Appendix Volume II, *Technology and the American Economy* (Report of the National Commission on Technology, Automation and Economic Progress, Washington: Government Printing Office, 1966), pp. 225–87.

well as the detailed job descriptions for five industries. They concluded that the over-all or net change in the skill requirements was remarkably small, especially considering that their study covered a quarter-century (1940–65). "There was considerable change in occupational requirements and content, but on balance, it was inconsequential or inconclusive with respect to over-all skill levels."[26]

The jobs examined in the study by Professors Horowitz and Herrnstadt were predominantly blue-collar. In another study, by the New York State Department of Labor, an effort was made to compare the (minimum) requirements and the (ideal) preferences of employers regarding education for jobs in 15 technical occupational groups, on the one hand, with the achievements of nearly 150,000 individuals who had worked in these occupations in New York State in 1962. The data show that employer preferences for college degrees ran ahead of the number of technicians with undergraduate degrees in only two of the 15 occupational categories. The educational achievements of technicians exceeded not only the minimum requirements but also the preferences of employers (with respect to degrees from technical institutes) in 10 of the 15 occupational groups. It is not possible to determine from the data whether the "excess" of institute graduates constitutes a trade-off against the "shortage" of college graduates, with shortage here defined as the workers' college achievements balanced against the employers' preferences.[27]

The popular assumption, supported by employers and, to some degree, economists, that widespread technological

[26] *Ibid.*, p. 287. In a preliminary report on the training of tool-and-die makers, the same authors conclude that performance (as rated by foremen) did not vary significantly among workers with different training paths. Furthermore, completing a given training path was not a prerequisite to success in the occupation. Morris A. Horowitz and Irwin L. Herrnstadt, "An Evaluation of the Training of Tool and Die Makers," Preliminary Report (Boston: Northeastern University, 1969).

[27] *Technical Manpower in New York State* (New York: State of New York Department of Labor, 1964), Vol. I, p. 47.

change in America is responsible for the demand for better-educated workers gained even less support from a recent study of the effect of technology.[28] From their data on workers' educational attainment and changes in output per worker (taken as a rough index of technological change) by industry, by sex, and by occupation, the authors infer that

. . . there is little, if any, relationship between changes in educational level [1950–60] and changes in output per worker. In those industries in which output per worker increased by less than 2 per cent annually (and employment increased under 15 per cent), 77 per cent of the employed men in 1950 had not completed high school, as compared with 72 per cent in 1960. At the other extreme, among those industries in which output per worker increased by 4 per cent or more per year (and employment increased by under 15 per cent) the proportion of dropouts fell from 83 per cent in 1950 to 76 per cent in 1960.[29]

Such data might well be *necessary*, but they are not *sufficient* to overturn the formidable body of beliefs in support of the rising demands of employers for educated manpower. It does no injustice to the authors' imaginative efforts to point out that their use of "output per worker" as an indicator of technological change begs important questions.

In order for such data to contribute to a *sufficient* argument, controls would have to be introduced for a number of potentially important contributing factors. One would wish to know whether, as might be likely, capital intensity is higher in industries with greater rates of increase in output per worker. Additional factors—such as the increasing educational achievements of *managers*—might vary a good deal from companies and industries with high rates of increase in productivity to companies and industries with low rates. When there

---

[28] A. J. Jaffe and Joseph Froomkin, *Technology and Jobs: Automation in Perspective* (New York: Praeger, 1968), pp. 85–97.
[29] *Ibid.*, p. 88.

are methodological obstacles to any clear-cut resolution, as is often the case, the conventional wisdom enjoys its alliance with attractive logic; its critics, however, are burdened with the chore of contesting the logic with data that are all too scarce.

In the remaining chapters of this book, we consider some of these data. They have been culled from the literature and re-analyzed, or they have been made available by managers of public agencies and private corporations. They permit extensive if not intensive examination of educational credentials in relation to performance in the workplace.

V Educational Achievements and Worker Performance

The search for evidence to give weight to economic arguments supporting the use of educational credentials for jobs has not been conspicuously successful. Aggregated data on income and education, favored in economists' researches, raise many more questions than they answer. The problems inherent in the economists' apparatus are compounded by those of a more strictly logical nature, problems that are more typically begged for analytical purposes than confronted in the simplifying assumptions of a general theoretical approach to reality.

The efforts of manpower and job analysts to identify the "real" educational requirements are of similarly problematical value; the difficulties of distinguishing employer *tastes* from employers' functional *needs* are in no wise eliminated by the use of the U.S. Employment Service's descriptions of jobs. These descriptions, while apparently based on today's practices, are themselves informed by preferences generated in the marriage of yesterday's labor-market conditions with prejudices honored too well by time. Thus margins of choice with respect to manpower utilization remain open to employers after technological determinants and the sorting process of market forces have shaped a firm's occupational structure.

And managers, upon whom there are strong pressures to be guided by evidence, usually offer little more than assertions in support of practices the benefits of which are assumed.

85

An alternative method is to examine the actual performance of workers in identical or similar jobs whose educational backgrounds are different to determine whether differential educational achievements might be related to differences in organizationally relevant behavior. It is to this point and to the related question of job attitudes that this chapter and the next two chapters are directed.

The chore is not a simple one, a fact for which many of us may be grateful. Indeed, there are few standards against which the adequacy of most employed Americans can be judged. Our occupational efforts are frequently bound up inextricably with the work of others in the production of goods —and, increasingly, services.

Where a man's (or woman's) work *is* extricable from the efforts of others, the results are substantially influenced by forces over which the individual has little control. It is a poor field representative whose declining sales record cannot be attributed to market conditions, and an unusual one who successfully competes with the advertising agency's claims to the credit for a rising sales curve! The acceptance by many Americans of the seniority principle in organizations is perhaps the best barometer of the implicit effect of these facts of complex industrial-bureaucratic life in America. In the absence of clear performance standards, most of us will choose job tenure as an indicator of capability and settle for the arbitrary seniority rule in preference to managerial definitions of the good worker. Where a man's contribution to an organization's work is not readily distinguishable, managerial judgments may be distrusted as whimsical, prejudicial, or both.

To be entirely convincing, of course, a comparison of the work performance of better-educated and less educated people would have to be systematic and statistically valid. Accordingly, one would prefer data that are representative of all occupations, and of all the people in these occupations, juxtaposed with all relevant dimensions of performance. It would also be desirable to be able to control in the data for other worker characteristics and attitudes to the extent that these influence worker performance, and also to control for managerial competence and an array of other factors that impinge upon employee behavior.

The data reported in the following pages fall far short of these requirements, but they are more than just suggestive of the truth. The cumulative weight of piecemeal evidence, after all, may be taken as a significant clue to truths that are not otherwise to be apprehended, and it is in this spirit that the materials are presented. Some of them are taken from previously published studies, but most were collected and analyzed in the course of the present investigation.

Blue-Collar Workers

In the first of the field investigations, data were collected in 1967 on the productivity, turnover, and absenteeism of 585 former and present female workers in a multi-plant Mississippi textile manufacturing company. We found that educational achievement was *inversely* related to performance thus conceived. Thus, where 57 per cent of the long-tenure employees had ten or more years of schooling, the figure for short-tenure employees was 71 per cent; the statistical probability that the observed difference would occur by chance is 5 in 100.

The data with respect to educational achievement correlated with productivity, which in this company could be measured accurately from piecework earnings, and absenteeism were somewhat less clear, but they gave no support to the contention that educational requirements are a useful screening device in blue-collar employee selection. The education of high producers did not differ from that of low producers to any statistically significant degree, although the *less* productive ones were slightly *better* educated. It is worth noting that the results can be generalized to the entire company since the groups about which the findings are drawn were constructed from a random 50-per-cent sample of over 1,000 former and nearly 850 present employees in the company's eight plants.[1] Since productivity data were examined only for long-tenure employees, the findings probably understate the magnitude of the inverse relationship between productivity and education.

In the same vein, there was no statistically significant relationship between educational achievement and absenteeism, another bugaboo of managers who are anxious to maintain smooth production schedules and continuous work flows, although there were slightly more high-school graduates among the "low" than the "high absentee" group.

In a comparable study of 762 workers in four departments of a Southern hosiery manufacturing plant, the same patterns were observed. Productivity and turnover were related to age, family stability, and a number of intra-organizational factors, but they were *not* associated with educational achievement among day-shift workers; education was *inversely* related to both measures of performance among employees on the night shift in this company.[2] We can speculate that better-educated workers were especially irritated by assignment to the night shift. Whatever the explanation, the employer did not benefit from having better-educated employees on either shift and actually lost out on the night shift with respect to productivity and turnover. Once again, the productivity measures were ac-

[1] For a more detailed analysis see Gordon Inskeep. "The Selection Process and Its Relationship to Productivity, Tenure, and Absenteeism among Garment Workers," unpublished doctoral dissertation, Columbia University, 1967, written under the author's supervision in connection with the present research.

[2] Michael Abramoff, "External Allocation, Socialization and Internal Allocation of Human Resources as Related to Performance," unpublished doctoral dissertation, Columbia University, 1968 written under the author's supervision in connection with the present research.

curate since they were constructed from piecework earnings for each employee.

It will be recalled, in our interviews regarding the "greater potential" of better-educated workers, that employers insisted that the elevation of education requirements reflects management's desires to build for the future by assuring a pool of labor from which promotions may be made. If their assumption is correct, we would expect to find that personnel who have been promoted are better educated than those who have not, especially in companies that are proud of the essential rationality of their manpower and personnel policies.

Although this expectation is not easily tested, we might well be skeptical of an intrinsically appealing analysis that protects its own flank by seeing long-term benefits in an approach to a short-run problem. In a parallel study, data were collected on the patterns of labor-force "attachment" among (1) installation-crew members in two privately owned urban utility companies, (2) workers in an auto assembly plant located on the periphery of one of America's great cities, and (3) nonmanagerial employees in two large urban department stores.[3] These data do not square with management's convenient rationale.

The patterns were substantially the same in all four employment settings; those of the installers are illustrative. In an effort to account for the promotion rates of these workers, educational achievement explained so few promotions that it could be discounted as a factor. The results were interesting, however, in that they offered some clues to the real nature of "organizational mobility," to borrow a barbarism from sociology, clues that are entirely consistent with the skeptical bias of the present study.

When the researcher who originally exploited the data examined the job titles in these four work settings, she dis-

[3] Marcia Freedman, *The Process of Work Establishment* (New York: Columbia University Press, 1969).

covered that although the titles were ordered into a pay scale, the resulting array did not correspond to a skill hierarchy except at the extreme ends of the wages continuum. It appears, then, that education may well be relevant to the "promotion potential" of workers in a shop or plant where title and pay changes reflect differences in job tasks and obligations, but it is not likely to be specifically relevant to promotions in settings where managers have developed a nominal hierarchy to legitimize wage differentials created by the numerous factors that operate in urban labor markets.

It is doubtful that the uncounted masses of Americans who are "promoted" each year are as easily fooled by nominal hierarchies as are some senior academics who conceive of occupational titles as ranks representing differential skills. Such ranks are merely included among the more socially significant rungs on the largely symbolic occupational "ladders." Assistant professors, we can be sure, will skillfully disabuse any academic coprolites who might challenge such a judgment.

Our strong suspicions about the nature of organizational careers, especially in the blue-collar fields, are not allayed by employers' assertions, especially in light of continuous efforts to rationalize and "bureaucratize" work. And theories purporting to account for labor unions' activities would be less than adequate if they did not assign a significant place to the occupational consequences of changes wrought by managers bent upon gaining benefits that accrue to "scale," specialization, and work simplification. In the four settings mentioned, education was a good predictor of initial salary and job title. But it will not surprise the reader to learn that seniority accounted for most of the promotions.

A final study, this time of "gray-collar" workers, gives further evidence concerning the specifics of educational achievement and worker behavior. Managers of a paper company (including a doctoral candidate on leave from his job as the

Director of Technical Personnel, who collected the data) were surprised that the wisdom of their preferences for better-educated technicians was not confirmed by relevant data.[4]

The data showed that short-tenure employees had a median of four and a half semesters of college training, while a matched sample of employees with longer service had completed only slightly more than three terms. It was an additional surprise to management that the longer-tenure (and therefore more valuable) employees scored substantially lower on an intelligence test, a test the personnel officials hoped would validate the practices of giving higher-scoring job candidates preferential treatment in placement.

There was, furthermore, no association between the educational attainments of these technicians and the evaluations they received from supervisory personnel, nor was there any association between education and absenteeism. And when the "reasons for leaving" given by former employees were reviewed, they revealed that over a third resigned well-paying jobs to return to school; another third left for jobs that offered higher starting salaries for their relatively advanced educational achievements.

These data and the observations of employers in our interviews suggest that better-educated people get ahead by changing jobs, and that their less educated peers stay behind and move into the higher-paying, if not always higher-skill, jobs vacated by employee turnover. Higher-skill jobs, meanwhile, are filled by the better-educated workers who have quit other employers.

There may, of course, be a higher wisdom than management's, according to which the materials discussed in this first section make a kind of sense. Perhaps turnover is simply a corrective process at the margins of the more rigid central

---

[4] These data were analyzed by Dr. Gordon Inskeep, now of Arizona State University, in connection with the work of a seminar conducted by the author at the Columbia University Graduate School of Business in 1966.

tendencies at work in a complex labor market; labor turnover is not all bad. And it is not likely that a perfect process of training, recruiting, placing, and paying workers will ever be devised. Nevertheless, we might hope that the value managers place on education as a screening device would be rewarded by a few *direct* associations between the achievements they prize and the productivity, attendance and loyalty they seek in their hired charges. It is probably fortunate that the ratios implied by these data are not included among those listed in annual reports since the wages paid to employees *are* directly correlated with education, a fact that may sadden proponents of efficiency in enterprise. Sadness gives way to anger among the spokesmen for those without academic credentials who continue to be told that their constituents "need more education."

White-Collar Workers

The facts are not more reassuring with respect to white-collar workers. An analysis of the merit pay increases awarded to over a hundred secretaries employed by one of the nation's largest magazine publishers revealed no discernible relationship between these rewards for performance and the educational achievements of the recipients who had attended various post-high-school programs but had not graduated from college.[5] Nor did any associations appear when the number rather than the amount of increases was considered. In fact, while a small number of college graduates received slightly more raises than the nongraduates, the education-evaluation data were otherwise *inversely* related.

[5] These data were made available by the magazine's personnel administrator and were analyzed by Dudley L. Post for a seminar conducted by the author in 1966.

A colleague who has been conducting studies of "debit agents" employed across the land by the Prudential Insurance Company has generously provided data on the sales accomplishments and education of each of four age groups among the 4,000 subjects that have been studied by Prudential's personnel researchers.[6] These data are especially interesting since they are broken down by the types of market in which the agents work, thereby holding constant a significant sales factor.

Three sets of progressively rigid sales and policy-retention rates for measuring the success of these agents were employed. The results were entirely anomalous when the agents' records were examined in connection with their educational achievements. The records of high-school graduates rarely differed by more than a few percentage points from those of comparably numerous college graduates of similar age operating in similar markets: sometimes the less educated men did better, although a few did not do so well as their better-educated compeers. The results are the same whether the data are examined in longitudinal or cross-sectional fashion. Prudential, which, unlike the companies discussed in Chapter IV, has done extensive research into its personnel practices, does not even consider formal education in the weighted application blank used in the selection of agents.

In another white-collar study, the results were in line with those already reported: Performance in 125 branch offices of a major New York bank, measured by turnover data and by the number of lost accounts per teller, was inversely associated with the educational achievements of these 500 workers.[7] The branches with the worst performance records were those in

[6] J. R. Milavsky, formerly of the Prudential Insurance Company, in communications to the author.

[7] Martin J. Gannon, "Employee Turnover and Productivity in a Branch Banking System," unpublished doctoral dissertation, Columbia University, 1969, written under the supervision of the author.

which a disproportionately (and significantly) high number of employees were attending educational programs after working hours! There was also evidence that performance was worst in precisely those branches in which, besides the educational achievements' being higher, the managers stressed education in consultations with tellers concerning their futures with the bank.

The fact that white-collar workers' job performances are more difficult to measure than those of blue-collar workers makes useful analysis in this area almost impossible. Salaried workers, for example, are not usually "docked" for the absences they incur whether they malinger, "go to the doctor," or attend to the myriad personal details of a folded, bent, and spindled society of forms, bureaus, licenses, and application blanks. Nor are formal records kept of the millions of hours spent on haircuts, apartment-hunting trips, brokerage-office visits, or headcolds by Americans whose salary checks presumably attest to their diligence and industry. The argument that these "breaks" are a factor in keeping employee morale high is rarely applied to the blue-collar worker who seeks to escape from the factory for no pleasure greater than his mother-in-law's funeral. The facts of life with respect to record-keeping guarantee that *any* criteria used by managers to screen employees can be *made* to work in the short run. And as my colleague and an authority on manpower problems, Professor Eli Ginzberg, has frequently observed, "The long run is, after all, only a series of short runs."

Professionals and Managers

Managerial and professional performance has long been a sticky issue in private enterprise, where handsome incomes are paid to highly placed leaders who preside over activities

that are even more vulnerable to influences beyond corporate
and managerial control than are those undertaken by insurance agents. It is a rare conference on "managing managers"
or "managing scientists"—and there have been many in recent
years—in which participants don't drink in frustrated fellowship at hotel bars where formal presentations on "management
evaluation" are reviewed by skeptical "executive development" personnel. None of the executives we interviewed felt
comfortable about his efforts in this much-plagued area, and
none was able to provide any information useful in an appraisal of his experiences in the recruitment and development
of managers and professionals.

Survey researchers at the Opinion Research Corporation of
Princeton, New Jersey, however, have sought to identify
some of the attitudes of engineers and scientists, including a
few with administrative responsibilities, in an investigation
sponsored by industry leaders concerned about the care and
feeding of these high-priced personnel. Because employers
had ranked the personnel ("A" or "B," according to their
"value") from whom demographic and attitude data were so-
licited, it was possible to make at least an empirical excursion
into the nettlesome issues involved.[8]

The personnel, nearly 620 of them, were employed by the
nation's six largest manufacturers of heavy electrical equipment and appliances; the education-income nexus could thus
be viewed in a comparative perspective, and logical inferences
drawn concerning the hiring and salary policies of the six
companies and the connections among company characteristics, personnel characteristics, and personnel satisfactions.

It may reasonably be assumed that the distributions of edu-

[8] The Opinion Research Corporation gave a duplicate deck of IBM cards
containing the data used in the present study to the Roper Center at
Williams College, Williamstown, Mass. We are indebted to the Director of
the Roper Center, Dr. Phillip Hastings, for making these data available to
us, and to the ORC for releasing the data for distribution by the Center.

cational achievements represented in each of the companies are indicators of that company's hiring policies. Engineers and scientists are more geographically mobile than most other occupational groups; moreover, each of the companies is large enough to recruit in a national labor market. Assuming, therefore, that the same types of men were available to all six companies, we can regard the fact that (for example) F had 62 Ph.D.'s among 96 employees whereas D had one Ph.D. in 100 to be the result of management choice. (See the cell numbers across the rows of Table V-1.)[9]

Table V-1 seems to show that income is tied to education more in some companies than in others: (a) The rank-order correlation (Tau Beta)[10] between education and income over-all is quite high (.32) and is even higher in some companies; (b) the mean income for Ph.D's is uniformly much higher than the mean for groups with other educational achievements, in general and within each company; (c) the standard deviation of incomes around the mean is generally smaller for M.A.'s and Ph.D.'s than for people with less education, indicating that the income of those with less than an M.A. is determined by factors other than education, whereas M.A.'s or Ph.D.'s are paid primarily on the basis of their degrees.

The three companies that pay roughly the same average salaries appear to have strikingly different policies with respect to educational requirements. Company D either purposely hires people with modest educational achievements or largely ignores the factor of education in hiring and salary decisions.

---

[9] It is possible that the educational achievements of these personnel reflect company turnover experiences rather than hiring practices, but we cannot pursue this possibility with the data available.

[10] For a discussion of the Tau Beta statistic, see M. G. Kendall, *Rank Correlation Methods* (New York: Hafner, 1955) and Robert H. Somers, "A New Asymmetric Measure of Association for Ordinal Variables," *American Sociological Review*, XXVII, 6 (December, 1962). We are grateful to Dr. J. R. Milavsky, now of the National Broadcasting Corporation, for his statistical advice, and for the services of the Columbia Bureau of Applied Social Research.

TABLE V-1
MEAN ANNUAL SALARIES OF SCIENTISTS AND ENGINEERS AT SIX COMPANIES, BY EDUCATIONAL ACHIEVEMENT, 1958

Company[a]		Education						Tau β
		Less than Bachelor's Degree	B.A. or B.S.	Some Graduate Courses	M.A. or M.S.	Ph.D.	Total	
A	Mean	$7,750	$6,720	$7,500	$7,480	$9,390	$7,750	.45*
	S.D.	1,710	1,410	1,380	1,180	1,730	1,780	
	Number	(4)	(36)	(6)	(29)	(28)	(103)	
B	Mean	9,670	8,410	8,920	9,110	10,710	8,930	.24
	S.D.	1,530	2,040	2,190	1,560	1,680	2,040	
	Number	(3)	(59)	(12)	(19)	(14)	(107)	
C	Mean	8,000	8,440	7,500	8,310	11,030	9,170	.44*
	S.D.	2,000	2,270	1,050	1,570	1,450	2,190	
	Number	(3)	(32)	(6)	(26)	(32)	(99)	
D	Mean	9,450	9,340	9,440	10,880	16,000	9,580	.06
	S.D.	2,290	3,000	2,880	1,640	0	2,700	
	Number	(38)	(44)	(9)	(8)	(1)	(100)	
E	Mean	—	8,840	9,000	9,430	10,910	9,850	.35*
	S.D.	—	2,640	2,680	1,660	1,840	2,310	
	Number	(0)	(32)	(6)	(21)	(44)	(103)	
F	Mean	—	11,110	11,860	10,890	12,840	12,240	.28
	S.D.	—	2,420	2,730	2,170	2,330	2,450	
	Number	(0)	(9)	(7)	(18)	(62)	(96)	
Total	Mean	9,230	8,500	9,110	8,980	11,370	9,550	.32*
	S.D.	2,210	2,510	2,580	1,990	2,290	2,620	
	Number	(48)	(212)	(46)	(121)	(181)	(608)	

[a] Companies are listed in order of increasing mean annual salaries.
* Significant at .05 level. For an explanation of Tau β, see p. 96, n. 10.

Companies B and E distribute an almost identical amount of money to about the same number of men, but they do not similarly tie increments of income to increments of education; the relationship is stronger in E than in B. Finally, F, the company with by far the highest average salaries, has an apparently "moderate" tendency to tie rewards to degrees; within each group there is room for the "effect" of factors other than education.

Table V-2 reveals even more: it shows that, at least with respect to men with graduate degrees, management in these six companies tends to reward educational achievement rather than performance! Men with master's degrees who were designated by *management* as among 20 per cent of their scientists who were "relatively most valuable in terms of present performance and potential" were paid an average salary which was $1,000 *less* than that paid to Ph.D.'s, who were reportedly less valuable. Other data show that Ph.D.'s are paid substantially more even when they are younger and less experienced. Small wonder that these Ph.D.'s were a happy lot!

The data do not support the blanket inference that employers always reward educational achievement more than performance, but they afford presumptive evidence that this is the case. It is entirely likely that the numerous discrepancies between the evaluations and incomes earned by the subjects in the Opinion Research Corporation's survey are artifacts of the initial salary differentials which reflect different educational achievements. These differentials are easily maintained when subsequent salary increases are clustered in such a way as to reduce the likelihood that personnel will make "coercive comparisons" among themselves. In these six companies, at least, it appears that some less educated men earn through *performance* salaries that men with Ph.D.'s are given for their degrees.

A thorough search of the published literature on turnover and absenteeism in industry revealed that the matter of education is rarely considered among the factors linked to these

TABLE V-2

MEAN ANNUAL SALARIES OF SCIENTISTS AND ENGINEERS AT SIX COMPANIES,
BY MANAGEMENT EVALUATION AND EDUCATION, 1958

Management Evaluation	Less than Bachelor's Degree	B.A. or B.S.	Some Graduate Courses	M.A. or M.S.	Ph.D.	Total	Tau β
Ordinary							
Mean	$7,780	$7,500	$7,840	$8,270	$10,850	$8,460	.41*
S.D.	1,550	1,720	1,570	1,590	2,060	2,200	
Number	(27)	(128)	(25)	(66)	(71)	(317)	
Valuable							
Mean	11,100	10,020	10,620	9,840	11,710	10,750	.17
S.D.	1,370	2,710	2,770	2,090	2,370	2,520	
Number	(21)	(84)	(21)	(55)	(110)	(291)	
Total							
Mean	9,230	8,500	9,110	8,980	11,370	9,550	.32*
S.D.	2,210	2,510	2,580	1,990	2,290	2,620	
Number	(48)	(212)	(46)	(121)	(181)	(608)	

Education

* Significant at the .05 level.

often-costly organizational problems. We reviewed hundreds
of these studies and conclude, as did Gaudet, that in

> . . . seeking to learn the relation of turnover to education,
> level of skill, and marital status we find many general statements
> which are valueless, or worse, for decision-making.[11]

In those few studies in which the present interests can be pursued, the results are entirely in line with those presented. Thus
a researcher and two executives examined the records of employees of the Bausch and Lomb Optical Company for a
period after World War II, during which recruiting and
training costs were "repaid" when an employee had worked
for nine months. When they compared 27 employees who had
remained on the jobs for nine months with those who had left
within three months,

> . . . the results . . . show quite conclusively that, at the time of
> employment, employees who stay at least nine months on the
> job and [more] have had less formal education, are more fre-
> quently married, and have more dependents than employees
> who leave the job prior to three months.[12]

A few years later the Bureau of Labor Statistics examined
the job changes of 1,700 apprentice and foreman tool and die
workers in 300 plants located in two labor markets and reported a high positive correlation between years of formal
education achieved and average number of job changes.[13]

And, in a study conducted at American Airlines of 2,015
"new hires" in all types of position, researchers concluded
that there were no significant differences with respect to edu-

[11] F. J. Gaudet, "Labor Turnover: Calculation and Cost," *AMA Research
Study No. 39* (New York: American Management Association, 1960), p. 79.
[12] Joseph Tiffin, "The Analysis of Personnel Data in Relation to Turnover
on a Factory Job," *Journal of Applied Psychology*, XXXI (1947), 616.
[13] "The Mobility of Tool and Die Workers, 1940–1951," *Bulletin 1120*,
Bureau of Labor Statistics (Washington: U.S. Department of Labor, 1952).

cation achieved between those who stayed and those who left.[14] Approximately the same results were reported in a comparison of the turnover rates of high-school and non-high-school graduates among 1,900 electronics technicians. Where 22 per cent of the non-high-school graduates had changed jobs, the figure for graduates was 25 per cent.[15]

Conclusion

The data in this chapter do not prove that educational requirements are bad; they do, however, reinforce doubts about whether the benefits that managers apparently believe accompany educational credentials do in fact materialize.

"But employers don't look for specific performance when they hire better-educated workers," some may argue. When they do, it is because they do not have evidence about the performance of the less educated workers who come to their personnel offices through contacts and references. Managers are concerned with generalized ability, and they believe that this can be ascertained through educational achievement.

Unfortunately, the data to test this hypothesis are not available. Some *pieces* of relevant evidence, however, suggest that the selection process is not so easily described. Professor Gary Becker (with an almost opposite purpose) sought to determine whether the individual returns on marginal investments in education are explained by the fact that higher-paid, better-educated workers are more able—i.e., more intelligent, and from backgrounds that make them more valuable to employers. His findings might embarrass an educator; they show that although there *is* a positive association between ability and educational

---

[14] Irwin W. Krantz, "Controlling Quick Turnover," *Personnel*, XXXI (1955), 514-20.
[15] James J. Treives, "Mobility of Electronics Technicians," *Monthly Labor Review*, LXXVII (1954), 263-66.

TABLE V-3

PROBABILITY OF ENTERING COLLEGE,
BY ABILITY AND SOCIOECONOMIC STATUS[a]

Ability Quarter	Socioeconomic Quarter			
	Low			High
	1	2	3	4
Males				
Low 1	.06	.12	.13	.26
2	.13	.15	.29	.36
3	.25	.34	.45	.65
High 4	.48	.70	.73	.87
Females				
Low 1	.07	.07	.05	.20
2	.08	.09	.20	.33
3	.18	.23	.36	.55
High 4	.34	.67	.67	.82

[a] The samples from which these probabilities were calculated were high-school juniors in 1960.
SOURCE: Flanagan and Cooley, *op. cit.*, p. 95.

achievement, the latter accounts for *much* more of the variance in earnings. Although each of the studies he considers is deficient in one or more of the particulars of research design, the cumulative weight of the evidence, as he correctly points out, is impressive indeed.[16] "Consequently," he writes, "it may be concluded that, even after adjustment for differential ability, the private rate of return to a typical white male college graduate would be considerable, say, certainly more than 10 per cent."[17]

Becker's results should not surprise informed Americans, so frequently reminded that 15 to 20 per cent of all high-school students who are intellectually capable of going on to and completing an undergraduate program do not do so.[18] Table V-3 was developed by Project Talent to show the

[16] See Gary Becker, *Human Capital* (New York: Columbia University Press), 1964, p. 88.
[17] *Ibid.*, p. 88.
[18] Lyndon Baines Johnson, *State of the Union Address*, January 1968.

cross-influences of "socioeconomic status" and ability on the probability of entering college. In every case, the probabilities increase with *both* status and ability: The "ability score facilitates college entrance to a considerably greater degree than does socioeconomic level."[19] For example, 70 per cent of the males in the highest ability, second-socioeconomic quarter go to college, compared to 36 per cent of the highest status, second-quarter ability group. Thus students from lower socioeconomic classes, especially those with ability, have some mobility, but this seems to be outweighed by the greater probability that *all* ability groups among the high-status groups will go on to college.

Again, Becker's findings on the returns from education and ability do not disprove the greater value of an educated worker over a less educated worker. Perhaps another researcher will be able to demonstrate that the credentialling process has somewhat more measurable benefits than have been uncovered in this study.

It is possible that there *are* benefits, and efforts to prove this point may betray a misguided empiricism on the part of researchers. But the faith of some in the benefits of education is perhaps no more valid than others' faith in the admittedly narrow issue of economic benefit. And one may well be skeptical, if not cynical, about how much *real* education can be utilized by most industrial organizations. Meanwhile, the contention that people are changed as a function of their education and thus can change the world gains at least as much horrifying as gratifying support from history. One should note that there are as many distinguished scholars advising the Department of State on Vietnam as there are among critics of that department, and that crackpot realism is no less prevalent among Ph.D.'s than among less educated members of advisory staffs in military

---

[19] John C. Flanagan and William W. Cooley, *Project Talent: One-Year Follow-Up Studies* (Pittsburgh: School of Education, University of Pittsburgh, 1966), p. 95.

and other governmental units. To argue that well-educated people will automatically boost efficiency, improve organizations, and so on may be to misunderstand in a fundamental way the nature of American education, which functions to an important, indeed depressing, extent as a licensing agency.

A search of the considerable literature on productivity, absenteeism, and turnover has yielded little concrete evidence of a positive relationship between workers' educational achievements and their performance records in many work settings in the private sector. While psychologists, sociologists, and other professional students of behavior have attended to the problem of worker performance, these students, like business researchers, tend to contemplate the more esoteric variables with their complex theories. The literature is replete with contingency tables, regression equations, and "sociometric" diagrams that trace in embarrassing detail the relationships between the "sentiments," "activities," and "interactions" of workers and the "orientations" of supervisors, on the one hand, and the work accomplishments, especially of "work groups," on the other.

While these studies are not directly relevant to the present study, they have a strong indirect bearing upon it. Since many of them deal with the relationship between worker attitudes and productivity—when they deal with productivity at all—they provide us with clues to the dynamics of the education-production nexus. The present chapter has suggested that all this is more complex than might be inferred from the litany chanted by education's worshippers. It is thus useful to "go the next step" in this seemingly infinite regression to determine whether educational achievements are associated with the attitudes so frequently assumed to be predictors of productivity. The evidence, meanwhile, points to the need for a balanced perspective on the modest benefits that accrue to employers from using education as a screening device.

VI Educational Achievements and Job-related Attitudes

The observation that job-related attitudes may intervene between combinations of workers' demographic characteristics, including their educational backgrounds, and their job performance is based on an abundant technical literature. The precise role of attitudes, however, is not clearly delineated. The theoretical relevance of job-satisfaction studies, for example—the type of study that dominates this literature—is less than established.

Few Americans would argue that high levels of job dissatisfaction or other "negative" worker attitudes should be disregarded. But there is no way to determine how much dissatisfaction is too much, and the methods for determining the losses associated with "alienation" in the workplace are even more obscure.

Consider that worker turnover may result from dissatisfaction, but that turnover is part of "occupational mobility," and, as we have noted, turnover may simply be a marginal "corrective" of the process by which human resources are allocated. Such a corrective can take many forms, only some of which are accounted for in theoretical estimates of economic events.

During the course of the present study, one highly placed executive in a mammoth insurance company commented that "tender-minded academics" were "downright naive" in their concern about worker turnover and wellbeing. It was his "informed judgment" that clerical personnel

> . . . are easily trained for their jobs, that if they stayed on in larger numbers they would become wage problems—we'd have to keep raising them or end up fighting with them; they would form unions and who knows what the hell else. It's better to hire girls who are too well educated to *stay* happy with the jobs we assign them to do. That way they get out before it's too late.

To balance these and other more commonly expressed values related to labor mobility is not simple. Conversations with economists do not reassure one that a reasonable "benefit-cost analysis" of job dissatisfaction can be made in the present primitive state of their art. One complicating factor is that satisfied workers are sometimes more and sometimes less productive than their "alienated" workmates.[1]

It is likely that this fact, which has been noted by all who have addressed the problem, is an artifact of the methods of social-science investigators. One reviewer correctly concludes:

> . . . the amount of productivity on the job varies directly with the extent to which productive behavior is associated with satisfaction, and inversely with the extent to which nonproductive behavior is thus associated.[2]

---

[1] This is not the place to enter into a discussion of the tortured uses to which the concepts of "alienation" in general, and "worker alienation" in particular, have been put. It must suffice here to point out that the terms are abused if we are to understand that the user believes he is fingering the Marxist rosary. For three urbane discussions by one who is bothered by the unfortunate history of the concept as Marx employed it, see Daniel Bell, "The Meaning of Work," *New York Review of Books*, October 22, 1964, pp. 21–23; "The Rediscovery of Alienation: Some Notes Along the Quest for the Historical Marx," *Journal of Philosophy*, LVI (1959), 933–52; and "Work and Its Discontents," *The End of Ideology* (Glencoe: Free Press, 1960), Chapter 11.

[2] Raymond A. Katzell, "Personal Values, Job Satisfaction and Job Behavior," in Henry Borow, ed., *Man in a World at Work* (Boston: Houghton Mifflin, 1964), p. 356. See also Victor Vroom, *Work and Motivation* (New York, Wiley, 1964), pp. 262–64.

This formulation, he notes, "accommodates equally well find-ings of positive correlations, negative correlations, and zero correlations between the two types of variables."[3] The upshot is that the researcher must determine whether productivity itself is a source of satisfaction in order that a study of satis-faction and productivity can precipitate meaningful findings on the "utility" of efforts to heighten worker satisfaction. Un-til investigations are designed accordingly, the anomalies in the reports in this troublesome area must not be gainsaid.

For present purposes, it is conceded that job attitudes are not the clearest of scientific variables for theory construction. While there may well be an element of efficiency accruing to managers from their efforts to improve morale, the issue is by no means a dead one.[4] Perhaps more to the point than the in-complete evidence on the beneficial effects of morale among workers is the belief that, in an affluent society, a satisfied work force is to be preferred to a dissatisfied one, produc-tivity, the "threat" of unions, and other questions quite aside.

Education and Job Satisfaction

On the score of job satisfaction, the evidence is somewhat more conclusive, if survey studies of worker attitudes are to be taken at face value.[5] From 1934 to 1963, employers have

---

[3] Katzell, *op. cit.*, p. 356.

[4] For a cogent discussion of the findings when such efforts are made from the point of view of an economist concerned with extensions of theories of the firm, see Harvey Leibenstein, "Allocative Efficiency vs. 'X-Efficiency'," *American Economic Review*, LVI (1966), 392–415.

[5] Daniel Bell argues that such attitudes are useless for most purposes, for they are expressed by people with no realistic alternatives to the meaning-less work they describe in response to the probes of social-science head-counters. See his remarks in a WBAI roundtable on "The Meaning of Work," summarized by Robert B. Cooney, "Democracy in the Work Place," *American Federationist*, LXIX (1962), 11.

cooperated with researchers who have produced no fewer than 450 percentage counts. The fact that "the median has fluctuated between 12- and 13-per cent dissatisfied for the past decade"[6] has not slowed or diminished the efforts of social scientists, nor has it stopped managers from seeking to document the malaise in their plants and offices or caused them to cut budgets for elaborate morale-building programs, complete with high-priced human-relations consultants, "sensitivity" trainers, and such exotic management gimmicks as "managerial grids."

Some—a small fraction—of these studies contain sufficient information to permit a review of the linkages between workers' educational achievements and the attitudes toward work that supposedly influence their work behavior. The following section points up once again the depressing fact that our faith in education gains little support from the social scientists.

Worker Satisfaction

Next to the findings that fewer than a quarter of all American workers are "dissatisfied" with their work, the survey result reported most frequently is that job satisfaction increases with job level. This finding is also consistently reported in other industrial nations, although the over-all percentage differences in satisfation among countries are considerable.[7] Thus, social scientists document the association of personal expectations

[6] H. Alan Robinson, Ralph P. Connors, and Ann H. Robinson, "Job Satisfaction Researches of 1963," Personnel and Guidance Journal, XLIII (1964), 36. This is the 22nd in a continuing series, the bibliographical notations for which are given in this 1964 report.

[7] See Alex Inkeles, "Industrial Man: The Relation of Status to Experience, Perception and Value," American Journal of Sociology, LXVI (1960), 1–31. For American data, see Frederick Herzberg et al., Job Attitudes: Review of Research and Opinion (Pittsburgh: Psychological Service of Pittsburgh, 1957), p. 20; and Vroom, op. cit., pp. 129–32.

with job attitudes;[8] workers who hold high-level jobs and whose occupational expectations have therefore been more nearly fulfilled are more likely to be satisfied than those with frustrated job dreams.

These findings point to the strong likeihood that worker expectations are the most promising subject of research with respect to job attitudes. And it requires little imagination to hypothesize that workers' educational backgrounds may be a major determinant of their occupational expectations and hence of their satisfactions. Educational achievements can predictably be associated with higher job expectations; consequently, attitudes toward work would be more favorable among better-educated workers as their occupational skills increase.

Unfortunately, this hypothesis is not examined even in studies in which investigators troubled to collect information on workers' educational backgrounds. There is a tendency, perhaps the result of a trained incapacity to confront the obvious in favor of status-enhancing scientism, to cross-tabulate attitudes with such exotic variables as ego involvement rather than with more commonplace demographic characteristics. To judge from the two dozen studies that do afford an opportunity to examine all or parts of the hypothesis, it is probably valid.

In one of the early and most widely cited studies of workers' satisfaction, Dr. Nancy Morse attributed the bulk of the observed differences between satisfied and dissatisfied clerical employees to variations in the supervisory styles to which these 742 low- and middle-skill-level white-collar personnel were exposed. A close examination of the data, however, reveals that the differences in satisfactions between the less and better-educated workers in each of several skill groups were as great as or greater than the differences among workers

[8] Katzell, *op. cit.*, p. 263.

broken down according to their supervisors on two of three dimensions of satisfaction employed in the study. With regard to the third dimension, the better-educated were "more satisfied," a reversal the author notes but does not fully explain, in a study that stresses the significance of supervisory "styles" for worker satisfaction.[9]

In a 1957 review, Professors Herzberg, Mausner, and Peterson located 13 relevant studies, and they reported that

> . . . five show no difference in job attitudes among workers differing in education; three show an increase in morale with increased education; another five show that the higher these workers' educational level, the lower their morale . . . . The three studies showing increased morale with education are in no case very conclusive . . . ; [they] were carried out either with groups having a restricted range of education, or with groups in unusual circumstances [e.g., retarded workers].[10]

A somewhat more specific test of the hypothesis was made in an investigation which concluded that the best-paid workers, who presumably were not doing tedious work and had lower educational achievements, were the employees with the highest levels of job satisfaction.[11] Herzberg's review indicates that this is indeed the case; the inverse relationship between educational achievement and work satisfaction in a given job category is reduced, *though not eliminated*, as the attitudes of successively older workers are examined.

Herzberg's conclusion is in basic accord with more general formulations in his field. Discussion in psychological circles in recent years posits a need to reduce dissonance among "cog-

9 Nancy Morse, *Satisfaction in the White Collar Job* (Ann Arbor, University of Michigan, Institute for Social Research, Survey Research Center, 1953). Efforts to recover the original data from the Survey Research Center and from Dr. Morse were not successful.

10 Herzberg *et al., op. cit.,* pp. 15–16.

11 Richard Centers and Hadley Cantril, "Income Satisfaction and Income Aspiration," *Journal of Abnormal and Social Psychology,* XLI (1956), 64–69.

nitions" and indicates that age, as well as educational achievement, should influence peoples' attitudes toward their work.
Discrepancies between what people believe to be true and
what they believe *should* be true, it is argued, are painful,
and people seek to reduce that pain by changing their beliefs,
or by elaborating them, so that beliefs and realities seem to
become consistent.[12] Thus, as better-educated workers with
lower-level jobs get older, they find various rationalizations
that explain away the continuing discrepancy between their
aspirations and rewards.

That an appropriately modified hypothesis has merit seems
to be a justifiable inference drawn from a brace of investigations. Howard Vollmer and Jack Kinney report unambiguous
results in a study of more than 2,220 civilians employed by the
Army's Ordnance Corps in the 1950's. The per cent of these
employees "satisfied" and "highly satisfied" goes down, and
the per cent dissatisfied goes up, as educational achievements
go up from grammar school, through high school, and up to
college. The hypothesis that the older, well-educated workers
may reduce "cognitive dissonance" by reappraising their jobs
is perhaps borne out by the authors' finding that "education
is more highly related to job satisfaction than is age, although
both seem to have a definite relation to the degree of job
satisfaction."[13]

The authors are careful to specify that "when management
wishes to develop people in certain positions in the light of
their long-range potentialities, [the] preference for younger
and higher educated applicants may be justified." This observation, while perhaps appropriate in a study that is substantially subversive of managers' theories about educated
workers, did not win support in the previous chapter, and

[12] Leon A. Festinger, *A Theory of Cognitive Dissonance* (Evanston, Ill.:
Row, Peterson, 1957).
[13] Howard M. Vollmer and Jack A. Kinney, "Age, Education and Job
Satisfaction," *Personnel*, XXXII (1955), 38–43.

there are some grounds for believing that many better-educated workers gain "real" promotions by interfirm rather than intrafirm mobility.

The data on the relationships between educational achievement and occupational accomplishment suggest a further refinement of the earlier hypothesis. One might expect, from the studies reviewed, that relationships between educational achievement, opportunities for advancement (real or perceived), and job attitudes parallel those bearing on education, occupational achievement, and attitudes. Once again, the work of previous researchers is less than fully revealing; their preoccupation with complex psychological and sociological constructs appears to get in the way of what are presumably more pedestrian, although they may be more productive, lines of inquiry.

It is likely that if the investigators traced their way back from "achievement motives," for example, they would be able to give such abstractions higher orders of specificity. It should be apparent that if "ego involvement" is a prerequisite to job satisfaction in a particular job setting, it would be useful to know what *kinds* of people are likely to experience such involvement, and what kinds of conditions encourage or reinforce it.

Employers, we may be sure, can more easily screen applicants than they can *shape* them; managers, after all, do not typically operate in a labor market in which they have *no* choice in the matter. And the tendency to screen out the less educated personnel may, in fact, have the effect of constraining choice on emprically questionable grounds. It is not insignificant that dissatisfaction is from two to four times greater among the better- than the less educated group in the Vollmer-Kinney study, while there is a regular difference of 10 percentage points between the satisfied and the highly satisfied among the better-educated subjects.

Two IBM researchers studied the educational credentials

and work satisfaction of 727 employees, half of the first-level supervisory personnel, in a large American corporation in the context of the so-called reference groups of these personnel. It was their hypothesis, in the curious language of their otherwise lucid report, that

> . . . college education or lack thereof constitutes a key input in the individual's self-evaluation. This self-evaluation in turn leads to expectations regarding salary opportunities which in turn affect satisfactions with present salary conditions. As a consequence, we would expect that having attended college would negatively affect satisfaction with pay since, for any given pay level, the college-trained person will be further away from the set of expectations he holds for himself. Further, if these expectations are held constant, then the difference between the college-educated and the non-college-educated should disappear because this would also partially control for reference groups, self-concept, and aspiration level.[14]

In addition to age and skill level, their analysis took into account the respondents' perceptions of getting comparable jobs elsewhere and of earning more money on their present jobs.

The findings were that satisfaction goes down with increasing education and that, although optimistic "external" expectations reduced the magnitude of the observed relationship, the differences by educational achievement remained greater than would be likely by chance. The differences nearly disappeared when satisfactions with present pay were compared in juxtaposition with the duties and responsibilities of the respondents, but the finding that "higher education in [this] sample is associated with relative dissatisfaction with pay" was not vitiated when the respondents' age and skill level were held constant.[15]

In the study of 550 bank employees reported in Chapter V,

[14] S. M. Klein and J. R. Maher, "Education Level and Satisfaction with Pay," *Personnel Psychology*, XIX (1962), 198.
[15] *Ibid.*, p. 204.

similar patterns emerged. When "better" and "less" educated tellers were compared, the former were overrepresented among those critical of management, and the latter were slightly overrepresented among those who were favorably disposed toward a long series of management practices considered in the study.

Some of the bank's managers tended also to emphasize the significance of educational achievement for promotions within the organization. One of the results of this practice—which is sometimes used by these managers to avoid acknowledging their impotence with respect to promotion policy, and sometimes to discourage valued employees from seeking transfers that would facilitate their own but not the manager's organizational career—is that approximately 150 of these tellers attended school after working hours. The modest educational differences were sharpened appreciably when these tellers' attitudes were compared to those of non-attenders. Indeed, the two most powerful predictors of dissatisfaction were the emphasis managers placed on education for promotion and the factor of attendance in after-hour educational programs, findings that parallel the results with respect to performance, reported earlier.

Dr. Edward M. Lehman, of Cornell University's Medical Center, examined the mobility patterns and satisfactions of men in practically every position within a regional affiliate of a large nationwide utilities industry.[16] His findings are altogether consistent with the theme in the present analysis. His sample included college and non-college men, and he reasoned that their "promotion satisfactions" could be interpreted only by examining their promotion experiences together with their educational backgrounds. After establishing the fact that the better-educated group had greater "initial opportunity," Lehman compared the satisfactions of more and less mobile men and

[16] Edward M. Lehman, "Mobility and Satisfaction in an Industrial Organization," unpublished Ph.D. dissertation, Columbia University, 1966.

found that although actual mobility experience is important in predicting promotion satisfaction, the prediction can be sharpened by considering initial opportunity. His findings are reported in Table VI-1.

TABLE VI-1

SATISFACTION WITH PROMOTIONS,
BY INITIAL OPPORTUNITY FOR MOBILITY AND ACTUAL MOBILITY

Initial Opportunity	Actual Mobility	% Satisfied	Number Satisfied
Low	Low	33.7	83
Low	Moderate	62.4	93
Low	High	76.2	42
High	Low	27.3	44
High	High	72.0	50

SOURCE: Lehman, *op. cit.*, p. 79.

Lehman also reports a close association between his respondents' satisfaction with promotion and their satisfactions with other aspects of the job.

Fred Goldner also considered the satisfactions with their promotions of 337 managers employed by a large electronics manufacturer in 1963; his findings are entirely in line with Lehman's.[17] He divided his managers into groups according to their length of service with the company, and reports that satisfaction is inversely related to educational achievements among managers in all three of the groups so constructed. The data are presented in Table VI-2. The percentages in the table refer to the percentage of respondents whose answers to the question "Are you satisfied with your advancement?" were below the mean of 7.5, which was used as the breakpoint for determining high and low satisfactions on a scale from 0 to 10.

[17] Fred Goldner, "Organizations in Motion," research in progress on management as a work force, Columbia University Graduate School of Business. Personal communication to the author.

TABLE VI-2

PERCENTAGE OF MANAGERS REPORTING LOW SATISFACTION
WITH THEIR PROMOTIONS, BY YEARS OF COMPANY SERVICE
AND EDUCATION

Years of Company Service	Education		
	Not a College Graduate	College Graduate	Advanced Degree
7 or less	—	30	36
	(2)a	(44)	(22)
8–15	14	35	47
	(29)	(101)	(43)
16 or more	36	45	—
	(58)	(33)	(5)
Total	28	35	43
	(89)	(178)	(70)

ª The numbers in parentheses represent the base on which percentages
were calculated; per cents are not shown for small bases.

SOURCE: Goldner, *op. cit.*

Corollaries of Dissatisfaction

That some job dissatisfactions are of more than routine interest is strongly suggested by the limited data available relating education with turnover and with workers' mental health.

Professor Bullock reports, in a study of 70 former employees and 100 present clerical employees of an Ohio company, that former employees had more job experience, were
older, and had more formal education than present employees.
The average scores of the two groups on scales purportedly
measuring their satisfactions were also significantly different.[18]
Form and Geschwender also discovered that there were
statistically significant inverse relationships between the sat-

[18] Robert Bullock, *Social Factors Related to Job Satisfaction* (Columbus:
Bureau of Business Research, College of Commerce and Administration,
Ohio State University, 1952).

isfactions and turnover rates of better- and less educated workers.[19]

These findings corroborate those reported in one of the most widely cited studies of "the occupational plans of workers" by Yale's distinguished labor economist, Professor Lloyd Reynolds. He reported, in the early 1950's, that workers with a high-school education or better showed a markedly greater desire to change jobs. In some cases their responses, as Professor Reynolds points out, probably reflected a desire to escape from manual work altogether.[20] He writes, "Of those with more than 12 years of education, 36 per cent [in one sample] and 48 per cent [in a second] wanted to leave their present job. Of those with four years or less of education, on the other hand, only 13 per cent . . . and none [in the two worker samples, respectively] wanted to leave."[21]

The deplorable quality of research on turnover makes it impossible to pursue this issue further in the present study. It is perhaps remarkable to note, in this connection, that though turnover was frequently mentioned as a problem facing the personnel executives with whom interviews were conducted, none had compared the characteristics, including the educational achievements, of short- and long-service employees despite the fact that relevant personnel data were retained in personnel files for long periods.

When better-educated people do not enjoy consistency between their educational and occupational statuses, they may also be more interested in union activities. In a study of New York cab drivers, Al Nash identified the success of their union with the efforts of a group of drivers who had attended a

---

[19] William H. Form and James H. Geschwender, "Social Reference Basis of Job Satisfaction: The Case of Manual Workers," *American Sociological Review*, XXVII (1962), 228–37.

[20] Lloyd G. Reynolds, *The Structure of Labor Markets* (New York: Harper and Bros., 1951), p. 80.

[21] *Ibid.*, p. 81.

training program conducted in New York City by Cornell's School of Industrial Relations. This group, which rated their "self-esteem" higher than the non-attending groups, was also disproportionately better educated than the more passive group of drivers.[22] One implication of such findings is that union leaders have better empirical reasons for concentrating on educational achievement in their recruiting efforts than do managers.

Finally, it would not be surprising, in light of the foregoing analysis, if better-educated workers in a given job category in fact suffered more than the frustration generated by the gap between their occupational achievements and the expectations to which their educational achievements may contribute. This is implied in an interesting study, *Mental Health of the Industrial Worker*,[23] in which the sample was broken down by skill levels according to official job titles, "clarified when necessary by consultation with automotive 'insiders'; the worker's own description of his duties, job operations, and training time required; and the rate of pay."[24] Mental-health scores were derived from six component indexes and two composite indexes constructed from coded responses to a carefully structured interview. The coding process was validated by a comparison of scores with clinical judgments of the interview material (for 40 cases) by "several experienced, highly qualified clinical psychologists and psychiatrists." The level of agreement,[25] especially as these things go, was remarkably high.

The over-all results do not confirm the expectations that better-educated men in routine jobs exhibit poorer mental health than do those with less education, possibly, as Kornhauser suggests, because the effects of education when skill

[22] Al Nash, "A Study of New York's Taxicab Union," unpublished Master's Essay, Department of Sociology, Columbia University, 1967.
[23] Arthur Kornhauser, *Mental Health of the Industrial Worker* (New York: Wiley, 1965).
[24] *Ibid.*, p. 56.
[25] *Ibid.*, p. 31.

level is held constant "are offset or overbalanced by *other* ways in which education relates to mental health."[26] Comparisons of school success did show a little support for the notion that "status inconsistency" can generate problems, although the support is shaky in that, while a relatively small proportion of the group in low-level jobs whose school success had been above average manifested good mental health, this group had relatively few respondents with poor mental health compared with those whose school accomplishments had been below average.

When Kornhauser undertook to perform a more refined analysis, however, the picture changed somewhat. Better-educated workers in lower skill-level jobs had lower "life satisfaction" and "self-esteem" scores, although the "personal morale" and "sociability" scores among the middle-aged and the younger middle-aged, respectively, were higher than among the less educated workers. While these tendencies are counterbalancing and thus tend to cancel out the effects of "inconsistency" between education and occupation,

> . . . the two particular mental health dimensions that do manifest the [incongruency hypothesis] relationship are precisely the ones that might be most expected to do so. Self-esteem and satisfaction with life can be presumed to depend to greater degree on vocational achievement in relation to aspirations than would feelings of social distrust (personal morale), social withdrawal, and other elements of mental health, which are more likely to derive from lifelong influences apart from the job.[27]

The relevant data are presented in Table VI-3, on the following page.

These findings can give precious little comfort to morale-conscious executives who might more easily improve the

[26] *Ibid.*, p. 136. Emphasis in original.
[27] *Ibid.*, p. 137.

TABLE VI-3

PERCENTAGE OF EDUCATIONAL GROUPS AT TWO
LOWEST OCCUPATIONAL LEVELS WHO HAVE HIGH SCORES
ON SELECTED MENTAL-HEALTH COMPONENTS

Mental-Health Components	Young		Middle-Aged		
	Some High School or Less	High- School Graduates	8th Grade or Less	Some High School	High- School Graduates
Life satisfaction	25	11	38	33	18
Self-esteem	18	11	22	14	12
Personal morale	25	21	19	32	59
Sociability	32	47	21	44	59
Number	(57)	(19)	(81)	(57)	(17)

SOURCE: Kornhauser, *op. cit.*, p. 137.

"human relations" climates and the "self-actualizing" potentials of their personnel by modifying their own attitudes toward educational credentials. It is no doubt a good deal easier to alter these attitudes than to manipulate the psyches of employees whose educations generate expectations well beyond those that the organization can fulfill.

The general line of analysis in this chapter was put to more refined tests in a revealing reinterpretation of data collected by the Roper organization. The fact that these particular materials have already provoked widespread interest among students of worker "alienation" and have even been the subject of one large-scale report[28] justifies the allocation of an entire chapter to their exploitation, the task of Chapter VII.

[28] Robert Blauner, *Alienation and Freedom* (Chicago: University of Chicago Press, 1964).

VII The Blue-Collar Worker: A Special Case

Several reasons have already been suggested for the seemingly perverse relationships between educational achievement and work performance. Contrary to popular belief, education does not always group people according to their abilities, especially the abilities to do specific jobs. This fact reflects, not only the great variations in standards among the nation's thousands of school systems and institutions of higher learning, but the parallel differences among the units within a system and even within a given school. In addition, there may be some truth in the adage that "you can't keep a good man down" in a society in which there are discrepancies between educators' and employers' definitions of a "good man."

Beyond the question of ability, however, lies the more subtle one of motivation, a question that can be tackled indirectly through an examination of the satisfactions of workers while their educational achievements and their job levels are held constant. The results help to explain why the oft-cited positive relationship between job level and work satisfaction is far from perfect.

We have already implied that Americans are influenced by the vulgarization of the argument that they have foregone incomes to complete their education. The popular culture plus experiences within the educational apparatus itself, with its implicitly or explicitly vocational aims, its placement personnel, guidance counselors, career-day programs, and employer interviews—all add independent weight to the widespread expectations among Americans that they deserve jobs that are interesting, that they will be promoted on the basis of abilities to which their diplomas and degrees give testimony, and that they will make money. "To get a better job, get a better education," reads the subway placard; "things are changing," says the disc jockey, "and so," he quickly adds, "finish your education to get a bigger piece of the action and a better job."

When their jobs are dull, when their chances of promotion are slim, when their salaries are dissappointingly low, then employees are dissatisfied, poorly motivated, and poorer employees; if they can, they change jobs. But if, over the years, they do not search out better jobs, or if family and other obligations limit their movement into more rewarding and gratifying work experiences, or if successive job changes have shown that their aspirations cannot be fulfilled, they begin to accommodate, to "settle in," to lower their aspirations, and to rationalize their circumstances; their dissatisfaction, though persistent, diminishes.

This argument is supported by data already presented. It is possible, however, to forge some of the links in the chain of reasoning through the detailed analysis of a special case—the blue-collar worker.

A "job satisfaction" study, conducted by the Roper organization for the editors of *Fortune* Magazine, provides information on the desire for promotion, the perceived chances for promotion, and the job satisfactions of 2,139 blue-collar respondents.[1] The survey was conducted among workers in 16 industries and, according to Elmo Roper and Robert Blauner, "Although not a random probability sample . . . [it was] 'a pretty carefully controlled quota sample,' and therefore representative of a population much larger than

[1] Data from this study were made available by the Roper Center at Williams College, Williamstown, Mass.; once again we are indebted to its director, Professor Phillip Hastings, and to his staff.

the 3,000 workers interviewed."[2] According to Elmo Roper and Associates, "Within the universe defined, the sample was so stratified as to contain the proper distribution of respondents by sex, geographic area, race, and age according to the Census of 1940,"[3] all of which is to say that the results, in their time, could probably be generalized to a substantial part of the blue-collar work force.

From the 3,000 workers originally interviewed, we removed the foremen and the women; our analysis is thus based on 2,139 males below the rank of foreman in 16 industries across the United States.[4]

Education and Skill

Our first analysis of the data consisted of a series of rank-order correlations[5] between each of 15 questions measuring satisfaction and the workers' background characteristics. The results showed that:

1. Education is indeed strongly associated with aspirations,

[2] Robert Blauner, *Alienation and Freedom* (Chicago: University of Chicago Press, 1964), in a citation from his correspondence with Mr. Roper, p. 16, note 11. Professor Blauner used these same "Roper data" in his book.

[3] Survey #58, *Fortune*, January, 1947.

[4] Since aspirations might reasonably be expected to be related to both educational achievement and job attitudes, 238 foremen were eliminated from the sample because they had reached the top of the blue-collar hierarchy, were more skilled, better educated, and had longer service than the larger group. Answers to such questions as "Does your job lead to promotion?" and questions dealing with aspiration to be foremen were uninterpretable when the respondents included both foremen and men of lesser rank. Women were also dropped because in an initial set of tabulations it became clear that the most interesting and crucial patterns in the results were substantially blurred by their inclusion. Women, particularly low earners, often work to supplement their husband's income and regard occupational issues as less salient than other issues facing them, a fact that argued for their exclusion.

[5] In this and later analyses of rank correlation the Tau Beta statistic was used. For a discussion of this statistic, see p. 96, *n.* 10.

whether those aspirations are measured in terms of a desire to be foreman or, alternatively, to be a union official;

2. Although education is weakly and sometimes insignificantly (though inversely) associated with work satisfactions, the "effects" of education are more intense among higher-aspiring workers.

3. Skill levels consistently "predicted" satisfactions and dissatisfactions. People with low-skill jobs were dissatisfied; the percentage satisfied increased in each category of increasing skill.[6]

The patterns of response to the question, "Is [your job] too simple to bring out your best abilities, or not?" are perhaps the most interesting and relevant to the present analysis. The question refers specifically to a dimension of work experiences that would involve a consideration of educational background.

The association between answers to this question and to others indicates that it can legitimately be construed as bearing upon dissatisfactions and satisfactions of workers. In survey research it is not uncommon to validate a question by comparing the responses it evokes with other seemingly independent measures. Judged by this standard, the validity, so-called, of this question is high. Respondents who stated that their jobs were too simple to utilize their abilities tended also to say that their jobs "do not enable them to try their own ideas," that their jobs permitted them "to do their work, and keep [their] minds on other things," and that they did not find their jobs "nearly always" or "mostly" interesting. They tended to reject the proposition that their "jobs would lead to promotion if done well." Moreover, these answers were most

---

[6] The data provided no direct information on skill level. In his book-length treatment of worker "alienation," based on these same data, Professor Robert Blauner assigned skill levels to the respondents in accordance with the number of months of training or experience they reported to be necessary to enable them to handle the jobs they held at the time of the survey. This procedure has been followed in the present study. Thus "skill level," the term used here, is really an indirect measure of job complexity.

strongly linked to one another among those with more education working in lower-skill jobs. In light of these patterns in the responses to the question of whether the job was too simple for their abilities, it has been used as an all-purpose measure of job satisfaction; those who regard their jobs as "too simple" are dissatisfied.

Table VII-1 shows a dramatic correlation between education and satisfaction. Reading across, we see that dissatisfaction, the feeling that the job is too simple for the worker's abilities, decreases with increased skill required except among those with less than a grade-school education. In the exceptional case, however, the numbers are too small for meaningful comparison.

Reading down, dissatisfaction increases with increased education among all but those in jobs requiring the most skill. The over-all rank correlation between dissatisfaction and skill is substantially increased for those with high-school or college education. (See the column on the far right.) This means that dissatisfaction is even more closely tied to skill level among better-educated employees than it is for the group as a whole.

Because of the empirical importance of skill for satisfaction, and because the logic of the argument calls for the comparison of better-educated with less educated men doing approximately similar jobs, the men were divided into four categories (Table VII-2);[7] these categories are descriptive of workers' "status inconsistency" because they indicate whether a man's skill level is in line with his educational level.

The four resulting combinations of education-plus-skill can be located on a continuum describing the degree of "fit" between education and job; this two-dimensional characteristic of workers closely approximates an accurate index of "status

[7] This procedure has the additional virtue that it creates categories large enough to permit further subdivisions according to age, length of service, and other characteristics.

TABLE VII-1

PERCENTAGE OF BLUE-COLLAR WORKERS DISSATISFIED, BY EDUCATION AND SKILL

Education	Skill (in training time required for job)					
	Less than 1 Month	1-3 Months	3-24 Months	More than 2 Years	Total	Tau β
None	20 (15)[a]	0 (4)	57 (7)	38 (8)	29 (34)	-.21
1-8 years	38 (275)	33 (116)	17 (217)	15 (219)	26 (827)	.20*
9-12 years	58 (216)	39 (107)	28 (279)	16 (271)	33 (873)	.31**
More than 12 years	50 (10)	75 (4)	29 (21)	16 (31)	29 (66)	.30
Total	46 (516)	36 (231)	23 (524)	16 (529)	-.07[c]	.24**[b]
Tau β	-.20	-.11	-.10	.01		

[a] The numbers in parentheses represent the base on which percentages were calculated.
[b] Tau β between dissatisfaction and skill.
[c] Tau β between dissatisfaction and education.
* Significant at the .05 level.
** Significant at the .01 level.

TABLE VII-2
EDUCATION AND SKILL COMBINED TO FORM A
STATUS-INCONSISTENCY VARIABLE

Education (in years)	Skill (months of training time required for job)	
	High (3 or more)	Low (Less than 3)
Low (0–8)	Inconsistent Most satisfaction (451)[a]	Consistent 3d most satisfaction (410)
High (9 or more)	Consistent 2d most satisfaction (602)	Inconsistent Least satisfaction (337)

[a] The number of men in the status-inconsistency category.

inconsistency"; that is, the relative discrepancy between a man's educational and occupational achievement.[8]

Accordingly, workers with high-skill jobs and comparatively low educational achievements would consider themselves fortunate and theoretically would be the most content because they enjoy rewards that are "inconsistently" high given their educational status. The next most content group would be the one in which work rewards match (in accordance with prevailing norms) educational achievement. People in low-skilled jobs and with low educational achievements would be less happy than those in the first two groups simply because their rewards are low; the *most* dissatisfied, however,

[8] The concept of "status inconsistency" or "status incongruence" is by no means new; indeed, the notion is often invoked in a variety of guises in efforts to understand social systems, large and small. See, for example, Gerhard Lenski, "Status Crystalization: A Non-Vertical Dimension of Social Status," *American Sociological Review*, XIX (1954,) 405-13. The idea in part is that social status has a number of hierarchical dimensions, that individuals occupy positions on each of these hierarchies, that social norms define the ranking of positions on each of these hierarchies, and that people whose position on one dimension is "incongruent" with their position on another suffer various social and psychological strains. The concept has been questioned both methodologically and theoretically, but it serves as a convenient shorthand for the two variables we are combining here.

would be those whose low-skilled jobs provide returns below
those perceived to be due people with relatively *high* educational achievements, and whose rewards are "inconsistently"
low in the light of their education. Once again, the concept of
status inconsistency in the present context refers to the identity or discrepancy between the rewards a person's status in a
social setting could be expected to earn him (according to
prevailing standards), on the one hand, and the rewards he
actually receives, on the other. The results of the analysis
throughout this chapter are consistent with this formulation
in almost every particular.[9]

Aspirations and Expectations

The explanation of the fact that men with more education are
more dissatisfied with low-skilled jobs than are those with
less education appears to lie in expectations: Better-educated
men expect to do better.

Table VII-3 shows not only that better-educated men want
to be foremen, but that more of these workers consider the
prospect likely. That their estimates are realistic may be inferred from the fact that better-educated men do have a better
chance: Foremen, excluded from our study, were indeed better educated. And better-educated men see more likelihood of
being promoted above the foreman's level. They are also more
likely to say that their "job leads to promotion" in general.

[9] The use of the concept "status consistency" borrows the very assumptions of the education-employment nexus this study undertook to explore.
If the nature of the link between education and job level is to be seriously
questioned, as argued in this book, then there is no educational level that
is *per se* "consistent" with any particular skill level. But the conventional
wisdom on the relationship of rewards to education and the linkage of income differences to occupational differences has been stamped into the wax
of culture and psyche; to question the value of these rigidities and prescriptions, one must first demonstrate their impact.

TABLE VII-3

PERCENTAGE OF BLUE-COLLAR WORKERS DISSATISFIED[a], BY STATUS
INCONSISTENCY AND PERCEIVED LIKELIHOOD OF BECOMING A FOREMAN

Perceived Likelihood of Becoming a Foreman[b]	Status Inconsistency					
	Low Ed– High Skill	High Ed– High Skill	Low Ed– Low Skill	High Ed– Low Skill	Total	Tau β
Likely	8 (60)[c]	16 (147)	18 (28)	40 (58)	19 (293)	.23
Unlikely	24 (74)	31 (108)	43 (79)	65 (79)	40 (340)	.31*

[a] In this and subsequent tables, those who are classified as dissatisfied are those who consider their job too simple for their abilities.

[b] This question was asked only of those answering affirmatively when asked whether they would like to be a foreman.

[c] The numbers in parentheses represent the base on which percentages were calculated.

* Significant at the .05 level.

When these aspirations are not satisfied, when their desire to be promoted seems likely to be disappointed, all of these workers are more dissatisfied with their jobs, but those with relatively more education and less skill are especially disaffected; the proportion who are dissatisfied increases by 25 per cent. Even among the relatively happy skilled men with little education, dissatisfaction triples, from 8 to 24 per cent, when they think it unlikely that they will rise to foremen.

Employers' notions about the desirability of hiring better-educated people in order to have a pool of promotable people, therefore, might well help generate discontent among better-educated, aspiring workers in low-skilled jobs, and particularly in shops and factories in which these workers perceive comparatively little chance of being promoted.

Furthermore, the predictions made in connection with "status inconsistency" are confirmed here as they are throughout the analysis: dissatisfaction increases uniformly, from the relatively contented man in a high-skill job despite low education (in the far left column), through the quite discontented man in a low-skill job. This stepwise pattern can be seen even among those who expect their aspirations to become foremen to be fulfilled. Forty per cent of the better-educated men in the lowest skilled jobs who think they *will* become foremen are unhappy.[10]

The impact of frustrated expectations on dissatisfaction is exactly the same when promotion possibilities are tapped by two other questions: "What are your chances of being promoted to a job above the foreman's level?" and "Does your job lead to promotion?" The pattern of the results was identical to that found in Table VII-3. Even the percentages were similar.[11]

Once again, the effect of status inconsistency is mitigated, but not eliminated, by (perceived) opportunities for promotion. Dissatisfactions which are born of the feeling that a job is too simple for one's abilities and which grow with increasing education among less skilled workers are only somewhat modified by opportunities for organizational advancement.

Employers who assert that better-educated workers are only temporarily "misplaced" in their firm, that they plan to promote these men, and that eventual promotion will mitigate the effects of the underutilization of educated manpower may well be correct. The tables indicate, however, that some skepticism is justified; even when these workers perceive that they will have the opportunity to advance, their dissatisfactions are relatively high. And there simply cannot be enough positions as foremen in industry to accommodate all who want them. The fact that foremen in American industry increasingly come from the ranks of college graduates makes the matter even more problematical.

[10] All of these men want to be foremen and think they will make it, yet a substantial minority see even this job as too simple. The contrast with the less educated men with high skills is particularly striking.

[11] Although differences between "aspirers" and "nonaspirers" were never more than four percentage points, they were always in the predicted direction.

TABLE VII-4

PERCENTAGE OF BLUE-COLLAR WORKERS DISSATISFIED, BY
STATUS INCONSISTENCY AND YEARS OF COMPANY SERVICE

| Years of Company Service | Status Inconsistency | | | | | |
	Low Ed– High Skill	High Ed– High Skill	Low Ed– Low Skill	High Ed– Low Skill	Total	Tau β
Less than 2	27 (85)a	17 (186)	44 (152)	54 (169)	36 (592)	.32**
2–5	19 (73)	27 (132)	39 (78)	48 (61)	31 (344)	.20
More than 5	14 (292)	23 (283)	27 (180)	51 (107)	24 (862)	.23*

a The numbers in parentheses represent the base on which percentages were calculated.
* Significant at the .05 level.
** Significant at the .01 level.

Settling for Less

With dissatisfactions of this magnitude, with the expanded opportunities for switching jobs in the "tight labor market" of 1947, the year the study took place, we can conclude that many of the most dissatisfied workers left for other jobs. The studies described in Chapter V indicated that better-educated men have greater tendencies to leave their jobs. Unfortunately, information on turnover for the men in the Roper survey is not available, but what may be assumed to be the indirect effects of turnover are visible in the data.

Table VII-4 squares well with the hypothesis that dissatisfied workers leave their jobs. Except for those with consistently high education and skill, dissatisfaction is greater among those with short service.

As men see their hopes still unrealized as they grow older,

TABLE VII-5

PERCENTAGE OF BLUE-COLLAR WORKERS DISSATISFIED,
BY STATUS INCONSISTENCY AND AGE

	Status Inconsistency					
Age	Low Ed–High Skill	High Ed–High Skill	Low Ed–Low Skill	High Ed–Low Skill	Total	Tau β
Under 40	19 (152)ᵃ	24 (400)	37 (181)	53 (268)	34 (1,001)	.28**
40 or over	16 (299)	16 (202)	34 (229)	46 (69)	24 (799)	.25*

ᵃ The numbers in parentheses represent the base on which percentages
were calculated.
* Significant at the .05 level.
** Significant at the .01 level.

they begin to rationalize, to reduce the pain of the discrepancy
between their expectations and their achievements, to find
reasons in the constraints or satisfactions of family life for
their lack of mobility, to diminish the importance of work in
favor of other, more pleasant parts of life; in short, to lower
their aspirations and neutralize their dissatisfactions. Table
VII-5 shows that dissatisfaction consistently diminishes with
age in every category of education and skill; the results are
like those in the study by Vollmer, discussed earlier. But even
in the face of these accommodations, dissatisfaction remains
quite high, especially among better-educated workers. And
the increase in dissatisfaction, as one looks from left to right
across the rows, remains striking.

Standards for Unhappiness: Relative Deprivation

Americans expect their lives to fulfill the prescriptions about
the higher rewards due educated workers, and they expect
their incomes and promotion prospects to be in line with
those of other similarly situated workers. Their satisfactions,

in fact, depend on these expectations. The question is not simply, "Am I deprived?" but "Am I deprived when compared with other men like me?"

Although the sociologists who have used the term "relative deprivation" to describe this phenomenon rarely articulate it, the term reflects the fact that there are no intrinsic, a priori criteria for the differential distribution of wealth that are independent of social conventions and the forces that determine them. Differences in income and, to some extent, in social station are thus determined by supply, demand, and power,[12] and the social norms that are reflected in them.

When men decide whether their jobs (and the incomes linked to those jobs) satisfy them, they have little standard to use beyond some sense of their own inner and material needs and the rewards and stations of similar men.

This argument underlies the "status inconsistency" hypothesis developed thus far, but it is possible to carry it a step furthur, to see if a man is more likely to expect his higher educational level to bring him a more skilled job if men at that level typically hold more skilled jobs. The plant in which a worker is employed would serve as a useful focus for comparison (a "reference group"), but the data did not provide information on the plant level. We therefore moved to industry as a conceivable focus for the worker in evaluating his job. The resulting hypothesis proposes that consistency between education and skill will determine dissatisfaction most in those industries in which increments of skill are most closely tied to increments of education.

To test this notion, industries were characterized by their "status consistency"; that is, according to the degree to which

---

[12] This is not the place to discuss the old argument that links rewards to demand and to "society's needs." Suffice it to say that striking sanitation workers in New York City had to let the city smell that its need for these workers required it to raise their rewards. These workers still wound up with wages far short of the income of gossip columnists, for example, people who, by some standards, only produce garbage.

TABLE VII-6

PERCENTAGE OF BLUE-COLLAR WORKERS DISSATISFIED,
BY STATUS INCONSISTENCY AND INDUSTRY STATUS CONSISTENCY

Industry Status Consistency[a]	Status Inconsistency				
	Low Ed– High Skill	High Ed– High Skill	Low Ed– Low Skill	High Ed– Low Skill	Total
Low	21 (262)[b]	22 (387)	35 (208)	48 (188)	29 (1,045)
High	12 (188)	22 (215)	36 (202)	57 (149)	30 (754)

a Industry status consistency is defined on the basis of the correlation between education and skill. High-consistency industries are those with a high and significant Tau Beta.

b The numbers in parentheses represent the base on which percentages were calculated.

skill level is tied to education. Utilizing the relationship between the education and skill levels of the workers in each industry to characterize the industry, a rank-order correlation (Tau Beta) was obtained for each of the 16 industries represented. These industries with high Tau β values between education and skill were characterized as "high consistency" industries; those in which skill level seemed almost unrelated to education were grouped as showing "low consistency."

Table VII-6 shows that the status consistency of industry makes little difference in the proportion of dissatisfied workers among those who *themselves* enjoy consistency with respect to education and skill: those with low education and low skill, and those with high education and high skill (see the two middle columns). The status consistency of the industry does make a big difference among those workers whose own educational achievements are inconsistently higher or lower than their skill level (see the first and last columns).

These two categories, and the life experience that they represent, exert so much influence that they stretch the differences in per cent dissatisfied (around 30 per cent for the population as a whole), from 12 per cent among the less educated men with high-skilled jobs in industries in which higher education is normally required for, or associated with, skilled jobs, to 57 per cent among men with relatively higher educational achievements who do not have skilled jobs although they work in industries in which education usually brings such rewards. Thus when "you need a good education to get a good job," the difference between "making it" despite that system or failing to "make it" despite that system mounts up to a 45 per cent difference.[13]

The results presented by Table VII-6 can be seen in further comparisons of columns 1 and 4. The status consistency of the industry has *opposite* effects for the "low educated, high skill" and the "high educated, low skill" groups. The already low dissatisfaction among the low-education, high-skill group *declines* even further as consistency of industry increases. But the already high dissatisfaction among those with high education and low skill *increases* as consistency of industry increases. Although they are quite unhappy (48 per cent say their job is too simple) in industries in which many similarly educated men are similarly deprived, dissatisfaction increases to 57 per cent in "highly consistent" industries, where most of their better-educated fellows are at higher skill levels than they, and education presumably "counts" in advancement.

---

[13] Professor David Caplowitz has pointed out that there is a certain amount of statistical constraint in these results: high-consistency industries are by definition industries in which there are few men with little education who have high skill. Thus such men may be exceptional and may differ significantly from similar men in less consistent industries. Similarly, better-educated men who have not reached high-skill jobs in consistent industries may also be strange: they may be characterological "losers" whose underachievement is justified. However, he concurs that the consistent patterning of the results makes relative deprivation at least as plausible an explanation, and perhaps more plausible, than personal idiosyncrasy. Note that high-education, low-skill men constitute 25 per cent of the entire group (see Table VII-2) and 15 per cent of those in high-consistency industries. Low-education, high-skill men are 19 per cent of the men in consistent industries.

Opportunities

We hedged our predictions about the low-education, low-skilled group while designing these cross-tabulations, recognizing that while their unhappiness might be diminished in "consistent" industries because the "system" explained their lack of advancement, they might, indeed, be less unhappy with jobs in those inconsistent industries where many men with relatively modest education had highly skilled jobs; although their "relative deprivation" could not then be blamed so easily on the system, the opportunity for advancement to a highly skilled job in the same industry might actually exist. Certainly the importance of opportunity for advancement in determining job satisfactions was demonstrated above.

To assess opportunities even approximately we must know the particular educational and skill distribution of jobs within each industry and the consistency with which skilled jobs were tied to educational level. Table VII-7 gives this information.

We see that more of the low-education, low-skill workers are unhappy in low-skill industries (35 per cent and 50 per cent), where their opportunities are few, and that they are most dissatisfied, even more than better-educated workers similarly situated, in those industries whose employees tend to be better educated and in low-skilled jobs. For in these industries these less educated men must compete with better-educated men for scarce skilled jobs. In these industries, on the other hand, the better-educated workers in unskilled jobs, for their part, need suffer less embarassment: though their opportunities are few, other educated men suffer the same deprivation. Here they register the least dissatisfaction.[14]

---

[14] We also attempted to assess the effect of the region by following a procedure similar to that evolved to determine the effect of the industry.

TABLE VII-7
PERCENTAGE OF BLUE-COLLAR WORKERS DISSATISFIED, BY STATUS INCONSISTENCY AND INDUSTRY EDUCATION AND SKILL COMPOSITION

| Industry Composition | | Status Inconsistency | | | | | |
Education	Skill	Low Ed– High Skill	High Ed– High Skill	Low Ed– Low Skill	High Ed– Low Skill	Total	Tau β
Low	High	19 (84)[a]	24 (95)	28 (58)	44 (25)	25 (262)	.16
High	High	12 (68)	18 (175)	22 (23)	47 (32)	20 (298)	.21
Low	Low	19 (233)	23 (229)	35 (266)	57 (210)	33 (941)	.30*
High	Low	14 (65)	23 (103)	50 (60)	41 (70)	31 (298)	.18

[a] The numbers in parentheses represent the base on which percentages were calculated.
* Significant at the .01 level.

Technological Complexity and Satisfaction

Professor Blauner, in the study mentioned earlier, concluded that dissatisfaction among the workers in that study could be largely attributed to "job conditions" in "different industries [where] . . . only the levels of training (skill) difference were of an equal magnitude";[15] his analysis was based on workers in four of the 16 industries on which data were available.

We found that although there *are* differences in the percentages of dissatisfied workers according to industry, these differences are not associated with any readily observable *patterns* of differences in the technologies of the industries when all 16 of them are considered. Thus we grouped the 16 industries according to several schemes and discovered that in none of them were the results at all related to the continuum of industries grouped according to worker satisfactions. "Capital intensity" data for these industries during the year of the original Roper study, which might be taken as indicative of technology, did not fit; nor did a continuum of "increasing technology," constructed around production techniques (conceived as "mass production," "batch production," or "unit production") help us to replicate or generalize from Professor Blauner's four-industry model, according to which workers are more satisfied in industries in which they have more control over their work.

Dissatisfactions associated with status inconsistency were greater in large than in small plants, a finding that led us to wonder whether work satisfactions were related to "bureaucratization" in industry. We therefore attempted to create a

---

The results, when controlling for regional education and skill distributions, were ambiguous. The only clearly interpretable feature in the data on region was that the proportion of those dissatisfied continues to increase with increasing personal status inconsistency.

15 Blauner, *op. cit.*, pp. 11–12, *n.* 16. Again, these are the same workers.

measure of "bureaucratization" by combining the size of companies with information on whether or not they were union shops; the idea was that workers who work in larger, more organized plants are more vulnerable to the power and control of organization. The attempt yielded fuzzy results.[16]

Thus although technological and organizational factors were not clear-cut in their effects, the effect of status consistency remained clear and strong.

As expected, increased education creates (and partially reflects) aspirations for jobs requiring greater skill and holding higher position within the industrial hierarchy. The desire for promotion and the expectation of promotion increase markedly as education increases.

Although the desire for jobs requiring increased skill is widespread, and people with these jobs are more satisfied on each of 15 measures of satisfaction, that desire is even stronger among people with more education, and the frustration of their wish for jobs of increasing complexity produces considerable dissatisfaction.

Job attitudes and aspirations are only somewhat tempered by age and increasing length of service. These "experiences" apparently lead to accommodation (and, presumably to the attrition from the work force, and therefore from the sample, of those with greatest dissatisfaction) but are virtually uninfluenced by other personal background characteristics. So great is the dissatisfaction among people with high education

---

[16] The relationship between job dissatisfaction and status inconsistency was stronger for union members than for non-union members. We reasoned that there might be relatively higher levels of dissatisfaction among non-union members and that union membership itself might be a way of coping with job dissatisfaction. Once they have organized, however, members' dissatisfactions might be lowered. The data do not permit a test, although they are consistent with such involuted reasoning: among all but the high-education, low-skilled men, non-unionists are relatively more often dissatisfied. It should be noted that the alternative hypothesis and prediction would also have been consistent with our biases: that more dissatisfied men join unions and *remain* dissatisfied. Union members would then be more dissatisfied. The results did not bear this out, however.

and low skill that even when they believe that they will be promoted, their dissatisfaction is considerable.

That stress on the importance of education for advancement tends to aggravate the unhappiness of educated, unskilled men is indicated by the finding that men with high education and low skill are even *more* unhappy in industries where a high association between education and skill exists, and men with limited education and high skill are even *less* dissatisfied.

Although the *magnitudes* of the relationship between "status inconsistency" and job dissatisfaction can be increased or decreased by introducing statistical controls for other background characteristics, for aspirations, for organizational and environmental, or even "reference group" variables, the basic *pattern* of the relationship (dissatisfaction decreasing from high-education, low-skill men through low-education, high-skill men) remains strong, with few exceptions.

These findings suggest that the use of educational credentials as employment criteria are at least as risky as Professor Seymour Harris argued twenty years ago. Other researchers may find, as Professor Harris suggested, that the dissatisfactions of "educated" workers who believe that their jobs are far below those for which their education qualifies them are a genuine threat to the safety of a democratic society. Nothing that has appeared in these data is inconsistent with the formulations of Columbia historian Richard Hofstadter regarding "status politics," frustrations, and the disaffected radical right in America. The rhetoric of employers, meanwhile, gains little support from these data.

Conclusions

The reader may regard the foregoing as a thorough exploration of data too tarnished by age to mean anything for the present and future, a point that deserves some attention. It is at least possible that the date of the original survey (1947) enhances its significance.

Nineteen forty-seven was a boom year. The labor market was as "tight" as in any period in our peacetime history, which suggests that demand produced by World War II had created economic expansion and, with it, some expansion in opportunities to transfer to other jobs, even given the return of millions of World War II veterans to the work force. At no time since that period have employment conditions been so favorable to the worker. In the survey, the men were asked whether they thought it "likely that they would be laid off in the next six months." The effect of status inconsistency was much stronger among men who felt that their jobs were insecure than among those who thought lay-off was unlikely.

In the face of deteriorated employment conditions from 1950 to the mid-1960's, in the face of a steady mass of unemployed workers, in the face, that is, of conditions of increased and continuing job insecurity, the dissatisfactions of the "underutilized" men in this sample must have been at least as severe until the present boom as it was when job insecurities increased dissatisfactions two decades ago.

The stress on education as a public and private panacea developed after these data were collected. The prescription "to get a good job, get a good education" has been thoroughly impressed on today's workers; if they have a good education, they now expect, more than did the men who answered Roper's questionnaire twenty years ago, to get a good job. Our whole argument has been based on the higher expectations of more-educated men and the dissatisfactions resulting from unfulfilled, and unfulfillable, aspirations. These aspirations have probably been heightened since 1947, as the attained education of the work force has grown since 1947, and as the pressure to "stay in school" has accelerated; the effects of increased education and rising aspirations in dissatisfactions, therefore, have probably grown and not diminished with the passing of time.

Moreover, while unskilled positions have been increasing at slower rates in the years since 1947, opportunities for advancement to foreman—let alone to positions "above the foreman level"—have diminished also as management has shown a penchant for hiring college men as foremen, converting industrial top sergeants into second lieutenants. If twenty years ago the belief that they would not be promoted tripled the dissatisfactions of the usually satisfied men with little education but highly skilled jobs and aggravated the dissatisfactions of the low-skill workers to the extent that 65 per cent of them were unhappy, and if twenty years ago 40 per cent of those better-educated, less-skilled men who *did* believe that they would be promoted were dissatisfied in spite of their good prospects, the unhappiness must be profound indeed for present-day blue-collar workers, whose education is even higher and who have heard and believed the promises made to diploma-holders.

One final test of management's rhetoric, and by implication of formulations concerning the value of education, may be made by exploring the job experiences of public employees. As a consequence of various public policies, civil servants and military personnel, compared to other employees, are somewhat less likely to hold their jobs because of their educational achievements. In the next chapter, therefore, some of the tables, literally and figuratively, are turned in a discussion of data on thousands of military personnel and on a 5-per-cent sample of nearly 200,000 civil servants.

VIII Education and Public Service

The growing concern of Americans with home rule, decentralization, and participatory democratic forms reminds us of the significance of public bureaucracies in the social, political, and economic life of the nation. The tragedy of Vietnam, the degeneration of the measures against poverty, the battles of city dwellers against negligent educators, the struggle of some law-enforcement champions against the enforcement of civil rights, the passionate crusades of students against government contracts with multiversities, all have triggered explosions on the Left and Right against the policies, practices, and strategies of government at all levels. Presidents, mayors, social workers, teachers, chancellors, generals, cabinet secretaries, police officers, human-rights commissioners, and professors have been loudly condemned by offended citizens of this nation, which maintains its historic links to populism and the pastoral romanticism that has informed its curious politics.

Although the criticisms and accusations pertaining to government may deserve more careful and dispassionate scrutiny than they are likely to receive when the times are out of joint, the *fact* of the growth of the so-called public sector can hardly be denied. And whatever the other consequences may be, the implications for manpower analysis of burgeoning public work forces cannot be ignored.

Consider that as long ago as 1963, or 18 months before the war in Vietnam was substantially escalated and a full year before the public virtually voted *down* the war in a presidential election, 16 of every 100 employed Americans worked for one of their various governments. We can speculate about what would have happened to this statistic had not the victorious candidates opposed an expansion of the war effort.

The attacks on the educational and defense establishments, in the meantime, have closely paralleled the very substantial manpower expansion in these two areas of public activity:

> During the decade of the 1930's, employment by the federal government (including persons on work relief as well as those in the Armed Forces) was the chief source of expansion. From 1950 to 1963, however, it was the increasing employment offered by state and local governments which accounted for the major share of the expansion in government employment. . . .
>
> When we review government employment by function, without regard to the level of government, we learn that employment for national defense purposes has been the single most important activity since 1940 . . . . Education was in second place in each benchmark year, and since 1954 it has become increasingly important as a field of government employment.[1]

Although attacks on government have illuminated the political problems that preoccupy the Left and Right, they have obscured manpower and employment developments that heartened more conventional liberals and conservatives for a time. In this connection, we recall that, in the last months of President Kennedy's tenure and the early years of President Johnson's administration, a politically moderate consensus was organized around the so-called new economics; according to one part of this Keynesian logic, the public services were regarded as an apposite arena in the effort to expand employment opportunities, particularly for disadvantaged Americans. While some sought to have government become "the em-

---

[1] Eli Ginzberg, Dale L. Hiestand, and Beatrice G. Reubens, *The Pluralistic Economy* (New York: McGraw-Hill, 1965), p. 120.

ployer of last resort," others pursued what their critics castigated as a program of vulgar pragmatism.

Daniel P. Moynihan, a former Assistant Secretary of Labor, and currently a member of President Nixon's cabinet, argued for a time that the Armed Forces should be utilized as an adjunct to manpower programs. Youngsters from low-income families, he contended, could get a start on work careers by participating in the military and would simultaneously acquire the discipline and skills required of young servicemen on active duty. This argument had the support of the former Secretary of Defense Robert McNamara. The war "shouldn't be a total loss." It was argued further, that civilian positions in the government could more readily be staffed by disadvantaged Americans because federal and state civil services preclude discriminatory employment practices.

An examination of the correlates of education among public employees is significant in a society in which public employment is regularly utilized as an instrument to distribute or redistribute work opportunities. The fact that he deplores the existence of large military forces and the destructive work in which they are engaged need not deter the analyst from using available data to cast light on the subject of the present study.

As it turns out, sufficient data are available on military personnel, on a 5-per-cent sample of the entire federal civil service, and on the highly skilled employees of one major federal agency to expand the discussion of issues explored in previous chapters. The performance and educational achievements of military personnel are a convenient starting point.

The Armed Forces

America's defense establishment, left to its own resources, would probably elevate educational achievement to the same place in the scheme of manpower policy accorded it by civilian employers. Indeed, the difficulties of manpower specialists at the upper reaches of this considerable pyramid of skills and numbers are compounded by deferment policies and the attitudes of most better-educated Americans, as well as by the personnel policies of civilian employers. Army manpower specialists would prefer to be spared the task of training "what's left" to them by American society, which has managed in recent decades to fight its wars, hot as well as cold, with a relatively small proportion of the nation's labor force; they would prefer to recruit and select people in accordance with their professional judgment.

It is precisely the fact that the military does *not* enjoy the specific labor-market advantages of private employers that makes the military experience relevant to the present study.[2] In addition to front-line combatants, modern warfare requires an enormous number of specialists whose skills represent a microcosm of the larger civilian system of employment. In the circumstances of the Defense Department, the military branches are obligated to train individuals to fit a vast, changing, and complex series of occupations, many of which have civilian equivalents.

Stories of military inefficiency are legion, of course, and have inspired countless songs, plays, novels, and films, both serious and comic. But the war machine does run, and it does so because men (and women) learn to navigate, type, and fly, to cook, grease motors, repair trucks, airplanes, and electronic equipment, to sort men, materiel, and mail, and to perform myriad other tasks. The military may justifiably take credit for doing its work as well as it does considering the magnitude of its task and, its spokesmen would add, the limited choice it has in selecting its personnel!

[2] The military does enjoy the comparative advantage of being guaranteed the *availability* of the "force levels" approved by Congress; these levels are always lower, however, than military manpower planners wish.

Fortunately for present purposes, all the military services have embarked on systematic efforts to develop and validate their techniques for assigning military personnel to military occupations. Personnel laboratories in each branch have designed a multitude of "screening" tests, the results of which can be combined with data about the backgrounds of a large segment of young American males for an analysis of individual performance.[3] In these ventures, knowledge of the educational achievements of military personnel typically adds little—sometimes nothing—to an effort to predict success in any of the Armed Services.

The performance measures used in many of these studies are inevitably inadequate in one way or another. Only a few studies bear upon general military "suitability"—that is, soldiers', sailors', and airmen's adaptation to the military life and their ability to survive without organizationally disruptive behavior.[4] Similarly, only a few studies have been conducted in which actual performance in the field, in combat, or on the job has been measured. Such undertakings require research designs permitting analysts to deal with standardized evaluations by trained raters working in controlled, homogeneous settings, and these conditions obviously are not easily met.

The results that *can* be reported are interesting, however, for they are based on performance records that may well relate to actual behavior in military billets. Most of these measures are based on the scores and grades that various personnel have achieved in training programs that take job tasks as well as pencil-and-paper examination grades into account. Electronic technicians, for example, are graded on their trouble-

---

[3] We are indebted to Dr. Harold Wool, until recently Assistant Secretary of Defense, who gave generously of his time and advice in the early stages of the research. He is, of course, in no way responsible for the use made here of data procured through his good offices, nor has he had any opportunity to review drafts of the present discussion.

[4] The normative question here of whether such adaptation is good or bad is begged. From a military viewpoint, of course, maladaptive behavior is undesirable.

shooting and repair skills as well as on written tests. These measures are in the same universe of measures as those used by private employers who generally see school success as a prerequisite to job performance.

In most of the relevant military studies, investigators have been concerned with improving the validity of classification and aptitude tests, or of items used in the construction of these tests, in conjunction with background information, in screening personnel for assignment to the hundreds of courses, long and short, that train them for military occupational specialties. While cynics may scoff at the utility of such tests—and few are the veterans who do not recall the "catch 22's" that made PX entrepreneurs out of experienced civilian sanitation workers—the researchers in military personnel laboratories have gone far in their efforts indeed.

In one of the first relevant post-World War II studies of Air Force personnel, high-school graduates, who at the time made up from 14 to 50 per cent of the monthly "input" of airmen, were compared with nongraduates in their performance on the Army Classification Tests and on 13 tests which were subsequently to make up the earliest Airman Classification Battery.[5] Dr. Dailey concluded that "high-school graduation, unless supplemented by other screening measures such as tests or the careful review of the actual high school record, does not insure that a basic trainee will be of high potential usefulness to the Air Force."[6]

Another investigator had noted that high-school graduates were not uniformly or markedly superior to nongraduates: the score distributions for the two groups overlapped on every test.[7] Nevertheless, the formal educational achievements of

[5] J. T. Dailey, "Comparison of High School Graduates and Nongraduates Among Recruits in the Indoctrination Division of the Air Training Command," Psychological Research and Examining Unit, Air Training Command, Research Bulletin 48-2, March, 1948.

[6] Ibid., p. 18.

[7] See William B. Lecznar, "Years of Education as a Predictor of Technical Training Success," Technical Documentary Report PRL-TDR 64-2, 6570th

airmen do appear to be related to their military suitability. According to a 1956 study by a senior Air Force investigator, high-school graduates have a lower probability of being discharged as unsuitable than high-school "dropouts,"[8] a finding that reflects the fact that "dropout" populations usually contain disproportionately more young people with low I.Q.'s and other "deficiencies."[9] In an extension of this study, investigators at Lackland Air Force Base were able to develop an equation, using data on age, years of education, and an aptitude index, for predicting the probabilities of discharge for unsuitability of the airmen included in the 1956 study.[10]

The findings in another study, however, indicate that the results of the 1956 study might have been influenced by the way in which education was treated methodologically. When education is treated as a dichotomous variable—that is, when discrete levels of educational achievements are considered simply, such as "high-school graduate" *vs.* "non–high-school graduate"—it may do some violence to education in the equations derived by the statistical technique known as regression analysis.

In 1963 Leland Brockaw undertook an extensive study of 4,458 graduates of eight technical military courses in order

---

Personnel Research Laboratory, Aerospace Medical Division, AF Systems Command (Lackland AFB, Texas, 1964).

[8] E. S. Flyer, "Factors Relating to Discharge for Unsuitability Among 1956 Airman Accessions to the Air Force," WADC-TN-59-201, DDC Document AD-230 758 (Lackland AFB, Texas: Personnel Laboratory, Wright Air Development Center, December, 1959).

[9] S. M. Miller et al., *School Dropouts: A Commentary and Annotated Bibliography* (Syracuse: Syracuse University Youth Development Center, 1964), pp. 31–77. It should be noted that in this particular work, however, there is considerable variation from one community to another in the capabilities of dropouts. In 1945–46, 5 per cent of youths who left school in the Midwest had I.Q.'s above 114; in another example, 30 per cent of St. Paul, Minn., dropouts had I.Q.'s above 100.

[10] W. E. Fisher et al., "Prediction of Unsuitability Discharges," WADD-TN-60-260, DDC Document AD-24807 (Lackland AFB, Texas: Personnel Laboratory, Wright Air Development Division, October, 1960); and Lecznar, *op. cit.*, p. 3.

. . . to evaluate a system of classification for assignment to technical school using aptitude information and reasonably comprehensive information on educational level, experience, and achievement . . . [and] to determine whether a brief questionnaire devoted solely to educational topics would be of sufficient validity to permit its use, in addition to the Airman Qualifying Examination, . . . in appraising a prospective enlistee as a desirable addition to the Air Force . . . .[11]

Brockaw's data are based on 16 questions about the characteristics of the courses and schools that the graduates of eight service programs had attended prior to military service and about their educational achievements. His techniques permitted him to establish the statistical weights of these items because they allocated the variability in final military technical-school grades achieved by the graduates among each of the separate and combined items used in the equation.

Brockaw's findings on the effect of educational achievement appear in Table VIII-1. The data reveal that there is a modest but positive relationship between high-school completion and course grades in only three of the eight programs. Several of these courses, it should be noted, are for occupations for which there are obvious civilian equivalents.

In addition, Brockaw computed two sets of mulitple correlations—between course grades for each technical program and "High School Graduation," and between grades and a

[11] Leland D. Brockaw, "Prediction of Success in Technical Training from Self-Report Information on Educational Achievement," AF System Command TD Report PRL-TDR-63-11 (Lackland AFB, Texas: Personnel Research Laboratory, Aerospace Medical Division, April, 1963), p. 1. The Airman Qualifying Examination is a screening device used by Air Force recruiters. The findings reported do not prove a great deal about tests. In many ways such tests can be almost as discriminatory as formal educational requirements, since many of them "measure" precisely what educational experiences are calculated to evoke: achievements of an intellectual nature. One must consider the data in this chapter, then, in light of qualifications that this footnote implies: the studies are interesting in that they apply to a selected and restricted population upon whom the tests are standardized and for whom, therefore, they are "valid."

TABLE VIII-1

CORRELATION OF EDUCATIONAL ACHIEVEMENT WITH FINAL SCHOOL
GRADE IN EIGHT AIR FORCE TECHNICAL TRAINING COURSES

Educational Achievement[a]	Technical School Course[b]							
	A	B	C	D	E	F	G	H
Grade school or less	—04	—10	—09	00	—04	06	—06	—05
Some high school	—30	—22	—28	—19	—22	—14	—31	—25
High-school graduate	23	24	26	01	00	01	15	12
Some college	18	12	08	14	21	12	17	18
College graduate	09	00	12	03	10	05	06	11
Number	738	690	593	267	820	554	759	433

[a] Each educational category is treated as a dichotomized variable; those with the education specified by the category are against all others.

[b] The courses, identified by letters in the column headings, are as follows: A-Reciprocating Engine Mechanic, B-Munitions Specialist, C-Organizational Supply Specialist, D-Accounting and Finance Specialist, E-Weather Observer, F-Control Tower Operator, G-Aircraft Radio Repairman, H-Fire Control System Mechanic.

SOURCE: Excerpted from Brockaw, *op. cit.*, Appendixes I and II, pp. 7–8.

"Selector Aptitude Index." The Aptitude Index showed uniformly higher predictive values than the education variable. When the two were combined, however, they produced "highly significant improvements in predictive efficiency." Brockaw concludes that information about educational achievement makes a significant contribution to an effort to predict technical-school success.[12]

The data in the tables lead us to interpret the word "significant" only in the narrowest statistical sense, however. Had it been possible to employ educational achievement as a five-step ladder corresponding to the items in Table VIII-1, rather than as five separate, dichotomized variables, the curvilinear character of the relationships suggested in Table VIII-1 would probably have modified the later correlation results quiet a bit. By splitting educational achievements into five *pairs* (*e. g.*, high-school graduation *versus* all other categories, item 3)

[12] Brockaw, *op. cit.*, Table 2, p. 4.

and treating the pairs separately, a great many of the realities of the results are lost. That the researcher did not notice this methodological problem is suggested by his unqualified observation that educational achievements add to his effort to make predictions; the facts are not so clear.

Even if we concede that increments of educational achievement contribute to the prospect that a young man will be found suitable for military service, the data in Brockaw's study suggest that these increments contribute relatively little to his prospects in technical programs. This, indeed, is the consistent finding in studies of the graduates of no fewer than 95 other technical schools and programs; in one such study, of 34 schools, the students involved numbered 11,408. In all of these studies, aptitude tests not unlike those employed in Brockaw's study correlate well with proficiency and performance scores, while educational achievements rarely account for more than 4 per cent of the variations in these measures of students' capabilities.[13]

In an unpublished memorandum, L. G. Humphrey, another Air Force researcher, commented on some of these numerous studies as follows:

Years of education are:
a) only moderately related to objective measures of aptitude;
b) a poor predictor of success in training;
c) almost unrelated to objective measures of proficiency on the job. . . .
Within the Air Force, completion of high school is thus not a useful criterion for assignment to school or on the job. . . .
It is believed that the relative insignificance of years of education for Air Force classification and assignment purposes is due to a changing philosophy of education which:
a) promotes children in accordance with chronological age rather than achievement;

---

13 See Lecznar, op. cit., p. 2, n. 2 and 3, p. 9, and pp. 11–14; and L. D. Brockaw, "Suggested Composition of Airman Classification Instruments," WADD-TN-60-214, DDC Document AD-252 252 (Lackland AFB, Texas: Personnel Laboratory, Wright Air Development Division, August, 1960).

b) provides a curriculum varied by type and difficulty level to fit the abilities of all the children in the school.

The apparent trend is toward less predictability from years of education rather than more.[14]

This last observation is particularly interesting because it is based on data that bear directly on the assumptions informing conventional judgments about education.

Of course, Air Force data do not tell us that education is unimportant or that formal learning experiences are irrelevant to the capacities, intellectual or otherwise, of the hundreds of thousands of men whose personnel histories are regularly reviewed at Lackland Air Force Base. Rather, these data point to the folly of confusing a man's driver's license with his driving ability. Just as different communities have different safety standards and variable skill requirements, so schools and school systems vary in their policies and practices. It should surprise no one that credentials alone predict performance so poorly. In none of the Air Force's studies does educational achievement account for more than a marginal portion of the substantial variations observed in the performance of very sizable numbers of airmen who have completed a large number of the most diversified courses.

The Navy's experience is entirely in line with that of the Air Force, although there are some variations in Navy personnel studies that make them immediately relevant. The Armed Forces have, for example, experimented with "salvage" programs in which illiterates and men who earn low scores on military classification tests are given remedial training to compensate for shortcomings attributable to social and other factors. These efforts have been uniformly successful; graduates develop into useful servicemen as often as the "average" and "normal" members of control groups with which they have been regularly compared.[15] Indeed, remarkably favorable

14 Cited in Lecznar, *op. cit.*, p. 3.
15 See Eli Ginzberg and Douglas Bray, *The Uneducated* (New York: Columbia University Press, 1953); S. Goldberg, "Psychological Procedures

changes in the adaptation and performance of low test-scorers have been produced through "recruit preparatory training" (RPT). In some instances these low-scoring candidates with modest educational backgrounds have performed at higher levels than better-educated men with higher GCT scores.[16] And, in a 1955 study, educational achievements were found not to be related to the performance of 1,370 Navy recruits who attended an RPT course. Neither were they related to the grades recruits received from their company commanders and instructors, nor to successes and failures in completing recruit training.[17]

On a related matter, the results are equally intriguing. A study of re-enlistment rates—always a vital figure to the military and to the Selective Service apparatus—revealed that re-enlistment rates of "acceptable" naval personnel were nearly twice as high for those who had completed less than twelve years of school as for those who had completed twelve or more years.[18] This finding, paralleling the earlier one that the job experience of better-educated workers in many private firms is

---

Employed in the Army's Special Training Units," *Journal of Clinical Psychology*, I (1945), 118–25; E. P. Hagen and R. L. Thorndike, "A Study of the World War II Navy Careers of Naval Personnel," Washington, D.C., *Research Report* Contract Hour-644, April, 1953; S. Mastropaolo et al., "A Study of the Relative Effects of Six-Week and Twelve-Week Experimental Training Programs on a Sample of Limited Aptitude Airmen," Technical Report 54-36 (Lackland AFB, Texas: AF Personnel and Training Research Center, September, 1954).

16 See C. N. Cofer, *Adjustment to Recruit Training: A Study of the Effects of Recruit Preparatory Training*. Technical Bulletin 54-22 (Washington: Bureau of Naval Personnel, December, 1954). This is a revealing study of considerable relevance to discussions of the "youth problem" in the "war against poverty." It also contains an answer, by implication, to civilian employers who claim that high-school dropouts have uncorrectable defects in their personal attitudes and capacity for disciplined work.

17 See Janet Eells, *Evaluation of Screening Standards for Recruit Preparatory Training*, Technical Bulletin 55-11 (San Diego, Calif.: U.S. Naval Personnel Research Field Activity, June, 1955).

18 Personnel Measurement Division, "Factors Affecting Re-enlistment of First Enlistees," Naval Personnel 18497; W2006.2.7 (Washington: U.S. Naval Personnel Research Field Activity, May, 1966).

shorter than that of their less educated coworkers, is probably related to the fact that the civilian economy does not favor ex-servicemen with modest educational achievements; many of these men re-enlist to exploit their military gains and to avoid labor-market disabilities.

Other Navy studies are virtual replications of those conducted by the Air Force. A study correlating the educational achievements of 415 electronic technicians with their proficiency scores on each of 17 concrete tasks, in conjunction with their age and pay grades (which is to say, the experience of these skilled men), found that educational achievements were *negatively* (though not significantly) associated with performance. The reseacher suggests that the negative signs of the correlations, reported in Table VIII-2, are

> . . . probably a reflection of [the] changing patterns of education in the United States. On the average, men entering the Navy in recent years have completed more time in school than men who entered the Navy several years ago. Since men with several years of experience, on the average, have higher check-list scores than their younger associates, the relationships between years of education completed and derived scores tend to be negative.[19]

These data take on added significance from the facts that (1) there is a high correlation between proficiency on the 17 tasks as measured by the technicians' *own* estimates and the ratings these technicians received from their supervisors on ships and posts in the two "theaters"; and (2) there is a tendency for re-enlistments to be higher among those who entered the Navy at a relatively young age than for those who were better educated and therefore entered the Navy when they were older.

[19] Adolph V. Anderson, *Training, Utilization and Proficiency of Navy Electronics Technicians II.* Technical Bulletin 62-13, *Technical Experience and Proficiency* (San Diego, Calif.: U.S. Naval Personnel Research Field Activity, September, 1962).

TABLE VIII-2
CORRELATIONS BETWEEN DERIVED CHECK-LIST SCORES AND AGE, EDUCATION, AND PAY GRADE

Check-List Score	Age PACFLT[a]	Age CONUS[b]	Education PACFLT	Education CONUS	Pay Grade PACFLT	Pay Grade CONUS
Basic measurements	26	24	−06	−05	38	26
Basic troubleshooting	33	43	−12	−15	52	58
Computation	32	29	−07	−17	47	39
Replace basic components	34	40	−08	−23	48	47
Records maintenance	42	65	−04	−08	50	68
Radio & teletype POMSEE[c]	20	24	−04	−08	29	22
Communications measurements	37	32	−11	−14	49	41
Communications check	33	29	−08	−11	44	38
Communications troubleshooting	36	20	−08	−12	45	36
Radar & Loran POMSEE	26	33	−10	−19	34	41
Radar measurements	26	33	−10	−23	38	53
Radar check, adjust, align	32	33	−13	−20	43	50
Radar troubleshooting	37	36	−12	−23	48	52
Use of an oscilloscope	41	41	−12	−21	51	55
Use of a VOM[d]	25	20	−03	−16	39	29
Use of a VTVM[e]	33	32	−05	−18	42	40
Use of a signal generator	32	30	−12	−10	46	45

[a] Pacific Fleet-based sailors.
[b] Continental United States-based sailors.
[c] Performance, Operation, and Maintenance Standards for Electronic Equipment.
[d] Volt Ohm Ammeter.
[e] Vacuum Tube Voltmeter.
SOURCE: Anderson, *op. cit.*, Table II, p. 18.

In a later report on the same investigation, the researchers examined the results of field tests of the competence of these electronic technicians asked to repair four different types of complex electronic testing equipment. The outcome was the same as reported in the study of the 17 tasks performed in the electronics training-school program:[20] experience is much more significant than formal education in accounting for performance in this demanding skill area.

Finally, David Kipnis reports that a "hand skills test" is a valuable supplementary screening device among lower-aptitude servicemen. An observed willingness to persist in tiring tasks, beyond minimum standards, contributed to both the school performance and the job performance (as measured by supervisors' evaluations) of low-aptitude men, but not of high-aptitude men, whose performance was better predicted by aptitude-test scores. The results of a study of 135 enlisted radiomen, 240 nuclear-power men, and 108 officer candidates indicate that less educated low-aptitude men may perform as well as high-aptitude personnel. These less educated men compensate for what would otherwise be deficiencies in their capacities for sustained effort.[21]

This review of Air Force and Navy data has perhaps been sufficiently detailed to spare the reader exposure to similar Army studies. This branch, too, has sought to rationalize further the selection of candidates for assignment to school and, in common with other branches, has produced many revealing statistics. In a 1967 communication to the writer, Dr. J. E. Uhlaner, Director of Laboratories, U. S. Army Personnel Research Office, Department of the Army, notes that the Army's Personnel Laboratory has for years sought to make the Army Classification Battery a more valid device for personnel assignment. Toward this end, the Laboratory compared

20 *Ibid.*, Part III.
21 David Kipnis, *Prediction of Performance Among Lower Aptitude Men*, Technical Bulletin 61-10 (Washington: U.S. Naval Personnel Field Research Activity, July, 1961).

enlisted men's test scores on this battery with their formal educational achievements in conjunction with performance in Army schools of all kinds. The "formal education" variable, he writes,

> . . . may be dismissed . . . . [Its] validity coefficients . . . were substantially less than the magnitude of the coefficients for the more valid ACB [Army Classification Battery] tests.
>
> After obtaining the above findings for occupational group after group in our prediction studies, we stopped mentioning the variable of years of education in our reports, although it is still included in the design.

In addition to the "salvage" programs and the validation studies already reported, data are available from another type of experiment applicable to all the Armed Forces. These findings confirm the judgment that when conventional screening standards are lowered, even substantially, no dire implications for performance ensue.

In the fall of 1966, the Department of Defense began accepting men who would not have met earlier mental or educational standards (95 per cent) or who had easily correctable physical defects (5 per cent). These men are trained in familiar fashion.

> While entrance standards have been revised, performance standards have not been lowered. The New Standards men are being trained right alongside other men in our regular training centers and schools. They are not singled out or stigmatized in any manner. Any special assistance they may require is provided as part of the normal training process. After completion of basic training, they are trained in a military skill either through formal courses or by on-the-job training.[22]

[22] *Project 100,000: Characteristics and Performance of "New Standards" Men* (Washington: Office of the Assistant Secretary of Defense, Manpower and Reserve Affairs, July, 1968), p. iv. The population this progress report considers actually numbers 125,152.

While the failure rates of New Standards men in advanced skill-training programs are higher than those of the control group with which they were compared, these rates have been dropping as a result of improvements in assignment procedures and training courses. And where 98 per cent of the control group successfully completed basic training, the corresponding figure for New Standards men is 96 per cent. About half of the small group that fails are discharged for medical reasons, primarily for conditions that existed prior to induction. Sixty-two per cent of these men are assigned to noncombat skill groups, most of which have direct or related counterparts in the civilian economy—food service, supply, wire communications, motor transport, and automotive repair.

That all groups of New Standards men do well in the service may be inferred from their progression up the military rank structure. Compared with other men, they are, according to the Assistant Secretary of Defense, "making very satisfactory progress." Eighty-four per cent reached the third pay rank, and nearly half reached the fourth, within the first 16.5 months of active service. The figures for the control group were 93 per cent and 64 per cent, respectively. "The gap in pay grade between New Standards men and control-group men is greatest in the Navy," according to the report, and "in part, this is due to the fact that in the Navy most New Standards men receive skill training 'on-the-job' instead of attending a formal school and thereby take longer to qualify for promotion."[23]

The military experience, which has been far more thoroughly documented than that of the so-called private sector, is substantially subversive of the prevailing ideologies that make so much of marginal increments of formal education. The results are interesting, not only because they include data bearing on relatively skilled occupational specialties, but

23 *Ibid.*, p. vii.

because they are suggestive of the productive potential of a labor market in a nation in which there has been chronic unemployment and, apparently, underemployment of large numbers of men and women with allegedly deficient educational credentials.

Consider, too, that the experience of the military is not altogether unlike that of the civilian economy during wartime. When the labor market is "tight," as it almost always is for the Department of Defense with respect to all but minority-group members of the labor force, people are hired less selectively, and with results that are largely gratifying. It can hardly be an inspiration to the unemployed youths of the 1960's and '70's to know that they have few deficiencies when their country needs soldiers but that they are otherwise expendable human beings. Were they to accept such a judgment with equanimity they would surely be faulted for their lack of initiative and for their stupidity.

That "dipping lower into the manpower barrel"—an unfortunate phrase used even by intelligent informants during the course of this investigation—is costly to productivity and efficiency is an argument with a slightly hollow ring in view of the data on the military's apparent ability to do well "with what it gets."

When we turn to civilian public servants, the data, like those on employees in the private sector, tend to be fuzzier. Civilians, whether in public or private employment, are rarely trained and indoctrinated in *formal* ways for *specified* technical tasks; consequently there are no data precisely paralleling those on performance in military-school programs. The data in the next section on the careers of a number of different government employees are nevertheless revealing, for they cut into the problem of educational credentials in yet another way. The fact that they contain detailed information on civil servants' promotions makes these data especially valuable.

Civilian Employees

Managers in government, no less than other managers, are eager to recruit qualified personnel for agencies with an internal labor market from which people can be selected to move up to more responsible positions; few organizations benefit from personnel programs in which all openings are filled from the "outside." To this end, voices are often heard proclaiming the need to obtain better—i.e., more educated—civil servants.

In New York City in 1966, for example, the Mayor's Task Force on City Personnel, after emphasizing the need "to identify, develop, and advance outstanding executive talent within its own ranks," found that "recent college graduates are now effectively excluded from management positions because these positions are filled almost entirely by promotion from clerical grades." The Task Force thereupon recommended that "the Mayor . . . stimulate the use of college graduates and persons with advanced degrees."[24] Such recruitment efforts in the public service are often complicated by the constraints imposed by a variety of policies designed to reduce, if not eliminate, formal requirements that operate effectively to discriminate unlawfully against one or another group of citizens. At the same time there may be policies of perferential treatment—as toward discharged servicemen—that confound efforts to use conventional hiring standards, including educational criteria, for many jobs. Finally, the use of competitive examinations may leave substantially open the question of the manner in which a job applicant *prepares* for government work.

[24] "Highlights from the Mayor's Task Force Reports," *City Almanac: A Bulletin of the Metropolitan Information Service* (New York: New School for Social Research, Center for New York City Affairs, 1966) I, 4, Section 2, unpaginated.

All this is to say that while educational credentials may be explicitly required for some jobs (for example, medical degrees for public-health positions) and implicitly required for other jobs (presumably only a law-school graduate will be able to pass a state bar examination and qualify for a variety of legal jobs in government), it is not necessary to attend college or high school to pass general informational tests, for which disciplined reading and native intelligence may be more than adequate. The upshot is that many federal and state civil-service positions are held by people who have not completed their studies for the standard diplomas and degrees awarded graduates of high schools and colleges.

In the face of this fact, it is useful to examine the determinants of promotion in government to see whether the career experiences of educated employees reflect their investments in their training; at the same time, their career experiences should also reflect their performance if a merit system is operative. The cooperation of the U.S. Civil Service Commission, which made it possible to construct a randomly selected 5 per cent sample of 180,000 males that is largely representative of the males among the 2.5 million federal employees, has facilitated such an examination.[25]

Promotion rates were defined by calculating the number of civil-service grades elapsed between entry grades and grades at the time of the study, and dividing the resulting number by the subjects' length of service in government.[26] The conse-

[25] The data were orginally collected in a larger Civil Service study; the data on male personnel from GS-5 through GS-15 jobs were retained for present purposes. We acknowledge our debt to the Civil Service Commissioner, Mr. John W. Macy, and to Drs. Albert P. Maslow and David L. Futransky for providing the data and their help and advice. They are, of course, in no way responsible for the ways in which the materials were processed or analyzed.

[26] It was necessary to analyze separately those who entered service at GS grades 1-4, 5-10, and 1-14. Since only GS-5 employees and above were sampled in the original survey, those who began at GS 1-4 had obviously received promotions to get into the sample, but for those in GS 5 and above, it was possible to have received no promotions. The GS-11-14 group suffer

TABLE VIII-3

ANNUAL PROMOTION RATES AND VARIATION EXPLAINED
BY PREDICTORS,[a] MALES IN THE FEDERAL CIVIL SERVICE,
BY ENTRY GRADE (1963)

	Entry Civil Service Grade		
	GS 1–4	GS 5–10	GS 11–14
Annual promotion rate			
Mean	.23	.26	.15
Standard deviation	.11	.16	.16
Per cent of variation in promotion rate explained by:			
Length of service	23.1%	4.3%	3.2%
Age	—	10.0	4.4
Current occupation	10.8	7.6	5.6
Education	3.2	3.3	6.8
In-service training	2.2	1.0	1.5
Number of agencies	—	—	1.1
Duty location	—	—	.8
Total variation explained	39.3%	26.2%	23.4%
Number	(4,204)	(3,182)	(481)

[a] Automatic Interaction Detector Program.

quent rates were then divided into the portions that arise from
each of ten sources that were considered *a priori* to have a
bearing on promotion. These "sources" included educational
achievement, seniority, type of occupation (accounting, administration, clerical work, etc.), and other items, including
organizational as well as personal characteristics.

The results, corroborating those of private firms reported
earlier, appear in Table VIII-3.[27] Except for the group in GS

a ceiling effect; those promoted beyond GS 15 would not appear in the
sample. Since it is rare for people to enter at GS 11 or higher, this is an
idiosyncratic, more educated group.

[27] The computer work and the detailed analysis from which these results
stem were accomplished by Gretchen Maclachlan, of Columbia University's
Conservation of Human Resources Project. This effort, which was an
extraordinarily exacting one, required a number of inventive trials and
readjustments. It is a pleasure to acknowledge her technical expertise, her
patience, and her helpful judgments on innumerable methodological issues.

grades 11–14, length of service and age are far more significant than education in accounting for the promotion rates of civil servants. For the GS-1–4 group, the ten factors together accounted for over 39 per cent of the variance in promotion rates, while length of service, by itself, accounted for fully 23 per cent. When age and length of service are considered together, as a surrogate measure of experience, the combination becomes the strongest factor in accounting for the promotion rates of the highest level, the GS 11–14 category, as well.

Generally speaking, promotions come early in the careers of civil servants, partly as a function of the shape of the hierarchy of GS ranks in government organizations. After long service (or, as in the case of GS 5–10's, age), the early advantages of educational achievement are cancelled out. Men of 39 years of age or over have about the same promotion rates regardless of education. This finding is remarkable when we consider that formal educational achievements are quite relevant to the work of some civil servants. A law degree, for example, is relevant to the work of National Labor Relations Board examiners; undergraduate training in the natural sciences is a reasonable background for a variety of jobs in the laboratories of the National Institutes of Health. Such "realistic" educational preparations should inject some upward bias in the role of education in promotion rates; the effect of educational achievement is nevertheless attenuated over a relatively short time.

Occupation is the second most significant factor in determining the promotion rates of the two lowest GS groups, accounting for 11 and 8 per cent, respectively. Among the highest-level personnel, the statistical influence of occupation is exceeded in importance only by that of educational achievement. Since educational credentials are more likely to have

---

The computer program used was the Automatic Interaction Detector (AID); see J. A. Sonquist and J. N. Morgan, *The Detection of Interaction Effects* (SRC Monograph 35, Institute for Social Research, University of Michigan, 1964).

been a factor in the hiring of the GS 11–14's than of the two other groups, however, this result is hardly surprising.

That educational achievement does survive this quantitative screening process in a fashion at all consistent with the conventional wisdom regarding education cannot be denied. It accounts, however, for a very small portion—3 per cent in the two lowest groups—of the observed rates of promotion for the employees in this large sample. In all, experience and occupation far outweigh educational achievement in determining the promotion rates of this large sample of civil servants.

Since educational achievements are highly correlated with the grades at which these government workers entered public service,[28] and since entry grade is closely related to the current grade of the subjects (Tau Beta = .22), the slightly more rapid advancements of the relatively better-educated men are a function of the boost that comes from being *hired* into higher ranks upon entering government services.

Thus, in Table VIII-4, it is clear from the first column that the over-all relationship between education and current grade, from which the force of education might be inferred, is reduced substantially when the civil-service entry grades of the subjects are held constant. Since the relationship between educational achievement and entry grade is stronger than that between education and current grade, controlled for entry grade,[29] the inference may be drawn that education has a greater bearing on the entry grades of these public servants than on their eventual promotion prospects. And, since education and entry grade are positively related while the relationship between education and current grade decreases for each successively higher entry grade, it is apparent that promotion experience is a function of these workers' *starting* points in the GS hierarchy.

---

[28] Tau β = .32, significant at the .01 level.

[29] The GS 1-4's are the exception (see p. 162, *n.* 26, in which this problem was anticipated).

TABLE VIII-4

THE EFFECTS OF EDUCATION AND LENGTH OF SERVICE
ON CURRENT GRADE, MALES IN THE FEDERAL CIVIL SERVICE,
BY ENTRY GRADE

| | Tau β Between | | |
Entry Grade	Education and Current GS	Length of Service and Current GS	Number
1–4	.31**	.31**	4,553
5–6	.32**	.47**	1,860
7–8	.26**	.51**	1,215
9–10	.24**	.45**	580
11	.22*	.50**	265
12	.02	.37**	153
13	.18	.40	77
14	.26	.10	21
All entry grades	.34**	.22**	8,724

* Significant at the .05 level.
** Significant at the .01 level.

To put this in another way, the better-educated civil servant is more likely to be hired at a relatively high grade, and the higher his grade at entry, the less relevant education will be to his prospects for promotion. In Table VIII-4, the statistical effects of educational achievement and length of service are compared; it is apparent that when entry grade is held constant, the effect of length of service is greater in every case. The main effect of education is on the GS classification upon entry into federal service; promotion prospects are largely determined by length of service or by the performance and other factors that longevity in an organization implies.

It is reasonable to infer that the organizational relevance of formal educational achievements tends to fall off in the careers of public servants. The fact that some of these workers *did* qualify for their early civil-service appointments by their educational credentials does not alter a general tendency for less educated people to move ahead, presumably on the basis of their individual merits as loyal and productive workers.

Once again, the promotability argument in defense of educational requirements suffers in confrontation with the facts of manpower utilization.

The data, of course, do not prove that the schooling of better-educated workers who are bypassed by colleagues with more longevity is wasted—indeed, the data may reflect the fact that better-educated civil servants leave public service for other jobs—nor that those better-educated workers who remain with the federal government do not utilize their schooling advantage. The data on promotion rates do suggest, however, that the quality of public service, such as it is, does *not* reflect the educational credentials of the federal work force and the upward movement of its promotable, well-educated members. At the same time, these data offer no basis for strong criticism of federal employment selection policies that reduce the significance of formal degrees and diplomas through veterans' preference, competitive examinations, and other components of the government's effort to eliminate discriminatory practices.

Such conclusions, derived from the civil-service materials, are buttressed by detailed analysis of some of the experiences of one federal agency whose performance in the public interest has been of demonstrably high quality, the Federal Aviation Administration (FAA). Few organizations in the United States must so often adapt to major technological changes and to discontinuously elevated demands for service. The FAA, which is responsible for the direction and control of all flights in the United States, operates the control-tower facilities at all public airports.

With the advent of jet-powered flight, the FAA had to solve almost overnight a horrendous technical problem with essentially the same work force of air-control personnel that had handled the propeller-driven traffic of the early 1950's. Since no civilian employers have manpower needs similar to that of the FAA in this segment of its statutory responsibilities, the agency was and is obliged to train its own technicians and control personnel. The agency confronted the challenge imaginatively by hiring and training many new people and by promoting (on the basis of "operational behavior") the people it already had. Between 1956 and 1959 the agency tripled in size.[30]

In 1966 the FAA inaugurated an Executive Selection and Inventory System (ESIS), which includes information on the civil-service grade, location, type of position, age, military-reserve status, education, experience inside and outside the agency, honors and awards, executive training, and other background data on all agency employees who reach grade 14 or higher. Its purpose is to enable the FAA to identify employees who are eligible for positions at grade 15 or higher, or who may be considered for additional training opportunities. As of 1968, there were almost 4,000 people in the ESIS system. The FAA was kind enough to furnish background data on 507 men, constituting *all* the air-traffic controllers in the system who had attained grade 14 or above.[31]

This complicated job, at a high civil-service grade, might well require, not merely the details of engineering or management science or mathematics, but all the supposed "correlates" of education—a disciplined mind, for example—and the more personal qualities that education is supposed to produce—reliability, steadfastness, responsibility, ability to think quickly, motivation, etc. Yet half of these men had no formal education

---

[30] Mrs. Ethel Cohen, Special Assistant to the Associate Administrator for Personnel and Training, personal communication.

[31] Data were furnished as of November, 1966. All identifying information was deleted to protect the anonymity of individuals. These 507 men are not a sample but the *universe* of controllers at grade 14 or above. It should be noted that 21, or 4 per cent, of these men, whose highest grade had been GS 14 or 15, were then in grade-13 jobs. According to the FAA Personnel and Training Branch, the reason for this apparent demotion was a change in program or in duty location at the request of a man himself, not downgrading for disciplinary or other reasons. Further evidence that they had not lost esteem in the agency is the fact that they were included in ESIS, which constitutes a pool for promotion to grades higher than 14.

beyond high school, although they did undergo very rigorous on-the-job technical training given by the FAA itself.

Of the 507 men in the study, of whom 410 had attained grade 14 and 97 were grade 15, 211 (42 per cent) had no education and no management training beyond high school.[32] An additional 48 men (almost 10 per cent) had no formal academic training beyond high school but had taken executive training courses. A few of these 48 men had more than three courses of managerial training, but most had only one. Thus, more than half the men had no academic training beyond high school. Further analysis of the data revealed no pattern of differences among educational groups by the position of the men in grade 15 or grade 14. That is, neither amount of education nor managerial training was related to higher grade.

It could be argued, of course, that the possibility of reaching certain positions depends on supply and demand at particular times and places, especially in an operation as decentralized as the FAA. According to such logic, given the scarcity of highly specialized skill, the agency was restricted to "low educated" manpower and was forced to promote what it had, regardless of merit. Nevertheless, the agency has been quite satisfied with the performance of its controllers, and the public has benefited from their remarkable safety records and their capacities for administering overcrowded airports.

In addition to the FAA's extraordinary record, the honors and awards received by tower controllers can be used as a rough measure of performance. ESIS records 21 different honors and awards, six of which were included in the data available. FAA personnel administrators were extremely uncomfortable about using these awards as a measure of performance. Honors are awarded on the basis of a subjective, unstandardized assessment of a man's work by his supervisor

---

[32] For personnel purposes, the FAA assumes that all employees have the equivalent of a high-school education. Since a diploma is neither required nor recorded, some of these 211 men may conceivably have been dropouts.

(for government-wide awards) or his supervisor's manager (for specific FAA honors).[33]

The number of honors weighs barely at all in consideration of a man for promotion. The agency has better information at its disposal. Not only is each man rigorously trained for his job and for the specific geographical subsection of his air tower's jurisdiction, but he is under constant observation. Traffic controllers work by talking to pilots, and every word they say is recorded and logged. A controller's records include every "confliction"[34] that occurs under his direction.

Unfortunately, the detailed performance data on each man are not available in tabular form.[35] Consequently, since major personnel decisions in private firms (especially decisions regarding white-collar workers) are often made on the basis of judgments such as those that go into the conferring of honors here,[36] it seemed reasonable to use honors as a rough measure of performance with the FAA's reservations in mind.

Table VIII-5 shows an impressive performance; only one third of these men never received an award, and 43 per cent earned more than one. College graduates were least likely to

[33] More specifically, such honors as Quality Step Increases, Sustained Superior Performance, and Outstanding Performance Ratings are common to the total government structure and are an innate part of the review of an individual's performance on an annual basis. Each of these awards is a specific recognition of unusual performance. On the other hand, Meritorious Service Awards, Certificates of Achievement, and Special Act or Service Awards are peculiar to the FAA award structure and are generally a little more difficult to obtain. The former category includes awards bestowed by the immediate supervisor with the blessing of the next-higher echelon, whereas the latter awards are bestowed only with the approval of a board or committee at a higher level (Mrs. Ethel Cohen, personal communication).

[34] When two planes come too near each other, the occurrence is called a confliction.

[35] The agency has an "up or out" policy and is eager to promote qualified people to the "journeyman" level. With such rigorous supervision, a move up in itself is a tribute to performance.

[36] Business journals are crammed with articles on how to evaluate employee performance. The elements are often quite personal, psychological, or of the grade-school report-card "deportment" variety.

TABLE VIII-5

EDUCATION AND MANAGERIAL TRAINING OF FAA CONTROLLERS,
G.S. 14 OR ABOVE, BY NUMBER OF HONORS AND AWARDS RECEIVED

		Honors and Awards Received, Percentage of Group				
Education	Managerial Training	None	One	Two or More	Total %	Total N
No college	None	30%	27%	43%	100	210
No college	Some	41	24	35	100	49
Some college	None	31	21	48	100	182
Some college	Some	38	24	38	100	16
College graduate	None	51	13	36	100	45
Total		34%	23%	43%	100	502

have received honors; the most awards were earned by non-college graduates *without* managerial training.

Here again, the FAA's cautions about the meaning of these awards must be taken into account; not all supervisors are willing to go through the red tape necessary to obtain them for their workers. Consequently, differences in the achievement of honors may reflect the personalities of supervisors more than the qualities of the men they supervise; there is a possibility that the high-honors men worked under supervisors who were more willing to take the trouble to arrange for awards than others. Furthermore, the small number of men in the "more educated" categories means that a few supervisors could strongly affect the data. However, there is no reason to believe that supervisors' idiosyncrasies were strongly correlated with the education of their men. Members of the Personnel and Training Section nevertheless felt that, although those who received awards did in fact deserve them, many among those not so honored were equally deserving and might have received them but for their supervisors.

Apart from these reservations, it should be noted that the FAA did very well with respect to government-wide awards. Half the men were chosen at least once; more than a hundred

TABLE VIII-6

EDUCATION OF FAA CONTROLLERS, G.S. 14 OR ABOVE,
BY NUMBER OF GOVERNMENT-WIDE OUTSTANDING
PERFORMANCE AWARDS

Education	Number of Government-wide Awards, Percentage of Group				
	None	One	Two or More	Total %	Total N
No college	51%	29%	20%	100	258
1 year of college	51	27	22	100	81
2 years of college	45	37	18	100	65
3 years of college	36	33	31	100	52
College graduate	67	20	13	100	45
Total N	50	29	21	100	501

of them, or one fifth of the total, were recognized for Out-standing Performance at least twice. The results when education is held constant (Table VIII-6) tend to mirror earlier findings: men with no more than a high-school education were just as likely to be outstanding in their on-the-job performance as those with one year of college. There *is*, however, a slight relationship with education: those with two or three years of college received more Outstanding Performance awards than did those with more or less education.

The performance of the better-educated tower controllers declines, however, when other, rarer awards are considered. Those with graduate degrees are underrepresented among the men honored for "Sustained Superior Performance," whereas those with two years of college did disproportionately well; those with no formal schooling beyond high school held their own.

When we look at "Quality Step Increases," which were awarded to only 12 per cent of the controllers, those with three or more years of college do better than those with less education (even the BA's hold their own this time), but neither of the two men who received more than one such award had attended college. There is little difference among educational groups in receiving the very rare merit-service awards and achievement certificates, but none of those with degrees received either.

In the logic of the enthusiasts of educational credentials, the FAA was "stuck" with the manpower it had. And because it was forced to train men and was unable to rely on formal credentials, the agency did not screen out men who would not have been permitted to take these positions in private industry or to undergo the relevant on-the-job training. Even if educational achievement *had* been used as a screening criterion, some of the excellent *better*-educated men would not have been hired; most of these men obtained their higher degrees only after their employment by the FAA.

Because it was "stuck" with less educated men—the expression may stick in one's craw—the FAA became a little laboratory in which the relevance of education for attainment of, and achievement in, important managerial and technical positions could be examined. Education proves not to be a factor in the daily performance of one of the most demanding decision-making jobs in America.

The FAA experience becomes even more significant in light of the fact that these positions are analogous to numerous posts in private industry, especially in the "technology industries." Many of these jobs are basically managerial, and any comparable management job in industry would be virtually inaccessible to anyone without at least a BA or BS degree, and often to those without an MA or MBA. If the requirement of technical knowledge of a highly specialized field prohibits the recruitment of managers from the outside, the FAA experience provides a compelling argument for advising technical industries, especially engineering companies, to hire without a compulsive regard for education and to promote from within. The highly technical and specialized industries that hire managers from the top and that insist on higher degrees for their engineers are exercising an irrational personnel policy. As was indicated in the earlier discussion of the rewards and evaluations accorded to more than 600 engineers and scientists, employers are not necessarily so economically efficient as the widows and orphans among their stockholders would like to believe.

It is saddening, especially in light of these findings, to report that FAA management expects that the educational attainments of future ATC's will be much higher, probably by FAA preference. They expect that increased job complexity and the introduction of automatic data processing will necessitate a knowledge of mathematics, air-transport economics, and "spatial relations"; at present the FAA is contracting with universities to teach these subjects.

Air Traffic Control Training would *still* have to be done by the FAA alone, however, and under repeated questioning they said that their desire to recruit more educated men does not reflect dissatisfaction with the performance of their present controllers. Rather, it reflects a *presumption* that ADP and other complexities will require more educated men, a desire to "keep up" with the rest of government, which they say is raising requirements, and a belief that, although educated men are not necessarily better, the increasing education of the population in general reflects invidiously on those with less education.

FAA spokesmen did express their intention of examining whether increased education actually is beneficial, once they accumulate a sufficient number of college men for comparison and their personnel records are sufficiently automated to permit tabulated comparisons of performance. An earlier effort to "build education into their testing procedures" was unsuccessful.

Assuredly, the managers of the public and military services in America are as education-conscious as those in private industry. At the same time, they must operate within the cir-

cumscriptions imposed by the realities of the labor market as
well as by those that inhere in financial and public-policy
decisions made in the name of government's many constituen-
cies. These circumscriptions shape the options facing public
leaders on the personnel front; willy-nilly, they must forego
whatever benefits are assumed to grow directly from the use
of formal educational criteria in the selection and assignment
of people.

The available evidence does not prove that the restrictions
on personnel policy have significant bearing on the job performance of those who do the people's work. There is, in fact,
more evidence to support the proposition that educational
credentials *as such* have relatively little bearing on performance; the extent to which public services function well is
apparently related to other factors, including the managerial
skills of those in responsible and accountable positions.

This conclusion need not be unwelcome in either educational or financial circles. Indeed, it should give heart to all
who would prefer that organizations maximize their returns
from the resources they are privileged to employ, as well as to
those whose objections to "bureaucracy" include the charge
that government agencies tend toward inflexibility in their
operations and toward a dread organizational disease that, for
lack of better terminology, may be called hardening of the
categories.

The irony will not be lost on some that the nonrational use
of formal credentials, which might be taken as a significant
symptom of "bureaupathology," is more likely to be found in
our great private enterprises than in our governmental apparatus. The capacity of industry leaders to temper the effect
of the marketplace in an age of subsidies, tax shelters, stock-
piling programs, depreciation allowances, and rulings that
facilitate the deduction of fines and damages for price con-
spiracies as "ordinary business expenses" is undoubtedly related
to the luxurious consumption of high-priced labor. As a con-

sequence, it is the public that shops in the competitive market so favored in economists' models. It is the public's hired managers who must act the role of the entrepreneur in imaginatively combining scarce human resources.

The argument that it might be more pleasant to deal with a well-educated employee of a business firm than with his less educated peer in public service will not be persuasive to most thoughtful readers, especially not to those who have had experiences with credit offices in leading department stores, managers of auto companies who are unwilling to honor their own and their dealers' obligations under corporate warranties, insurance claims representatives, or employers who have used armed plant policemen in response to union organizing efforts.

Certainly, as the relevant chapters indicate, the writer had greater success in government than in business in getting at the problem of the utilization of educated manpower. His hopes for the future of private enterprise received no boost from his interviews about manpower with business leaders who were otherwise among the most articulate and charming people one could wish to encounter.

IX The Great Training Robbery

Of all the arguments that have been mobilized with respect to education's central place in American life, the hardest to confront are those that emphasize the "social returns," including the so-called external benefits, and the "social costs" attending education. The issues in this realm are singularly hard to frame, for they bridge empirical and philosophical questions that force a simultaneous consideration of methodology and values; such universes of discourse do not lend themselves to ready amalgamation.

Still, it is possible, without treating these major questions in detail, to pinpoint a few specific problems generated by the present-day enthusiasm regarding formal education before presenting the tentative conclusions supported by this study. First, we can pause to examine the correlates of the emphasis on education within the educational establishment itself that parallel those discussed in earlier chapters. Second, it may be useful to suggest briefly some of the implications of this emphasis for the quality of education in America. Finally, we will submit some general recommendations in the context of a few observations about what can be called liberals' responsibilities.

The Educational Establishment

In the academic year 1966–67, total expenditures for formal education in the United States were nearly $49 billion, including $32 billion for elementary and secondary education. The sums devoted to public schooling, which comprised 2.4 per cent of GNP in 1938, comprised 3.8 per cent in 1966–67.[1] Clark Kerr, formerly president of the University of California and now with the Carnegie Foundation, has recently estimated that over the next decade, expenditures on higher education alone, excluding expenditures on federally sponsored contract and grant research, "will need to rise . . . to 3 per cent of the Gross National Product,"[2] a proportion close to the proportion of the GNP currently being spent for *public* education.

An interesting aspect of these developments is that they have an immediate impact on the structure and functioning of the educational apparatus itself. This apparatus is growing by leaps and bounds and has become vulnerable to the problems of most growing systems, including consolidations calculated, like mergers, to yield economies of scale, unionization, and "bureaucratization."[3] For present purposes, however, the most interesting effect, an effect related to those generated by rapid growth, has been the expansion of demand for educated manpower within education.

Education, as was noted in the previous chapter, is the most important nondefense activity in the public sector as a field of government employment. Its growth has been accompanied by a dramatic change in the academic achievements of teachers—so dramatic that today as many as three fourths of all jobs defined as requiring college degrees are teaching jobs

---

[1] These and a number of other intriguing facts on education appear in a useful booklet by the Committee for Economic Development, *Innovation in Education: New Directions for the American School* (New York: Committee for Economic Development, 1968).

[2] Clark Kerr, "The Distribution of Money and Power," *The Public Interest*, XI (1968), 100.

[3] See Michael Moskow, *Teachers and Unions* (Philadelphia: University of Pennsylvania, Wharton School of Finance and Commerce Industrial Research Unit, 1966), for a fine discussion of these and related developments.

TABLE IX-1
PERCENTAGE DISTRIBUTION OF YEARS OF SCHOOL COMPLETED
BY TEACHERS,[a] BY SEX, 1950 AND 1960

Years of School Completed	1950			1960		
	Males	Females	Total	Males	Females	Total
8 years or less	3.2	1.6	2.0	0.8	0.5	0.5
1-3 years of high school	2.4	1.0	1.3	1.2	1.4	1.3
High-school graduate	5.5	5.0	5.2	3.5	4.6	4.3
1-3 years of college	12.7	29.3	25.1	7.8	22.3	18.2
College graduate	76.2	63.1	66.4	86.7	71.2	75.7
Number (in thousands)	(287.9)	(842.2)	(1130.1)	(476.9)	(1205.5)	(1682.4)

[a] Includes elementary- and secondary-school teachers plus "teachers not elsewhere classified"; excludes college instructors and professors.
SOURCE: 1950 Census, *Occupational Characteristics* (Special Report P-E No. 1B), Table 10; 1960 Census, *Occupational Characteristics* (Subject Report PC (2)-7A), Table 9.

(see Chapter III). Not all teachers have such academic achievements, of course, but the figures are impressive (Table IX-1).

Meanwhile, the number of teachers increased by almost 50 per cent from 1950 to 1960, a rate of increase much higher than that sustained by the work force, which grew about 15 per cent in the same decade.[4] One can conclude, accordingly, that the mounting demand for education feeds in no small part upon itself. And this conclusion leads to the further conclusion that an examination of the correlates of the educational achievements of teachers is as important as the examination of these correlates among the populations considered in earlier chapters.

[4] For more extensive data on the educational achievements of teachers, see John K. Folger and Charles B. Nam, *Education and the American Population, 1960 Census Monograph* (Washington: U.S. Department of Commerce, Bureau of the Census, 1968), pp. 84–86.

Not many reasonable people are skeptical about the utility or relevance of undergraduate degrees for teachers in the nation's schools. But we might ask about the relevance of the postgraduate training these educators pursue.

Consider that it is not at all unusual for school systems to pay differential salaries according to the educational achievements of their teachers. In addition, and to encourage them to undertake further studies, teachers are generally awarded salary increases for academic work pursued after hours or during their summer vacations and sabbatical leaves.

These personnel practices may redound to the advantage of pupils, but there is no evidence that relates their performance to their teachers' educational achievements. There is some evidence, however, that teachers, like employees elsewhere, tend to become dissatisfied with their occupational achievements and to look to greener economic pastures. Data from the postcensal study conducted in 1962 by the National Opinion Research Center and the National Science Foundation on nearly 4,000 teachers are illustrative.[5] In a comparison of the positions held by these teachers in 1960 and 1962, there is no evidence that better-educated teachers are more likely to move out of education than are less educated teachers of a given age or level of teaching. Indeed, this type of teacher turnover was negatively related to educational achievement over this very short period.

There is strong evidence, however, that over a longer period both elementary and secondary teachers are less likely to stay in teaching as they move up the educational ladder (see Table IX-2). It is a matter of speculation whether this is a good thing, whether school systems benefit from the pat-

[5] These data were made available by Professor Seymour Warkov, of Teachers College, formerly of NORC. They are more fully exploited in Harold Oaklander, "The Career Perspective of Teachers" (Doctoral dissertation, Columbia University Graduate School of Business, in progress under the writer's direction).

TABLE IX-2
PERCENTAGE OF TEACHERS WHO HAD HELD THREE OR MORE POSITIONS,
BY EDUCATION, SEX, AND SCHOOL LEVEL, 1962

	Education			
	Not a College Graduate	College Graduate	Some Graduate School	Master's Degree
Males				
Elementary	37	17	22	40
	(30)[a]	(41)	(117)	(114)
Secondary	36	24	28	38
	(76)	(153)	(343)	(422)
Females				
Elementary	54	40	41	48
	(411)	(469)	(254)	(176)
Secondary	52	40	48	50
	(71)	(268)	(198)	(227)

[a] The numbers in parentheses represent the base on which percentages
were calculated.
SOURCE: Oaklander, *op. cit.*

terns implied by the table. It is probable, however one evalu-
ates the results, that if communities wish to reward their
teachers' loyalty, they are not conspicuously successful; the
table implies that systems of salaries for teachers enhance the
labor-market potentialities of teachers at least as much as they
serve the interests intended.

Other data, collected in 1962 by the Institute of Administrative Research, Teachers College, on three suburban school
systems bordering New York City and Philadelphia, have also
been analyzed in the detailed study by Harold Oaklander
cited above. They serve to amplify the patterns observed in
the postcensal materials.

There is no evidence in these data that the more educated
teachers in the three systems are more likely to wish to continue as classroom teachers. The data can be broken down in
a variety of ways—by sex, by age, and by the school levels
on which these 933 teachers work.

TABLE IX-3

PERCENTAGE OF TEACHERS HAVING HELD POSITIONS IN MORE THAN
ONE SCHOOL SYSTEM, BY SEX AND EDUCATION

	Education	
	Bachelor's Degree	Master's Degree or Higher
Males	16 (85)[a]	25 (238)
Females	20 (359)	36 (251)

[a] The numbers in parentheses represent the base on which percentages were calculated.

SOURCE: Oaklander, *op. cit.*

When the teachers are grouped according to whether they have acquired at least a master's degree, we find that 32 per cent of those with postgraduate degrees want to leave classroom teaching, compared to 25 per cent of those who hold only a bachelor's degree. Male elementary and junior-high-school teachers and female senior-high-school teachers who wish to move away from the classroom into other educational jobs, or out of education entirely, account for the sizable difference between the two groups.

The teachers in these three systems are not unlike those in the much larger postcensal study in that those with relatively high educational achievements are more likely to have had jobs in school systems other than the one in which they were employed at the time of the survey (Table IX-3).

Although there are many forces that result in the occupational transitions in these tables—the jobs of spouses and the family plans of female teachers come readily to mind—the educational differences are at the very least suspiciously parallel to the other patterns that have been identified throughout the present study.

The Quality of Education

Inner-city school critics are much more concerned with other aspects of performance than with those that reflect the dissatisfactions of teachers. They would remind us that the deterioration of urban education has been unaffected by the rising educational credentials of teachers. While turnover rates may in part reflect teachers' quests for rewards commensurate with their educational achievements, these achievements are viewed skeptically by many Americans, both in and out of city school districts.

This skepticism gains some force through these data. By emphasizing teachers' academic credentials to the degree we do in America, we substantially subvert the reform of programs in the nation's schools and departments of education. An incentive and salary system linked to academic credentials not only may backfire, as the turnover data strongly imply, but may serve to subsidize teachers' colleges by guaranteeing them large numbers of clients. Therefore, these institutions are under little pressure to institute much-needed changes in their efforts to train educators.

The poor and their stymied young are not the only ones, of course, who complain about education in America. The numbers of more privileged groups may not match the volume or character of their protest; they may not be proportionate to the hideousness and perversions in education to which they point, but there is plentiful evidence that youths who are favored with an opportunity to attend "better" schools at all levels are less than happy with their experience.

Student demonstrations like those at Columbia, Cornell, and Harvard rattle many citizens on and off campus, just as the uprisings in some urban high schools and the "liberated" behavior of suburban adolescents offend the sensibilities and

upset the equilibria of whole communities. These developments should not distract attention, however, from the objects
of the students' wrath and the substance of young people's
complaints that inform (if they do not precisely illuminate)
the logic of their behavior. Their teachers, perhaps surpris-
ingly, do sometimes pinpoint the issues, though with fewer
obscurantist trappings. Witness the following formulation:

> . . . as Americans move into the end of the twentieth century,
> there is one institution which can no longer afford the luxury
> of waiting to see how the story turns out, and that is the institu-
> tion of education itself. Not simply because education has a
> stake in the notion that self-consciousness is a good thing but
> because education, especially at its higher reaches, now plays a
> leading part in the plot. . . .
> What troubles American education today is the simple fact
> that it has no choice between [two] simple alternatives. It must
> meet both demands. It must serve power and yet make that
> power humane. Whether it can or not is at the bottom of what
> troubles American education today.[6]

This speaks to the point that many young people seek to
make when they protest government contracts with universities and the irrelevance of contemporary education. They
charge that education focuses on vocational placement in a
society of buttondown personalities and grey-flannel mouths,
competing to breathe the technicians' polluted air, to drive
the engineers' beached whales on crowded cement ribbons
that choke the planners' cities. Education mirrors a society,
they argue, in which liberation is confused with "upward
mobility," and in which human relationships are confounded
with the ritual behavior of the polite middle class. One may
conjure up an image of an educated community in which the
inanities of cocktail-party patter regularly pass for conversa-

6 John William Ward, "The Trouble with Higher Education," *The
Public Interest* (No. 4, Spring 1966), p. 88.

tion, in which clam dip serves as social cement, in which work is a job and not labor, crabgrass is the evil goddess to whom one kneels in Sunday terror, spiritual values are high-proof, neutral, and pure grain, and suburban husbands are handymen with sex privileges.

These charges are not lightly dismissed, as educable teachers realize and as most parents of teenagers are obliged to learn. It is the adult culture, especially its educated culture, the young argue, that has most truly gone to pot.

Education, Class Barriers, and the Liberal Creed

The defenders of the educational establishment point out that things could be worse and that critics have overstated their case. Education, they assert, produces thoughtful citizens and material well-being; the economic benefits to the society are accordingly stressed and linked, by assertion, to social welfare. But surely, in a discussion of education, the definition of social welfare must go beyond aggregated tallies of material benefits to include the matter of education's role in the distribution of social product. And when the issues are thus joined, the defense is less compelling.

Educational credentials have become the new property in America. Our nation, which has attempted to make the transmission of real and personal property difficult, has contrived to replace it with an inheritable set of values concerning degrees and diplomas which will most certainly reinforce the formidable class barriers that remain, even without the right within families to pass benefices from parents to their children.

As a number of my colleagues have suggested, employers can derive benefits from the employment of better-educated workers that outweigh the pathological correlates of "excessive" education; after all, the intent was only to open up the narrower economic issues. But the use of educational credentials as a screening device effectively consigns large numbers of people, especially young people, to a social limbo defined by low-skill, no-opportunity jobs in the "peripheral labor market."[7]

Barriers against greater mobility are not made less imposing by public policies that reinforce the access to formal education of middle- and upper-income youngsters through subsidy and subsidy-like arrangements. Today, tax-supported and tax-assisted universities are full of nutant spirits from families whose incomes are well above those of the average taxpayers. The personal advantages to those who hold academic credentials are sufficiently well known that the majority of Americans do not even pause to question the TV spots or subway posters that warn of the lifetime hazards facing "dropouts."

If the barriers to mobility are not fully visible to the disinherited, poverty warriors have been armed with weapons to subdue the poor in skirmishes against the "disadvantaged" which have distracted attention from a much-needed war against poverty. Substantial funds from that war chest have been consumed by educational mercenaries who campaign against the personal—which is to say educational—deficiencies of the youthful poor. Foot-long ads addressed to "educational technologists" offer grand salaries and extensive benefits to induce men and women (many of those who respond are public-school teachers) to enroll in the legions who will train impoverished youths in encampments across the land, financed by profitable cost-plus contracts.[8]

During the life of the office of Economic Opportunity and

---

[7] See Dean Morse, *The Peripheral Worker* (New York: Columbia University Press, 1969).

[8] See Ivar Berg and Marcia Freedman, "Job Corps: A Business Bonanza," *Christianity and Crisis* (May 31, 1965).

the thousand community-action programs it spawned, unemployment rates among the nation's less educated have
dropped; black workers had an unemployment rate of 6.8 per
cent in 1968—"the lowest," according to the Department of
Labor, "since 1953."[9] But it is not at all clear what portion of
this gain—modest as it is—is attributable to the war against
poverty. The Labor Department's estimate that "the sharp
Vietnam buildup began, largely unexpectedly, at the very
time the economy was already being propelled toward full
employment by surging civilian demand" must be balanced
against its own statement that "in the two years after mid-
1965, increased defense expenditures generated a total of 1.8
million jobs—some 700,000 in the Armed Forces and about a
million in private industry."[10] Whatever can be said in favor
of our wars, it is unsettling that they are among the significant
mergers of our time.

The quality of public education available to the poor and
near-poor is almost uniformly low, a fact that contributes increasingly to the visibility of the barrier between the haves
and the have-nots. For the have-nots, especially black Americans, there is a special pain in all this, for they are underrepresented in the policy-making councils that have decreed the
frightful mess in urban education and the segregated style of
American living and learning, but they are overrepresented
among those who suffer the penalties in foxholes overseas and
ratholes at home.

At least as sharp a pain must afflict some thoughtful liberals
in America. For them formal education has been the equili-
brating mechanism in a progressing industrial democracy
that has been relatively free of class conflict. It was the liberal
who helped to sell America on education and who saw in ed-

[9] *Manpower Report of the President* (Washington: U.S. Government
Printing Office, 1969), p. 23. White unemployment rates were 3.2 per cent.
Ibid., p. 44.
[10] *Ibid.*, p. 25.

ucation the means by which merit might ultimately conquer unearned privilege. He must now acknowledge that he is the defender of a most dubious faith. For while he struggles from the edges of hard-earned privilege to help the poor, he must live off these privileges in the education of his own children.

Consider, in this context, that over one third of all school-age children in New York City, many of them the sons and daughters of earnest liberals, attend private and parochial schools.[11] It is at least ideologically convenient for the parents of these children to champion the cause of the neighborhood school and the decentralization of desperately sick urban public-school programs. The serious question of whether this makes educational and political sense may be effectively begged in favor of a willingness to "allow others" the control *they* have over their children's school experience.[12]

The position that such reforms will reverse educational inequities does put a good face on their ruggedly individualistic pursuit of their own narrow self-interest; it may be doubted whether the ragged individuals thereby left to fend for themselves will necessarily benefit from this quaint version of egalitarianism. The middle-class children of liberal and conservative parents in silk-stocking districts are doubly blessed, of course, with relatively good public schools and a self-serving ideology about the seemingly neutral principle of the neighborhood school that has now become an article of faith for many inner-city dwellers. These desperate people have gained the ideological support—and sometimes the financial support—of progressive whites, many of whom are masters at converting liberal principles into a tasteful though

[11] David Rogers, *110 Livingston Street* (New York: Random House, 1968), pp. 56, 59.
[12] Private-school parents, of course, may point out that their control over their children's school experience is limited to choice of school—not by any means an unlimited choice at that—since the demand for private-school services has fostered a certain indifference reminiscent of the public-school pathologies in large cities.

distracting pragmatism. Since the logics in defense of urban educational reforms are presented only less delectably by Southern politicians, the long-run advantages of such tinkering will unquestionably depend in part on the success of reformers in demonstrating that they do not mean simply to raise the hopes of their repressed protagonists. Such a demonstration must take account of the credentials barriers and the employment levels that help to sustain them; again, the education-employment nexus becomes strategically important.

Conclusion

The results of the present study do not give much weight to the economic argument in its detail, although it would be foolish to deny that education is involved in the nation's capacity to produce goods and services. No benefit would accrue from reviewing the detailed findings in this concluding chapter. Let us state, however, that they give grounds for doubting that it is useful to regard education in America within a simplified framework in which a person's *years of schooling* are taken as a significant measure; schools are too diverse and people too differentiated to permit the routine and automatic confusion of the morals, motives, and capabilities of the licensed with their licenses. The experience with marriages in Western society may illustrate the point.

Another general conclusion from the data must be that we could profitably and sensibly redirect our educational investments in order to improve primary and secondary public education. It is consistent with the observations in preceding chapters that America should be doing a far better job in assuring that *all* of her people reach adult life with twelve years of quality training and education. Employers, for example, indicate that their educational requirements reflect their dissatisfaction with what public education is accomplishing. Added expenditures for higher education, which already constitutes 34 per cent of direct educational outlays, is not likely to change all this.

Within the educational establishment there is further room for redirection.

> The missing link in education is development research as it is practiced in industry. . . . Though there is great need for more basic research in education, there is an immediate demand for more extensive developmental work which will evaluate and apply the findings of research and demonstrate their practical worth. At present only 10 to 12 per cent of the funds expended on educational research and development are devoted to development.[13]

It would also be desirable from all points of view if those who failed to take full advantage of their educational opportunities in their youth had a second chance, after discovering themselves and developing the attitudes that serve the learning process, in a system of adult education. Under present circumstances, life-long consequences stem from decisions made by, for, and against youths. And it may be questioned whether a citizen should suffer all his life with the disabilities that come of having been exposed, for example, to a poor grade-school experience, where "functional illiteracy" paves the way for disenchantment, delinquency, or deprivation.

Education needs to be reformed in America by striking a balance between "too much" for some and "not enough" for others. The tendency on the part of employers to raise educational requirements *without careful assessments of their needs, in both the short and the long run,* can benefit neither managers nor the system they extol.

This purposeless credential consciousness further handicaps

---

[13] Committee for Economic Development, *op. cit.*, p. 30.

education, especially higher education, in the pursuit of its promise to liberate people and to help preserve for a society its better traditions and commitments. This part of our cultural heritage is already in danger of being obscured by a growing materialism, stifled by know-nothing "status politics" and radical rightism, and weakened by the radical, disenchanted Left.

There is no escaping the fact that in America the political and social wellbeing of the individual are bound up with his economic opportunities. It is therefore a matter of great moment to the society whether the economic argument in favor of education takes far more account of the complexities involved in measuring the relationships among abilities, educational achievements, and job requirements. The efforts presented in the present volume give abundant support to the position that the issues involved in these relationships have not been adequately joined and that a more differentiated line of analysis needs to be considered in framing public policy toward education. Policies calculated to generate job opportunities for a growing population would seem to deserve higher priority than those designed to rationalize, by their stress on education, the considerable difficulties imposed on those without academic credentials.

At the same time, the data give reason for concern about the personal wellbeing of the growing numbers who do not find that their investments in education are earning them the rewards they were taught to anticipate. The political consequences of latent discontent are not necessarily less threatening to democratic institutions than those of the noisier versions of American dissaffection.

Finally, it is appropriate to call attention to the role of the American academic community in the processes by which credentials have come to loom so significantly in the lives of their fellow citizens. A Columbia University colleague has put one major aspect of the matter well:

Is it not dangerously presumptuous to insist, despite our lack of understanding about the contribution of college schooling to occupational performance, that nevertheless, all professionals must pay a toll to the schools and the teachers? University administrators and college professors have been put into a position that all too closely resembles the old robber barons on the Rhine. They exact not just coin from those who wish passage to professional employment but also the more valuable asset, time—four to eight years of students' lives. . . .

For those who want to do more than pass through to a career . . . college has much to offer for its cost. The offering takes the form of perspectives, understanding, and insights rather than lucrative techniques and productive skills. . . . [However] not all persons find such an education to their taste or in their interests; some may wish to pursue a career as immediately as possible, postponing until later, or doing without, the contribution education might make to their lives. At present, choice is denied. Entrance to a career is through college, where schooling all too often is masked as education. Would not the colleges, teachers, students, and those who look forward to professional careers be better served if other entry ways were open, available, and used?[14]

It is by no means clear that Professor Kuhn's questions are easily answered, but they deserve the attention of educators who manage the sluice gates that determine so substantially the directions of the nation's manpower flows.

Another major aspect of academics' role in credential-making catches them up in the apparatuses that maintain the status quo with respect to the distribution of America's wealth. Data presented earlier call attention to the "class bias" that attends the economics of education, a development that exacerbates the increasingly conservative implications of education in America.

14 James W. Kuhn, "The Misuse of Education: The Problem of Schooling for Employment," speech presented at the inauguration of Dr. Gordon C. Bjork as President of Linfield College, McMinnville, Oregon, May 20, 1969.

The significance of this development gains additional force in a study of "the methodology for estimating the benefits and costs of higher education for a state, and . . . the relationship of these benefits and costs to legislative policy," by Professors Hansen and Weisbrod, of the University of Wisconsin.[15] Using data on the California system of higher education, the authors, distinguished students of the economics of education, report:

> Public subsidies for higher education in California tend to go disproportionately to students from relatively high-income families and are received in quite different amounts by people even within given income classes. Almost 40 per cent of the student-age population receives no subsidy whatsoever, while a relatively small group receives very substantial subsidies. Whether this pattern of subsidy distribution is consistent with the social objective of equality of educational opportunity is certainly open to question.[16]

The academic community may, of course, uphold high standards for admission to their institutions, both public and private, on the basis of hallowed academic principles. The fact is, however, that the "educationally disadvantaged" students will *not* receive credentials for the well-paying jobs in the economy to which high academic standards and degrees stand in problematic relation.

Perhaps the academic community owes it to the losers to re-examine the talents and capabilities of the considerable population groups to which current educational measures, tests, and examinations do not attend. Perhaps such a charge relates to the matter of "relevance," about which more is said than done on America's comfortable campuses these days. One's

---

15 W. Lee Hansen and Burton A. Weisbrod, *Benefits, Costs and Finance of Public Higher Education* (Chicago: Markham Publishing Co., 1969), p. vii.
16 *Ibid.*, p. 84.

own experiences as an educator are not heartening, but pessimism in respect to reforms that would be responsive to the needs of losers is a most inappropriately self-serving emotion for the innumerable subsidized tenants of America's academic mansions.

Index

10
PRAYERS
YOU CAN'T
LIVE WITHOUT

How to Talk to God about *Anything*

RICK HAMLIN

Executive Editor, *Guideposts* Magazine

Guideposts

New York

10 Prayers You Can't Live Without

ISBN-10: 0-8249-3218-8
ISBN-13: 978-0-8249-3218-3

Published by Guideposts
16 East 34ᵗʰ Street
New York, New York 10016
Guideposts.org

Distributed by Ideals Publications, a Guideposts company
2630 Elm Hill Pike, Suite 100
Nashville, Tennessee 37214

Guideposts and *Ideals* are registered trademarks of Guideposts.

Acknowledgments

Every attempt has been made to credit the sources of copyrighted material used in this book. If any such acknowledgment has been inadvertently omitted or miscredited, receipt of such information would be appreciated.

All Scripture quotations, unless otherwise noted, are taken from the *New Revised Standard Version Bible*. Copyright © 1989 by the Division of Christian Education of the National Council of the Churches of Christ in the United States of America. Used by permission. All rights reserved.

Scripture quotations marked (CEB) are taken from *Common English Bible*. Copyright © 2011 by Common English Bible.

Scripture quotations marked (KJV) are taken from *The King James Version of the Bible*.

Scripture quotations marked (NIV) are taken from *The Holy Bible, New International Version*. Copyright © 1973, 1978, 1984, 2011 by Biblica, Inc. Used by permission of Zondervan. All rights reserved worldwide. www.zondervan.com

Scripture quotations marked (RSV) are taken from the *Revised Standard Version of the Bible*. Copyright © 1946, 1952, 1971 by Division of Christian Education of the National Council of Churches of Christ in the United States of America. Used by permission.

Library of Congress Cataloging-in-Publication Data has been applied for.

Cover and interior design by Müllerhaus
Cover photograph by Shutterstock
Typeset by Aptara, Inc.

Printed and bound in the United States of America
10 9 8 7 6 5 4 3

For Sweetie

"Funny. Healing. Thoroughly attention-grabbing. Peek into Rick Hamlin's transparent prayer life and the prayers of many others such as Corrie Ten Boom, Catherine Marshall, and Mother Teresa."

—MARION BOND WEST, author of *Praying for My Life*

"If you find yourself struggling with prayer, as many people do, Rick Hamlin's *10 Prayers You Can't Live Without* is here to liberate you. Through anecdotes from *Guideposts* readers and the wisdom he has acquired from a lifetime of praying, Hamlin shows how prayer can become an effortless conversation with God. And he does so in a humorous, inspiring, and poignant way. Highly recommended!"

—MARCIA FORD, author of *The Indispensable Guide to Practically Everything: Prayer*

"I love this book! I pray that you will read it and experience the power of prayer in your life."

—JON GORDON, author of *The Energy Bus* and *The Seed*

"Rick Hamlin is a praying man for whom praying is as natural as breathing. In the years I've known him, I've often asked myself how he does it. Now I've got an answer. Rick's amazing book *10 Prayers You Can't Live Without* is full of bold insight and practical wisdom about the practice that is the very breath of our spiritual lives. The fact is the more I learn about Rick, the more I learn about prayer."

—EDWARD GRINNAN, editor-in-chief of *Guideposts* and author of *The Promise of Hope*

"Here are ten words to describe *10 Prayers You Can't Live Without*: charming, inspiring, liberating, delightful, engrossing, moving, wise, healing, thoughtful, beautiful."

—BOB HOSTETLER, author of *How to Survive the End of the World*

"Prayer has long been, for me, more a source of worry than of comfort or strength. I don't pray as often as I'd like or as meaningfully. With insights and instruction woven almost invisibly through his little compendium of prayer stories, Rick Hamlin not only transformed my prayer habits but banished my insecurities about prayer. 'To try to pray is to pray,' he reassures in the very first sentence. By the end of his book, under his gentle tutelage, I was trying all the time."

—PATTY KIRK, author of *The Gospel of Christmas* and *A Field Guide to God*

"Whether you're a newcomer to prayer or a lifelong prayer warrior encountering an occasional dry spell, *10 Prayers You Can't Live Without* is a book you can't live without. From his own daily appointment with God on the subway to the experiences of people he knows—both famous and unknown—Rick Hamlin has distilled guidelines to make every prayer a true 'conversation with God.'"

—ELIZABETH SHERRILL, author of *All the Way to Heaven*

CONTENTS

Contents

INTRODUCTION

TO TRY TO PRAY IS TO PRAY.

You can't fail at it. Nobody can. Open your heart, open your mouth, say something, say nothing. Shout if you must. Raise your hands, clasp them in your lap. Sing if you please. You can start with a "Dear Lord" and end with an "Amen," or you can dive right in. You can close your eyes, get on your knees, use whatever language you like or no language at all. You can pray when you're walking, running, driving to work, setting the table for dinner, lying in bed before you turn the light out.

To try it is to do it. It's the only human endeavor I can think of where trying is doing. Reaching out is holding on. Joining in is letting go. Prayer is as natural as breathing. It's fun. It's a relief. It's comforting. It's a solace. You can tell yourself it's an obligation or that it's a terrific waste of time, but how often do you get to waste time with a purpose? If you're like me and think every minute of your day has to be accounted for, you really do need prayer. You'll run out of steam without it.

You can do it in private. You can do it with a friend at your kitchen table or in a church pew or with your family at dinner. You can do it in a windowless basement with a twelve-step group or out under the stars on a summer night. You can practice it all you like, but the practice itself is perfect. No need for a dress rehearsal. All your false attempts, your back-up-and-try-again efforts — they're it.

You will wonder if you're doing it right. You will want a little more guidance. You'll want to hear from others who take it seriously and learn from their example. Even the finest cooks look for inspiration in a new cookbook. But the masters will affirm that prayer is a school for amateurs because doing it from the heart is all that matters. That's the only expertise you need.

For thirty years I've made a conscious effort to work on my prayer life. I do it religiously, faithfully, absentmindedly. I often forget to pray, but I don't forget how. I don't think you really can. A need, a friend, a worry, a piece of bad news or a cause for celebration pulls me back. Returning is part of the process. So is waiting. Besides, being critical of your prayers defeats the whole purpose.

What has helped me? The Bible, especially the Psalms. A faith community that challenges me and keeps me on my toes—Sundays at church, I get recharged. Writers who know more than I do. Friends who give me working models of passionate faith. A family that prayed together and still does at every dinner. And for almost all those thirty years I've worked for a magazine where I've been expected to ask boldly, sometimes brazenly, about other people's prayer lives.

"Do you ever pray?" I ask, or "When did you pray?" or "Did you pray about that?" You'd be surprised by the answers and how committed people are to prayer. I remember the actress whom I had written off as a spiritual lightweight because she showed up in glossy fashion magazines. "I pray all the time," she said without a pause. Or there was the newscaster who spoke profoundly and humbly of the people in disasters she prayed for, disasters she had to report on. "Easy enough for you to say," I thought, until I discovered quite by accident how she followed up those prayers with substantial financial help. (No, I can't say who she was. Giving anonymously was a crucial part of her faith.) And there have been the countless subjects who have promised to put me in their prayers. One recently e-mailed me because she had a sense that I needed urgent prayer. (She was right.)

To tune into people's prayers is to look into their souls. It's to learn how to love them and stretch my own soul. Through my job I've heard the prayers of farmers battling drought, athletes pushed to their physical limits, people dealing with disease and financial turmoil and incalculable loss. I can't begin to say what an effect all these stories have had on me except to give you a glimpse of the ones that I still retell myself.

I've called this book *Ten Prayers You Can't Live Without* because it's an attempt to break down and categorize the prayers I find the most helpful. Do I expect you to pray exactly the prayers that I have in the same way? Goodness no. Prayer is personal. Find the way that works best for you. Even the Lord's Prayer can be said in different ways. I hope I can expand your thinking about it and help you find other prayers to use. There's "*Nooooooooo!*" and "Thanks" and "Forgive me, I blew it" and "Hi, God!" At other times I turn to more formal prayers like the one a mentor taught me: "Jesus Christ, have mercy upon me. Make haste to help me. Rescue me and save me. Let thy will be done in my life."

As I said, we're all amateurs at prayer. You can practice a prayer in your head, like a conversation you expect to have with your boss. You want to get the words right. You want to make sure you're understood. But don't forget that every thought you've phrased and rephrased in your mind has been heard and understood better than you could have expressed it.

"Search me, O God, and know my heart," the psalmist says. "Try me and know my thoughts."

Every writer hopes to be read, but I would be just as happy if you stopped reading me, dog-eared a page or marked a spot in your e-reader and prayed instead. A doctor I interviewed once told me that for him, reading was a form of prayer. I believe that. Would that reading this book feels like prayer to you (writing it certainly has been for me). A good read makes me want to talk to the author. But in this case if you talked to our Maker, I would feel like I really accomplished something.

CHAPTER ONE

Pray at Mealtime

———◆───◇───◆———

*"Bless this food to our use, us to your service,
and bless the hands that prepared it."*

It all started with a nightly blessing.

My father's rambling graces were famous in the neighborhood. Whenever one of us invited a friend over for dinner we usually warned, "Dad always starts dinner with a prayer. Just bow your head. Don't eat anything until Dad says amen.

"And it might take him a while to get there."

I was one of four kids, each of us two years apart. We lived in an LA suburb that looked like any suburb we saw on TV. Our street was lined with palm trees that wrapped themselves around my kites. We had rosebushes in front, an orange tree and a flowering pear that dropped white petals in January like snow. The flagstone walk was lined with yellow pansies leading to a red front door.

We ate dinner in a room Mom insisted on calling the lanai. It had once been a back porch and had been converted with the help of plate glass, sliding glass doors, screens and a corrugated fiberglass roof that made a tremendous racket when the rain hit it. But this was Southern California so it wasn't often.

Dad came in from his commute on the freeway, kissed Mom, hung up his jacket, poured himself a drink, checked out the news on TV. One of us kids set the table. Mom took the casserole out of the oven with big orange pot holders and set it on the counter. "Ta-da!" she exclaimed. She tossed the salad in a monkey pod bowl they had picked up on a trip to Hawaii. "Dinner!" she called in her high-pitched, musical voice. "Dinner's ready."

We converged on the lanai from different parts of the house, my sisters from their rooms upstairs or the sewing room where my older sister, Gioia, was always re-hemming a skirt in the constant battle of fashion vs. school rules. I seem to remember a three-by-five card being slid between the floor and the bottom of her skirts when she was kneeling. The hem had to touch the card or the girls' vice principal would send her home. My older brother and I slept in a converted garage, which was convenient for whatever motor vehicle he was working on. Howard could roll the minibike or go-cart right into the room from the driveway. No steps to climb. I slept with the familiar smell of gasoline, and my brother had to put up with the old upright piano next to my bed.

We were as different as two boys could be. He never held a tool he didn't know how to use. I never heard a Broadway show that I didn't want to learn the lyrics to. He was physical, mechanical. He could fix anything. He was outdoors racing the minibike up and down the driveway with his neighborhood fan base cheering him on. I was inside, listening to a new LP, learning a song inside my head. I was overly sensitive. He pretended to be thick-skinned.

It's a wonder we didn't pummel each other, although as the older brother by twenty-two months, he pummeled me enough. I didn't circulate in his orbit. Not even close. Howard would wake me up early in the morning to go work on one of his forts and I would find an excuse to return to the house to work on a watercolor. Sometimes we had great talks as we were falling asleep. Most of the time, though, we did our own thing, Howard soaking an engine part in a Folgers coffee can of motor oil, me studying the liner notes for a record album.

Then came the blessing.

Dad's graces were a call to worship, an effort to pull these disparate family members together, to get us all on the same page. We gathered at the big teak table and the dog was sent outside to bark. We squirmed, we giggled, we kicked each other under the table, we rolled our eyes, but we were forced to see that we were all one and we had to be silent for a minute or two. We scraped our chairs against the linoleum floor (eventually it was covered with a lime-green indoor-outdoor carpet). We left homework, the kite caught in the tree, the news on TV, the seat for the minibike, the Simplicity pattern laid out on the floor, the rolls in the oven. We rushed in from school meetings and play practice and afterschool jobs. My younger sister, Diane, put her hamster Hamdie back in his cage and we could hear the squeak of the animal running to nowhere on his wheel.

"Let us reflect on the day," Dad began. We closed our eyes.

Then he paused.

There was a whole world in that pause. Silence. Nothing to do but think. I have been in Quaker meetings where we sat in silence waiting for the Spirit to move and it was just like that pause. I have worshipped in churches where the minister was wise enough to be quiet for a moment as soon as we bowed our heads. Every Monday in our office we gather in a conference room at 9:45 and read prayer requests that have come in to us over the past week; then we close our eyes, pausing in silence before we remember those requests.

At first all you hear is ambient noise. The drone of an air conditioner, the hum of a computer, a car passing by, my sister's hamster squeaking in his cage, your stomach rumbling. You think, "That hamster wheel needs some WD-40.... That car needs a new muffler.... Boy, I'm hungry." Then you listen to what's going on in your head.

Back then my head was spinning with a million thoughts. I was replaying what my best friend and I had talked about under the walnut tree at school or what Miss McGrath had said about my paper in class or what I wished I could say to the cute girl who sat behind me. What I wished she thought about me. Reflect on the day? There was too much noise going on inside. What did that have to do with prayer?

All we had to do was listen to Dad. Like a great preacher warming up, he cleared his throat and began, usually with something he heard on the radio or saw on TV.

"God, I ask you to be with us in the coming election," he prayed. "May the voters make the right choices in the primary."

"Remember our president as he makes his State of the Union address.

"Be with our astronauts in tomorrow's flight.

"Remember the Dodgers in tonight's playoffs.

"We are sorry about those who suffered from the recent tornadoes.

"We mourn the death of your servant Dr. Martin Luther King."

"It's like the six o'clock news," one of my brother's friends said. "You don't need the radio or the TV. You can get all the headlines from your dad's grace at dinnertime." Prayer can be a way of conveying information. It can be the means of processing history, even recent history. Think of all those passages in the Psalms that rehash the Israelites wandering in the desert: "Forty years long was I grieved with this generation, and said, It is a people that do err in their heart, and they have not known my ways: Unto whom I sware in my wrath that they should not enter into my rest" (Psalm 95:10, KJV).

A modern-day psalmist in a button-down shirt and a bowtie, Dad prayed us through the 1960s and 1970s, the Watts riots, the flower power of Haight-Ashbury, the turmoil of the Vietnam War, the stock market's rise and fall, inflation, Kent State, Cambodia, Watergate, Nixon, Agnew, Ford, Carter. Dad dumped everything in his prayers, all the noise in his head, all the stuff he worried about. They were throw-everything-in-but-the-kitchen-sink prayers.

Let me extol the benefit of such prayers. First of all, this is a *great* way of dealing with the news.

I have friends who get so riled up about what they've seen on TV or read on the Internet or in the paper that they can't sleep at night.

The first moment you see them you have to let them unload, let them chill. "I can't believe what a terrible trap our president has got us into," they'll exclaim, or "Congress is ruining our nation" or "I just read a terrible story about corruption in government." They're so anxious that you can't have a normal conversation until they've let go of their worries.

Of course, the news can be devastating. The headline splashed across the front of a newspaper in bold type sends a chill through me. The nightmarish scenario on the TV news has me double-locking the doors and tossing and turning at night. But most of those news stories were crafted to make us scared. Fear sells newspapers and magazines. The cover line about the ten most dangerous toys that can hurt your children makes you want to pick up that parenting magazine at the supermarket checkout. Fear about how your house might have a poisonous noxious gas seeping into it keeps you glued to the TV. Scary Internet headlines are designed to make you click through. You're supposed to get upset.

I do. All the time. If I read too much bad news it puts me in a foul mood. Talk about controlling my thoughts. I once stared at a provocative headline in a tabloid at a newsstand and screamed right back at it. My nerves were jangled. Something about the wording set me off there at Madison and 34th Street, right around the corner from the office. I was so shocked I slunk away hoping no one had heard me. Who was that jerk making all that noise? What got into me? The tabloid could have winked and smiled back at me: *Gotcha!*

Bad news can become a dangerous loop in my head. It's usually about stuff I have no control over: the national debt, the unemployment rate, the decline of the dollar, war, the weather, the poverty level, the stock market, the trade imbalance, the decline of the West, the decline of civility, growing pollution, the polar ice cap melting. It's essential to be well informed. I'm a junkie for all kinds of news. Good thing all those reporters and columnists keep me up-to-date. But there's no reason for the bad news to consume me.

If the news pulls you down it can rob you of the creativity you need to get your best work done. A study has shown that getting your blood pressure up by reading a depressing story in the newspaper or watching a disturbing report on television prevents your mind from doing the intuitive wandering it needs to make creative connections. That sounds like the work of prayer to me (and no, the article didn't put it that way). Save the news for times when your mind doesn't have to be at its best. Or take it in early and then toss it away.

Dad put the news back into God's hands. He asked God to intervene in places God was not necessarily considered. What did God know about the Dow and runaway inflation? What would God think about Nixon and Watergate? The point was, if we were thinking about it, the good Lord deserved to hear it. The good Lord would care.

As Dad's graces continued, he moved on to matters closer to home.

"We look forward to seeing our daughter Gioia march in the drill team at the football game tonight, bless her," he prayed.

"Bless Rick at the piano recital on Sunday."

"We're grateful for the new minibike Howard bought. We pray that he uses it safely and ask him to receive your blessing."

"We're thankful for Diane's good tennis match today."

"We look forward to Back to School Night and meeting our children's teachers. We know you know what good work they do. Bless them."

What a valuable lesson in prayer and parenting. Dad prayed for us. He noticed what was going on in our lives. Not the secrets that lurked inside, like my crush on the girl who sat behind me in fifth grade, but the events that were on his radar. The football game, the homecoming parade, the senior class musical, a tennis tournament, finals, dance class, the prom. He paid attention. At Back to School Night he graded our teachers and came back home to tell us how they measured up, which was to say how we measured up. He wrote it all down on a piece of paper with letter grades. When he gave my fourth-grade teacher, Miss McCallum, an A, I felt like the luckiest kid on earth. You can never underestimate a child's need for love and attention from his parents.

Francis McNutt, the great advocate for healing prayer, would often ask when he spoke to groups how many people remembered their parents praying for them. How many had heard their mother or father pray for them when they were sick, for instance? How many remembered a time when a parent had prayed out loud for them? Maybe twenty percent could recall a moment when their moms had prayed for them, but their dads? Only three percent of them.

I read that figure in astonishment, wondering how my father managed it, especially for a man of his generation, a buttoned-up World War II submarine veteran, the suffer-in-silence type. How did he ever learn to open up like this to us? How did he get over the natural embarrassment that comes from praying out loud in front of your loved ones? I'm far more the wear-it-on-my-sleeve sort, and even I fumble when I have to pray extemporaneously with my family. For Dad it came as naturally as breathing. There must have been something healing in it for him, blessing us and dinner every night.

I thought of Dad's graces recently when we ran a story about a dad, Kevin Williamson, who, with his two teenagers, was celebrating his first Thanksgiving after his wife, Bev, had died of cancer.

Kevin didn't want to get out of bed that morning, let alone celebrate. Long before his children were up, he trudged into the kitchen and got a cup of tea. The only sound was the rumble of the refrigerator. The quiet time reminded him of Bev and the mornings they had spent planning their days and their future, a future that had turned out different from what he'd ever imagined. The phone rang. It was their neighbor who was having them over to dinner. "Can I bring anything?" he asked.

"Just yourselves," she said. "And bread...we could use some bread."

"Sure." He figured he'd go out and buy some at whatever supermarket was open. Then his eye landed on his wife's recipe box still sitting on the counter. He thought of Bev's yeast rolls, the same recipe that had been handed down in his own family for generations. His mother had taught Bev to make them. He could remember the scent of them wafting from the wood-burning stove at his great-grandmother's home.

Kevin found the recipe card, written in his own mother's handwriting. He put on an apron, got out a mixing bowl and lined up the ingredients on the counter.

"What are you making?" his daughter asked, wandering into the kitchen sleepy-eyed.

"Mom's yeast rolls." He stirred the yeast into warm water, beat an egg, added the flour, kneaded the dough and let it rise. He separated the dough in balls and put them on a baking sheet. Perfect for dinner. But there was still some left over.

Bev had always made an early batch just for the family. Maybe he could do the same. With the leftover dough he made a few more rolls and put them in the oven. Soon the kitchen smelled like all those Thanksgivings of the past. He thought of Bev, how she made her family laugh, how she taught them to love and to live. The timer buzzed. He took the pan out of the oven, then called his kids into the kitchen.

"Let's all have one," he said, putting the rolls on a plate.

They sat at the kitchen table and joined hands, and he bowed his head to say grace. "God, it's been a tough year for us. We miss Bev so much. We thank you for the time we had with her. We're grateful for the little reminders, each day, of her presence in our lives still. And we're blessed that we have one another."

The story was from Kevin's point of view, not the kids', but I don't doubt they were suffering the loss of their mom just as acutely and were comforted by their dad's grace. They knew they had been loved and still were.

My dad's prayers were filled with his love for us and for Mom. He prayed for President Nixon, the astronauts, Sandy Koufax and *us.* We were on equal footing with the famous people who dominated the news. We were stars. What he couldn't always articulate in a conversation he could say in a prayer. He bowed his head and his heart opened up. He told us the good things he thought of us.

Dad was a far more complicated person than my straightforward, sunny-tempered mother. He worried more, hurt more, suffered more and internalized most of it. He smoked, he drank—the clink of ice cubes in a glass was an enduring part of the soundtrack of my childhood. He could be self-involved. He got angry and didn't know how to express the anger. He could burst out in a frightening tirade, most often directed against himself. The sound of Dad throwing his tennis racket against the fence and chastising himself—"Thornt!!"—was a familiar feature of Sunday's mixed doubles with Mom. You could tell which rackets were his in the hall closet because they were usually bent or patched up with tape. But in his prayers he loved and was lovable.

From Dad's graces I picked up a tool I use almost every day when I pray. It's one of the most valuable things I know and it was a long time before I recognized how helpful it was.

When you close your eyes to pray and start listening to your heart, you're going to face a slew of distractions. You'll hear a kid bouncing a basketball down the sidewalk, a radiator will rattle, a bus's brakes will squeak. You'll start thinking of all the stuff you need to get accomplished that day, and soon you'll exclaim, "Geez, what am I doing? I haven't prayed at all."

Dad's graces were frequently interrupted. Our dog Andy barked. The next-door neighbor's dog barked. The phone rang. A passing car honked. Mom's kitchen timer went off. We started to giggle.

Dad put the interruptions right into the prayer:

"God, be with our dog Andy. Help him protect us."

"Thank you for our daughter's popularity. We know that whoever is calling for her will call back." In case Gioia hadn't dashed to the phone already.

"Bless Mom's rolls in the oven. We look forward to eating them." In case Mom hadn't gone to get them.

"Bless our children's high spirits. You know their energy is a good thing."

If you fight an interruption in a prayer, it becomes much bigger. If you fold it into the prayer loop, it becomes part of the weave of your thoughts, the cord that becomes your lifeline. Even monks who devoted hours to meditation, star athletes in the spiritual life, get distracted in prayer.

Thomas Merton, the brilliant writer and Trappist monk at the Abbey of Gethsemani in Kentucky, wrote one of the greatest modern prayers of spiritual yearning: "My Lord God, I have no idea where I am going. I do not see the road ahead of me. I cannot know for certain where it will end. Nor do I really know myself, and the fact that I think I am following your will does not mean that I am actually doing so. But I believe that the desire to please you does in fact please you. And I hope I have that desire in all that I am doing. . . ."

Reading his journals, you see evidence of how even someone as spiritually focused as Merton could be distracted. In one passage he mentions staring at the pattern of lariats and cowboys on a visitor's shirt during worship, his mind wandering. If Merton could get distracted like that, so could I. Just because you're trying to be otherworldly doesn't mean that the worldly won't slip right into your head. Don't fight it. Listen to it. Pray your way through it.

"Praise the Lord from the earth," goes the psalm, "fire, and hail, snow, and vapors, stormy wind fulfilling his word, mountains, and all hills, fruitful trees, and all cedars, beasts, and all cattle, creeping things, and flying fowl" (Psalm 148:7–10, KJV). You praise God for everything you see and hear, everything on your wavelength. Andy barking, horns honking, the timer buzzing, the phone ringing, the hamster on his squeaking wheel, the kids giggling, praise the Lord.

The end of grace came with the single line that Dad repeated night after night: "Bless this food to our use, us to your service, and bless the hands that prepared it." There was the blessing.

"Amen," Dad finally said. "Amen," we responded. Mom went off to rescue her browning rolls, the mac-and-cheese made the rounds from the cork trivet, we asked Dad about what he heard on the news. Soon dinner would dissolve into a three-ring circus. We got up from the table to demonstrate some exercise we'd learned in phys ed. Diane did a somersault on the lime-green indoor-outdoor carpeting. Howard did a handstand and then showed us how many push-ups he could do. "Not on a full stomach," Mom exclaimed.

If we failed to appreciate the tomatoes in the salad, Mom would remind us, "These tomatoes cost nineteen cents a pound," as though that would add to our pleasure. If we wondered why we were getting an unfamiliar brand of cookies or brown-and-serve rolls, she would say sheepishly, "They were on sale," a holy refrain in a family with four growing children.

Our manners deteriorated. We made a boarding-house reach across the table, grabbing the butter. "No, no, no," Mom said, tapping the back of a hand with the back of her knife. Dad would go into a lecture on etiquette. "When I was in submarine corps during the war," he began, "some of the fellows told me I should give up on 'please' and 'thank you' and 'please pass the rolls.' Well, I told them I wasn't planning on spending my life on a submarine. I would say please..."

We hardly listened. We were in a rush. If there was any light left after dinner we would go back outside for a game of kick the can or freeze tag. There would be baths to take, books to read, bedtime. Still we'd had this quiet moment together when Dad asked God to bless our food and to bless us.

◆ ◆ ◆

The idea of blessing anything is not that common today. It means stopping and slowing down. We usually like to jump in and do something. We want the car to start right away, we want the computer to be ready to go, we hate delays when we get on the Internet. We want dinner now. But blessing is as ancient as faith and central to it. What did Jesus do before he fed the five thousand? He blessed the bread and broke it. What did he do when all the disciples were gathered in the Upper Room for the Last Supper? "Jesus took bread and blessed it and broke it and gave it to them, saying, 'Take, eat; this is my body.' And he took the cup and when he had given thanks, he gave it to them, and they all drank of it."

This was the opposite of fast food. A nutritionist I know makes the point that saying grace is good for the digestion. It gives us a chance to slow down before we eat. We smell the casserole cooling or the steak waiting to be cut, the gastric juices get going but we don't start shoveling in immediately. "Bless this food to our use" could be a prescription on the back of the bag of groceries. Thankfulness at the dinner table is good for the body *and* soul. You certainly enjoy your food more when you season it with gratitude. You've thanked God and the cook.

Getting dinner on the table is a nightly miracle and in families it's so easy to forget the miracle makers or even to acknowledge them, especially if they do their duties well and effortlessly. Efficiency can make the work dangerously invisible. I was a newlywed when I worked on a story from a writer who was listing the reasons for her fifty years of happy marriage. "Tommy has never once forgotten to thank me for a dinner I've cooked," she wrote.

Note to self: thank your wife for dinner. Be like Dad blessing Mom.

We are not wholly responsible for the food on our table. Not only are there the "hands that prepared it," but also the farmers who toiled, the rains that watered, the soil that nurtured, the sunshine that blessed and all that help we got to earn the money we spent at the supermarket. The self-made man is a fiction, the luck we credit for our good fortune an illusion. Thankfulness reminds us of that. Even the most rudimentary grace has the essential ingredient of gratitude, whether it's the standard "God is great, God is good. Let us be thankful for our food" or the summer camp classic, "Rub-a-dub-dub. Thanks for the grub. Yeah, God!"

Asking for a blessing means acknowledging that someone has power over you or can give you something you want. Now it's just a courtesy to ask your future in-laws for their blessing on your marriage, but there was a time when it was a make-or-break conversation. When a minister or priest blesses the congregation it's a reminder that God is the great source of our well-being: "May the Lord bless you and keep you. May the Lord make his countenance shine upon you and be gracious to you. May the Lord turn his countenance to you and grant you peace."

In the Bible, Esau, the firstborn, came in from the fields so hungry that he sold his birthright to his younger twin brother, Jacob, for a bowl of lentil stew. (My wife, Carol, likes to remind me of this every time she serves up her lentil stew.) When Esau was away, Jacob fooled his blind father Isaac by pretending to be Esau. At his mother's urging, he dressed in his brother's rough clothes so that he would smell like Esau and put goat hair on his arms so he would be hairy like Esau. (As a kid in Sunday school I thought that Isaac must have been pretty dense to mistake a furry hide for a hairy forearm.) The ruse worked and Jacob won his father's blessing: "May God give you showers from the sky, olive oil from the earth, plenty of grain and new wine. May the nations serve you, may peoples bow down to you…Those who curse you will be cursed, and those who bless you will be blessed" (Genesis 27:28–29, CEB).

Enigmatic and deceptive as it is, the blessing holds. Jacob becomes the patriarch of a new nation after wrestling with the angel who changes his name to Israel. I think the longing for a parent's blessing is just as deep and hard-wired in us today, even if we might not use that word. To hear your father bless you night after night is bound to have its effect. Sometimes I wonder why I was never tarred with the brush that turns religion into a dark thing and God into the big scary Father in heaven ready to condemn us for our least faults. If I knew that God loved me, it wasn't just because I was told so—and I was, countless times—but also because I experienced the love of God through Dad's prayers.

Monasteries observe the offices of the day, praying at specific times. "Seven times a day I praise you for your righteous laws," says the psalmist in Psalm 119:164 (NIV). Making grace a habit keeps prayer on the agenda.

◆ ◆ ◆

As brave as I am in writing about prayer, it's taken me years to be brave about saying grace in public. In a New York restaurant where there are waiters hovering, ready to sprinkle some parmesan cheese on your pasta or grind some fresh pepper, I won't ask my friends or colleagues to bow their heads before we dig in. When I'm with some holy person in a clerical collar I've learned to pause before lifting my fork. "Is he going to say grace?" I wonder. Will we be like that grandmother and kid in the Norman Rockwell painting who are praying to the rest of the diners' bemusement? I'm self-conscious. Are all eyes on us, the only two people praying in this restaurant?

I've decided it really doesn't matter. First of all, it's magnificently self-centered to think that anybody else is looking at me in a restaurant filled with people who all have their own concerns. Second, self-consciousness is often a prelude to prayer. "Who am I to pray this? Why would God be interested?" you wonder and then you jump in. Faith often requires an attitude of "I can't believe I'm doing this but I'm going to do it anyway." Be bold. Mighty forces will come to your aid.

At home when we have friends for dinner, I have fewer qualms. I used to wonder, "Should I say grace if they're not believers?" Will they find it awkward? Will they be bored? I've given up that too. Let them see this as my little eccentricity, like people who collect paperweights or make their dogs do tricks at the table. I say grace at dinner. Who am I to guess what they believe or don't believe? They won't mind. I might go a little faster when guests are here or give them a signal so they don't eat half their salad before I've bowed my head, but grace is what we do. It's the habit of the house.

Carol and I started saying grace at home when our two boys were young, the apple falling not far from the tree. I couldn't then and I still can't extemporize a grace as sweet as the ones I heard in my childhood. As the boys grew older, I asked them to participate. We went around the table, each of us in charge for a night, Carol, Tim,

Will, me, then back to Carol. If you want to know what's on your children's minds, ask them to say grace.

Like my father, I could see all those reasons for gratitude.

I remember pausing outside our apartment and looking in one winter night when the boys were young. Carol was boiling water for spaghetti, the steam already fogging up the windows. William was sitting at the kitchen table, writing in a school workbook, his hand curled around his pencil, his mouth forming a word. Timothy was dashing in from the living room, the tuft of his milkweed hair moving across the bottom of the windows like a duck in a shooting gallery. The light was on above the piano and Carol was reaching in the cabinet for the box of pasta. She wouldn't pour it in until she saw the whites of my eyes.

At once I could see my life from the outside, how fortunate I was, how blessed. Soon I'd be on the inside. A kiss to Carol, put away the briefcase, hug the boys, settle any fraternal disputes. It was always a race. Could we get it all done? Set the table, eat dinner, wash the dishes, read to both boys before bed, hear their prayers, get them to sleep, talk to Carol, pay the bills, get to sleep ourselves. There was hardly a moment. But this. I could see my life from a different view, as others might have seen it, maybe as God saw it. I was the luckiest guy on earth.

It made me understand why Dad would sometimes pause during grace, overwhelmed by emotion. If only we could see how beautiful our lives are. If only we could just reflect on the day. Dad was the weeper in the family. He had what my wife would call "the gift of tears," a trait that has been passed along to my older son, Will.

Let me not gloss over Dad's outbursts of anger, but when they occurred at the dinner table we usually found something funny in it. When he threw his fork down after a bite of Mom's chicken broccoli casserole with a risky teaspoon of curry in it, he barked, "Who put that India stuff in here?" Mom said meekly, "I wanted to try something different." We giggled, then laughed till tears rolled down our cheeks. Even Dad laughed.

I once provoked Howard into throwing a fork at me—the argument was about Bill Cosby, if you must know. I cried. Then someone pointed out how funny it was, and we laughed. Even Dad got his chances back. He could come up with a one-liner that put us in stitches. In old age, he moved mighty slow, his joints aching from arthritis, his back bent over from spinal stenosis, his feet in their clunky lace-less white sneakers. He followed several steps behind our energetic tennis-playing mom.

"I just pray and pray for patience," Mom said.

"That's one prayer God hasn't answered yet," Dad muttered from his walker.

We laughed then and we laughed again when Howard retold that story at Dad's memorial service. Everybody in the packed church laughed. Mom laughed from the front pew. Laughter is as healing as gratitude, maybe even more so.

When I hear Paul's extraordinary statement in Romans 8:38–39— "For I am persuaded that neither death, nor life, nor angels, nor principalities, nor powers, nor things present, nor things to come, nor height, nor depth, nor any other creature, shall be able to separate us from the love of God which is in Christ Jesus our Lord"—I think of my family. It's the feeling of safety and security that I grew up with. It's the satisfying love I find at my own dinner table when I say grace with my wife and my children. Here is love. Nothing can separate me from it.

Dad's graces continued through his mid-eighties. Wracked with pain, he got to a point where the only place he was comfortable was lying in bed. The neuropathy in his feet made walking downstairs for breakfast a trial. Still, whenever the family got together for dinner or even if it was just him and Mom in the breakfast room, he said grace. The words came haltingly, the thoughts were briefer. There was little of the six o'clock news but more of us, our spouses, his nine grandchildren. He always ended by saying, "Bless this food to our use, us to your service, and bless the hands that prepared it."

Mom and her much-blessed hands took magnificent care of him until the day he simply couldn't get out of bed. He spent the last five months of his life in a nursing facility on the lush grounds of a home for retired Presbyterian ministers that took in local residents when they had an empty bed. He flirted with his nurses and befriended his roommate. We pushed him in his wheelchair through the gardens of oaks, palms, roses, citrus trees, birds of paradise. He was confused sometimes and he slept for hours, but he wasn't unhappy.

I flew out to visit every month. Once, our younger son, Timothy, and I drove straight from the airport to his bedside. "We just flew in, Dad," I said.

"From Puerto Rico?" he asked.

"No, Dad, from New York," I said.

"Close enough," he responded, as though it was a nice joke. Why should he have to bother with such geographic details when he was on a larger cosmic journey?

I remember thinking we should have some big profound conversation about the end of things. Perhaps he would want to pass on some advice or share some memory of his childhood. He didn't. We would sit in the sun by his old convertible that I drove on my visits and he would point to a passing truck or admire the statue of Jesus in one corner of the garden. The last time I saw him still conscious, I kissed him good-bye on his forehead, the same place he kissed me as a boy after my bedtime prayers. "I love you, Dad," I said.

"Tell your wife," he said, the cylinders in his brain moving slowing, searching for the right words. "Tell your wife," he said, "that I am loved."

He was loved. That much we knew.

Less than a month later my sister Gioia had the last conversation anybody had with him. He was in hospice care and too weak now to go on wheelchair jaunts. He didn't move from his bed. "Dad," she said, teary-eyed, "I'm going to miss you so much."

He looked up at her and asked, "Am I moving?"

Yes, sort of.

He slipped into a coma or some state of minimal awareness and I flew out to see him for the last time.

We sat by his bed for five days while he slowly left us, his vitals winding down, his hands getting colder, his feet getting bluer. He could squeeze hands, but then his hand became weaker. He had no water, no food, no nourishment. Every day we thought would be his last, but he rallied when we appeared, his four children, our spouses, his grandchildren, their spouses, talking around him and above him like we did at dinner. He waited until four in the morning, when none of us were present, to die. Never the first to leave a party, he wouldn't go when we were still there.

We all spoke at the funeral, each of us wearing one of his bowties (the girls wore them on their wrists). Gioia talked about following in Dad's footsteps in her career, becoming a professional fundraiser and non-profit executive like him. Diane described his generosity of character and his tireless volunteer work. Her husband, Mike, spoke of his submarine service, three war patrols in the Pacific during World War II. Our son Will confessed that when he was eleven and his fifth-grade teacher asked the class what their goals were, Will said that he wanted to have four children and nine grandchildren, just like his grandfather. I sang a song that Dad loved and then reminded the packed church how he had prayed for all of them. "I'll hold a good thought for you" was how he put it.

But Howard got it just right, Howard who had sat holding his hand at his bedside, hardly letting go. "When I was sitting with Dad these last few days," he said, "I tried to think if there were any things that I needed to talk about. Were there any things I still needed to say?

"All I could come up with was thanks. You see, Dad let me be me. That's what he gave all of us. He let us be ourselves. He encouraged us to do just what we wanted."

I don't know what comes to people's minds when they say, "We were blessed." But what comes to my mind is a childhood when Dad prayed for us night after night at the dinner table. Such prayers must be called grace because they offer a heaping serving of God's grace. We were blessed by them, richly blessed.

CHAPTER TWO

rayer as Conversation

"Hi, God."

O ur church youth group was putting on the worship service for Sunday. I was picked to lead the congregation in prayer. At age fourteen I'd sat through plenty of prayers led by one of our robed ministers, solemn, stately, dignified. But I wanted to do something different. What was the most honest thing I could say about prayer? How would I address God if nobody else were there?

I walked to the lectern clutching my notes, my bellbottoms that I'd already grown out of billowing above my skinny ankles, my hair an unruly mess. "Let us pray," I said. The congregation bowed their heads. I took a deep breath, looked down at the words I'd scribbled with a ballpoint pen and went to the top of all my polished phrases. "Hi, God," I said as boldly as I could into the microphone. Not "Dear Heavenly Father" or "Dear Lord" but "Hi, God," because it seemed like the best way to open this conversation. "Hi, God," because that was the way you'd start a frank conversation with anyone you loved.

Prayer is conversation. It's a conversation you can have all day. It's a conversation that has gone on for most of my life—give or take a few years of the silent treatment on my part. Bob Hostetler, who has a terrific blog on prayer, suggests in his book with the winsome title *Quit Going to Church* that it could be just sitting in a chair with a cup of coffee the first part of the morning. "You might tell him about your hopes and plans and fears and worries for the day or you might ask him to tell you his.... The important thing is not so much the words you use as the habit you pursue."

That's it. Make it a habit. If I could only pass on one piece of advice about prayer, this would be it: Pick a time and place for prayer and try to do it every day.

Don't be too ambitious about how much time you devote to it. Better to take on a challenge that's manageable than one that's going to overwhelm you and frustrate you until you finally give up. If it's only going to be five minutes, then five minutes it is. Perfect. Five minutes of quiet with just you and your prayers and God listening, or you listening to God, is impressive. If you can do that, congratulate yourself. It's an accomplishment you should be proud of. You've made a place for God in your life. You will reap the benefits.

Whenever experts talk about New Year's resolutions, they always stress that you should give yourself an achievable goal. Working out at the gym for an hour and a half five days a week is not going to hold if you've barely set foot in the place in the last year. Do something small. Better that it can grow into something bigger than you slacking off and giving up altogether.

My insistence on a particular place for prayer might surprise you. Can't you pray anywhere? Isn't God everywhere? "If I take the wings of the morning," the psalmist says, "and dwell in the uttermost parts of the sea, even there thy hand shall lead me and thy right hand shall guide me" (Psalm 139:9, KJV). Yes, God is everywhere. But the external stimuli of a familiar place are going to help you connect. Familiarity does not breed contempt in the spiritual life. Familiarity makes it all the easier. You're here for a regular conversation, "Hi, God." You don't want to be thinking about the furniture or what color the drapes are. The background should be so comfortable that you don't even have to pay attention to where you are.

There are a thousand ways to pray in the middle of a busy day. You'll say something quietly to yourself, you'll hold the lyrics to a song in your head, you'll scroll a picture of calm and comfort through your brain when you're feeling anything but calm. You'll take a few deep breaths and remind yourself of God's love. You'll sing along with the car radio. You'll stretch your hands, releasing tension. You'll flex your toes. You'll read a passage of Scripture on Facebook. In your imagination you'll zap someone with God's love across the conference table at a particularly rancorous meeting. You'll smile. You'll laugh. You'll thank someone for something they did that they thought no one noticed. You'll praise a colleague or a cashier or the janitor at your kids' school. You'll tell a friend how much you care about them. You'll buy an "I'm thinking of you" card and mail it. You'll send a quick e-mail to a troubled soul, reminding her that she is in your prayers.

If you give yourself some concentrated, uninterrupted, dedicated time of prayer every day, all those other ways of praying will come easier. It's the unpolluted aquifer that will feed your best intentions. It will give you perspective on the whole day.

A couple of years ago my brother Howard sent me an e-mail with one of those two-megabyte attachments that make you wonder what you're going to have to scroll through. This turned out to be a picture of a beautiful Alpine meadow, yellow flowers in green grass beneath a cerulean sky, a brooding black helicopter in the background. "We flew here for lunch," he wrote, "only twenty minutes from home."

Howard and his wife, Julie, are helicopter pilots, among other talents, and their helicopter, when it's not being rented by the local police department, sits in the airport near their home in the middle of a dense, smoggy megalopolis of jammed freeways. All they had to do was lift off and fly to the mountains to get this view. *Flee like a bird to your mountain.*

"Just the sort of trip I look for in prayer," I wrote my more skeptical brother. To lift off, be airborne, look down on my troubles as they shrink into proper size, and take myself to a mental meadow.

My prayer habit is sustained by my morning commute on the New York City subway. My mind is freshest in the morning, my need to set my thinking right is also great. Not for nothing did the psalmist say, "My voice shalt thou hear in the morning, O Lord; in the morning will I direct my prayer unto thee, and will look up" (Psalm 5:3, KJV). If I have scanned the news at breakfast, I can be in an ornery mood. As I've said, there is always a story to get me riled up or irritated.

Anything bad about the economy is sure to convince me that I'm headed for the poorhouse. The fear rattling my confidence is reason enough to pray.

I take the elevator down to the subway platform and wait for a train. I often run into some neighbor but we all have our morning habits. We want to be in different cars on the train, we stand at different spots on the platform. Most of my pals know that I use my commute for prayer and meditation. But they're taking out newspapers, Kindles, iPads, paperbacks or documents they've downloaded onto their phones. My Jewish brethren are reading Scripture in Hebrew; there's always a Hispanic neighbor studying the *Santa Biblia*.

We live in the upper reaches of Manhattan near the end of the A train. I'm usually lucky enough to get a seat. I have two old battered, dog-eared copies of the New Testament and Psalms printed by the Gideons International. One was actually picked up on a subway seat and has someone else's underlining and scribbling, the pentimento of its previous ownership. Both copies have been taped at the spine. I keep one in my gym bag, one in my briefcase so I'm never without it. I used to be able to read the small type without glasses. No more. When my neighbors see me take out my Bible it's a sign that I have something else in mind for my commute rather than chatting. Some of them must think, "Yikes, a Jesus freak. I sure hope he *doesn't* talk to me."

Several years ago the *New York Times* was doing a story on prayer and after the reporter interviewed me they sent a photographer to take a picture of me praying on the subway. "I'm sorry," I said, "you can't do that. If I know a photographer is taking a picture of me I won't be praying. I'll be too self-conscious. I'll be faking it." We settled on a compromise. The photographer would take a picture of me reading my little green Bible. Then he would get off at the 125th Street station and I could pray then.

The subway has become such a natural place for me to pray that I sometimes fear if I don't have a morning commute, I'll still put myself on a train just to pray. It's my meditation chapel, my Chartres. All the external stimuli tell me it's time to pray. The white noise of the wheels rumbling along the tracks, the squeak of the brakes at each station, the jostling movement of the train, the opening and closing of the doors, the sound of the people shifting around me, the conductor's voice. "Watch the closing doors, please," could be my prayer call.

Choose a place to pray and you anoint what's around you to help you in your spiritual journey. You make it holy in the most mundane way. Sleep experts will tell people who suffer from insomnia to use their beds just for sleeping—not eating, catching up on work, watching TV. You want your bed to trigger all your impulses to relax and fall asleep. When I go to my office and sit at my desk I'm stimulated to work. When I click on my computer I'm ready to sort through a million e-mails. When I sink into the sofa in front of the TV I'm ready to be entertained. When I get onto the subway train in the morning I'm ready to pray.

I usually read a psalm or some fragment of Scripture before I close my eyes. It helps me concentrate, but I don't insist on it. Some days I'm ready to close my eyes the minute the train pulls out of the station.

For any novice in prayer I must immediately defuse any misconceptions you hold about this plunge into the otherworldly, this reach for the divine. When I'm praying there is no celestial buzz about my head, no flutter of angel wings. I don't go into a trance. I'm not on a magic carpet ride. Prayer is not an escape. That's what you get from drugs and alcohol, or at least that's their short-lived promise. In the words of Sister Joan Chittister, "Prayer enables us to be immersed in what is fundamentally and truly divine in life right now. It is not meant to be a bridge to somewhere else because God is not somewhere else. God is here."

God is here. Go meet him.

"Aren't you afraid you'll miss your station?" someone once asked me. Of course not. You're always aware of what's going on around you. At times I find myself leaning into the world around me. Other times I lean away from it. The external noise can keep me focused or become part of my meandering: "125th Street," the conductor can say, "next stop 59th Street." That's a reminder of a long uninterrupted stretch underground before I need to change trains, an alert to make the most of this time.

Some writers talk about the discipline of meditation and prayer as though you have to take a mental whip to the thoughts that swirl around in your head and corral them back to your intention. You're supposed to seek a sublime emptiness to find the presence of God. In all my years of praying I've never been very successful at that. The brain is too active (at least mine is). Instead I think you should be very forgiving about all the thoughts that enter your head when you pray.

They are not just distractions. They might be the main event. This is what you came for, to hear what's happening in your head. Listen to it. Pay attention. Ask God where you need help. Drop your worries in God's lap. Look for where you are needed.

When you say "Hi, God," God can say "Hi" back in the most startling ways. It could be when you're praying, but it might be when you're driving home from work, standing in line at the supermarket or watching TV at the end of a long day.

Back in the late 1980s a Massachusetts couple was watching a made-for-TV movie called *God Bless the Child*. Mare Winningham played a single mom who lost her job and her apartment. She and her daughter ended up sleeping on cots in homeless shelters. A social worker finds them a house, but things go from bad to worse. The daughter gets seriously ill and the mom feels she has to put the girl up for adoption so she can get the care she needs.

James and Terry Orcutt had been asking themselves if there was something more they could do for God. They'd raised their kids, they both had decent jobs, they were living in a small rented house. As the credits of *God Bless the Child* rolled across the screen, tears ran down Terry's face. James almost jumped out of his recliner galvanized, as though someone had grabbed him by the shoulders and shaken him. "All that woman needed was a room like one of ours," Terry said, "until she could get back on her feet."

The Orcutts had flipped on the TV to unwind before bed. Now they stayed up until 2:00 AM talking. What could they do? They couldn't take in the homeless in their house; their landlord would never accept that. But maybe they could help out in other ways. What if they collected food, clothes, furniture, money to pay an electric bill, to give to people who were in desperate straits? Their grown son's bedroom had a bed and dresser in it that they could easily give away. "God," they prayed, "we'll do whatever it takes."

The next night they drew "We Collect for People in Need" signs and posted them around town. In a matter of days their basement was filled with chairs, sofas, bedding, food, plates, silverware, pots, micro-waves. Others wanted to help too. James opened up the yellow pages and called up homeless shelters and halfway houses. Then he loaded up his car, a Chevy Cavalier with 120,000 miles on it. He borrowed a roof rack, and he and Terry started to make deliveries. They'd carry a sofa up two flights of stairs to a mom and two kids who had only one small mattress. They'd deliver a mini-fridge to a man whose only source of power was an extension cord strung from an upstairs neigh-bor's apartment. They made sure his bill was paid so that his power could be turned back on.

At one moment James wondered if they were being too soft and unsophisticated. "Should we ask people to fill out anything to show they're qualified?" he asked Terry.

Terry shook her head. "In all my readings of the Bible," she said, "I don't believe there's one time when Jesus ever asked if a person was worth helping."

They started an organization called My Brother's Keeper. They would accept donations to cover expenses but they wouldn't ask any-thing from the government. The government *would* want paperwork and that's not who they were. When someone asks where the furniture and supplies come from, they're given a small wooden cross. My Brother's Keeper now has a fleet of trucks and a 15,000-square-foot warehouse. They've helped tens of thousands of families.

The Orcutts prayed regularly. "Hi, God" was a habit with a question at the end: "What else can we do?" It's like that question you ask someone going through a crisis, an illness, a death in the family: "Is there anything I can do?" James and Terry were pretty insistent about it, repetition in prayer being a good thing. But the answer didn't come when they had their heads bowed or were on their knees. It came when they were watching a made-for-TV movie.

If you listened to my head in prayer, you'd be surprised at the racket going on in there. None of it is going to sound that holy. I'm irritable, I complain, I replay conversations at work and e-mails I sent. I self-justify and talk nonsense. I obsess about my health and my appearance. Prayer is reaching for God. Be suspicious of anyone who promises you heaven each time you're out of the gate. More often you'll be mentally balancing the checkbook and wondering when the adjustable-rate mortgage is going to bounce back up. Take it as a chance to ask God to help you trust him with your finances.

"Hi, God," I'll say, "it's me, Rick. Remember all that stuff I told you about yesterday and what I was really worried about? Well, today, something else just hit me..." If God seems silent, does it really mean he's not listening? The best moments with the people you love can be filled with silence. Think of the down time you spend with a spouse. You're both puttering around the house. One of you is reading a book, the other is washing the dishes or wiping the table after dinner. The kids are watching TV. Neither of you says anything but you feel each other's presence. One of the greatest pleasures of marriage is being with someone and not having to speak. God time is like that. It offers the gift of companionable silence.

Some days on the subway, when I'm ready to close my eyes and pray, somebody will sit down next to me and I'll know I need to talk. "Hi, Rick. How are you?" says a neighbor I haven't seen for a long time. I sigh. *Don't you see my Bible in my lap? Can't you tell I'm busy?* What arrogance! Maybe the thing God had in mind for me that morning was to listen to what my neighbor had to say.

One June morning it was a guy I hadn't seen much since our boys played Little League together. He's a high school teacher and was a terrific coach for our boys. I loved hanging out with him, but I wasn't in a chatty mood just now. "Hi, Rick," he said. "Hi, Bob," I said, "how are you?" I reluctantly slid my Bible back into my gym bag.

"I'm doing okay," he said. We talked about our boys first, where they were, what they were doing. Small talk. But then he said, "I'm heading downtown to hand in my resignation. This is my last year of teaching."

"Wow," I said. "What are you going to do next?"

He talked about some of his plans and how he was feeling in the lurch, untethered, uncertain exactly what the future would hold. He seemed glad to share this milestone with someone, his last official day as a public schoolteacher. By the time I got off the subway I knew that conversation was more important than any of the prayer chitchat that would have taken place. "Hi, God," you say, and God comes in the form of a friend who needs to talk. *Just as you did it to one of the least of these you did it to me.*

Another morning I was meditating on a verse from the Psalms (30:5, KJV), trying to remember what I'd read ("Weeping may endure for a night, but joy comes in the morning"). From the other end of the train I heard the strident voice of a West Indian woman I think of as the A-train evangelist. "READ THE BIBLE," she said. "Listen to the message of the Bible and be saved. God wants you to read the Bible. Hear God's word."

I sighed. *She's so loud. I didn't want loud this morning. I want peace and quiet. I wish she'd go back the other direction.* She meandered through the crowded subway train, chanting at top volume. Still with my eyes closed, I could hear people stepping aside to make room for her. I could imagine none of them were making eye contact or taking any of her tracts. "I wish she'd shut up," someone muttered. I echoed the thought. What a holy, kindly, forgiving soul I am!

Then just as she came to my end of the car, she started reading a psalm from her Bible. "Weeping may endure for a night, but joy comes in the morning," she proclaimed, just the passage I'd been saying to myself. So much for the word of God transforming me. I opened my eyes, looked at her and smiled. I stood up to get off the train. "Thanks," I said. "That's one of my favorite psalms too."

"READ THE BIBLE," she said.

◆ ◆ ◆

How do you know if God's talking to you in this conversation you've started? How do you know he's saying something back to your "Hi, God"?

Here's a bit of wisdom I got from job-hunting expert Richard Bolles. "The Holy Spirit is the Lord of our time," he said to me when I was interviewing him for a *Guideposts* story. He is the author of the book *What Color Is Your Parachute?* a perennial bestseller and an essential text for anyone looking for a job or changing careers. Bolles also happens to be an Episcopal priest and in fact wrote the book after going through his own career change from parish ministry to a different way of helping people.

We met in Washington, DC, on a luminous April day. I had listened to him give a talk to a group of priests in the shadow of the National Cathedral, and then we drove to the cherry trees out by the Jefferson Memorial. Sitting under the trees as they were dripping blossoms while a surprising number of Japanese tourists swirled around us taking pictures, we talked about time management. We were discussing how in an office there were always interruptions to whatever you hoped to get done. I was telling him how I tried to give myself goals each day but rarely accomplished all that I set out to do. Something was always coming up. A phone call, a last-minute meeting, a demand for a new article, a request for a rewrite of a story that I'd already rewritten two times, a conversation with a colleague, a book landing on my desk, unexpected news from home. There were days I wanted to throw up my hands in frustration.

Think of all those interruptions as coming from the Holy Spirit,"

"Think of all those interruptions as coming from the Holy Spirit," he said. "Instead of trying to control time, be open to what time is offering you." And then he gave me that phrase: "The Holy Spirit is the Lord of our time." It wasn't at all the subject of the article I wrote, but it's what I remember most from that interview. I say it to myself all the time, especially when I don't think I'm getting anywhere. *The Holy Spirit is the Lord of our time.*

Be open to what the Holy Spirit is saying. Pay attention to the nudges that come. If a colleague wants to talk about her frustrations raising her teenage son or has chosen this moment to reveal some deeply held insecurity, it is not a moment to stick to the schedule. Listen. A golden opportunity has come your way. You are being asked to do something important. Instead of choosing someone else, God has chosen you. You in all your own insecurities and uncertainties, you in your ham-fisted attempts at kindness, are being given a chance. This is a tremendous benefit of prayer. To make us aware of how we can serve. To give us the courage and the insight to know when we should drop everything and help someone else. Over the long haul, the goals on the schedules that we give ourselves get met, especially if they're entrusted to a higher power. The torturing, niggling anxieties shrink to a manageable size when the big needs have been addressed.

Take a moment to say "Hi, God" and you can get something that you didn't even know you were looking for.

Emily Procter is a beautiful LA actress, known for her role as Detective Calleigh Duquesne on the long-running TV show *CSI: Miami*. Before she was famous, before she landed the part that gave her financial security and an enviable measure of stardom, she was just another aspiring Hollywood actress going from audition to audition. Each lucky break was supposed to lead to another, a supporting role here, a sitcom there, a drama in the works, the chance to make a valuable contact. But as she was making her way in a brutally tough market, she found herself becoming too self-absorbed. Had she lost enough weight? Did her hair look right? Was there a reason she hadn't gotten called back after that last audition?

Just to get out of herself she volunteered at the soup kitchen at the church a couple of blocks from her apartment. Every Monday in her very unglamorous green overalls and clogs, she'd serve the homeless and the hungry and those who were just down on their luck. Her father was a doctor back in North Carolina. Her mom volunteered with AIDS patients. She was used to signing up for service projects at her church back home. What to do with herself while waiting for that big break? This soup kitchen was where prayer led her.

For most of us—and I'm including myself—that would be the end of it. Emily would volunteer at the church every Monday until Mondays became too busy. It's easy serving the homeless in an institutional setting. It's safer to relate to a needy person when you are simply dishing out lasagna and salad.

But there was one homeless guy in a wheelchair on Wilshire Boulevard who never came to the soup kitchen. He sat in his shorts and red windbreaker reading. One December Monday, as Emily was heading to the church in her green overalls, she stopped and asked him, "I work at the soup kitchen at All Saints. Want to come with me and get lunch?"

"Yeah!" the guy said.

"I'm Emily," she said.

"I'm Jim," he said.

She grabbed his wheelchair and started pushing but couldn't maneuver it very well in her clunky shoes. Finally she had to tell Jim that she couldn't do it in her clogs. "I'm going home for Christmas," she said, "but I'll be back the first Monday after New Year's. We'll have lunch then."

"Okay," Jim said. He probably didn't believe her. Who would? But true to her word, Emily Procter showed up the Monday after New Year's in tennis shoes and whisked Jim off to the All Saints soup kitchen.

It became a ritual with her, and the best of spiritual growth comes through such rituals. Every Monday Emily pushed Jim in his wheelchair to the soup kitchen. It was a relief to talk to somebody who wasn't in show business, who wasn't bragging about what part she had been offered or what movie she hoped to be cast in. It was good to know Jim. One day three months after they'd met—this was the part of the story my mom loved the most—Jim took Emily's hand and pressed some money in it. Forty dollars. A lot for a guy who lived on the streets.

"Jim, what's this for?" she asked.

"I want to tell you something," he said very solemnly. "I think you're very pretty, but you really need to buy a new outfit. I saved up this money."

Emily realized that he had never seen her in anything but her grungy green overalls. "Thanks, Jim," she said. "I guess I've never told you: I'm an actress. I have lots of other clothes." They laughed about that.

Jim remained a good friend of Emily's for years and still is. They ate breakfast at a coffee shop. She helped him get a place to live in affordable housing. He'd been a terrible alcoholic and almost died before he got sober, he told her. "God stood by me even when I wasn't standing by me," he said. Jim was the voice of reason Emily needed when she feared she was getting too wrapped up in her career. He gave her perspective on life, a larger view. He was an answer to prayer, the friend she didn't know she needed until she found him.

There's another story of an actress who paid attention to the meandering of her prayers. Marcia Gay Harden played one of her best parts for an audience of one. Marcia is probably best known for her Oscar–winning role as Lee Krasner, the artist Jackson Pollock's wife, but she's been in a ton of movies and plays. I first heard about her from my friend and prayer partner Arthur Caliandro (for more about the prayer help I got from him, see chapter eight). He was for many years the senior minister at Marble Collegiate Church on Fifth Avenue, not far from the Guideposts office. Marcia was a member of the congregation, and as Arthur said, "She's got a terrific story."

In her early days as an actress, she lived in DC, doing a lot of theater and supporting herself as a waitress. Someday she hoped to work full-time as an actress, get her Screen Actors Guild card to do TV and movies and move to New York, but for now, this was it. One day two women came into the restaurant where she worked, sat down in her section and told her they recognized her from a play she'd been in. They had a special part to offer her, not on stage but at the Georgetown University Hospital. They were from the Make-A-Wish Foundation, which grants wishes to terminally ill children.

"A seven-year-old girl named Bonnie is dying of cancer," they told her. "She doesn't have much more than a month to live. *Snow White* is her favorite movie and Bonnie's wish is to meet Snow White. Could you be Snow White?"

Marcia didn't hesitate. How could she? She promised she'd be available to play Snow White whenever she was needed.

The trouble was, the day that the Make-A-Wish Foundation settled on was the day she had a casting call to be in an Oliver Stone film. It was the only day Oliver Stone would be in DC casting for his movie, an opportunity a budding actress like Marcia couldn't afford to miss. The casting director didn't need to stress how important it was. "Whatever conflicts you have, reschedule them."

Marcia called the Make-A-Wish ladies. "Couldn't you make it another day?"

"I'm sorry," she was told. "Bonnie's running out of time."

A promise was a promise, especially a promise to make a sick little girl's wish come true. It was one of those "Hi, God" moments when you've prayed to do the right thing and the right thing feels like it's all wrong. Marcia feared she was making the worst career mistake of her life, but she forced herself to say no to the casting call. She immersed herself in the role of Snow White. She found a good costume, reread the story, watched the Disney movie and could rattle off the names of the seven dwarfs backwards and forwards. She had the part down cold.

Still, the morning of the performance she was full of doubts about the choice she'd made. She drove to the hospital in Georgetown in her yellow VW dressed in her Snow White costume, wiping the tears from her eyes. She made one last call from a pay phone to the casting director to beg for a chance to reschedule. "No, Marcia," she was told. "This is it."

She was running late. This *was* it. She wiped away her tears, then asked for directions at the hospital's reception desk. She dashed down a hall and found Bonnie's mother and sister standing outside the girl's room. They gave her some presents to give to Bonnie. Marcia took a deep breath and went inside. A small, painfully thin girl looking much younger than her years was sitting on a pallet on the floor. Her pale face lit up. "Snow White!" she said. All of Marcia's doubts vanished.

"Hello, Bonnie," she said. "I'm so glad to see you. I'm so sorry Grumpy, Sneezy, Sleepy, Doc, Bashful, Happy and Dopey weren't able to make it."

They talked for a while about the handsome prince and Marcia gave her the presents. Then Bonnie took Marcia's hand and asked the toughest question of all: "When I die, will the prince kiss me and then I'll wake up again?"

What could Marcia say? How could you answer a child's question like that? She closed her eyes for a second and tried to imagine how

Bonnie was feeling, how lonely it must be to be this young and this sick. She'd always felt there was an inherent mystery to acting, that when she found a role she connected with—a role she was meant to play—it felt like God was using her for something good. This was such a moment, as though everything she did was a prayer.

"No, Bonnie," she said, "it's even better. When you go to heaven, God will kiss you and then you'll wake up again."

Bonnie died a week later. Marcia eventually got her Screen Actors Guild card and moved to New York. She spent more years going to acting classes, waiting tables, living in crummy apartments before she got her big break and ultimately her Academy Award. But the role she played for a sick seven-year-old was one of the most important she had ever played.

◆ ◆ ◆

Would that all my prayers ended up with such noble results. I like to think I would have done the right thing like Marcia, but I don't know. The inner voice has to contend with tons of well-meant advice urging us to look out for number one, to go for the big chance, to do what we have to do to get ahead. "It's a nasty world out there and nobody's going to give you a prize for being unselfish," someone will say. Nice guys finish last. Look out for yourself because no one else is going to. Even my big-hearted dad had these grumpy, Eeyore-like, woe-is-me moments when he would mutter that he would have done better in life if he hadn't looked out for the other guy. "What am I supposed to do with that?" I would wonder. "How is that supposed to help me?" I'm glad Marcia could admit to her doubts. Up until the moment she stepped into Bonnie's hospital room she wasn't sure. How could she help? Was she doing what God wanted her to do? Only then was there clarity.

Prayer is a way of slogging through the inner conflicts, looking for the truth. It requires honesty. That's one reason I've called this section "Hi, God." A spontaneous conversation with God, one where you say what's really on your mind, is more likely to lead to a satisfying conclusion than anything you could have planned. Sure, you can give yourself a pep talk but when you're at your wit's end, spell it out to God. Say the worst. Expose yourself. Come clean. Just articulating it will help. Later you might even find yourself telling someone else just what you were telling God. It could be just the right person.

Susan Peabody was a single mom in Berkeley, California. Ever since her husband died, her teenage son Karl had become more and more withdrawn. She tried to talk to him, but the more she reached out, the more he pulled away. His junior year of high school, his report card revealed that he had been absent ninety-five times from classes and had six failing grades. She sent him to the school therapist, grounded him, pleaded with him. Nothing worked.

Finally she got down on her knees. She didn't mince words. "God, I can't do anything more for my son. I'm at the end of my rope. I'm giving the whole thing up to you."

She was at work when she got a phone call. A man introduced himself as the school guidance counselor. "I want to talk to you about

Karl's absences," he said. Before he could say another word, Susan choked up and all her frustration and sadness came pouring out.

"I love my son," she said, "but I just don't know what to do. I've tried everything to get Karl to go back to school and nothing has worked. It's out of my hands."

There was silence on the other end of the line. The guidance counselor solemnly said, "Thank you for your time, Mrs. Peabody," and hung up.

Amazingly enough Karl's next report card showed a marked improvement. Eventually he made the honor roll. His senior year, Susan attended a parent-teacher conference with Karl. The teachers marveled at the way he had turned himself around. She was so grateful for this answer to her desperate prayer. On the way home Karl said, "Mom, you remember that call from the guidance counselor last year?"

Susan nodded.

"That was me. I thought I'd play a joke but when I heard what you said, it really hit me how much I was hurting you. That's when I knew I had to make you proud."

Give yourself a time, pick a place and pray. Do it a little bit every day. Check in. God will find you wherever you are and you can find God. You don't have to say much. "Hi, God" will do. At that long-ago youth service at church when I was close to Karl's age, my voice barely changed, my shirt rumpled, my sideburns just wishful thinking, I walked down the aisle with the rest of the group. We passed out daisies on the way. Some of the girls danced in leotards at the altar. We played Simon and Garfunkel's "Bridge Over Troubled Water" because we knew how precious friendships were. Then I said my prayer.

A small shock wave passed over the congregation's bowed heads, like a breeze ruffling a mountain lake. But that generation gap we talked about in those days was mostly a figment of our imaginations. I remember one of the older members of the congregation coming up to me after the service, clutching my hand in a cloud of perfume. "I don't always say it the way you do, but when I pray it's just like a conversation with my best friend. I think that's what you meant, wasn't it?"

Oh, to be heard. Oh, to be understood.

CHAPTER THREE

Pray for Others

"Be with those I love and the ones they love..."

When you're not sure what to pray or how to pray, say a prayer for someone else.

John Howard works for Lowe's near his home in Elizabethtown, Kentucky. One November morning, earlier than usual, he got in his Ford pickup, grabbed a cup of coffee at the drive-through and took a shortcut through a new subdivision. In the pre-dawn darkness he spotted a glow up ahead. He thought maybe somebody put up Christmas decorations early, but no, it was a big piece of plywood, about four feet by three feet, painted white with a message bathed in floodlights: "Please pray for Baby Layne."

Questions bounced around in his mind: Who was this Baby Layne? What was wrong with Baby Layne? And who would go to the trouble of putting up a lighted sign asking for prayer?

John wasn't a particularly religious guy and not very confident in his prayers. Praying felt pretty mechanical and he wasn't even sure God heard him or would answer, but there was something about the honesty of this request on its plywood background that touched him. He would pray for Baby Layne, whoever Baby Layne was.

It became his morning routine. Get into the truck, grab some coffee at the drive through, cut through the subdivision, slow down at the sign and pray for Baby Layne. He finally told his wife, Susan, about it and what he'd been doing. Like many wives, she was a little more practiced in prayer and often prayed for others. "Isn't it nice to start your day by thinking about someone else?" she said.

"I just wonder how Baby Layne is doing," John said.

"Why don't you knock on their door and ask?" she said.

He didn't want to bother a family caring for a sick child, and anyway what would he say? That praying for a complete stranger had helped him? That keeping this regular appointment with God was a comfort and a blessing? Besides it was so early in the morning when he passed the house. Better to say nothing.

Then one spring afternoon, on his way home from Lowe's, he passed the house and sign and saw a man out in front. Fiftyish like him, in a white baseball cap, mowing the lawn. *Now's my chance*, John thought. He pulled into the driveway and got out of his truck. The man reached down to shut off his lawn mower.

John hesitated for a moment. I know exactly how he must have felt. Do you really want to tell some complete stranger that you've been praying for him or for his family? Doesn't it sound completely outlandish? And who are you to think your prayers mean anything?

How presumptuous of you, how intrusive, how foolish. But John had stepped out of the pickup truck.

"I just wanted to tell you," he said. "I . . . I saw your sign a few months back and I've been praying for Baby Layne ever since."

The man in the white baseball cap stood there; then his eyes pooled with tears. "I'm Kenny," he said. "Baby Layne is my grandson and hearing that really means a lot, sir. Thank you." Then he gave John a bear hug.

There is a sublime intimacy to praying for someone else that breaks down all barriers. Jesus exhorted us to do it, even saying that we should pray for our enemies: "Love your enemies, bless them that curse you, do good to them that hate you, and pray for them which despitefully use you, and persecute you." What a challenge that is. Praying for strangers seems a good deal easier.

I love the Apostle Paul's expressions of prayer. What he writes in his letter to the Philippians, a letter that's almost two thousand years old, sounds as fresh as an e-mail I got yesterday: "I thank my God every time I remember you, constantly praying with joy in every one of my prayers for all of you" (Philippians 1:3). What a way to say "I'm keeping you in my prayers." Nothing perfunctory about it. His passionate tone fills me with awe. "And this is my prayer, that your love may overflow more and more with knowledge and full insight to help you to determine what is best, so that in the day of Christ you may be pure and blameless, having produced the harvest of righteousness that comes through Jesus Christ for the glory and praise of God" (Philippians 1:9–10). What a model for prayer. Go out on a limb when you pray for others.

Take a risk. Be outrageous. Be passionate. Wish for the biggest thing you could possibly wish for. Take a leap. Love a lot not just a little.

My friend Rick Thyne sometimes calls me from California in the middle of the day, in between clients in his psychotherapy practice. "Just thinking of you and Carol," he'll say. "You know how much I love you both. Hugs, prayers." I feel like one of those Philippians or Corinthians, anyone who received one of Paul's letters must have felt, zapped by outrageous love. In the unguarded language of faith Rick refers to me as one of his "beloveds," part of his spiritual community. Of course he struggles in his faith. He's faced devastating losses. Lord knows, he's stumbled more than a few times, but this is what he does. He prays for people whenever he can. His patients are blanketed in prayer whether they know it or not (most of them probably don't). It's his gift to them, an essential part of his work.

The truth of the matter is that when you pray for someone else, you're helping yourself. Love is disinterested but love has this side benefit of making you bigger, stronger, less selfish, more interesting—in a word, lovelier. Praying for others is a bellwether of mental health for me. If I'm sinking into self-absorption, if I'm worried too much about what's happening to me, I know what to do. Pray, for goodness' sake. Pray for myself, yes, because I can't avoid that (no use hiding my feelings). Then pray for somebody else. Pray for all those who need God so much more than me. Dad always put it in his graces, "Be with those we love and the ones they love..." and he'd name a few. He'd tell them too, "I'm holding a good thought for you."

You should see my desk, littered with yellow Post-It notes with names of people I'm praying for: "Jerry, chemo...Emma, loss...Emily, healthy baby...Roberta's girls.... David, job interview...Monty, business...Rebecca, job...Renee, lawsuit...Pat, peace...Chuck, addiction...Mary Lou, ankle..." I'm not great at it but I just keep doing it. You just do. Thank God for e-mail. I can send a quick e-mail with a follow-up question—"How are you? You're in my prayers"—and keep track, updating the Post-It notes.

I know, I know. It can be embarrassing and cringe-making to tell someone that you're praying for them, especially people who don't believe in prayer and think it's utter nonsense or worse, delusional. "You're in my thoughts," I'll say, or borrowing Dad's language, "I'm holding a good thought for you." I've been known to put it in all caps— "HOW ARE YOU?"—because the prayer feels so urgent, a shout-out to God. The pain is immediate, the worry grave. I have to trust that all the people I pray for know it's out of love. Affection and fondness can cover a world of awkwardness. May my agnostic friends, whom I adore, forgive me if my prayers seem presumptuous or intrusive. "Be with those we love and the ones they love" is a crucial part of prayer.

I've even turned my prayer list into a memory exercise. Forgetfulness has been a problem of late, a sure sign of age. Coming up with people's names is the worst. I sputter and draw a blank. If Carol's anywhere close I turn to her for help: "You know who I'm talking about, honey. That guy we went to college with who played hockey and used to go out with what's her name and then got married to her roommate instead..." She usually *does* know who I'm talking about. She's my hard drive for names, but like a good wife she'll wait as I go through my game of Twenty Questions. She makes me search my own hard drive just to see if it's running.

"Memorize the names on your prayer list," I told myself. "It'll be good for your spiritual life and good for your aging brain."

I put the names in groups of five. Easier to remember that way. I'll look at one of my Post-It notes, then close my eyes and go down the list in my head. The mental search is part of the prayer. Who e-mailed me the other day? Who is struggling? Who is going through a rough patch? Who asked me to pray? I can almost feel myself opening a file in my brain, one of compassion and care, one that needs plenty of use or it would disappear.

On that spring day in Kentucky, John got the whole story about Baby Layne. Kenny's grandson had been born four months premature, weighing just over a pound, and had to have open-heart surgery. "The doctors didn't think he would make it," Kenny said, "but I wanted to do something to help so I made the sign." Look what happened. A guy found a prayer routine on his morning commute. A premature baby survived. And two strangers became friends.

Baby Layne is a healthy kid now, running around on his grandfather's lawn. John and his wife drop by to see him and his grandfather. And all because of how John responded to a simple request on a plywood sign.

◆ ◆ ◆

Prayer expands your world. You learn to care about people you would never have known otherwise, and you find out what makes them tick.

You grow in your ability to love. I have a Facebook friend I pray for. She's suffered some setbacks over the years and reached out to me, so I added her to my list. Following her on Facebook can be alarming. She posts and links to stuff that seems outrageous to me—polemical screeds. Every time I'm ready to hit the delete button, there's an inner voice that urges me, *Maybe there's something important here that you need to understand. Grow. Listen. Learn.* We all live in our little bubbles and certainly the New York City bubble I inhabit can seem mighty small and parochial (funny, how a city of eight million can be small). Prayer stretches me and takes me outside of my limited universe.

River Jordan is a novelist in Tennessee. Her two sons were in the military and a couple of years ago at Christmastime she learned that both boys were going to be deployed, one to Afghanistan, one to Iraq. She was devastated. What if this was their last Christmas as a family? What if this was the last time she saw them together? How was she going to get through this year that they were gone?

Then she had one of those crazy, out-of-the-blue, wake-up-in-the-middle-of-the-night inspirations. For her New Year's resolution she decided that she would pray for at least one stranger for every day that her boys were gone. Raising the stakes, she decided she should also, whenever possible, tell the strangers that she was praying for them.

This seemed like an impossible challenge, harder than promising to lose fifty pounds in the new year. River is an introvert, a self-described "say-my-prayers-in-private" kind of person. How was she going to handle going up to a stranger and saying, "I'm praying for you"? Why had she ever made such a difficult New Year's resolution?

The first time she did it she was at the bus terminal in Nashville. She felt drawn to the woman at the ticket counter. Mustering up all her courage, she walked up to the woman and said, "Hi, my name is River…and I have this resolution to pray for a stranger every day, and today you're my stranger so I'll be thinking about you and saying special prayers for you."

The woman was stunned. "Oh, honey! My name is Annie. This is unbelievable! Do you know what I was saying to God just this morning?"

"No, ma'am…"

"I was saying my prayers when I asked God, 'Is there anybody in this whole wide world who is praying for me?'"

"Well, it looks like I am," River said.

Pretty unbelievable. All that year, every day, she'd look for a stranger to pray for. As she says, "I can't say I chose them exactly. Sometimes it seemed like they were chosen for me. I'd turn the corner and a person would come into view and it was like an inexplicable urging: *This is the one.*"

Sometimes River thought she'd chosen the wrong stranger, like the time she was in a restaurant and her eyes landed on a gorgeous young woman wearing killer shoes and an artfully tied scarf. Not exactly a "please pray for me" poster child, she seemed to have everything together. But River felt drawn to pray for her. Only when she talked to her did she discover that this "Miss Perfect" was a victim of the economy, out of work and worried whether she'd find a job.

Appearances can be deceiving. Everybody needs prayer, as River said, "even beautiful women wearing designer shoes."

Keeping her New Year's resolution forced River Jordan to get out and meet people. She couldn't get swallowed up in her worries. She was constantly discovering what other people's worries were, what kept them up at night. Her own prayers were answered when both her sons came home after a year of deployment. By then, though, praying for strangers had become an essential part of her life and well-being. She's still at it.

I'll admit that when I read River's story I told myself, "She could do that because she lives in the South, near the buckle of the Bible Belt. Everybody talks about prayer down there, but I live in New York. No one's going to buy that from me. No stranger will want to know I'm praying for them."

Then one summer day I was sitting on the steps in front of a sky-scraper and a young guy sat near me and started to talk. Unlike River, I am no introvert but the son of a man who always assumed that elevator operators, concierges, desk clerks and hardware salesmen wanted to be asked about more than the weather. Mind you, New Yorkers also like to talk. This guy told me how tough his job was and how awful his boss was and how he wasn't sure he could take it anymore. The stress was terrible. He feared he wasn't measuring up. He might never succeed.

"Do you have a family?" I asked. "Anybody who cares about you?"

"Yes," he said. "My girlfriend cares."

"Maybe you can remember that when things are stressful," I suggested.

"I'll try."

"It also helps to come outside and take a break like you're doing now, doesn't it? It's really a beautiful day."

"Yeah, it is."

At this point I took a big breath and asked, "What's your name?"

"John," he said.

"Okay, John, I'll pray for you." I stood up and shook his hand, and his name went on a Post-It note.

As I mentioned, praying for others is how we start our week at the Guideposts offices.

I remember the first time I did it, 9:45 on a Monday morning, sitting at the conference room table. I reached for a stack of the letters our readers had sent in. I rolled up my sleeves and began reading. What a catalog of suffering and misery. In those days the letters were mostly handwritten and you could see a world of pain in small, jittery handwriting or desperation in harried script on yellow lined paper. Cancer, death, divorce, job loss, alcoholism, addiction, financial troubles, family issues, marriage struggles, grief, imprisonment, infertility, infidelity. I quickly learned to search for the letter that expressed gratitude for a blessing or asked for something comparatively minor, like the teenager who wanted us to pray that she make it to cheerleading camp.

But I still have the same feeling I had that first day. Like River Jordan, I'm incredibly grateful for my blessings.

Today most of the requests come through the Internet, tens of thousands of them every month. We have hundreds of volunteers around the world praying. Every request gets prayed for at least once. Nobody has to pay. (Yes, there are sites that will charge you for prayer!) If you want to read some touching prayer requests—and people's answers to prayer—visit OurPrayer.org. Try it when you're having a bad day. One scroll down through the heartache of others will convince you how blessed you are and remind you that you are not alone in your struggles.

"Hi, I am so devastated about giving my dog away," came one recent request. "I believed with all my heart that I was doing the right thing. I believe he went to a home that could give him more than I could. But I loved my dog and miss him so much. It has been two months now and I cry almost every day. I want to get over this and I have prayed that God will heal my broken heart. Next to the Lord, he was my best friend. Please pray for me."

Ouch.

"I am going through a hard time right now. My husband is having an affair with a woman at his job. He comes home late every night. My daughter is a senior in high school and told him about her awards ceremony, but he didn't show up. What have I done wrong? Please keep us in your prayers."

Ugh.

"Please pray for my friend. He hasn't been able to find work for two years now. No public program seems able to reach him or help him. He is behind on his electric bill and his rent. He is pitiful and angry.

I can't help him anymore. Please, any prayers and kind thoughts for him would be MUCH appreciated. I did not tell him I am doing this but I think that is okay."

I prayed for all of them. Every week I pray for requests like these. A priest at our church, Elizabeth Maxwell, used a helpful phrase when she described prayer as a process to help us metabolize sorrow. Without prayer, sorrows can make us bitter. With prayer, we can transform sorrow and anger into empathy, understanding, compassion. Every Monday I take on that task.

And yet, I can still feel I'm not up to it or that really somebody else should be doing it, somebody more qualified. Our volunteers, mind you, get training.

One busy morning at work the phone rang. An unfamiliar number was on the caller ID but I answered it. (Just so you know how easily distracted I am, I always answer my phone. I always think, "Maybe it's one of my kids calling from some unknown number.") "Hello," I said in a brisk businesslike tone.

"I'm Bernadette," a faint voice said.

"This is Rick Hamlin. Can I help you?" I asked, searching my memory to see if I knew a Bernadette. Someone whose story I had worked on? Someone who had sent me a manuscript?

"I need someone to pray with me," she said. "My friend Mary is very, very sick from cancer and is in hospice care. I don't know what to do. I'll miss her so much . . ." She sounded like she was crying.

In addition to OurPrayer online, we have volunteers and employees who will pray for people on the phone. Clearly this woman needed to be transferred to someone who could help her, someone who'd been trained to. What number should I give her? I looked at my bulletin board. Where had I written that down?

"Tell me more about your friend," I said, stalling.

She went on and everything she said—how quickly the cancer had spread, how hard it was to know whether to pray for a miracle or a quick passing, how alone she felt—told me that it would be the biggest cop-out to bounce this grieving woman around, to put her on hold or ask her to dial another line. Maybe she'd gotten my number for a reason.

"Can I pray with you right now?" I finally asked.

"Yes," she said.

I did my best, lowering my voice, saying what came into my head. Did I help? I don't know. I hope so. I do know it was the right thing to do.

◆ ◆ ◆

When you get to be known, however modestly, as a praying person, people will ask you quite openly if you will pray for them. I worry all the time that I will forget to pray for someone I've promised to pray for. Hence the Post-It notes. It doesn't work just to say, "I'll remember." I might, I might not. Any reminders are good. Over a decade ago, when we got new computers at the office, we were told that we needed to change our passwords every month. I did okay for a while, using some variation of my name, my kids' names, my wife's names, everybody's birthdays, my mom and dad's birthdays. Eventually I ran out of good mnemonic methods. Then I looked at my prayer list.

"Use someone on the prayer list for your password," I decided. I typed in a name. The next morning, of course, I couldn't remember why I couldn't log on. Then I thought, "Who are you praying for?" Bingo. Thirty days is a good time period to pray for someone. They're not going to necessarily be out of trouble or on easy street in thirty days, but their situation will definitely have changed. It's always satisfying to retire a name. Prayer answered.

For many years my dad was a volunteer for the Tournament of Roses, the organization that puts on the Rose Bowl and Rose Parade in Pasadena. He rose up through the ranks, directing traffic, managing crowds, checking on the safety of the floats, going to endless meetings. In the early eighties he became the vice president. What was his job that year? They told him he was in charge of the weather.

Now, as anyone who has seen the Rose Parade and Rose Bowl on TV knows: it's always on the first of the year. (Except when January 1 happens to be a Sunday, then it becomes a moveable feast, the wise souls of the Tournament believing the Sabbath should be observed.) And it's always beautiful weather. At that point it hadn't rained on a parade in nearly thirty years, not since the year I was born.

"Thornt," they told my dad, "you've got a good relationship with the Almighty. You make sure it doesn't rain."

What do you know? The skies on New Year's Eve that year were gray and cloudy. Shortly after midnight the rains came down, one of those torrential storms that surprise you in balmy Southern California. The people camped out on the parade route huddled under umbrellas and tarps. The waiting floats were covered with plastic to protect the flowers, the bands put on their foul-weather gear, and the queen and her court were issued umbrellas.

But just on the dot of eight, when the parade started heading down Orange Grove Boulevard, the sun came out. Another beautiful day.

"Good job, Thornt," Dad's pals told him. "You've got friends in high places." I can see Dad's blue eyes crinkle and hear him murmur modestly, "I was just holding a good thought." Good prayers come with a dose of humility and awe.

Why should our prayers convince the Almighty to do something he'd want to do anyway? Why should a thousand prayers change his mind? I suspect it's not about God but about us. God wants us to pray for others because it helps us focus on what's most important and brings out the good in others in us. It spreads hope. It reverses the momentum of despair and pain. God doesn't need to hear from us to be convinced. But we need to reach out and speak up, to convince ourselves. We become co-laborers with God. We welcome the sun or meet the rain. For the person prayed for, it's an extraordinary gift. When you've been on the other end you feel it.

Lee Woodruff and her husband, Bob, went through a terrible ordeal but as far as they're concerned they wouldn't have gotten through it without the prayers of others. Lots of others.

I met Lee and Bob in their sun-drenched Westchester, New York, kitchen a year after he'd been wounded in Iraq. Bob is a reporter for ABC News, and he'd gone to Iraq in his role as co-anchor of the evening news. He and his cameraman were filming a segment from a tank hatch, on the lookout for insurgents, when the tank hit a roadside

IED. As they say, you never hear the bomb that hits you, and Bob didn't. But as his body fell back into the tank, he remembered being enveloped by a pure white light and floating above it. Then he was on the floor of the tank, spitting up blood. That was the last thing he knew.

Lee was at Disney World with their four children that January morning when she got the call. The president of ABC News gave her the news, choosing his words very carefully. "Bob has been wounded in Iraq. He's alive but he may have taken shrapnel to the brain." He was being flown to a military hospital in Germany.

This was Bob's fifth trip to Iraq. Going to dangerous places was part of his job. Lee had learned to put the worst of her fears out of her mind, to avoid them as much as possible. She was busy enough taking care of the children. But now it looked like the worst of her fears had come true. A head wound, shrapnel to the brain. Would Bob survive? She wanted to shout out to God, "Why us?"

She flew back with the children to New York. A network of friends and family stepped in to help while Lee went to Germany. Nothing could have prepared her for that first sight of her husband in the ICU. His head was swollen to the size of a rugby ball, deformed at the top where a piece of his skull was missing. There were cuts and stitches on his cheeks, forehead and neck. His lips were swollen. His left eye looked like a dead fish, she said. He was unconscious. She leaned down to kiss him and spoke, hoping he somehow heard: "I love you, sweetie. You've had an accident, but you're going to be all right."

The doctors were guarded. Bob was young and in good shape. He could recover. But for the first time Lee heard a phrase that would be repeated again and again over the next thirty-five days: "It takes a long time for the brain to heal. Remember this is a marathon, not a sprint."

She couldn't fly with Bob to the hospital in Bethesda, Maryland. Traveling on her own, she handed her passport to the customs agent through the Plexiglas window. The woman looked at it and her face softened. She handed the passport back and squeezed Lee's hands. "The nation's thoughts and prayers are with you, Mrs. Woodruff," she said. It was Lee's first indication of the prayer support she'd get.

In Bethesda Lee started a routine that would last weeks. She'd go to the ICU in the morning and talk to Bob in that overly cheery voice a mother uses with her baby. She would let him know about the kids and tell him stories of how they met. She would play music for him. His eyes were blank, his face expressionless. *Somewhere there's a brain in there healing,* she tried to remind herself.

Then she'd go to the YMCA for a swim, talking to God as she did her laps. Would she be all right? What about the kids? What would Bob be like when he woke up? The doctors and nurses had warned her, "Prepare yourself, Mrs. Woodruff. Bob will have to learn things all over again. Think of him as a baby learning to speak, then read and write..."

The prayers kept coming, e-mails, notes, cards, a cross that he could hold in his hand, homemade angels made out of paper clips. "We're praying for you," people said, praying in churches, synagogues, mosques, community centers, living rooms and YMCAs. Lee read the notes to Bob and hung some of the cards up on the hospital room wall. When her own faith felt weak she turned to the faith of others.

One day when the children were visiting, Bob's older daughter kissed him and Lee saw a tear roll down his cheek. Wasn't that a sign of hope? Another time as she sat next to him, talking to him, telling him, "I love you, I'm with you," he grew agitated. He seemed to be trying to talk through the tracheotomy tube. He pulled her hand towards him and she was sure he mouthed the words, "I love you, sweetie." The nurse had to give him a shot to calm him down. Lee clung to that image of him trying to speak as much as she clung to the prayers on the walls around them.

The fourth week the trache tube came out and Bob was moved to another ward. Lee felt her own energy flagging. She missed being with her children back in New York. Their visits to Bethesda were too short and too few. Her fears of the future haunted her. The conversations with God on her morning swim grew desperate. Doctors warned her that Bob's personality might have changed because of the brain injury. What if he were violent when he woke up? What if he didn't know who she was? He'd grown so thin and fragile. How much longer could she go on?

She went for an early swim one morning, then headed to Bob's hospital room. She pushed open the door and froze. He was sitting up in bed, a big smile on his face. He saw her and lifted his hands in the air. "Hey, sweetie," he said, "where have you been?" Overjoyed, incredulous, she wanted to say the same thing back to him: *Where have YOU been?*

There were many months of therapy ahead. Bob came back to New York and spent his days as an inpatient at Columbia University Medical Center. He would struggle to find a word and Lee got good at playing charades, but when he came up with something like "unsettling" all on his own, she knew he was well on his way. Bob was back.

You don't go through something like that without being changed. For Lee she gained a new understanding of the power of prayer. When she was weak, when she was struggling, when she feared she was at the end of her rope, others were thoughtful enough to pray for her. They covered for her. They gave her strength.

◆ ◆ ◆

When I talked to Lee Woodruff about her story I must have said something about Columbia University Medical Center. It's a sprawling complex in upper Manhattan and we live only fifteen blocks away. After a few years of having doctors all over the city, we figured it would be good to find a primary care physician who was affiliated with Columbia, who could refer us to any of the specialists there. Worst-case scenario, if anything went wrong in the family, we would have a hospital with doctors we knew nearby.

A couple of months after Lee's story came out in *Guideposts*, one of those doctors, a lung specialist, was worried about a chest X-ray I'd had and sent me for a CT scan. On a cool sunny November Saturday I walked down to the hospital for the exam and walked home. That afternoon I planted my tulip bulbs in the little garden in front of our apartment. I wasn't thinking about my health. I was more concerned about making sure the bulbs were deep enough so the squirrels wouldn't get to them. I was a little alarmed when the specialist called

Carol at home—the only number she had—and told her I should call back immediately. "Your lungs look fine," the specialist said, "but you've got an aneurysm in your aorta that looks really big. You'd better do something about it."

A tremor of fear passed through me. An aneurysm? In my aorta? Didn't people die when an aneurysm burst? I'd always had a heart murmur, an indication of a defective valve. I went to a cardiologist every two years just to get it looked at. He'd told me there was a weakness to the walls of my aorta and this could cause major trouble someday, but I didn't think much of it. After all, I was in good shape. I ate well, got plenty of exercise, had strikingly low cholesterol levels. An aneurysm? He never mentioned that was a possibility.

The next thing I knew I was in my cardiologist's office and he was tapping his yellow pencil on his desk and using it to point out the aorta in a large model of the heart. "You'll need to have open-heart surgery," he said. "And soon."

Fear swept over me like a cold wind. Open-heart surgery would be a huge ordeal. I'd be under anesthesia for hours, lying on a table in the operating room. The idea of it gave me the creeps. A machine would take over for my heart and lungs. I wouldn't even be breathing on my own.

"Isn't there some less invasive way of doing this?" I asked.

"No," he said simply.

I headed back to work. On the subway I took out my green pocket Bible. I turned to the Psalms and tried to pray. But nothing would come. The rhythm of the cars careening along the track, the usual background for my spiritual ritual, jarred me and cranked up my fears. All I could think of was being in that operating room, unconscious, cut off from the world, cut off from God.

I called my old college roommate Jim. He and I have prayed each other through tons of situations over the years. We're godparents to each other's kids. "It looks like I'm going to have to have open-heart surgery." I filled him in.

"We'll keep you in our prayers," he said.

I talked to Carol that night. Open-heart surgery. Soon. Maybe in an attempt to deal with her own fears, she told a few friends and relatives the news and it spread like wildfire. Family and friends e-mailed her and then more friends e-mailed back, asking to be put on her list for updates. Her collection of e-mail addresses started to look like a Christmas card list gone haywire. We heard from people we hadn't seen in years, friends from college and high school, parents from our boys' kindergarten days.

Two days before the operation, we met with my surgeon in his office. Still wearing his scrubs, fresh from surgery, he gave us a Power-Point presentation on how he'd repair my aorta and replace the defective valve. It was a polished talk, meant to allay my fears. "I do this operation two hundred times a year," he said, "and I've never lost a patient." *Of course*, that made me think, *I could be the first*. I knew my rising panic wasn't rational. I trusted the surgeon, the hospital. But to tell yourself a fear is irrational doesn't make it go away. I couldn't get out of my head the image of me with a machine pumping my blood and breathing for me while I lay there dead to the world.

I checked into the hospital and got prepped for surgery, my chest shaved and marked as though my heart were a bull's-eye. Carol brought me a big salad for dinner and the nurses were in and out of my room, checking my blood pressure, monitoring my heart. But then they all left.

I lay there in the cardiac ward feeling very much alone, unable to sleep, unable to pray. I turned to a prayer I've relied on for years: "Jesus Christ, have mercy on me. Rescue me and save me. Let thy will be done in my life." But that night saying those familiar words, I felt no sense of spiritual connection. All I felt was fear.

Carol came by in the morning with a friend who promised to distract both of us. We talked about everything but surgery. All too soon visiting hours were over. Carol kissed me and was gone. The nurse came for my things. I took one last look at my Bible and handed it over. Any minute now I'd have to go to the operating room and be put under. I almost didn't answer the phone when it rang. "Hello," I said.

"Rick," came a warm, familiar voice.

"Tibby!" My friend the writer Elizabeth Sherrill and her husband, John, on the other line.

"You are the last person I would ever expect to be in the hospital for heart surgery," she said.

"That's what I thought," I said.

"How are you?" she asked.

"Pretty anxious," I admitted. "I didn't sleep at all last night. I keep thinking about the anesthesia and being on the heart-lung machine. It's like being dead. I can't even pray."

"We'll pray for you."

John and Tibby did pray for me, right there on the phone. I didn't say anything. I let go and let their words do the work for me. What I couldn't do for myself, others would do for me. I would depend on all the people who had promised to pray for me. They would keep me connected to God. Just as a machine would do the work of my heart and lungs, I could trust my friends and family to do the work of my soul.

That moment, waiting for the techs and their gurney to take me to the OR, closing my eyes and clutching a phone, was a revelation. That's why I take very seriously the request, "Keep me in your prayers." Praying has a huge effect on the object of those prayers, all the better if they know it. When your connection to God is fraying, there are others who will keep you in touch. When you can't pray for yourself, let someone else pray for you.

"Amen," Tibby and John said.

"Amen," I echoed.

The surgery was a success. These days I go to the gym, I run a lot and I eat carefully. And I try not to miss an opportunity to pray for anybody who needs it.

CHAPTER FOUR

Praying the Lord's Prayer

———————◆❖◆———————

"Our Father, who art in heaven, hallowed be thy name…"

I'm not the first person, and I trust I won't be the last, to point out that the Lord's Prayer is in the first-person plural. It's not "Give me this day my daily bread" or "Deliver me from evil" or "Forgive me my sins" (or my debts or my trespasses) "as I forgive those who sin against me." It's "give us," "deliver us" and "forgive us." We're in this together. What we ask for ourselves, we ask for others. When we say "Our Father, who art in heaven…" we're not alone. Even if you pray it by yourself on a deserted island, you're including yourself in the community of faith with every word. "Wherever two or three are gathered together in my name," Jesus famously said, "there I am in the midst of them" (Matthew 18:20, KJV). The very words of the Lord's Prayer echo that thought.

Praying with others is different than praying by yourself. I don't focus half as well as I'm in a pew praying with people around me. It feels like I'm closer to God when I'm all by myself, bombarding him with my worries, closing my eyes with the words of a psalm on my lips. We have Jesus' example of going off by himself. After feeding the five thousand, "He went up on the mountain to pray" (Matthew 6:46). No wonder. Multiplying the loaves and fishes must have been a lot of work, not to mention talking to all those people afterwards. (The coffee hour to end all coffee hours.) But then he also prayed with his disciples, showing them how to pray together.

The Lord's Prayer appears twice in the Bible. In each case the context and set up is a little different. As Luke describes it, Jesus was praying, apparently by himself, and when he had finished one of the disciples asked him, "Lord, teach us how to pray the way John taught his disciples" (Luke 11:1, CEB).

Jesus responded, "When you pray, say" and then he gave the disciples the familiar words "Our Father..."

In the book of Matthew the prayer appears towards the end of that good advice usually called the Sermon on the Mount. Jesus is urging the disciples not to pray ostentatiously with long empty phrases and lots of words.

"Do not be like them," he says, "for your Father knows what you need before you ask him. Pray then in this way..." And he gives his listeners the Lord's Prayer. In this case it seems more like a guide. *Pray in this way* vs. *When you pray, say.* It's as though Jesus is urging his disciples, here's what you should do when you pray: Be direct. Make it simple. Don't be long-winded. Cover all the bases. Forgive. Relinquish. Pray for others as you pray for yourself.

A guide for prayer or the specific words of a prayer, it works both ways. What Jesus must have realized is that we humans need something to hold on to, words we can use in any situation, a lifeline of phrases, even though he's assured us that God hears us before we say anything. I can almost see him rolling his eyes at the disciples, thinking, "O ye of little faith, if you really need something, here it is."

Guess what? We do need it.

Talking to people over the years, hearing their stories, I'm often surprised how the Lord's Prayer doesn't necessarily feel like the right prayer, but it's the only one they can think of. And it's effective. I remember one woman, a hard-driving New York real estate developer who was constantly in tough negotiations. She drummed her manicured fingernails impatiently on her desk as we talked and scowled at a ringing phone. I wouldn't have wanted to be on her bad side. Once, in the middle of a deal when she was sure she was being cheated, she was so angry she knew she needed to calm down or she simply couldn't function. "Pray, pray," she told herself. But what could she pray? "The Lord's Prayer," she thought, even though it had no apparent connection to getting the loan or dealing with her colleague's machinations.

"I stood outside that conference room and pretended to rummage through my briefcase while I said the Lord's Prayer to myself. You know what?" she said to me. "I couldn't come up with the words. I was too angry. It took me a whole minute to remember, 'Our Father, who art in heaven...' In that time I was able to collect myself and go back to the meeting."

"What happened with the colleague?" I asked.

"Later he apologized. It was a misunderstanding. I don't work with him anymore, which is just as well, but we're friends."

"What about the loan?"

"I got it," she said with a crisp smile.

She felt all alone, trapped by her feelings, then reached for the Lord's Prayer. It was that very act, searching for the words when she couldn't find them, that gave her a necessary measure of peace.

Back in the 1980s, Elaine St. Johns, a writer I worked with when I first came to the magazine, got a call at midnight from a friend of a friend. "Walt has had a massive heart attack," the woman said. "Mona wanted me to let you know. They're in an ambulance right now. Mona said, 'Pray for us.'"

The shock of the news, the fear, made Elaine's well of prayer run dry. All she could think of was her friend Mona sitting by her stricken husband Walt. Elaine could picture the ambulance rushing to the hospital. She could envision the doctors and nurses scurrying back and forth in the ER. The prospect of loss devastated her and made prayer impossible.

"Help me pray," she asked God. Quick as lightning the thought came to her: *Pray the Lord's Prayer.* Just as quickly her mind rejected the idea. She'd said the Lord's Prayer many times. She'd prayed it often with Mona. But it didn't speak to the current situation. There was nothing in it about illness or racing ambulances and raging fears. *PRAY the Lord's Prayer,* the inner voice said again. This time she obeyed, and prayed the familiar words more carefully and thoughtfully than ever before. She paused over each phrase.

This was before the era of cell phones and e-mail. Elaine didn't find out what happened for several days. At first the prognosis looked dire. Walt not only had suffered a heart attack but also had three clots in his lungs, pneumonia and a temperature of 107 degrees.

But Walt recovered. Better yet, he became a different person. He had been "a borderline agnostic," but after that night there was a complete change in his attitude toward God. Elaine didn't think it was coincidental.

She continued to pray the Lord's Prayer slowly and intentionally as she had that night. The results were satisfying, and as she said, often unexpected. An ugly tumor, scheduled for surgery, simply disappeared from her finger. A financial crisis and a family squabble of some duration both evaporated without her taking any action or giving it further thought.

"There is no way to pray this prayer for one person or one family alone," she wrote. "The minute I consciously addressed 'Our Father,' even though my immediate concern was Walt and Mona, I was also including my family, friends, strangers, enemies. I was praying for them as well. As I contemplated this I realized the universal intent of Christ when he gave the prayer to us. When we pray 'Thy kingdom come, thy will be done on earth as it is in heaven,' we make supplication not only for our own known and unknown needs but also for the needs of his children everywhere. This, to me, was the source of those unexpected results in my own experience—the healing of my finger, my finances, my family relationships. The implications on a worldwide scale were overwhelming."

My mother first taught us the Lord's Prayer when we were kids gathered around the teak table in the lanai, the dog looking quizzically at us through the sliding glass doors, waiting for his dinner. We'd finished ours. A lifelong learner and a budding Sunday school teacher, Mom wanted us to know this one prayer, her blessing to us. We repeated the words after her, Dad at her side. It didn't take long to get it down. Perhaps we already knew it from church. What surprised me was her directive.

"You should pray this prayer whenever you're in trouble," she said. We nodded.

Never an alarmist, rarely given to think the worst, she still added, looking straight at Howard, "If you're in one of your forts and it falls down or if you're in a tunnel and it collapses, you can say this prayer." Howard was always building a stratospheric fort at the top of a swaying eucalyptus or digging a secret tunnel under the fence in the backyard, no doubt inspired by some movie we saw of POWs escaping from a Nazi prison camp. Perhaps her trust in the prayer's power could explain her usual equanimity. Still, I remember thinking, "Why all these big words? Wouldn't 'Help me, God' do just as well?"

Now I believe there's something to the way Elaine St. Johns put it. When you say the Lord's Prayer you're praying for your own needs, known and unknown, and praying for everyone else's too. You're making powerful links to your family and your community. Your helplessness is part of the world's helplessness, and your faith is shared with theirs. This feels like the foolishness of God that Paul writes about: "For God's foolishness is wiser than human wisdom and

God's weakness is stronger than human strength" (1 Corinthians 1:25). Jesus taught the prayer to us and we teach it to one another, passing it along from generation to generation. As any teacher knows, when you teach something, you learn it and your students become your teachers. If you've taught it to your children, they'll be sure to remind you of it.

On a May Sunday morning in 2010 there were terrible floods in Nashville. Services were canceled at the church Colleen Coury and her family usually attend. No one would be praying the Lord's Prayer there that morning. Colleen caught up on some work, but then realized they needed to do some shopping. The fridge was empty. She and her husband, Joe, and their twelve-year-old son, Clay, piled into their Chevy TrailBlazer for a quick grocery run.

The TrailBlazer's big all-weather tires gripped the road in the rain. It made it through a low spot near a creek, spraying water in all directions. Clay splashed through the puddles in the supermarket parking lot. They grabbed a few staples—a pound of turkey, a loaf of bread, a gallon of milk and a couple of pizzas—and were back in the Trail-Blazer in no time. Ten minutes and they'd be back home.

But when they came back to that low spot on the road, the puddle had swollen into what looked like a turbulent lake. Joe started to back up but there was a pickup right behind him. Figuring the water was about a foot deep, he eased the SUV forward. Halfway across, a wave rocked the truck and swamped the engine. Joe turned the key in the ignition. Dead. Colleen looked out her window. The water was halfway up the door.

Joe clicked his seatbelt loose, powered down the window—the electrical system still worked—and climbed into the churning water. It was waist deep. "Get out," he yelled to his son. "Hurry!" He helped Clay onto the hood. Colleen squeezed through the window and climbed onto the roof. Joe clung to the TrailBlazer's door. There was no room for him on the top of the truck.

Rescuers weren't far off. A fire truck pulled up and two men tethered to shore waded into the water and tossed them life vests. The current sucked the vests downstream. "I'm in trouble," Joe hollered. "I can't hold on much longer."

Colleen was starting to panic, fear surging through her. If her strong husband couldn't hang on much longer, how could she? Her hands were cold and trembling. Any moment she'd slide off the rain-slicked roof. She looked down at her son Clay, still on the hood. His eyes were closed, his head bowed. Then she heard him above the noise of the storm: "Our Father, who art in heaven, hallowed be thy name."

How many times had they said those words together? They were part of his bedtime ritual. She had taught Clay that prayer and now he was reminding her of just when to use it.

"Get on the roof!" Joe yelled to his son from the churning water. "Stay up there." Clay crawled up the windshield. "When the truck moves," Joe continued, "ride it to the trees, then jump off." With that he let go of the door.

The TrailBlazer began rocking. The current lifted it from the road and pushed it downstream like a bobbing cork. Colleen held her son tight. "Do something! Now!" she screamed to the rescue workers.

"Don't panic," they called back. How was that possible when her husband was clinging to a clump of ivy, his head barely above the water? The TrailBlazer was moving faster. It started tilting, capsizing. "Jump!" Joe yelled. "Get clear of it. Grab the first tree you can." The SUV sank from view.

Clay grabbed hold of some vines, and Colleen wrapped her arms around a small tree. Joe was yanked back into the current, grabbing a big elm leaning out into the water downstream. The water was cold. Colleen's heart was pounding. Then she heard Clay's voice again: "Our Father, who art in heaven..."

He was right. This was exactly what they should do. She prayed along with her twelve-year-old son. "Hallowed be thy name, thy kingdom come..." The words gave her some sort of hope.

"We're going to get through this," she yelled to Clay. "Keep praying."

"I'm getting tired," he said.

She saw a truck arriving with a small boat. "They're coming to get us. Just hold on a little longer!"

She was swept into the water, plunging helplessly into the current. Then she felt a hand grab her. Joe. She grabbed the trunk of the elm. Clay was sucked into the water too, but Joe was able to grab him. All three of them clung to the large elm.

Finally the men with the boat were able to get close enough to toss them life vests and a rope. They held onto the rope as they were pulled through the rapids to safety. The elm, the rope, the rescuers in the boat had saved them. But Colleen was quicker to say that prayer had been their lifeline. A prayer she had taught her son to say years earlier. A prayer they could say together.

◆ ◆ ◆

The Lord's Prayer pops up in the most unexpected places. Before writing this chapter I thumbed through stacks of back issues in my office—I've got loose copies of the magazine going back to 1977. I was amazed at how often the Lord's Prayer was a crucial part of the story. From home Bible studies to football huddles to AA meetings in church basements to people thrown together in natural disasters, the Lord's Prayer creates instant spiritual community. It provides healing words for what cannot always be said.

Roberta Rogers was not close to her father, "a complex and distant man," as she described him. She was vacationing on Topsail Island in North Carolina when she received news that at age eighty-four he had been diagnosed with inoperable cancer. Walking on the beach, where a rough tide had washed up hundreds of small stones and pieces of broken shell, she was reminded of the broken relationship she had with her dad. Losing him would mean also losing the hope that she would ever gain his unconditional love. The stiff sea breeze whipped through her hair. She looked down at the jagged-edged shells. A wave swept across the beach. Studying the sand, she bent down and picked up a few perfect shells.

Holding them in her hand she was able to recall a few untarnished memories. She remembered accompanying her dad on business trips when she was young and feeling important to be with him "calling on the trade." And there was the trip she and her brother took with him on the Mohawk Trail. Up early one morning they went for a walk on a misty country road and her dad showed them the flowers and told them their names. Once when she was eight she fell into a deep depression. It was the only time she remembered her dad opening up to her. He told her about his own fears and how he tried to believe God could help. His halting faith, so uncharacteristic of him to speak about, gave her hope.

Now, determined to keep hold of the good memories and let the other painful ones go, like the broken shells, she flew up to New England to be with her father. It wasn't a perfect visit. There was so much more she wanted to say but she couldn't find the words. She flew home. After that his condition deteriorated rapidly. He sank into a coma so deep he needed no painkillers, yet he held on tenaciously. One of the hospice nurses said she had never seen anyone survive so long in such a condition. It was as though he was waiting to see someone.

Roberta made one last trip. She sat next to her dad's bed and held his hand, listening to his hard, irregular breathing. She told him of those happy memories she had had, that walk along the country lane, the words he had used to comfort a frightened eight-year-old girl. A healing force flowed between them. Her brother joined them, sitting on the other side of the bed. They had never been a praying family, certainly never praying out loud, but the thought came to her: *We should pray the Lord's Prayer.* She fought the idea, but then her brother made the same suggestion. He whispered to their dad, "You want to say the Lord's Prayer." It was more a statement than a question.

For the first time they prayed together, "two of us loud and one silently," as Roberta said. "Our Father, who art in heaven...forgive us our trespasses as we forgive those who trespass against us..." all the way to the end of the prayer. Then she leaned over, kissed her Dad's brow and said, "I love you," the reconciliation she had longed for happening in an instance, all her remorse gone. The next day he died. The hospice nurse said he was at peace. So was Roberta.

Actor Ricardo Montalbán (of *Fantasy Island* fame) was appearing in the musical *Jamaica* on Broadway in the late fifties. The run of the show kept getting extended. At first his family was able to be with him, but they moved back to California and he felt marooned. Often he went to St. Malachy's Chapel with his dresser Charlie after the Saturday show. One Saturday he was fed up and lonely. When he knelt in the well-worn pews, all he could mutter was, "Lord, I want to go home. I miss my family." Then he heard Charlie pray, "Our Father..."

In those two small words was the reminder he needed. He was not alone. There were others he needed to look after. "Jesus, in teaching us how to pray, had made it clear that we were to speak not only for ourselves but for all members of his family—not just for me, Ricardo, but for all those around me," he wrote. The ache of homesickness melted away into caring for those he was with, like Charlie, like his cast members, like those worshiping in the chapel.

If you look into the different scientific studies testing the effectiveness of prayer, the results of some seem very helpful, proving that prayer offers benefits for a longer, healthier life. But the ones that strike me as foolish or in fact wrong are the ones that seek to set up controls—say, one group of hospital patients that will be prayed for and one group that will not, with researchers looking to see the differences between the two groups.

First of all, how do they know that the "un-prayed-for" really went without prayers? They might have had secret advocates that they didn't know about, never mind the researchers. Maybe we all do. Second, if I were a prayer volunteer in the study, I would have to point out that prayer is not something that limits itself to one small universe. Prayer is generous, indiscriminate, compassionate. It knows no bounds. How could you honestly say you are only going to pray for one group and not another? What kind of prayer would that be? Again, it's "Our Father," not "My Father."

Bill Butler and his wife, Simone, were lost at sea, a thousand miles from the nearest coastline. Their thirty-nine-foot sailboat had sunk and they were in an inflatable six-foot raft in the Pacific. As Bill put it, "Finding our little raft in this vast ocean would be like locating a Volkswagen Beetle somewhere between Florida and Oregon." Among the few crackers and canned goods on board Simone found some prayer cards. Time and again she would grasp Bill's hands and pray her way through the Lord's Prayer: "Our Father, who art in heaven..."

They caught fish with the one pole and hook they had. They drank water using a desalination pump. They fended off sharks and sea turtles. The sharks kept their distance during the day but at night they smacked the fragile raft with their tails and bumped it with their snouts as though it were a bath toy. The floor was so thin Bill and Simone could feel the sharks' snouts. One small tear in the raft would send it to the bottom of the ocean. *Whack!* A shark gave the raft a jolting blow with its tail. *Bang!* Another hit it from underneath, sending it spinning.

A huge freighter appeared out of nowhere and came so terrifyingly close that it almost rammed them. Despite Simone and Bill's screams, despite the flare they set off, the freighter rumbled on. The wind and water dragged them ever further from any shipping lanes. The sun beat down on them mercilessly. At night the sharks kept at it. Each day Bill managed to catch enough fish to keep them alive. Each day Simone grasped Bill's hands and said the Lord's Prayer. Initially Bill didn't join her—he wasn't a praying man or much of a believer, really—but as the weeks went on, he spoke out loud with her: "Thy kingdom come, thy will be done." It would take a miracle for them to survive.

After sixty-six days the currents brought them close to the shores of Costa Rica, where they were picked up by a patrol boat. Bill was a seasoned sailor with forty-eight years behind him. He knew how unlikely their survival was. "The odds against us making it were astronomical," he wrote. "Impossible even." They had lost weight, suffered terrible sunburn, their very clothes fraying on their emaciated bodies, but they lived. And from their prayers Bill found something he hadn't had when they first set off—a faith that gave him hope day after day. That prayer Simone said over and over became a part of him.

Julie Garmon is a forty-something mom with a son at home and two grown daughters. A prolific freelance writer, she works tirelessly at her craft and her faith. Recently she wrote about going to her yoga class after receiving discouraging news from her doctor. She'd been diagnosed with two autoimmune disorders—celiac disease and Sjögren's Syndrome—and she was scared. What would be next? How would her life change? Everything she read on the Internet only ratcheted up her worries. She almost skipped the class. Usually the different poses and the deep breathing served to clear her mind. Not that day. At the end of the class, she lay on her mat, still tense, when her teacher did something unexpected.

"Our Father, who art in heaven..." she began to say. Others joined in, saying the familiar words. Julie did too. Her mind calmed, her worries diminished. It was the only time her yoga teacher had ever prayed like that in class.

"Give us this day our daily bread" is a reminder not to worry about what will happen in the future. Sufficient unto the day. All we need to ask for is what we need today. I can get really worked up about stuff that's far off: Will I have enough for retirement? Will I be able to take care of my wife? Will I ever pay off my mortgage? Will I have a stroke or be struck down with cancer? The Lord's Prayer tells me: Ask God for what you need now. Our daily bread. That's good enough.

I don't think of certain prayers as lucky charms or talismans. You don't have to pick the right one or it won't work, as though prayer were a heavenly doctor's prescription: "Repeat the 23rd Psalm three times daily for stress" or "Take four Lord's Prayers for loneliness." It's not a question of what will get God's attention. As Jesus pointed out in Matthew, "Your Father knows what you need before you ask him." What matters is finding words that get *our* attention, that will focus us. The Lord's Prayer might be the only praying words you've ever known. Good. Use them.

Remember back in 2002 when the DC area was terrified by the Beltway Sniper? Ten people were killed and several wounded in a three-week period, all of them in the Maryland, Virginia and DC area. The killings were so random, usually with one bullet, often in parking lots and filling stations, that parents refused to send their kids to school. People were jumpy just filling their gas tanks. Truckers who came through the area were sending bulletins on their CB radios, looking first for what was said to be a white van and then more specifically a blue Chevy Caprice with New Jersey license plates.

Of course people were praying. Ron Lautz, a trucker from Ludlow, Kentucky, was one of them. He hadn't been much of a believer until his only son, Ron, was dying of multiple sclerosis. One October day, between his runs in his 18-wheeler, Ron visited his son at the nursing home. The boy was sitting on the edge of his bed, hands raised over his head, praising the Lord. For more than a year he hadn't been able to sit up on his own.

"I'm leaving here," the son said. "Someone's coming through that door tonight to take me home." He looked hard at his father. "Dad, I don't want to be up in heaven waiting for you and you don't make it. I want you to go over to my church right now and give your life to the Lord."

Ron did exactly that and gave his life to the Lord. His son didn't last the night, but Ron was a changed man. I don't know how a mom or dad could ever bear the pain of losing a child, let alone get out of bed in the morning. I can only admire their faith all the more. Ron got active in church, headed the men's fellowship, led retreats, was on the Sunday school board. And he never started a run without kneeling by the bed at the rear of his eighteen-wheeler cab and praying.

In those days of terror, with frequent trips through the DC area, Ron wondered what he could do. "I got to thinking about what I'd learned in church," he wrote, "how a bunch of people praying together can be more powerful than a person praying alone." What if he got on his CB to see if a few drivers wanted to pull off the road to pray with him?

He pressed the button on his microphone and said if anyone wanted to pray about the Beltway Sniper, Ron would meet them in half an hour at the eastbound sixty-six-mile-marker rest area of I-70.

One trucker answered right away, then another and another. Ron hadn't gone five miles before a line of trucks formed, some coming from behind, others up ahead. The line stretched for miles. It was getting dark when they pulled into the rest area. There must have been fifty rigs there. Everybody got out of their cabs and stood in a circle, holding hands, sixty or seventy of them, including some wives and children.

"Let us pray," Ron said. "Anyone who feels like it can start." He said the first one to speak up was a kid maybe ten years old, standing to his left. The boy bowed his head and prayed, "Our Father, who art in heaven..." They went around the circle. Some prayed their own words. Others repeated the Lord's Prayer. One phrase seemed particularly applicable: "Deliver us from evil." What could be more evil than this random violence?

Ten days later Ron was making his run through the DC area again, headed westbound on I-70. At the rest stop at the thirty-nine-mile marker near Myersville, Maryland, only a few miles from where everyone had gathered in a circle and prayed, the blue Chevy Caprice with New Jersey plates was spotted. Ron's eighteen-wheeler blocked the exit and the Beltway Sniper was caught and arrested—two men as it turned out. That was the headline in the next day's paper and on TV. I like the story of the truckers praying the Lord's Prayer at the sixty-six-mile marker even more. It's one of those rest-of-the-story moments you probably won't see on the news.

Fear was what gripped the nation and everybody in that Beltway area for those three weeks. Fear tends to feed on itself. When you're with people who are constantly looking over their shoulders, you start doing the same. Fear, as has often been pointed out, is love's opposite. Not hate, fear. Fear is what blocks you from loving someone, fear of being ridiculed, fear of rejection, fear of failure, fear of the unknown. Fear of dying can be so paralyzing that all faith disappears. When I was in the hospital getting ready for heart surgery, fear was what blocked me. "There is no fear in love, but perfect love casts out fear," the Bible says in 1 John 4:18 (RSV). How do you find that love when you're in a terrifying situation?

Toni Sexton and her husband, Rickey, were a sweet couple living in Wytheville, Virginia. I say "were" because Rickey is surely no longer with us. When we ran their story a dozen years ago he was wheelchair-bound from ALS—Lou Gehrig's disease—and as I knew only too well, having just lost one of my best friends to ALS, its progress is sure and devastating. But what I also knew from my friend was how precious those few last years could be.

Rickey had been a construction leader for the Virginia Department of Transportation, full of energy, always willing to help a neighbor. Three years after he was diagnosed, his muscles had wasted away. He'd stopped working. He lost his voice. Confined to a wheelchair, he could only nod his head and use his fingers a little. When he wanted to communicate to Toni, he spelled out the message and she interpreted it.

When he was well, Rickey made "power bands" for his friends, little leather bracelets knotted with colored beads. Each one was symbolic, a green bead for spiritual growth, yellow for heavenly glory, white for trust and forgiveness. After he got sick, his brother-in-law made them for him. He'd give them to his many visitors.

That April day Toni was headed to the mailbox. A car came screeching around the bend, turned into the driveway and skidded to a stop. A couple jumped out and ran towards her. The man had long, messy hair, wore faded jeans and a ripped T-shirt. The woman, a few years younger, probably in her twenties, had a pretty face and curly brown hair. Toni froze in her tracks. Both of them were carrying pistols.

"Get in the house!" the man yelled. He pushed Toni forward, slammed the door behind them, and ran into the living room, pulling down the blinds. The girl trained her gun on Toni. "Don't try anything," she said. A police cruiser tore down the road, siren blaring.

The man stared at Rickey in his wheelchair. "What's the matter with him?" he asked.

"He's got Lou Gehrig's disease," Toni explained. "He can't move anything but his fingers."

The man's name was Dennis and the girl's Angel. They stared out between the blinds. "There's cops everywhere!" Dennis said. More squad cars had pulled up and police swarmed around the house. "What are we going to do?" Angel asked. The two of them pushed furniture in front of the doors and covered all the windows.

"You got any drugs in this house?" Dennis demanded, waving his gun.

Toni went to get some of Rickey's muscle relaxants from the medicine cabinet in the bathroom. Dennis snatched the bottle from her and popped a few pills in his mouth, then tossed the bottle to the girl. Toni was swept by a fearful wave of recognition. She realized she'd seen them on the news. They'd assaulted two police officers and stolen their guns. The police were hunting them in two states.

She looked to her husband. Rickey spelled out something with his fingers: "Give them power bands."

The couple was dangerous, waving their guns around, high on pills. What would power bands do? But Rickey insisted. Toni dug them out of the bag in his wheelchair. She held out the bracelets.

"What's this?" Dennis snapped.

"A power band." She held out one for the girl, who put it on.

"What do the colors mean?" she asked.

Toni explained.

"Nobody ever gave me nothing before," Dennis said.

The day wore on. Angel clicked on the TV. Toni discovered that she was on the news. She made some Spam sandwiches. Dennis paced the front room, smoking. The phone rang. He barked at hostage negotiators. He slammed down the phone. They took more of Rickey's pills. There was tense silence.

Then Angel said in almost a whisper, "Would you do me a favor, ma'am? My mama used to read me the Lord's Prayer before I went to sleep at night. If you have a Bible, I sure would appreciate it."

Rickey nodded. Toni took the Bible from the shelf. Even though she knew the words well she found it comforting to read them and feel the weight of the book in her hands. "Thy kingdom come, thy will be done, on earth as it is in heaven." When she finished there was a longer silence, different this time.

"We're not going to get out of here alive," Dennis said. "We'll kill ourselves before we give up."

Rickey started spelling another message. Toni interpreted it out loud: "Please don't hurt yourselves. God loves you. I love you. God will get you through this. Trust him."

Nine hours had passed since Toni went to get the mail. Angel slumped at the kitchen table. Dennis's head dropped on his chest and he passed out. Toni leaned over and took Rickey's hand. He pressed it firmly. Then Angel got up, went to the phone and called the police. "We're ready to give up," she said. The siege ended without a shot being fired. "It was Rickey. He was the one who calmed them down and saved us," Toni said. Rickey, his power bands and a timeless prayer.

◆ ◆ ◆

Each phrase of the Lord's Prayer is worthy of a book, but the one that catches me, the hardest to live by and accept is "Thy will be done." For me, it only comes after a battle of wills, that point of surrender. You can't really be helped by anyone unless you acknowledge your need. I can get so defensive when I hear criticism that I'm unable to listen to the good in the critique. Same thing happens spiritually. If God knows what I need better than I know myself, why put up so much resistance? The old adage (not to be found anywhere in the Bible) "God helps those who help themselves" is true...until it's not true. We can sail through a dozen trials until we hit a wall. God's right there to lend a hand but usually we're so stubborn—or at least I am—that we're not willing to reach out and grasp it. We get so used to punching the wall, our hands balled into fists, that we don't know how to relax and accept the helping hand.

Have you ever watched someone parallel park? I can look out from my bedroom window down to the street below, a God's-eye view. I'll see a car pull out, a car behind waiting to take its place. The driver will check to see if there's enough room. "You've got at least a foot at either end," I want to shout. I watch the driver pull forward and back up, turning the steering wheel. Some drivers are great at it. Others are miserable even with plenty of extra space, rolling up over the curb, bumping the car in front. From my exalted position I can see exactly what they need to do. "Turn now!" I've been known to say. If they'd only listen. If they'd only hear. I suspect I'm often like those hapless drivers.

"It's good to remember that not even the Master Shepherd can lead if the sheep have not this trust and insist on running ahead of him or taking side paths or just stubbornly refusing to follow him," wrote Catherine Marshall in her *Guideposts* story "The Prayer of Relinquishment."

So when do we say "Thy will be done?" When to relinquish? Apparently all the time. At least if we follow the guidance of the Lord's Prayer. It's there up towards the front of the prayer: "Thy kingdom come, thy will be done, on earth as it is in heaven."

Usually when people refer to this powerful phrase, they mention Jesus in the Garden of Gethsemane on the night before his Crucifixion. He knew what was ahead and dreaded it. The fear must have been palpable, the horror immense. He didn't say "Thy will be done" right away. First he prayed, "Father, if you are willing, remove this cup from me." Then he exclaimed: "Yet not my will but yours be done." If he had to struggle with it, should we be surprised that we do too? Asking is a part of prayer. All that talk. But then give up when you need to give up. I've never been able to get there without a lot of work.

Catherine Marshall was married to longtime *Guideposts* editor Len LeSourd. She died in 1983, just about the time I started writing for *Guideposts*, so I never knew her personally but from all accounts she was a very demanding person, setting high standards for herself. It's what makes her a compelling writer. Her book about her first husband, Senate chaplain Peter Marshall, *A Man Called Peter*, was an instant bestseller and her novel *Christy* a perennial favorite, but the book I found most helpful was a slim volume about her day-to-day challenges of faith, *Adventures in Prayer*. She made no claims about prayer without testing them firsthand and tells her own powerful story about getting to "Thy will be done."

As a young woman she was bedridden with what she called "a widespread lung infection." No specialist could help her. No drug could cure her. Neither did her faith make a difference. "Persistent prayer," she wrote, "using all the faith I could muster, had resulted in nothing. I was still in bed full-time."

Then one afternoon she received a pamphlet about a missionary who had been an invalid for eight years. The woman had prayed and prayed that God would make her well. After all, if she were well she would be able to better do God's work. Nothing doing. Finally, all worn out, she prayed, "All right. I give up. If you want me to be an invalid, that's your business. Anyway, I want you even more than I want health. You decide." In two weeks the woman was out of bed, completely well.

None of this made sense to Catherine. Until she came to her own point of abject acceptance. She'd prayed and prayed with no answer. "I'm tired of asking," she finally said. "I'm beaten through, God. You decide what you want for me." Tears flowed. She had no faith anymore, at least not faith as she understood it. She expected nothing. And the result?

"It was as if I had touched a button that opened windows in heaven," she wrote, "as if some dynamo of heavenly power began flowing. Within a few hours I had experienced the presence of the living Christ in a way that wiped away all doubt and revolutionized my life. From that moment my recovery began.

"Through this incident and others that followed, God was trying to teach me something important about prayer. Gradually, I saw that a demanding spirit, with self-will as its rudder, blocks prayer. I understood that the reason for this is that God absolutely refuses to violate our free will; that, therefore, unless self-will is voluntarily given up, even God cannot move to answer prayer."

This is the hardest kind of faith to have because, as Catherine acknowledges, it involves a giving up of faith. A giving up of everything. In my own prayers it's where I land at two or three o'clock in the morning after I've failed at everything else. "Thy will be done" is a struggle. I can say it about relationships or even health easier than I can ever say it about something financial. God might know something about healing a broken heart or shrinking a nasty tumor, but what does he know about the S&P 500 or the check that's about to bounce? What does he know about the job market? What does he understand about adjustable rate mortgages and IRAs? I once interviewed a man who claimed that losing his dream house to foreclosure was the best thing that had happened to him. "I learned to trust God more than ever," he said. All I could think was, would I feel the same way?

"Faith is a gift but we can ask for it," Fulton Oursler, author of *The Greatest Story Ever Told*, wrote in *Guideposts* many years ago. Prayer is the asking. Bow your head and say the Lord's Prayer. Sing it in a crowded church, say it to yourself in the car on your way to work, run through the checklist of all it covers. It's like the Pledge of Allegiance or "The Star-Spangled Banner," repeated so often that you can forget how powerful it is. Say it in a time of need and you'll discover your faith anew.

The Lord's Prayer is so simple you can memorize the words in an hour. And you can spend the rest of your life learning how to live it.

CHAPTER FIVE

Praying for Forgiveness

———————◆◇◆———————

"I blew it, God."

My brother, Howard, was the first to call me on it. "You still haven't forgiven Dad," he said.

Dad had died and we'd mourned him with honest eulogies of all the good he'd given us. We counted ourselves lucky to have had such a father. Why bring up ancient history now? "Sure, I've forgiven him," I blithely told Howard. I could remember exactly when I'd done it eighteen years earlier, shedding the hurt like a eucalyptus tree shedding its old bark. It was all gone. Water under the bridge, as they say.

Then I paused and thought harder. Howard was right. My resentment was still there. Yes, I had forgiven Dad but I needed to go back and do it again. Forgiveness is like that. We need to do it all the time. Consciously, deliberately, jumping right back in the same murky waters until they become clear. To forgive and forget? Easier said than done and impossible without invoking a higher power. I wouldn't even try.

Corrie ten Boom knew a lot about forgiveness and had a lot to forgive. During World War II she and her sister Betsie had concealed Jews from the Nazis in their home in Holland. They were arrested and sent to the concentration camp at Ravensbrück, where Betsie died. A passionate Christian before the war, Corrie felt compelled in its aftermath to return to Germany to spread the message of forgiveness. It was the only way to heal from the horrors of the past, the only way she could possibly recover. "When we confess our sins," she often said, "God casts them into the deepest ocean forever."

In those brutal postwar days Germany was still a bombed-out, bitter, occupied land. Corrie had just given a talk in a church basement when a balding heavyset man in a gray overcoat came up to her, a hat clutched between his hands. "There were never questions after a talk in Germany in 1947," she wrote. "People stood up in silence, in silence collected their wraps, in silence left the room."

A look at this man's face immediately took her back to Ravensbrück, where he'd worn a blue uniform and a visored cap. She could see the huge room there with its harsh lights, the pathetic pile of dresses and shoes in the center on the floor and the shame of walking naked past him. She could picture her sister's frail form, the ribs sharp beneath the parchment skin. He had been a guard at the camp, a leather crop swinging from his belt.

Now he stood in front of her and thrust out his hand. "A fine message, fräulein," he said. "How good it is to know that, as you say, all our sins are at the bottom of the sea."

Corrie pretended to look for something in her purse. Here, she had just given a talk on forgiveness and she couldn't begin to forgive this man who had been one of her captors. Her blood seemed to freeze. "You mentioned Ravensbrück," he went on. "I was a guard there. But since that time I have become a Christian. I know that God has forgiven me for the cruel things I did there, but I would like to hear it from your lips, as well." He extended the hand again. "Will you forgive me?"

Anyone who has ever spoken to a group about some laudatory aspect of faith will be familiar with a moment like this. You've just said, "We should do . . ." or "God wants us to . . ." and you're suddenly asked to put into the practice the very virtue you've extolled. You want to squirm right out of it. You want to exclaim, "I didn't mean a situation like *this*, God," but there you are on the spot.

Two things I find very helpful about Corrie's depiction of forgiveness: One, you can't wait for the good feelings to come. You often have to act before you feel anything. "Forgiveness is an act of will," she wrote, "and the will can function regardless of the temperature of the heart."

"Jesus, help me," she prayed silently in that church basement. Woodenly, mechanically, she thrust her hand into the guard's outstretched hand. Only then did any healing warmth race through her. "I forgive you, brother," she could honestly say. They grasped each other's hands, the former guard and the former prisoner. It was done.

And her second point: Just because you have managed to forgive someone for some unspeakable wrong doesn't mean forgiveness is all over. Corrie described another incident in which she had to forgive, a betrayal by friends she knew and loved. She was seething. She acted against her feelings, proclaimed her forgiveness and a measure of peace came. Done, she thought. But she awoke in the middle of the next night, still rehashing the whole affair. How dare they! What terrible behavior and from people she considered her dearest friends! She sat up and switched on the light. "Father, I thought it was all forgiven. Please help me do it again!" And again.

A pastor gave her a helpful analogy. Think of a bell in a church tower. You pull on a rope and let go, the bell keeps ringing and ringing. Ding, dong, ding, dong. Slower and slower until it finally stops. "When we forgive someone," he said, "we take our hand off the rope. But if we've been tugging at our grievances for a long time, we mustn't be surprised if the old angry thoughts keep coming for a while."

Working an old grievance can be a guilty pleasure, self-justification a repeating refrain in our heads. Talk about a clanging bell. Our hurts can so define us that letting them go is like erasing our personalities, a frightening prospect. I used to think forgiveness would come easier as I grew older. I'm not so sure now. Emotional pain can magnify with age when left unattended. Not long ago I listened in wonder as my colleague John Sherrill declared he needed to see a therapist because his new pastor, a woman, brought up some painful memories from childhood. "I found myself resenting her in a way that had nothing to do with her. It all went back to my own mother," he said. "She was a strong domineering woman and I needed to forgive some things she had done." This from a man in his mid-eighties.

A forgiving spirit is a lasting grace but prayers of forgiveness are meant to be said again and again. Not for nothing is it part of the Lord's Prayer. *Forgive us our sins as we forgive those who sin against us.* John Sherrill's best friend from childhood, Van Varner, was the editor-in-chief who hired me at *Guideposts.* He had his own poignant example of learning how to understand and let go of the past when he too was in his eighties.

Van was a warm, courtly, charming Kentuckian who spent most of his life in New York City. He loved old movies, Broadway shows, walking his dog in Central Park and betting on the horses, having grown up in horse country. Impeccably dressed and urbane, he had an impish sense of humor and a way with puns. We met first through his godson Ty, a college classmate of mine. "Blessed be the Ty that binds," Van said the first time I met him. I had just submitted my first story to the magazine. "No, this story isn't quite right for us," he said, "but you should keep trying." As for the Ty/tie pun, it took me another ten years to figure that one out.

I adored Van. We all did. He was a marvelous teacher and editor. "The tears should be in the eyes of the reader," he often said, drawing a penciled line through any sentences on my drafts that were over-wrought or too purple. Plain prose was the best way to tell a story. Don't have your subjects weep buckets of tears. Don't signal too much. If you've told a good story well, your readers will feel it.

He claimed he never cried over a story. He only wept singing "My Old Kentucky Home" at the start of the Kentucky Derby, which he generally watched by himself in his apartment on television, perhaps for that reason. There were hurts buried deep in his past that those who knew him could only guess at.

Van was the middle of three boys reared in Louisville. When he was five his parents divorced. Van prayed fervently for his parents to get back together. He prayed for them to love each other. He loved his father and was sure his mother still did too. Whatever had happened between them could be undone, couldn't it? His father sent the boys postcards almost every day, met them after school and was always present for Sunday dinner. Later his mother remarried, unhappily as it turned out, and the family moved to upstate New York. Van's prayers were never answered. He couldn't quite forgive God and couldn't quite give up hope for a rewrite to a story long finished.

None of this were we wholly aware of until Van, deep in his retirement, sent in a remarkable story of his own. (Tears in the eyes of this reader.)

Years ago, when his mother died, she had left behind an envelope that said: "Letters of Importance from Joe W. Varner." Van put the envelope in a safe-deposit box and for nearly half a century never looked inside. The memory of his parents' divorce was too painful. Why risk being hurt all over again? Every time he saw the envelope in the safe-deposit box he left it alone. "You figure that by the time you reach my point in life," he wrote, "things are what they are."

Then one day on a visit to the bank, he slipped off the rubber band on the yellowed envelope and finally looked inside. They weren't legal documents, as he'd assumed, but love letters his father had written *after* the divorce, always addressed "Dearest Mary Milam."

His mother had even saved a telegram his father had sent shortly before her remarriage: "IF NOT YET TOO LATE FOR YOU TO RECONSIDER…" His father frequently mentioned Van and his brothers. He was contrite and full of apologies. "You have been hurt…You have and do come first always in my heart."

Van had a new understanding of his parents. The bittersweet proof was in his hands. "They loved each other supremely," he wrote. "Their love was not perfect, as I had so believed when I was a boy. No, not ever that. But, oh, how human, and in its own imperfect human way, how lasting." After decades Van could finally let go. He could forgive God and his own expectations. He could see how his childhood prayer had been answered after all.

As an editor Van would urge us to look for stories that weren't simply front-page, dramatic, made-for-TV-movie situations. We all can imagine how hard it must be to forgive a loved one's killer face-to-face. We can read about it and admire the faith of a saintly Corrie ten Boom and say to ourselves, "I don't know if I could do that." But it can be just as hard to forgive—and just as admirable—in our day-to-day struggles. Think of the grudges we nurse and cling to long after their expiration date. The sister we stopped speaking to when she took the heirloom tea service out of the dining room right after Mom's death. The colleague who poisons the workplace because of jealousy. The husband who bitterly resents the demands of his wife's career yet says nothing to her about it. The child whose prayer never seemed answered. Simmering resentments are deadly barriers to a godly life.

"When you are offering your gift at the altar, if you remember that your brother or sister has something against you, leave your gift there before the altar and go, first to be reconciled to your brother or sister and then come and offer your gift," Jesus said (Matthew 5:23–24, RSV). We can't be reconciled to God if we're not reconciled to each other and to our loved ones. Doing that can take a big gesture, something extravagant and bold. You're trying to rewrite a script that has gone awry, redoing a story. I think of something Beatriz Sandoval—or B, as her friends and siblings call her—did when she wanted to reconnect with her mother after a deep chill. I wish I could show you the picture of her we ran in the magazine, a beautiful dark-haired woman surrounded by flowers—"a fragrant offering," to use Paul's words for it.

B is from a large Latino family in Southern California. She and her mother had had a rocky relationship for years. She remembered being teased as a child for being chubby and wearing glasses. "You'll never get a boyfriend the way you look," relatives would say—and her own mother wouldn't defend her. She hated that. Moreover, she resented being at her mom's beck and call as a girl. No matter how hard she worked she felt she could never earn her mom's approval. Even after she moved out of the house and became successful in her career, B never made peace with her mom. After one bad argument, B told her mom that she never wanted to talk to her again. And for five years she didn't.

"You should call your mom sometime," her husband said. B brushed off his suggestion. She wasn't about to back down. If her mom was being stubborn, she could be stubborn too. They were alike in that.

Then B's sister Leticia announced that she was getting married and wanted B to be the maid of honor. B was thrilled. She could picture the shower she would put on and wanted to do all she could to make her sister's wedding unforgettable.

One problem: Her mother would have to be included in all the events and the silence between the two of them would be unbearable. Already the family held separate holiday gatherings so that B and her mom wouldn't have to be in the same room. B could see how their feud had the potential of dividing the entire family. She should put an end to it. But how would she reverse things? How could she find words to express everything she felt?

"Okay, Lord," she prayed, "I know what I need to do, but I can't do it without you. I'm really going to need your help with this one."

One day on her way to work, B stopped at a florist's. Her mom loved flowers. B held the cooler door open, trying to choose between a red bouquet, a pink bouquet and a white bouquet. Suddenly with a sweep of her arm she grabbed every bouquet from the cooler and carried them to the counter. Eight dozen roses. She paid quickly and hustled to the car. "This is crazy," she thought, but it was what she needed to do.

B pulled into her mother's driveway. She saw her mother standing in the garage. Was her mother crying? B gathered the bouquets in her shaking hands and stepped out of the car.

Her mother *was* crying, her proud, stoic, stubborn mom. For the first time B realized how the separation had hurt her mom.

B rushed to the garage, set the flowers down and took her mom in her arms. "You don't have to cry, Mom. I'm here now," she said.

"*Mi hija*," she repeated over and over. "My daughter, my beautiful daughter."

"Let's not talk about it, Mom," B said, forcing back her own tears. "What do you think?" She pointed to the flowers. "Did I get enough?" They both laughed and went inside to find vases.

The flowers expressed what B couldn't possibly have said with words. She felt relief, exhaustion, excitement and peace rush through her. She had done something that she had desperately needed to do for a long time. Not just for those five years of angry silence but for a lifetime of pent-up resentment. Eight bouquets to express her love. Who was at fault? They both were. B could see that now. "Forgiving and being forgiven are two names for the same thing," said C. S. Lewis. They work in tandem.

"Let all bitterness and wrath and anger and clamor and slander be put away from you, along with all malice," Paul wrote in his letter to the Ephesians (4:31–32, KJV). "Be kind to one another, tenderhearted, forgiving one another as God in Christ forgave you." In one wild beautiful generous gesture, B said that with flowers. Don't think for a minute that those roses were not also a prayer.

◆ ◆ ◆

Not forgiving, not praying for forgiveness, not letting go, can be dangerous not only to your spiritual well being but also to your physical health. Anger turned inward is poisonous. Old wounds left untreated fester. One of the things I find freeing about praying the Psalms is the expression of anger. The psalmist speaks honestly about evil, entreating God in Psalm 139, "Do I not hate them that hate thee, O Lord? Am I not grieved with those that rise up against thee? I hate them with a perfect hatred. I count them my enemies." Before you can forgive your enemies you have to know who they are.

Carolyn Maull McKinstry was afraid something terrible would happen if she got too close to other people, even her husband and her two young daughters, so she barely talked to anyone. She found herself drinking in the middle of the day. She didn't sleep. She picked at her food. She lost weight. Her hands were always breaking out in rashes. She was in a state of constant misery and didn't know why.

Her husband, Jerome, walked in on her in their Atlanta home when she was on the phone to a suicide hotline. "I just wanted someone to talk to," she told him. "I was lonely." Jerome insisted she speak to their doctor and she ended up in a psychologist's waiting room.

Carolyn had grown up in Birmingham, Alabama, at the height of the civil rights struggles. The city had been nicknamed Bombingham because of all the bombs that had destroyed black homes, businesses and churches. Her father had done his best to shelter his family from the troubles. Strict rules were observed, the politics of desegregation never discussed. Carolyn was not allowed to go anywhere without being escorted by one of her brothers. Church was the only place she could go alone.

The family went to Sixteenth Street Baptist Church downtown. Carolyn was baptized there at age thirteen, and remembered staring at the tender face of Jesus in the stained-glass window after her pastor lifted her from the water. "It seemed as if he were telling me, 'I'm here, watching over you.'" She'd been happy, trusting, carefree, not constantly afraid like she was now.

The psychologist asked her about her symptoms, the sleepless nights, the drinking during the day. Finally he said, "What you're dealing with is depression. It's treatable but you won't survive if you keep on like this.

"I can't help but think there's something, maybe in your past, you need to let go of. We need to figure out what's bothering you."

Something in her past? Carolyn had tried not to dwell on it, but it would never go away. She would never forget.

She drove home from the doctor's and took down a box of old things from her closet. On the top was the Bible her parents had given her when she was baptized. She'd had it with her on that terrible day she had never been able to forget: September 15, 1963, Youth Sunday.

She'd been laughing with her friends in the restroom at the church—Cynthia, Denise, Addie and Carole. She was the Sunday school secretary and had to go upstairs to hand in her attendance and offering report by 10:30. When she was in the office the phone rang. She held the receiver up to her ear. A man's voice said, "Three minutes," then hung up. What was that about? She still needed to collect the report from the adult classes. She walked into the sanctuary, toward the stained-glass image of Jesus.

Boom! The floor swayed. Glass fell at her feet. Someone shouted, "Hit the floor!" She dropped flat on the ground. There was a stampede of feet. Sirens. She had to get out. She looked up and saw a hole in the stained-glass window where Jesus' face had been.

The streets were filled with people screaming and crying. She found her father behind a police barricade. They drove home in silence, too scared to talk. Why would anyone bomb their church?

That afternoon their phone rang at home. Carolyn remembered her mother answering it, listening, then hanging up, her face filled with sorrow. There were four girls in the restroom who never made it out. Carolyn's four friends. Dead.

That night Carolyn burrowed deep under the covers, but it was hours before she was able to sleep. Why did people want to kill her congregation, her friends? Why would they bomb a house of God? And that mysterious phone call, was that a warning? Could she have done anything? The world would never seem safe again. A terrible emptiness opened up inside. It haunted her, through high school, college, her marriage. No one had ever asked her what she thought. She hadn't gone to the funeral because she wanted to remember her friends as she'd last seen them, in the restroom laughing in front of the mirror. What she really wanted was for their killers to suffer. She wanted them to feel as much pain as she did.

Now she sat with her old Bible. "God," she prayed, "I am in so much pain. Please fix my body. Take away my craving for alcohol. Please touch me with your healing." She felt the weight of the Bible in her hands. It fell open. There was an old church bulletin tucked inside. September 15, 1963, the day of the bombing. Youth Sunday.

She read through the hymn selections and the names of the people who were to give the prayers. Then she saw the pastor's sermon title, "A Love That Forgives." The Scripture text was Luke 23:24. Carolyn turned to the passage: "Father, forgive them, for they know not what they do."

Tears streamed down her cheeks. She thought of that stained-glass window of Jesus reaching out to her. He was still doing it, all these years later, years that she'd carried a terrible burden inside. "Forgive me, Lord, for not coming to you before now," she prayed, "for not trusting you." She could picture the bombers and their fear. She could understand the enemy. *Forgive them as you have forgiven me.* She could feel the hardness in her heart melting, the anger and bitterness flowing from her.

Carolyn's depression didn't disappear overnight but she'd taken the first step. Like Corrie ten Boom, she would have to return to prayer again and again. Forgiving wasn't something she could do on her own. She kept seeing the psychologist, kept growing in her faith. She and Jerome moved back to Birmingham and became members of Sixteenth Street Baptist Church. Eventually she went to divinity school so she could spread her message.

"The church holds a special status in the history of the civil rights movement," she wrote, "a symbol of faith and hope for all who enter its doors. For me it will always be a reminder of God's infinite grace and love for all his children, and how we are given that love in order to forgive what seems unforgivable and release our burdens to him."

◆ ◆ ◆

Every Sunday in our church we say a communal prayer of confession that comes right out of the Book of Common Prayer: "Most merciful

God, we confess that we have sinned against you in thought, word and deed, by what we have done and by what we have left undone..." I especially like that phrase "by what we have left undone," a reminder of the dangers of spiritual sloth, a goad to do something. Faith requires giving up, letting go. And yet it is anything but passive. It is work. Asking for forgiveness means taking a moral and emotional inventory. Not burying the least attractive parts of ourselves but bringing them to light. That seems so counterintuitive. I would rather consider myself Mr. Super Nice Guy rather than admit to those moments when I blew it. Quite frankly if it weren't on the weekly agenda at church I would probably skip it. And yet how would I move forward in faith if I didn't look for those things "done" and "left undone" and let them go?

I'm reminded of a liturgical gesture I've seen in some worship services, particularly with my Catholic friends, when the priest raps at his chest with his fist. What a great way to express the pain. "I hurt you, God, and I have hurt myself. Forgive me."

Confession seems the most private of moments, and yet there is wisdom in a community praying for forgiveness together. A whole community suffers when it doesn't forgive. "Now if anyone has caused pain, he has caused it not to me, but in some measure—not to put it too severely—to all of you," Paul wrote in his second letter to the Corinthians. "For such a one, this punishment by the majority is enough, so you should rather turn to forgive and comfort him, or he may be overwhelmed by excessive sorrow. So I beg you to reaffirm your love for him." One of the most extraordinary recent examples of communal forgiveness was in an Amish community after the killing and wounding of ten schoolgirls. Some in the media criticized them for their quickness to offer forgiveness—as though it weren't authentic or didn't fully acknowledge the evil—but it was so obviously at the heart of what knit them together. They lived by it.

Let me get back to that conversation I had with my brother, Howard.

Our dad was not perfect. He had his demons. I've already hinted at them, but that doesn't make it any easier to write about them. Maybe if I first emphasized Dad's deep faith and his heartbreakingly honest prayers, I've told myself, you could read this in the forgiving spirit in which it's meant. But it took me a long while to understand it myself. "God is not always choosy about the vessels of his grace," wrote the Canadian writer Robertson Davies, a line I underlined and circled when I first read it.

The biggest difficulty I had with my dad was his drinking. If he had too much, as he often did in my late teens and twenties, he didn't become more jovial or jolly. He became less than himself. His natural sentimentality turned mawkish. His deep sensitivity veered into self-pity. His extraordinary spirituality seemed gone.

As children naturally seek to understand their parents, I looked for clues. I asked my closest minister/therapist friend, Rick Thyne. We talked about all my dad's strengths. "Your father would drop everything to help someone," Rick said.

I knew he would. Yet how could a man be so spiritual and good and generous but also unable to cut back on the cocktails when he was, to use my brother-in-law's phrase, "overserved?"

Dad was our faith mentor at home, an upright Presbyterian with deep roots. Mom taught Sunday school. Mom had a spiritual awakening at one of those famous Billy Graham crusades that transformed LA after World War II. But Dad was the reason we went to church. On Sunday mornings Dad was an usher, the gold embroidered cross on a burgundy background displayed on his suit-coat pocket. Dad served on the board of deacons, then the board of elders in our church long before Mom ever did (probably before women were allowed in those roles). I've known people who had problems with the concept of a heavenly father because of what their earthly fathers were like. Not me. Dad was a righteous man.

"Does he drink because of something that happened to him during the war?" I asked Rick. Was it some lingering response to the trauma that he had suffered in the submarine corps during World War II? Some late and long-running sequel to *The Best Years of Our Lives*, which I'd seen on TV as a kid?

"Do you think he's self-medicating for some post-traumatic stress?" I wondered.

Dad served on a submarine through two war patrols. Unlike other dads who never spoke of the war, he didn't hesitate to give us a vivid picture of what it was like—if we were listening. At the dinner table, he described what happened when his sub dove deep under some Japanese vessel searching for them, crawling at the bottom of the Pacific. "We could hear the depth charges dropping around us," he said. "We walked around in our socks and whispered as if the Japanese could hear us."

"What would happen if they found you?" we asked.

"They would take down the whole sub. That was the thing about the submarine corps. You all died or you all survived."

He took us to a museum to show us a submarine just like his. It was tiny. I would have been terrified to spend an hour, let alone months, on a boat like that. I didn't even like it with the hatch open and sunlight streaming in. He came back from the war rail-thin and jumpy, according to old letters, and he probably drank a lot. His whole generation drank a lot. But he wasn't rail-thin and jumpy when I was in my teens. Not externally at least.

Drinking as a response to some long-ago war trauma? I didn't completely buy it.

The conversation with Rick Thyne and my siblings and others went on for decades, as such conversations do. Rick happened to introduce me to the writings of M. Scott Peck, author of the wildly popular *The Road Less Traveled*. In a later book Peck wrote about alcoholism being a spiritual disease. Alcoholics, if my dad had been one—he would never have said he was—were often very spiritual people, Peck said. When they couldn't fulfill spiritual longings, they turned to drink as a substitute. Not for nothing was hard liquor called "spirits."

That made sense to me. Dad was comfortable in his faith, but sometimes he went to the wrong place for a spiritual fill-up.

Then there were glimpses we'd get of some lingering sadness, a story or two he'd tell at an unguarded and yes, lubricated moment. His mother had breast cancer when he was twelve years old, a double mastectomy in the late years of the Depression.

"I didn't see her for a whole summer," he said to me. "She went into the hospital and they didn't tell us why. I didn't know if she was going to live or going to die. Nobody said anything."

Imagine what that would be like for a sensitive kid like my dad. Like me.

My prayer for myself was to just let go of the whole thing. Drinking didn't get in the way of his work. It didn't seem to harm his health. It didn't bother Mom. It was under control—mostly. But it bothered me. I didn't enjoy him when he drank too much. It marred my image of who my father was. I didn't like being so judgmental of someone I loved and admired deeply. "Help me let it go, God," I could say, but I couldn't let it go. It gnawed at me. I wasn't able to sort the good Dad from the troubled one who drank and the drinking one threatened to overshadow our relationship. I couldn't forgive.

When I was in my late thirties, I had my own wake-up call. It was as though God was shaking me by the shoulders and saying, "Sure, you can forgive. Look for the big picture. See your dad the way I see him."

Carol and I lived in New York with our two sons. Mom and Dad were frequent visitors to our apartment. We loved seeing them. They were good grandparents. But whenever Dad came he needed a bottle of vodka and I could never bring myself to buy it for him. I would let him go to the liquor store. I cringe at the memory. It seems inhospitable, ungracious, unloving. I say now, "Rick, why didn't you give him a break? He was so good to you in so many ways. Why couldn't you be as generous?"

That spring we hit the roughest patch we ever had in our young family. Tim, age four, broke his femur in a tricycle accident at nursery school. Will, age seven, came down with the chicken pox a day later. Tim had to be in traction for twenty-seven days at the hospital. Will was sick at home. Carol and I were darting back and forth between the two places.

Mom came out for a week and was her helpful, upbeat self. Then she went home. She'd done more than her duty as mom, grandmother and mother-in-law.

In the midst of all this I was diagnosed with a tumor on my parotid gland. It had to come out. Soon. So while Tim was in traction at the hospital and Will was recovering from chicken pox, I had surgery. It was supposed to be an easy procedure, a quick recovery—or so the doctors said. But I came home after a night in the hospital in misery. Half the nerves in my face were bruised and unresponsive. I could only half smile, couldn't blink one eye or squint. Worse, I couldn't sleep but was groggy from the general anesthesia. How was I going to take care of a kid with chicken pox if I couldn't take care of myself? Carol was busy enough with Tim at the hospital.

Mom and Dad called me that night. "Hi," Dad said, "how are you?"

"Not so great," I said. I gave a synopsis, then hung up. Dad called back five minutes later. "I'm taking the night flight out, the red-eye," he said. "I'll be there in the morning."

First thing in the morning, with the dawn, Dad pulled up to our apartment, stepping out of a cab in his red sweater vest. I replayed the words my friend Rick Thyne had said to me years before. He was right. My dad would drop anything to help someone. He did the big things right. The drinking shrank back into proportion. Forgiveness came easy then. Didn't even have to try.

◆ ◆ ◆

But remember how I said forgiveness was something you had to go back and do again and again? Hence my conversation with Howard. He saw something and was calling me on it. I had to figure out what it was. Where was this new anger coming from? Why the resentment only months after Dad's funeral, a spiritual send-off that was as cleansing as anything I'd known? Hadn't I forgiven?

I realized it was a borrowed resentment, an unforgiving heart that came not just from Dad but also from my anger at alcoholism on my wife's side of the family. One of the great gifts of the twelve-step movement is the insistence on honesty, and now I had to be honest with myself. I was angry with my mother-in-law, even all these years after her death. *You need to forgive her too*, I thought.

Carol's mother's given name was Moon. She was a brilliant, charming, clever woman who did *The New York Times* crossword puzzle in ink—finished it by 9:00 AM—and could cook anything. Soft-shell crabs dipped in batter, sweetbreads for Carol's birthday, lobster with tons of butter, pecan pies at Thanksgiving. She was a voracious reader, going through books so fast she gave most of them away to the library because there was no room left on her shelves. Moon loved her dogs, coddling her pugs and addressing her German shepherds in German as though it were her native tongue.

She'd been a beauty in her youth, tall and blonde with blazing blue eyes and a strong chin. She was the queen of the annual pageant in the Mississippi River city where she grew up, and sometimes I wondered if that was part of the problem. All that attention before she was twenty, posing at civic events in her tiara, having her picture in the paper. It would have to be all downhill from there.

By the time I knew her she'd been divorced for a dozen years, although there was always some man in the picture enjoying her humor, her cooking and, truth be told, the chance to drink together. For by then my mother-in-law had a serious drinking problem, far worse than anything my dad ever had. The morning began with vodka. She'd drink it from a jam jar while she did the crossword, and the drinking continued throughout the day. There were times of day when Carol simply didn't call her.

This was always most noticeable in the fall when Moon wanted to know about our Christmas plans. As early as September she'd call and ask: "Tell me, what should I get the boys for Christmas? What do they want this year?"

Carol steeled herself for these conversations. She checked caller ID and looked at her watch—any time after five was hopeless. She wanted to be sure her mother was lucid. She didn't want to be disappointed again. "Okay, Mom," Carol would finally give in. She'd pick something off of Santa's list and send Moon a catalogue, the right page dog-eared with the perfect present circled in red.

The conversations continued intermittently all fall. "What was it that the boys wanted for Christmas?" There were other talks about

Christmas: Whose family would we be with, when, and what should we eat this year, turkey or roast beef? But it was the conversations about the boys' presents that were the hardest to take.

The final call always came a week or two before the twenty-fifth. Carol answered. Moon sighed. "Could you buy something for the boys and tell them it came from me? I'll send you a check later."

I wished I could have protected Carol from the despair she plunged into after this last conversation. I prayed I could relieve her sorrow. Sometimes I was tempted to say, "Don't do it. Don't buy them anything from your mom." What was a gift if it didn't involve some effort for the giver? Instead, Carol had to wonder if her mom really loved the boys; she could do so little for them when she was under the influence. Moon made promises but was too unwell to keep them. That realization didn't relieve the anguish. Dutifully, Carol wrapped up something for the boys from their grandmother and buried her pain.

Then the year the boys turned twelve and nine, Carol and her sisters gathered together, determined that their mother get some help. They organized an intervention. On an August morning at seven o'clock we arrived at Moon's house. We sat around her dining room table and asked her, as lovingly as possible, to go into a twenty-eight-day inpatient treatment facility. She listened to us with strained patience. The jam jar was full, the crossword was waiting. "All right," she sighed. "I'll go."

I can't fathom how hard this must have been. For a sixty-nine-year-old woman to leave her comfortable home, bid farewell to her dogs, her kitchen and her garden and live in a dormitory with total strangers, all going to mandatory lectures, AA meetings, group therapy and one-on-one sessions. Like a prison sentence. None of us had any hope the treatment would really work—this wasn't the first time we'd tried. But none of us could tolerate the status quo any longer.

Moon came out of the program looking great. She even managed to thank us. "I will never let that happen again," she promised. She went to meetings regularly. She started seeing a therapist. She talked about the changes she would make in her life. We were hopeful but wary, Carol wariest of all.

That fall there were none of the usual phone calls from Moon about what she would get the boys for Christmas. "It's just as well," I said. "She's got other things on her mind. She's working on her sobriety." If we had only known what was really wrong.

In November Moon collapsed at home with what seemed to be a massive stroke. She had no speech, little movement. It wasn't even clear if she recognized any of us at the hospital. Every day for ten days Carol was at her mother's bedside. At first there was some faint hope that she would recover. Then the doctors determined that the stroke had been caused by an aggressive cancer that riddled her body. All we could do was wait and make sure she was in no pain.

Moon died two days before Thanksgiving. At her burial service we gathered around her grave, all of us crying. It was hard not to ask ourselves a hundred what-ifs. What if we had done the intervention earlier? What if we had worked harder at getting her to give up drinking? Maybe she would have discovered the cancer sooner. Maybe we wouldn't be standing around a grave but celebrating birthdays and Thanksgivings and Christmases for many years to come.

An old family friend, another recovering alcoholic, held up a coin. "This was to commemorate Moon's first ninety days of sobriety. Nothing made her prouder."

Our mood that Christmas was muted. Carol was only going through the motions. She bought the presents, did the decorating, read the Christmas cards, sang the carols, but her heart wasn't in any of it. "You don't have to go to any parties this year," I told her. "Everybody will understand."

The packages piled up. Presents from relatives, from friends. Boxes from websites and catalogues where we'd shopped. We knew what was in those boxes. Something I ordered. Something Carol ordered. But one day a package arrived from a company that neither Carol nor I had ever heard of. "Do you know what's in here?" I asked. And why was it addressed to the boys and not to us? It was a big box.

I cut through the tape and dumped out all the Styrofoam worms. I put my hands in and pulled out a globe. A beautiful globe of the world. "Who's this from?" I asked Carol.

She fished out the order form. She looked and then turned away. It was from her mother. A Christmas present for the boys.

There is a story, surely apocryphal, about a Filipino peasant who claimed to have spoken to Jesus. The woman was passed along from parish to parish until finally the bishop interviewed her. Had she really seen Jesus? Could she really speak to the Lord? With an apparent attempt to trap her, the bishop said, "If you truly speak to Jesus, will you please ask Jesus what my sins are? He would know all about them. I've confessed them to him often enough."

A few weeks passed and the peasant woman came back to the bishop. "Did you speak to Jesus?" he asked.

"Yes," the woman replied.

"Did you ask him what my sins are?"

"Yes," she said. And then with the utter simplicity of the saint, she added, "He forgot."

Our sons got other presents that year. Lego astronauts, a baseball bat, football jerseys, a set of Narnia tapes, but nothing quite like the present from their grandmother Moon, who loved them and was finally able to express that love because she was at long last well.

No, I don't think I can ever forget. I'm not that holy. But I can forgive. And I have to, again and again. I can hear that bell Corrie ten Boom spoke of ringing and ringing. This can mean forgiving someone I've already forgiven or wasn't even the person I thought I was angry with. It can take me back to resentments I thought were long gone. Anger, particularly anger from childhood, has a way of lurking below the surface and when the waters get churned up, it can rise to the top. Watch out. Hurtful behavior from one person can remind you of other hurts. Just because you've buried the dead doesn't mean you've forgiven them.

"Thanks, Howard," I said. "I haven't completely forgiven Dad." Or Moon. The realization was enough. There were healing stories I could turn to. But I suspect if I live into my eighties, I'll still be at it like Van Varner and John Sherrill.

God knows there are ways I've hurt others. Forgiving is the only way to a clean slate.

CHAPTER SIX

Pray through a Crisis

———◆◇◆———

"Nooooooooo!"

The calls came when I was at lunch. I returned to the office to find my voice mail full of urgent messages from California. First from my older sister. She was breathless and in a hurry, jumping into her car to drive to the hospital in Long Beach. "Ricky," she said, "we need your help. There's been an accident. Mike was in a plane crash. Right at the airport. He's the only survivor. Five other guys died. He's being rushed to the ER. Please pray. Pray."

My mom was the next to leave a message: "Honey, I don't know if you heard but it's Mike. He was in a plane crash at the airport in Long Beach. I'm heading down there now. He survived. I don't know how he survived but it's very, very serious. We need your prayers. Poor Diane and the girls."

Diane called too. "Ricky, Mike's holding on, but we all need to pray. Please pray."

I listened to the messages with a sinking feeling. Mike is my younger sister Diane's husband. He's a big boisterous guy with bottlebrush blond hair, a loud voice, a louder laugh and thighs the size of tree trunks. His idea of fun was to ride his bike a hundred miles before breakfast on a Saturday morning. It was impossible to imagine that anyone so physically fit could be hurt. He was wired and funny and full of energy, always forwarding some e-mail about politics or faith or some combination of both. He worked hard running a small business and worked just as hard at his faith, filling up notebooks with Bible verses. He led grace at family dinners with a greeting that could be heard down the palm-lined block: "DEAR GOD..."

I felt so helpless. I wanted to be with my sister Diane and her three girls in the hospital waiting room, getting constant updates. I wanted to hug them, talk to them. I wanted to hear it straight from a straight-talking doctor coming out from the swinging ER doors. Was Mike going to survive? I needed to know exactly what the damage was. "Ricky, please pray." What else could I do? It was as though prayer was the only refuge of the helpless.

I returned calls. Got my older sister, Gioia, on the line. "What happened?"

"Mike and five other guys were on a business trip," Gioia said. "They took off from the airport in a small plane. It crashed right after takeoff. It's all over the news. The engine must have caught on fire. The plane was in flames. When they put the fire out, Mike was the only one alive."

How awful. Horrific. "Where are his burns?"

"All over."

What about brain damage, internal damage? What about his heart? What about his lungs? When would they know?

"Who was with him?" I asked.

"Guys he worked with, colleagues, friends," she said, "the pilot, the owner of the plane."

"*Ughhhhhhhh.*" I can't even put down the sound I made. "This is terrible."

"We've all got to pray. Please pray."

"Where's Mom?"

"She's in the car with me," Gioia said. "We're driving down there right now."

"Keep me posted," I said. "I'll pray." But what would my prayer be? All I could come up with was an awful groan. "No, God, *nooooooooo!* Don't let him die. Not Mike. Not with those other guys already dead." What an awful thing, a horrendous tragedy. I could barely take it in.

I put down the phone and rocked in my chair, leaning forward, hugging my stomach, trying to hold the pain in and hold back the sound. A month earlier, almost exactly a month earlier, Dad had died and we'd all been together. There are prayers for moments like that, prayers for a natural passing, prayers of mourning and loss. But there was no prayer for a moment like this except "*Noooooooooo!*" I couldn't find anything else.

I called Carol. "I have this feeling that Mike's going to make it," I said, wanting to reach for hope. Grasping at straws. "He's really strong. He's got a strong faith, a strong will to live." Who was I spinning things for? It didn't take away the pain I felt. "*Noooooooooo!*" went the prayer loop in my head.

How can an inner scream be much of a prayer? "You're a writer," I tell myself. "You're an editor. Can't you come up with fancier words for a prayer than that? Can't you articulate it?" But at that moment there was nothing else.

I prayed in stunned anger and fear. I called our sons to let them know: "A terrible thing has happened to your uncle Mike..." I e-mailed friends and texted them, widening the network, sounding just like my mom and sisters when they called me. "Pray, please pray," I said. That was all there was to do. The only possible response.

Prayer connected us those first twenty-four hours. All of us were desperately clinging to hope, the believing and non-believing, those of us praying fervently and those stumbling at prayer. I did some of both. I had to check in hour by hour for progress reports. I'm not the sort who can retreat to a mountaintop, unplug my connection with the world and devote myself to prayer. Not by a long shot.

Mike and Diane's friends gathered at the hospital. Many of them knew the other guys, the ones who hadn't survived. Their focus was on Mike, the sole survivor. He had to make it. I could picture the scene, the kids pretending to do homework in the orange plastic chairs, the parents whispering to each other.

Mike and Diane's minister showed up and led the group in prayer. The hospital served sandwiches. In a crisis it's easy to forget to eat. Night fell. Everybody left. Diane kissed her daughters good-bye and stayed at the hospital. My sister Gioia stayed with her, the two of them prepared for an all-night vigil.

The doctors worked on Mike all night. They gave him forty pints of blood and ran him through a battery of tests.

There is a litany of medical terms to describe a patient's state, putting into clinical language what is too terrible to describe: "The patient is in critical condition...serious condition...critical but stabilized." We were looking for words to tell us not only if Mike was going to survive but also in what state. Where were the burns? How bad were they? What bones were broken?

Around midnight my "*Noooooooo!*" changed to a "Please, God, please." The doctors had been feeding us small nuggets of information. There was no apparent brain damage. His heart, his kidneys and his liver were all right. There was hope for his lungs, even after all that noxious smoke. What a miracle. But second- and third-degree burns still covered a third of his body. Once he was stabilized he would have to go to a burn unit for the painful scrubbing of old scarred tissue and grafting of skin. He would be there for a very long time.

I felt greedy praying, "Please, please" in this terrible disaster. Five good men had been killed, leaving behind wives and children, empty desks, empty beds, empty offices. "Please, God, can't some good come from this? Can't there be one ray of hope? Don't give up on Mike."

After thirty-six hours it looked like Mike would survive. In what shape, with what capacities, it wasn't clear. But an ambulance could take him to the burn unit for the long struggle and painful treatment ahead. My "*Noooooooo!*" faded into a brief sense of relief and a moment of thankfulness but *"Noooooooo!"* had served its purpose, keeping me connected when I was feeling undone.

There's a tendency to whitewash God, to make the Lord into some cosmic Santa Claus, always jolly, perennially upbeat, never displeased, never angry. But when I'm angry, I'm not in the mood for a laughing Santa Claus. I need a God bigger than that, someone who can understand my pain, someone who can match the depth of my feelings. Let's not be so quick to diminish God's power or wrath. "O Lord, do not rebuke me in your anger, or discipline me in your wrath," are the sharp words of Psalm 6. "Be gracious to me, O Lord, for I am languishing. O Lord, heal me, for my bones are shaking with terror...I am weary with my moaning. Every night I flood my bed with tears. My eyes waste away because of grief."

"Noooooooo!" is the sound of my prayer when I turn to God in desperation. I don't look for him to smile at me with bland reassurance. The people I turn to when I really need help are big, passionate, caring, generous, knowledgeable about human frailty. They can match my anger, they understand my fears, they can love me when I'm at my most unlovable. They're right there with me when I'm "weary with my moaning" and my eyes "waste away because of grief." The same is true of the God who loves me and whom I love back, in spite of the worst.

"If I believe that he can love me, I must also believe that I can love him. If I do not believe I can love him, then I do not believe him who gave us the first commandment: 'Thou shalt love the Lord thy God with thy whole heart and thy whole mind and all thy strength and thy neighbor as thyself,'" wrote Thomas Merton. Loving God means being willing to shout to him "No!" Sometimes I think he's saying *"Noooooooooo!"* right back with me.

◆ ◆ ◆

Marian and Chris Hammaren had one child, their daughter Caitlin, a nineteen-year-old sophomore at Virginia Tech. The Hammarens lived in upstate New York, an eight-hour drive from the campus, but Marian kept in touch with Caity by texting. In fact, that August day when the Hammarens dropped Caitlin off for freshman orientation, they weren't ten minutes north of Blacksburg when Marian got her first text: "I LOVE my room, Mom. And I know I'm going to love it here. Don't worry. XXC."

Caitlin was busy with wall-to-wall activities, prelaw classes, church, her job as a resident advisor, her sorority. "If you're too busy to call," Marian told her daughter, "just text me an OK. If you're too busy for that, just type an 'O.'" Caitlin laughed.

On the night of April 15, 2007, a nor'easter blew through the Hammarens' upstate town. "The radio's predicting floods," Marian texted her daughter. "Can you BELIEVE it?"

The Hammarens had to dig a trench that night to keep their house from flooding. Two hours later, they came inside, dried off and Marian checked her cell phone. Caity had left a message: "Let me know how it turns out! XOC."

"All's well," Marian typed back. "Dad has it under control. Love, hugs and kisses. Talk to you tomorrow."

There was no message the next morning, but that wasn't unusual. It was still early. Marian headed in to work where she is an occupational therapist. She'd just walked into her office when Chris called. "Turn on your computer. There's a problem at Virginia Tech." Then her cell rang. It was a classmate of Caitlin's. Had Marian heard from her? "No," Marian said. "What's going on?"

"I don't know," Caitlin's friend said. "But it's something really serious. Police are everywhere."

Marian clicked onto the news. Shock ran through her at the lead headline: "Two dead at Virginia Tech. Gunman still on the loose." *Only two*, she tried to reassure herself. Couldn't be Caitlin. But there was still no message. Deep inside Marian, like a mother, knew something was wrong. She reached to shut off her computer and saw that the headline had changed. The number of dead had now climbed into the twenties. She raced for her car and called Chris. "Get ready to leave," she said. "We're going down to Virginia."

The weather was still bad. They hit snow going through the mountains. Traffic slowed, then came to a halt. While Chris gripped the wheel, Marian called every hospital and police station within a hundred miles of Virginia Tech. No one could tell her anything. On the radio the news grew grimmer. The death toll rose. The names of the first two victims were released. At least thirty more names would follow. All the while Marian checked her cell phone for the one message she was desperate to get. No "OK." No "O." Nothing.

They finally pulled up at Virginia Tech. Police ushered them through the crowds to a room at the rear of the inn where other families were gathered. A police office and a minister walked up to them. "Part of me wanted to run," Marian wrote, "to run so fast I could get back to yesterday when the only worry I had was a flooded house. Instead, I stood stock-still, bracing for the shock."

"Mr. and Mrs. Hammaren," the officer said, "I'm sorry. Your daughter was pronounced dead at five minutes after ten this morning."

Caitlin's sorority sisters helped them get through the week. In a haze, forcing themselves to move forward, they spoke to the police, cleaned out Caitlin's room and attended a service with more than six hundred other people. Just before they headed back to New York, Marian was given Caitlin's laptop. She looked at it with grief. No more funny e-mails sent from it, or photos with Caitlin's sorority sisters.

Then Marian opened the laptop and saw a small strip of paper taped above the screen. "God," it said, "I know that today nothing can happen that you and I can't handle together."

At home every time Marian picked up her cell phone she expected to hear her daughter's voice. She couldn't go into Caitlin's bedroom. Could barely go upstairs at all. She could talk to Chris but he was suffering just like she was. She needed to talk to someone. The only person she really wanted to talk to was Caitlin. With nowhere else to turn, she started talking to God.

"Why?" she asked again and again. She screamed. She yelled. "How could something like this happen? Why did you let my daughter get taken away from me?"

She picked up books on spirituality at her bookstore and burned through them. She read the Bible. She was looking for something, a response, an answer. In the middle of a book, those earnest words taped to Caitlin's computer would pop into her head, "God, today nothing can happen that you and I can't handle together." What did that mean?

One August day four months after Caitlin's death, Marian was sitting in her backyard, reading. It was a gorgeous summer morning, with the sun pouring down and the breeze shifting the branches of the trees. Not unlike that morning when she and Chris had first loaded up the car and driven Caitlin down to Blacksburg.

Out of the blue, that prayer of Caitlin's sounded in Marian's head: "Nothing can happen that you and I can't handle together." This time the words were being said to Marian. They penetrated her. Deep in her bones she believed them too. She knew with utter conviction that she would see her daughter again. "Lord," she prayed, "I don't understand Caitlin's death. I'm pretty sure I never will. But I know that you're here with me. Because I know you—because you're present in my life—I know that Caitlin is here with me too." She felt God present with her in her misery, God echoing her sorrow.

I once worked on a story with a minister, of all people, who stopped talking to God when his son was born with severe birth defects. The man was in too much of a rage. "After all I've done," he told himself. "After giving myself to others, to God's service, he would do this to me. How dare he!" He preached, he read the Bible to his congregation, said prayers with them, he visited the sick and elderly, but he refused to address God directly. Not a word. He was fed up with God, unspeakably angry.

After a year of this holy silent treatment, he had a disagreement with a friend. They patched it up quickly—it had all been a simple misunderstanding. "I'm so glad you told me you were angry," the friend said. "I needed to know." *I needed to know.*

The parallel in the minister's own spiritual life pierced him with immediate understanding. If he was angry with God, didn't he need to say it? The least he could do was speak out.

He got down on his knees and prayed, all his pent-up anger spewing forth. He told God what he thought, the angry "No's" finally coming out, the recriminations, the hatred, the wounded pride. He couldn't begin to ask for help and he probably couldn't have been helped until they'd had it out.

To not tell God how angry you are is to risk not telling yourself, to keep your feelings bottled up. Marian had every reason to be in a rage. It seems miraculous to me that she understood enough to yell and scream at God, praying "Noooooooooo!" when the news went from bad to worse to devastating. Only then, only when she kept the connection going, refusing to hide her anguish, was there a hint of healing. I don't doubt that she has to relive that prayer of "No" every time April 16 comes around. The pain will always be there, even in the midst of comfort. A friend who lost his daughter twenty-one years ago to a horrific accident says that every anniversary is different, but every anniversary needs to be observed. Sometimes you need to remember the bad times with God to get to the good.

◆ ◆ ◆

Negative emotions get in the way of prayer, especially if they go unacknowledged. "I don't feel like praying," we say. "I'm too angry with God." For me fear is the biggest culprit. I have no desire to pray when fear is driving peace and love right out of my heart. I don't know how to find God when I'm trembling inside and the inner voices block all hope. Where is he? Will I even know him when I see him? On the day of the Resurrection, two of the disciples were headed to a village called Emmaus. They were talking about what had happened when Jesus approached them. They didn't even recognize him.

"What are you discussing with each other?" he asked.

This was when one of them, Cleopas, the only one named in the Gospel, said, "Are you the only stranger in Jerusalem who does not know the things that have taken place there in these days?" (Luke 24: 18). He was incredulous and maybe a bit arrogant, blinded by grief. How could this stranger not know?

"What things?" Jesus asked innocently enough.

Cleopas gave him the full rundown. That Jesus was condemned to death and crucified. That they had hoped he would be the one to redeem their people. That nothing like that had happened. The only disturbing thing was that very morning some women of their group had found Jesus' tomb empty and a vision of angels appeared, saying he was alive. What a frightening story to hear, impossible to comprehend.

"Oh, how foolish you are and how slow of heart to believe," Jesus said. He went on to explain how Scripture had been fulfilled.

Near the village Jesus seemed prepared to leave them, but in keeping with the ancient rules of hospitality, they urged him to come with them. "Stay with us, because it is almost evening and the day is now nearly over."

When he was at the table with them, he took bread, blessed it and broke it and gave it to them. Their eyes were finally opened, they recognized him and then he vanished from sight. Only then could they acknowledge how they'd felt when he first appeared. Only then could they see. "Were not our hearts burning within us while he was talking to us on the road?"

I can hear the cynic say, "If he really was Jesus, why didn't they figure it out? They had enough time with him, after all." I can also think of times when fear and sorrow prevented me from seeing a truth blazing before my eyes. Praying "*Noooooooooo!*" is a way to push back at the fear, send it packing.

I've already mentioned how our son Timothy, at age four, broke his femur. It was one of those times when everything seemed to be going wrong.

Of all days, it was Maundy Thursday. I came back to the office from a dentist appointment. One of our assistants looked gravely at me. "Call your wife," she said. I got back to my desk and found several messages from Carol. With each one she sounded a bit more frazzled. The first: "Tim's been in an accident at nursery school. It sounds like he broke something. I'll let you know." Then another message: "We're heading to the doctor's office. It looks bad." Then a third: "The doctor sent us to the X-ray lab at 59th Street. Can you meet us there?"

Obviously this was before the days of cell phones.

I dashed out the door, leaving a quick message at church. "I don't think I'll be able to sing at the service tonight," I told our choir director. "Timothy broke his leg."

The X-ray lab was in a dreary building near St. Luke's–Roosevelt Hospital. I went to the lab on the sixth floor. Then I was sent to the pediatric lab on the tenth floor. Carol and Timo weren't there. "But were they here?" I asked. There was no record, said the receptionist. I called the doctor's office and didn't get a response. I called work to see if Carol had called there—all of these calls made from a corner pay phone. Finally I played back a message on my voice mail from Carol: "Hi, it's me. We're at the Hospital for Joint Diseases down on East 17th."

I considered taking a cab, but now it was rush hour and the subway would be faster. The A train to the L train. At the hospital I asked for Pediatrics. Someone sent me up to the thirteenth floor. I stepped out of the elevator and into the conversation of two doctors.

"It's the worst break I've ever seen on a kid," one said to the other, shaking his head. "Right through his femur. He got hit by a tricycle."

Were they talking about my son? The worst break he'd ever seen on a kid?

"Could you tell me where the pediatric X-ray lab is?" I asked politely.

"You've got to go back downstairs. It's on the third floor."

Finally I found Timothy and Carol, Timo looking small and shocked. He was actually shaking. Carol explained: He'd been in an accident at nursery school. Some kid ran into him with a tricycle.

"That's what some doctor upstairs was saying. The worst break he'd ever seen." The fear started cranking up. ("This is the reason hospital staff is asked never to discuss a case outside of an office or some private space," a friend who works in a hospital told me.)

According to the X-rays the break was in the femur, a big bone to heal. Carol, trying to be brave, with both of us trying not to be alarmist in front of Timo, said, "The doctors say he has to be in traction for twenty-seven days."

In traction?

"He can be at home, can't he?"

"He has to be in traction here at the hospital."

A four-year-old in traction in a hospital bed for twenty-seven days? That sounded like being stuck on a plane for twenty-seven days with a toddler, trying desperately to entertain him and distract him. It was frightening. Unthinkable. How would we handle it?

I spent that first night with Timothy. He was on his back, his leg in a contraption in the air, the sides of his crib like bars on a jail cell. The parents of the kid in the next bed were watching a shoot-'em-up cop movie on TV to distract them from their crying child. At midnight the show was still going on. The loud soundtrack made it impossible to pray. I wouldn't have known what to say anyway.

"Daddy, we're stuck," Timo said, grabbing the bars.

"You'll be okay, honey," I said, struggling to believe it. All I could do was echo his thought: We're stuck. We're stuck. We're stuck. When he finally dozed off, I tried to sleep in the hospital chair. And I tried to pray. Fear was making it impossible. Jesus could have been standing right there in a hospital gown—probably was. I couldn't see him. The only word I could pray was *"Nooooooooo!"*

◆ ◆ ◆

What comes to the rescue when you're saying no? How do you get out of it? Maybe it's by just saying no that you open yourself up for help. It leads back to that spiritual relinquishment that Catherine Marshall talks about. Say no loud enough and someone will hear. I've already mentioned how Mom and Dad both came out to help us through that rough patch. Our good friends did too. One neighbor actually coordinated a crew to cover our needs. Every night we got the call: "Need anybody to watch the kids? Anybody to do an errand?"

How did Diane and Mike get through his two months in the burn unit? How did my sister manage to take care of her girls, visit the hospital and remain positive through that long ordeal? You can't stay in a high-adrenaline emergency zone forever. You finally collapse. Family and friends came to their rescue too. Their refrigerator was so full of dropped-off meals that I don't think Diane went grocery shopping for two months. People came out of the woodwork. Our prayers, their prayers, became ones of hope and comfort instead of those monstrous prayers of fear. No one would ever ask for any such disasters to come into their lives, and yet, when you live through one, when you get to the other side, even if all you can pray is "No, God, no," you find your faith changed.

Patrick and Carter were fraternity brothers at Birmingham Southern College in Alabama, Patrick a premed. At the end of August, before classes started, they decided to go camping with some other frat brothers in the Sipsey Wilderness, a remote part of north-central Alabama, about seventy miles northwest of Birmingham.

They drove up on a Saturday morning, parked at the end of a rutted dirt road, grabbed their backpacks and tents and made their way up sandstone bluffs into a dense forest. Far from civilization, so far there was no cell phone signal, they set up camp on a rock ledge overlooking a fork of the Black Warrior River. There was a sheer sixty-foot drop to the cold waters below.

After hiking down to the river and swinging like Tarzan from a tree that hung over the waters, they hiked back up to start a fire, put up their tents and build their campsite. They gathered wood, cooked burgers and hot dogs, sang songs around the fire as it got dark. The fire was burning down. "Carter," Patrick said, "could you grab some more wood?" Carter was a sophomore, a year younger than Patrick.

Carter went to their woodpile, picked up a branch that needed to be broken to fit on the fire. He hauled it off to jump on it. No one was paying much attention, but somehow while jumping on the branch, Carter lost his balance and fell. One of the guys turned around and noticed. "Guys, Carter fell off the cliff!"

"Oh, my God, oh, my God, no!" Patrick thought. For a second he couldn't move, couldn't pray, couldn't do anything. Then he cried out, "God, don't let Carter die!"

Maybe it was his premed training or maybe it was the motivation that came with prayer, but Patrick went into action. "Call 911," he told the guys. Then remembered. No cell service for miles. "Forget that. Drive into town and get help!"

Patrick scrambled down the hill. First he looked for Carter on a rocky promontory just thirty feet below the campsite. Nope. He must have fallen all the way into the river. How could he have survived? Patrick raced back to the campsite, got a lantern and a flashlight, and ran down to the water with some of the other guys.

It was pitch dark. He held up the lantern, and could see nothing. At least five minutes must have gone by. Patrick knew from his pre-med classes that if Carter were underwater without oxygen for eight minutes or longer, he'd be brain dead.

Jump in, a voice urged Patrick. The voice was quiet and insistent. He dropped the lantern, clamped the flashlight between his teeth and dove in. He stayed down for thirty seconds. Couldn't find him. Swam to a second spot and dove again. Nothing. One more time and his foot hit something. Carter. Patrick grabbed his friend under his arms and dragged him to the surface, then swam him to shore. It was like pulling a dead weight, Carter's mouth wide open, his eyes vacant.

Their buddies were ready to reach for Carter, but again something urged Patrick, *Don't pull him out of the water*. "Just keep his head above water. Hold his neck and stabilize him." He didn't want to risk spinal cord damage.

He listened for a heartbeat. Nothing. Then began mouth-to-mouth resuscitation and chest compressions. He kept trying and trying. Patrick figured his friend had been oxygen-deprived for twelve minutes. No way would he survive. Then came a slight gurgling noise.

Probably the last bit of air escaping Carter's body. But the gurgling came again. And again. Very weak. Was that a heartbeat?

The rescue crew finally arrived. In a matter of minutes they had Carter in a harness and in a medevac helicopter. Patrick and his buddies followed. Patrick didn't say what was on his mind, that if Carter somehow survived, he wouldn't be Carter anymore. He couldn't possibly be. He'd been without oxygen for too long. "No, God, no," came that prayer. *Noooooooooo!*

The only encouraging word from the ER doctor was that they'd done the right thing by keeping him in the river. "The cold water lowered his core temperature and kept him alive. Good thing you knew how to do that."

Patrick couldn't take credit for it. Something—or was it someone?—had told him what to do.

For two weeks Carter was kept in a medically induced coma. Brain scans showed he'd been without oxygen for at least ten minutes. Doctors told his parents to expect the worst. But his family didn't give up hope. Patrick tried not to. Finally the doctors brought Carter out of the coma. "He was the same Carter," Patrick marveled. No permanent brain damage. "Miracle Kid," they started calling him. All those "No's" had turned, amazingly, astoundingly, into a Yes.

Patrick had never been as scared as he was when his friend fell off a cliff into the water, but he never lost touch with God. He acted and his friend survived.

◆ ◆ ◆

A time of mass fear came for the nation on 9/11. Most of us can recall the moment when we looked at TV and said, "No, God." I wasn't in New York that day, but I remember being so frightened after what I saw that I walked outside in the sunshine, just to get away from the brutal images of flames, smoke and massive skyscrapers disappearing in billows of dust. "No, God, no, this can't be happening."

The next day in midtown Manhattan, a familiar view was gone from our south-facing windows at the office. Two enormous buildings that had dominated the skyline were conspicuously missing. We were stunned, numb, angry. Soon all over town eight-by-eleven Xeroxed posters of the missing appeared on lampposts and phone booths, husbands, wives, daughters, sons pictured in happier days. "Have you seen?" "Any information on..." The wanted were the lost. Twenty-four hours after the disaster, police sirens wailed, jangling our nerves. But as the stories were coming in of the people who were gone, there were still stories coming in of the people who were saved. We held on tight to every one of them.

Can I say there's something saintly about Brian Clark and Stanley Praimnath? They wouldn't say that about themselves, but ten years after, they still exude the faith they both say helped them that terrible day. For the tenth anniversary of 9/11 they came into the office for a photo shoot. Stanley brought the business shoes he had worn walking down some eighty stories of the World Trade Center. They still smelled of smoke.

I have met other people who have survived appalling tragedies and still seem haunted by them, the nightmare never ending. Or they haven't wanted to talk about what happened. These two, Brian in particular, have made a point of sharing their story.

They were strangers at the time. Stanley was an assistant vice president in loans operations at Fuji Bank on the eighty-first floor of the South Tower, while Brian worked for Euro Brokers on the eighty-fourth floor. Ever since the first terrorist attack on the World Trade Center back in 1993 Brian had volunteered to be a civilian fire marshal. When the North Tower was hit at 8:46 that morning, he grabbed his flashlight and ordered everyone in the office to evacuate the building. "People are jumping!" someone said from the window. He couldn't bear to look.

Stanley had actually taken the elevator down to the lobby after the North Tower was hit. "The safest place to be is back in your offices," he was told, and he returned to his desk. The offices were still eerily empty when he glanced out the window and saw the plane coming up from the southern tip of Manhattan, traveling unbelievably close to the ground. He watched in horror as it got closer and closer. He could actually see the lettering on the sides. Its nose seemed pointed right at him. He dove under his desk. No, it couldn't be happening. *I'm in your hands, Lord.*

It took him a few moments after the plane hit to stop shaking. His legs felt like jelly. He crawled out from under the desk. The walls in the office had been knocked flat. Papers drifted everywhere. He was chest-deep in plaster and broken furniture. Through the ripped ceiling he could see the floor above.

Brian was escorting a colleague to the ladies' room, flashlight in hand, when the plane hit. The lights went out. Ceiling tiles and air-conditioning ducts broke loose and clattered to the floor. Dust was everywhere. The floor beneath him lurched up. His fire marshal training kicked into gear and he led a group through the darkness toward the stairwell. On the eighty-first floor he ran into two people coming up. "We've just come off a floor in flames," one of them said. "We have to get above them."

Up or down? What was the best thing to do? Both could be deadly.

Just then Brian heard a sound, a muffled voice coming through the stairwell wall: "Help me, somebody. Please help! I can't breathe."

Brian followed the voice. The air was worse than on the stairs, and there was another sharper smell, what he later realized was jet fuel. He wondered if he should turn back. Again came the cry: "Help me!"

"Hang on," he called. He shined his flashlight around. All he saw was a massive wall. Then at the very bottom something moved for a second, caught in the beam of light. A hand. "I see you," he cried.

Stanley was overwhelmed. He wanted to say a thousand prayers right then and there. He couldn't keep his faith to himself. "I have to ask you," he said. "Do you know Jesus?"

"Yes," said Brian, "I go to church every Sunday." Neither of them thought it was an odd conversation to be having at the time.

Stanley pounded on the wall. Brian did too. Piece by piece, they widened the hole. Finally Brian reached in and grabbed Stanley and pulled him through the opening. "My name's Brian," he said.

"I'm Stanley, and you're my brother for life."

The air was getting thicker. "Let's get you out of here," Brian said. They started down the eighty-one flights of stairs. The first flight was almost blocked by wreckage. Stanley hesitated. "Come on," Brian said. "We can do this." He led the way, sliding down a pile of debris.

The sprinklers were running. At about the seventy-ninth floor they saw long cracks in the wall and flames. The heat was terrible, but it was too late to turn back. By the seventy-fourth floor, the air started to clear. They went down, flight by flight, seeing no one. At 9:55, they staggered out onto the concourse. The place was empty. "Go through those doors and run!" a rescue worker told them.

They sprinted across Liberty Street past a maze of trucks, police vehicles and dazed survivors. They didn't stop until they came to Trinity Church. "This man saved my life," Stanley said to a minister standing outside. "He's my guardian angel." They wanted to go inside to thank God and pray for those who were still trapped. For the first time they could look back and see the Trade Center. Brian was struck with horror at the thought of his coworkers who had gone up instead of down. How had they survived? There was a rumbling sound and the top of the South Tower disappeared from sight. Dust filled the air.

They ran for their lives again. At one point Stanley pulled out his business card and put it in Brian's hand. Then they slowed to a walk. Arms around each other, they joined the thousands of others moving toward the East River and the bridges leading out of Manhattan, leading to safety.

Just before they reached the river, Brian and Stanley got separated. For a moment Brian wondered if it was really true. Did Stanley really exist? He reached into his pocket and pulled out the business card.

Later people would say to Brian, "You saved Stanley's life." But as Brian saw it, Stanley saved *his* life. If he hadn't rescued Stanley, what would have been his fate? Ready to give his life to save a stranger, he ended up being saved himself.

Stanley is still a banker but he's also a minister. He often thinks of what Joseph said to his brothers: "You meant evil against me but God meant it for good" (Genesis 50:20). The soles of the shoes he wore that day are melted and caked in ash. He's kept them in a shoebox with the word "deliverance" written on it. "They're kind of like my ark, a reminder of God's presence and the life I owe him," he says.

I was just one of millions who prayed in horror when I watched the disaster unfold on 9/11. None of our prayers reversed the tragedy. The evil had happened. We couldn't rewind the clock or send those fuel-laden jets back. But there is truth in the mystery Stanley Praimnath observed. *You meant evil against me but God meant it for good.* Prayer is a means for extracting the good out of what can only seem bad. At times of crisis anger, fear and shock hit you hard. You don't think you can even move forward. You're trapped, numbed. You cry out to God, "Noooooooooo!" It seems a futile outburst, but that's all you could possibly say. And it's the prayer that keeps you connected. It's the way of reclaiming the good. Both men in Tower Two prayed to God for help. And then they found each other.

CHAPTER SEVEN

Sing Your Prayer

———❖———

"Alleluia."

In fifth grade, I was finally old enough to sing in the kids' choir at church. We ran over from school, raced across the flagstones in the church courtyard, kicking up petals from the Iceland poppies. The choir mothers fed us doughnuts, Lorna Doones, Fig Newtons, Dolly Madison cupcakes or whatever they figured would keep us subdued for an hour-long rehearsal. We dashed up the linoleum stairs and took our assigned seats, the boys filling one row—at least I wasn't the only one. The choir director pounded out chords on the piano, then poked at the air, gesturing at our notes in space. We opened our mouths. "God is in this place," we sang. *"Ah-lay-lu-ee-ya."*

I've sung in big, trained church choirs that appeared on national TV and little ones that barely fielded a voice per part. I was part of the tenor section of the cathedral choir in Florence, Italy, when I sang the "Hallelujah Chorus" one Easter Sunday, failing to make the slightest dent in the way my Italian cohorts pronounced the English words:

"Hay shall r-r-reign for aye-ver and aye-ver." I've happily bellowed out rough-hewn Appalachian tunes in our church choir, pounding my feet against the floor. I love spirituals and gospel and singing praise music with a rock band, rhythmically challenged though I am, but truth to tell, I'm happiest with the old standbys, from "Rock of Ages" to "Amazing Grace."

I would feel robbed if I didn't get to sing in church. With age I can't sustain a long phrase like I used to, and I fear I'm developing a wobble. At some point our choir director is going to tell me, "Rick, you've got a vibrato you could drive a truck through," but with my dying breath, I will sing.

"Dad, don't sing here," my kids exclaim when the spirit moves and I break out in song on the streets of New York or on the subway. Not long ago I was on a subway train heading to work and I heard a West Indian woman singing, "Holy, holy, holy, Lord God Almighty!"

She was coming down the car, passing out Bible tracts. "That's not the tune I know," I told her. "How does that go again?"

"Holy, holy, holy," she sang again and I joined in (I'm a better follower than sight reader). "Which wert, and art, and evermore shall be," we sang together.

The doors opened. "I've got to go. That's my stop," I said, stopping the singing.

"Amen, brother," she told me.

"Amen, sister," I said right back and exited the train.

The Bible is full of singing. The Psalms were all written to be sung, with "lute and harp," "tambourine and dance," "strings and pipe" and "loud clashing cymbals." St. Francis of Assisi and his sworn-to-poverty brothers sang psalms as they wandered the Umbrian hills, preaching to the birds and begging. Paul and Silas sang in jail with their feet in stocks. In a preliterate, preprint era, putting a text to music was a way of remembering it. When you couldn't carry a pocket Bible or have a Bible app on your cell phone you could carry the words in your head, surely the best place for them anyway.

The early church created hymns that clarified their beliefs. Paul is probably quoting one of those early Christian hymns in his epistle to the Philippians (2:10–11): "That at the name of Jesus every knee should bow, of things in heaven and things in earth and things under the earth. And that every tongue should confess that Jesus Christ is Lord." Every tongue confessing like every tongue bursting out in song. In Ephesians 5:14, he quotes another hymn: "Sleeper, awake! Rise from the dead, and Christ will shine on you." Makes me think of a four-part Bach chorale we sing at Advent, "Sleepers, Wake," which is more specifically a reference to the parable of the virgins waiting for the bridegroom with their lit lamps.

I'm terrible at memorizing Bible verses, but certain passages stick with me because I've sung them or heard them sung. "Many waters cannot quench love, neither can the floods drown it" (Song of Solomon 8:7). "O clap your hands, all ye people, shout unto God with a voice of triumph" (Psalm 47:1). "I am the bread of life and he that believe in me shall not slumber" (Job 6:34). When someone reads this passage from Job (19:25) at a funeral—"I know that my Redeemer liveth and that he shall stand on the latter day upon the earth"—how can you not hear it as Handel set it to music in the

Messiah? Or for that matter, how can you hear the word *Hallelujah* without singing it? It's alleluia with an "H," impossible for my Florentine choir friends to do.

"But I *can't* sing," I can hear you protesting. "I can't carry a tune in a bucket. Ever since I was in second grade and our music teacher told me to just mouth the words, I've been afraid to sing."

Maybe you can't sing. (How I wish I could give those bad-news music teachers of yore a piece of my mind.) But you can learn. I have a friend who says she can train anyone, even the most tone-deaf, to sing a respectable "Happy Birthday." More importantly, I'd rather stand next to someone singing the wrong notes than think they are too intimidated to sing at all. We'll call it harmony.

My dad always sat in the front pew at church and sang at the top of his voice. The tone was great, the pitch varied. He had about four notes that he could carry—sometimes they were the right notes. What did it matter? My dear colleague Edward Grinnan claims he's the family lip-syncher, the guy who moves his mouth but makes no sound. His tone-challenged mom was more like my dad; she sang at top volume. "God loves my voice," she declared.

"Make a joyful noise to the Lord" says the psalmist (100:1, RSV). Nothing there about making a perfect sound.

Even if you insist on lip-synching, you can still use music to pray. Put the ear buds in, crank up the volume and be that singer of your dreams. Long ago in that upstairs choir room of my childhood, I used to stare at a sign that said in ecclesiastical Gothic script, "He who sings prays twice." I didn't have a clue as to what it meant then. Still not sure I do, except that I know music is a great amplifier of the spirit. It can connect you to the emotional heart of something when you're spiritually numb. I'm sure you've had the experience of listening to some song and being transported right out of a self-pitying, preoccupied state. When you can't find words to help you pray, reach for a song.

Dad's last five months of life were spent in a nursing facility. The wheelchair-bound residents gathered every day in a bright community room for meals and activities, coaxed by a remarkably good-natured staff. They played bingo, watched *Singing in the Rain* on a wide-screen TV and heard Sunday morning church services.

We didn't fool ourselves by saying, "Dad will be coming home soon." This was it, his last spot on earth, a shared room at the end of the hall near a plaque that read, "I was sick and you visited me (Matthew 25:36)." He'd be there till the end. For the rest of the family it was within an hour's drive. For me it was a five-and-a-half-hour cross-country flight. I made the trip once a month, which never felt like enough. When I was back in New York I was always thinking of where Dad lived.

"You should sing for them," Mom suggested.

"Who?"

"Daddy and the others in the community room. They would like that."

"Okay," I said, trusting Mom's instincts.

I printed out words from my big yellow Rodgers & Hammerstein songbook: "Oklahoma!" "Some Enchanted Evening," "Edelweiss,"

"Hello Young Lovers." These were tunes he loved to hear me play on the piano when I was young. It would be a trip down memory lane. But also in those heartbreaking days, practicing the songs was a way of staying in touch. Walking down 34th Street in a cold rain singing to myself the tango of "No Other Love" linked me to a family drama on the sun-drenched West Coast. There is some intriguing research about how loved ones can share the same thoughts though separated by hundreds of miles. We've often run stories of people who had urges to pray for a loved one only to later discover that was just the moment of danger or need. Could Dad sense me singing songs for him far away? I don't know. But I could keep him close through the music.

"Your dad must love to have you sing," friends would say.

"I'd go nuts if I weren't doing it," I would say. It was too hard to process this leave-taking with only monthly cross-country flights.

At the care facility, many of the patients had slipped into dementia. One woman spoke to me only in Korean as though I could understand every word. Another showed off her doll, assuring us that this was her baby. One man always asked me where I'd gone to high school. One woman rocked back and forth in her wheelchair, moaning, "No, no, no, no."

"We have a real treat today," said the activities director when they gathered in the community room. "Mr. Hamlin's son Rick will sing for us."

No piano, no guitar, no music in front of me. I looked at everyone and launched into "The Surrey With the Fringe on Top," hoping I could remember what I'd memorized on Manhattan's cold streets.

Scanning the faces of my audience, I wondered if they were following. What was going on in their minds? Did they recognize the song at all? Halfway through, one woman joined me from her wheelchair. She didn't miss a word, even the tricky part about the "isinglass curtains you can roll right down." Wouldn't you know it, it was the woman whose only word until then had been "No, no, no, no."

I thought I was there for Dad. Maybe I was there for her. She kept on singing from *Oklahoma* and *South Pacific* after my mini-recital was done. She finally went back to her refrain of "No, no, no, no" but at least it had a tune beneath it now, a cheerier one that spoke of a surrey with fringe on top. He who sings prays twice? My prayer had been for some peace of mind. Amplified by the music, it was as though it spread to her.

◆ ◆ ◆

Music cuts right through to our emotional and spiritual needs. It can say what we can't. Not long ago I was working on a *Guideposts* story with *Good Morning America* anchor Robin Roberts. She wrote about her mother, Lucimarian, one of those extraordinarily lucky people who can sit down at a piano and play any tune. From a young age Lucimarian took refuge in singing hymns and accompanying herself at the keyboard. She married Larry Roberts, a career officer in the Air Force and one of the famous Tuskegee Airmen who integrated the military during World War II. After the war, in the early days of their marriage, they were stationed in Japan.

Lucimarian was living with a toddler in a few rooms of a Quonset hut far away from home. "Nothing prepared me for the isolation I felt as the only black woman on a base in a foreign country," she wrote in her memoir, *My Story, My Song*. "On days when the loneliness became almost unbearable, I would go to the base chapel, which was open twenty-four hours a day. I'd slip inside the empty chapel, go straight to the piano and begin to play hymns and sing. By the time I left an hour or so later, I felt revived. I have often wondered what I would have done without the hymns and scripture to comfort me then and countless other times."

Many years later, after a long happy marriage, Larry died of a sudden heart attack. Lucimarian was bereft. She lived in Pass Christian, Mississippi, where they had retired. That first Thanksgiving she went to New York to be with Robin for the holidays. The two were invited to join Robin's colleague Diane Sawyer and Candice Bergen, among others, for Thanksgiving dinner. Robin assured her mom that they didn't have to go. They could do something small, just the two of them, but even in grief, Lucimarian wanted to be with others. She'd always thrived around people.

They went to dinner with Robin's friends (Lucimarian was amused to think that Murphy Brown was passing around the hors d'oeuvres). When they gathered at the table, everyone was asked to make a comment or offer a reflection. *Mom, you don't have to say anything*, Robin thought. Everybody would understand. But when it was Lucimarian's turn, she did what she'd always done.

Her voice soft but still true, she began to sing the old spiritual "We'll Understand It Better By and By." The song contained her sense of loss along with her hope and faith. "By and by, when the morning comes, when the saints of God are gathered home, we'll tell the story how we've overcome..." Soon Diane Sawyer joined in. "For we'll understand it better by and by." How else to take in the unexplainable, how else to get to the other side of grief? When you sing with someone else you share your sorrow. Just two voices in harmony—"wherever two or more are gathered"—is reassurance enough that you're not alone.

Contemporary music has shown us the range of emotion a song can contain. The blues, rap, hip-hop, folk, country, rock can take on remorse, rage, sorrow, pain and praise. The Psalms are prayers with the same outrageous range. What could be more mournful than the opening of Psalm 137? "By the waters of Babylon we sat down and wept." All the misery of a displaced people far from home is in that line. But less often will people quote the end of the same psalm: "Happy shall he be that takes and dashes the little ones against the rocks."

What are we supposed to do with verses like that? They're disquieting, disconcerting. Part of me wants to edit them out of the Bible. What a mistake that would be, like censoring a prayer. I've never heard that vengeful verse set to music but I can imagine singing it with full-throated anger. "God, I'm so angry and lonely and miserable, here's what I wish you would do!" I can also imagine feeling much better after I've sung it. Cleansed, purged, getting something out of my system. We all have enemies. We're supposed to pray about them. Even sing of them. Why should we be surprised when a psalm gets raw? The words that we need to pray or sing can be counterintuitive.

A Jewish friend of mine was talking to me about mourning her mother's death. She decided to observe the religious tradition of saying Kaddish, the Jewish prayer of mourning, for a year. A busy ob-gyn, she managed to go to her synagogue before work every morning and pray with a small gathering. One important part of saying Kaddish is that you are urged to pray with others. In grief you shouldn't be alone.

"What are the words of the prayer?" I asked. "Is it a prayer of lamentation?"

"Not at all," she said, surprising me. "The words are mostly words of praise." On the Internet I found a translation. The key line of the Kaddish prayer is the congregational response: "May his great name be blessed for ever and to all eternity."

Praise. Praise when you've gone through loss. Praise for a year of mourning. Why praise? Because praise is healing. Words of praise said with others take you out of yourself. Praise also puts you back into God's world. Praise, even when it's just said, is a song.

Elizabeth Sherrill has written eloquently of suffering from depression, especially in her early days of marriage, when she was raising young children. She could barely get through a day, frozen in despair. Caring for her children was a daily marathon. John would come home from work and she'd dash upstairs to the attic just to be alone with her sorrow. John would have to listen to her sobs coming through the closed door.

At one point his boss, Grace Oursler, the first editor of *Guideposts* magazine, sat John down and asked him how things were. At first he started by explaining what Tibby was going through. "No," she said, stopping him, "I want to know how *you* are. What is happening with *you*? When someone is sick, everyone in the family suffers. Tell me about you."

John explained how weary he was, how frustrated and angry, how it tore him apart to find his two young boys listening at the door of the room where their mother lay crying, how watching the woman he loved more than anyone in the world suffer was more than he could bear.

"Be praiseful," was her advice.

"Thankful?" he asked.

"No," she corrected, "give praise. Think about the difference between praise and thanksgiving. Thankfulness is us-centered. When things work out the way we want, we're thankful. Praise is God-centered. Praise means becoming aware of God in your life right now. Praise is the beginning of healing."

"Praise him, alleluia" is a phrase we've sung at church, and it circles around in my head. It can be repeatedly endlessly. "All that have life and breath, praise ye the Lord. Sing to the Lord, alleluia." Praise can be the most outrageous, unexpected, wonderful, right thing to do. Think of the hymns we sing. When a minister in our congregation died at a tragically young age, we abided by his wishes and opened the funeral with the most glorious of Easter hymns: "Jesus lives! Thy terrors now can no longer death, appall us. Jesus lives! By this we know, Thou, O grave, canst not enthrall us. Allelluia!"

He demanded that we celebrate a victory, tears in our eyes. The thing is, if you're crying, you can't sing and if you're singing, you can't cry. That day we sang.

◆ ◆ ◆

Singing gives us courage to do what we don't think we can do, from Anna in *The King and I* whistling her happy tune to civil rights activists marching with hymns and spirituals.

Not long ago Leymah Gbowee won the Nobel Peace Prize for helping to bring peace to Liberia. The country was torn by a brutal civil war that had left hundreds of thousands dead, families broken, children maimed, villages abandoned. The women of Liberia were fed up, and through Leymah's leadership they began a series of protests in a field near the fish market of Monrovia, the capital.

"In the past, we were silent," Leymah could say to the crowd. "But after being killed, raped, dehumanized and infected with diseases and watching our children and families destroyed, war has taught us that the future lies in saying no to violence and yes to peace. We will not relent until peace prevails."

The women all wore white, as Leymah wrote in her memoir, *Mighty Be Our Powers*. "Liberian women love to dress up, but we'd come to the field completely bare of makeup and jewelry, in the kind of 'sackcloth and ashes' described in the Book of Esther, where the heroic queen stands up to save her people from extermination."

There was a very real threat of violent reprisals from President Charles Taylor. His security service was notorious for torturing and killing opponents. His control over the country was brutal.

The women sat outside in the fierce heat, a hundred degrees in the sun, holding up signs that proclaimed, "The women of Liberia want peace." They prayed for courage, the Christians turning to the Psalms, the Muslims praising Allah, and all of them sang. In the remarkable documentary about Leymah and the women of Liberia *Pray the Devil Back to Hell*, you can hear them chant and sing. The music of their voices rises from the field, magnifying their power, connecting them with their Creator. Even the slogan "We want peace, no more war" they turned into a song.

Those protests were the beginning of change. Leymah herself is quick to admit her flaws and honest about her need for faith. Like Moses, she seems the unlikeliest choice for a leader, an unwed mom, the survivor of an abusive relationship, a woman who had to struggle to find her own voice. At one point someone warned her father, "Talk to your daughter – she's putting your family at risk."

He shook his head and said firmly, "God sent that girl. You will see something good come of it."

"We are tired of suffering—we want peace," the women chanted, the sound of their voices giving each other courage. "We are tired of running—we want peace." The battle for peace was fought with prayer and song.

In another international trouble spot, Haiti, the poorest country in the Western Hemisphere, hymns seemed to be all that were holding the people together. After the earthquake that devastated Haiti in 2010, rescue workers noted people singing. Alison Thompson was one of them.

Alison became a full-time volunteer almost by accident. A freelance filmmaker, she was living in New York when the World Trade Center was hit. As soon as she heard the news on 9/11, she put on her rollerblades and skated downtown, thinking she might be able to help. After all, in her native Australia, her father was a preacher and her mother ran a hospital. She often volunteered at her mother's hospital but she didn't really have any disaster-relief training.

She was skating against the traffic, people covered with dust and ash looking frightened and dazed, trying to get away. She reached Ground Zero and heard a loud rumble. She darted under a UPS truck. The second tower was collapsing. She said a quick prayer for help, then darted out. How could she help?

There were plenty of first responders and professionals looking for survivors trapped under the debris. They had the right training and skills. But who was going to rescue them when they collapsed under the daunting workload or the hopelessness of the task? No one wanted to leave the area but they were spent. They needed encouragement and rest. She could help them. With a friend, Alison commandeered an abandoned bar, put out a sign that said "Ground Zero First Aid Station" and spent the next few days cleaning faces, giving water, offering hugs to exhausted workers. When she was too tired to do much more she skated home to get some rest, but then skated right back, eventually volunteering with the Red Cross. As she puts it, she skated into a whole new role: professional volunteer.

When a terrible tsunami hit Southeast Asia in 2004, she was watching the news. "I'm going there," she told herself. Once again, she had no idea how she could help, but she emptied her minuscule bank account, borrowed a friend's frequent flier miles and flew to Sri Lanka, staying there for the next fourteen months. In a small, devastated village she helped build a hospital and an open-air soup kitchen. She played with the children and organized other volunteers like herself to bury the dead. She even established a tsunami early-warning system.

She went to New Orleans after Katrina, no longer an inexperienced amateur. Within days of the Haiti earthquake she gathered enough medical supplies and equipment to fill an airplane and flew to Port-au-Prince, the stricken capital.

Her group quickly established an outdoor hospital on a golf course in Haiti. Soon they were treating a thousand people a day. That first night, though, as she was trying to sleep, Alison heard singing wafting through the bushes and trees. Three o'clock in the morning and people were singing. A disaster had devastated their impoverished country and their response was music. Hymns. It sounded like a chorus of angels. Where was it coming from?

She got up from her tent before the dawn and followed the sounds. She found lines of refugees, survivors of the quake, waiting in line for food, their stomachs empty but their spirits full of praise.

In the days that followed, a pastor formed an open-air church near the hospital, and every day, when Alison was exhausted from her work at the hospital, she would go to the spontaneous services, raising her hands and singing with the people. The music became her source of healing, praise an unexpected response to misery. She sang to renew her spirit, praying with song.

"Have an eye to God in every word you sing," wrote John Wesley in his preface to *Sacred Melody*, written in 1761. "Aim at pleasing Him more than yourself or any other creature. In order to do this, attend strictly to the sense of what you sing, and see that your heart is not carried away with the sound, but offered to God continually."

Music is inspired and inspiring. Songs can come straight from the Holy Spirit and can administer the comfort of the Spirit. They can be offerings *to* God, but they can also be offerings *from* God. "Come down, O Love divine/Seek Thou this soul of mine,/ And visit it with Thine own ardor glowing," goes the old hymn, a tune that makes me feel it's doing the work of the words. No wonder we often picture angels singing, God's messengers reaching out to us with music. I once interviewed Noel Paul Stookey, songwriter and singer in the folk trio Peter, Paul and Mary, and he told me about a song that came straight from the Almighty. In this case even the words were God's.

Noel dropped out of college and moved to New York City. He had no career plans. He gravitated to the coffeehouses in Greenwich Village to play chess. One night he noticed a stage being constructed in the corner of a coffeehouse and the manager told him auditions for entertainment would be held later in the week. Relying on nothing more than the songs he had written in high school and college, he was suddenly in show business.

He was put together with Mary Travers and Peter Yarrow and they formed Peter, Paul and Mary. Soon their songs, like "Lemon Tree," "If I Had a Hammer" and "Puff (The Magic Dragon)," were on the radio and on top of the charts. The fame was heady. They were performing 150 nights a year, appearing on TV, making recordings, but Noel felt something was missing. He felt he was losing touch. "Read the Bible," a friend advised. He began at Genesis and read right through. He started praying regularly too, asking God the smallest questions: "Shall I take this elevator?" "Shall I sit here?" "What would you have me say?"

When Peter was getting married he asked Noel if he would bless the wedding by singing at it. "Of course," Noel said. But what would he sing? He would have to ask God.

Home from a tour, Noel retreated to his basement studio. He tuned up his twelve-string guitar and then sat in silence. "Lord," he prayed, "nothing would bless this wedding more than your presence. How would you manifest yourself?"

The lyrics came:

I am now to be among you at the calling of your hearts,
Rest assured this troubadour is acting on My part.
The union of your spirits here has caused Me to remain,
For whenever two or more of you are gather in My name
There am I, there is love…

He put them together in a song. About an hour before the wedding he sang them first to his wife, Betty. "It's beautiful," she said, "but they won't understand 'I am now to be among you.' They're going to think you're presuming to be God."

He took his wife's advice and changed the words at the last minute to "He is now to be among you..." He sang it that way for Peter's wedding and expected that he'd never sing the song again.

But several weeks later at a Peter, Paul and Mary concert Peter asked, "When are you going to sing that song you sang at my wedding?"

"But it was just for you, just for your wedding," Noel explained.

"My bride is out there," Peter said. "Would you sing it for her?"

He sang it that night and for the rest of the tour. The song seemed to have larger appeal than he expected. "Is this what you wanted, Lord?" he asked God. "Did you mean the song for everyone?"

The answer seemed to be yes. But this posed a technical problem for Noel. He wanted to include "The Wedding Song" on an album he was recording but how would he copyright it? The song hadn't come from him.

I remember sitting with Noel over breakfast at a New York diner when we talked about this, my tape recorder running. "Other songs I've written have been inspired by my faith, but this one really did come directly from God," he said. Witness the lyrics. "If I didn't copyright it somehow, the record company would get all the profits and that didn't seem right. But I couldn't rightly copyright it in my name either."

In the end he copyrighted the song to a foundation to oversee the publishing rights. Any money the song earned could be distributed to worthy causes. By now millions of dollars have gone to charitable organizations all over the US. "It belongs to every bride and groom who ever had a good friend strum a guitar and sing at their wedding," Noel says. "God gave me a song. It was mine to give away."

◆ ◆ ◆

The people you sing with become a part of you. After they're gone, you can still hear them. I think the sound of everyone who has ever sung at our church is buried in the walls of the place, and all their "alleluias" come echoing back whenever we sing. They make up that "great cloud of witnesses" the Bible talks about. If you've sung harmony with someone, you especially miss their part when they're gone. When Mary Travers died in 2009, Peter and Noel went back on the road to do a series of farewell concerts, one in each city where they had performed together. On Mary's parts in classics like "Leaving on a Jet Plane," they would encourage the audience to sing her line. The tours weren't meant to go on forever. Just this last good-bye with the two-thirds of the trio that was still left. She was gone but she was still there.

Charley was one of my dearest singing buddies. We met in a small, close-harmony, all-male a cappella group in college at Princeton. He was a baritone, I a first tenor. On a winter's night my freshman year, I was initiated into the group when Charley and some of the other guys burst into my dorm room, startling my roommate as they burst into song: "My comrades when I'm no more drinking, but sick with gout and palsied lie...believe me then the end is nigh." An old song that was the group's rallying cry. Their serenade meant I had passed muster. I was in and this was the proof, a bunch of guys waking me up at 2:00 AM.

We sang "My Comrades" on campus under neo-Gothic arches, our voices bouncing off the old stone walls. We performed it on road trips to Florida and at homecoming concerts. We did it at women's colleges, where we teamed up with all-female a cappella groups. In diminished numbers, Charley and I and another pal crooned it on backpacking tour in England. We sang it at graduation, a reminder of how we'd bonded in our bright college years, and sang it at reunions with wives and kids in tow. Even though the lyrics promised death: "When I die, this day or tomorrow, my testament's already made…" we never thought of death singing it. That was the arrogance of youth. It was just an old drinking song that made us giddy, especially the way the group performed it, breaking our semicircle and shaking each other's hands.

Then we sang it at Charley's funeral.

In his early forties, Charley was diagnosed with ALS, Lou Gehrig's disease. There is no cure. The first sign was an ache and tremor in Charley's hands. He was a college professor, editing countless papers and pounding out comments on his computer. He thought he had carpal tunnel syndrome. It was something much worse. The first time I saw him after the diagnosis he was walking with a limp and using a cane. He had two sets of twins, one year old and three years old, and they were tumbling all over him like puppies. "If this is death," I thought, "it wouldn't be so bad." His super-organized wife, Lynn, had already installed wheelchair ramps in their suburban Boston home. She would be ready.

"So I know this ALS has hit your hands and your legs," I said to him, "but I sure hope it hasn't affected your voice."

"Hambone," he called me by a college nickname, "you haven't changed a bit."

"Can you sing?" I asked, ready to launch into a verse of "My Comrades," at least for the kids' benefit.

He shook his head and spoke in an awkward, unmodulated tone: "My breathing's not so good. It's hard to hold a note."

I visited Charley six months later at his family's place in Maine. By then he couldn't feed himself. He was fine with a straw but needed help with a spoon. We sat on the deck, Charley in a wheelchair. I spooned him his yogurt as I'd done with my kids, and I kept missing his mouth. I started giggling and he did too as it dribbled down his chin.

"Hambone," he said, "you were never good for much."

The next time I saw him he was on a feeding tube with round-the-clock care, mostly physical therapy students on eight-hour shifts. He was in a hospital bed set up in his living room. He had a computer close by to communicate with the outer world, and a TV across the room so he could watch *The Little Mermaid* and *Beauty and the Beast* and *Peter Pan* with his kids. They would race through the room while one of the students and Lynn would lift him up with the help of a harness—it took two of them—so they could change the sheets or he could sit in his wheelchair. Every twenty minutes the aide would use a suction machine to suck out the phlegm in his mouth that could choke him or saliva that he couldn't swallow.

He couldn't speak, couldn't nod, but he could blink and he could smile. He had an alphabet on a small board in three rows and if he wanted to say something, you pointed at each row until he smiled or blinked; then you halted there and went through the letters, "H, I, J, K, L, M, N, O..." until he stopped you.

You couldn't finish a word for him. You had to let him have his full say. I remember asking, innocently enough, "How are you?" We spent fifteen minutes working through the answer: "O-U-T T-O L-U-N-C."

"Out to lunch," I leapt to the conclusion.

But he gestured with his eyes. There was more. We went back to the letters and he spelled out: "A-S A-L-W-A-Y-S." No use finishing his thoughts. With ALS your body gives out but your mind doesn't go and I couldn't deny Charley a chance to complete a self-deprecating thought. He was still Charley.

This was the deal he and Lynn had made. It would have been easier to have him in a nursing home, but he wanted to live as long as possible with his kids around so that they would at least have some memory of him.

For two years Lynn and Charley kept life in the living room going. I went up to Boston a couple of times just to offer another pair of adult hands. Frankly I wasn't much help with Charley but I could read books to the kids and give them their baths and wash the dishes for Lynn. I remember giving their three-year-old son Nick a bath and launching into an old cowboy song, "Out in Arizona where the bad men are, there's nothing there to guide you but the evening star..."

"That's a song your daddy taught me," I said. Charley and I sang it in England as we wandered around the gardens at Blenheim and later when we strolled down the streets around Piccadilly, American boys singing about cowboys and the prairie. "You should hear him do it."

Then it dawned on me. Little Nick had never heard his daddy sing. He'd never been to any of the reunions where we lined up for the old repertoire. He'd never known what his dad sounded like on a lullaby. Without that, how well could he know his dad? Was Charley really Charley without song?

I dried Nicky off and went downstairs. "I taught him the tenor part to 'My Comrades,'" I told Charley. "That's all he'll ever need."

Charley gave me his "out-to-lunch-as-always" look.

One summer weekend I drove up from New York and walked into the house—the door was always open. Lynn and the kids had gone to the town pool. "Hey Charley," I said, "it's Hambone." He still had that dazzling smile. The PT student was in the middle of bathing him, an extraordinarily complicated process involving the harness to raise Charley's six-foot-four frame. I sat in a chair and waited. A visiting nurse arrived. With help from the PT student Charley explained how he'd almost choked. For a moment he couldn't breathe. It was very scary. He could have died. You could still see the fear in his eyes.

"Of course you could have died," I thought. "You are dying. That's what's happening. That's what ALS means." And yet he wasn't dying. He was living. Life was raging on around him. He was there for the report cards and piano practicing and Suzuki violin squeaking. He could admire the soccer trophies and the Halloween ballerina and see the ball thrown across his bed or rolled under it. He listened to the stories of Madeline and Eloise and Bambi and Barney.

Charley had almost finished his bio for our college class's twenty-fifth reunion book. One finger could still wiggle enough to register yes or no on the computer as it scrolled through the alphabet, his finger picking out the words in the same way that his mind picked out letters from the alphabet board. In December he had a stroke and slipped into a coma. He died two days later. It was a shock even if it wasn't a surprise. Somehow I expected him to go on for many more years.

I thought the funeral was going to be miserable, Lynn looking brave in the front pew with the two sets of twins, the rest of us weeping uncontrollably. But it was a joyous occasion. Everybody in that church had somehow participated in Charley's long battle with ALS. They'd brought casseroles or babysat the kids or raked the yard or given books and videos or sat by Charley's bed. We'd been part of Charley's life, not death.

We sang something dignified and holy at the service, full of alleluias, but after the service in the church hall, it was "My Comrades" once again. "But die I this day or tomorrow, my testament's already made, my burial from your hands all borrowed but without splendor or parade..." The words rang truer than we could ever grasp when we first learned them. Life was long or short but the important thing was to go out singing with your comrades.

The songs that help me pray are not all religious or spiritual. I don't think God minds. As long as they link me back to him. "God, how can I get through sorrow? How am I going to manage the misery of survivor's guilt?" With every milestone I thought of all the stuff Charley was missing. That is the heartbreak of someone you love dying too young. Charley, you would have had a blast at our reunion; Charley, you should have heard us old grads singing again—boy, we could have used you on the baritone line. Charley, you would have been proud at your kids' graduations and their school plays and their soccer games and concerts and seeing the girls dressed up for the prom. Charley, you missed most of Harry Potter. Charley, buddy, I still hear you sing.

Charley taught me that how we die is not something we do just for ourselves. It is the last thing we do for those who love us. I like to think I'll be as feisty and good-natured and funny as Charley was to the bitter end, but even now, a dozen years after his death, I'm not so sure. As long as I have music to help, music around me to ease the way, singing friends even if I can't sing, a million hymns in my head to help me pray. As long as I have alleluias.

CHAPTER EIGHT

A Classic Prayer to Focus Your Thoughts

———◆◇◆———

"Jesus Christ, have mercy on me, a miserable sinner.
Make haste to help me. Rescue me and save me.
Let thy will be done in my life."

The Jesus Prayer is a prayer from the Eastern Orthodox tradition going back to the Desert Fathers. "Jesus Christ, have mercy on me, a miserable sinner" is the heart of it.

It's easy to learn and so short you can repeat it in your head without anyone knowing you're praying. I find it a godsend when I'm sitting in a meeting, going cross-eyed trying to follow some boring PowerPoint presentation. Who needs to know I'm praying silently? I've found it useful in church meetings too (just because a meeting happens at church doesn't mean it can't be a trial of Christian charity). "What am I doing?" I ask myself. "Why am I here?" The Jesus Prayer restores my focus.

My first acquaintance with it came in college when I read J. D. Salinger's novella *Franny and Zooey*. It's really two short stories back to back, and in the first Franny Glass is on a date with her boyfriend. They're headed to the Yale game, played at what I like to imagine is my own alma mater, Princeton, and over lunch she is spiraling into a meltdown. What she clings to is a book, *The Way of the Pilgrim*, about a Russian peasant who wanders the countryside repeating to himself the Jesus Prayer: "Jesus Christ, have mercy upon me, a sinner..." He repeats it a thousand times a day, then several thousand, the words calming the spirit. I could picture Franny at one of those restaurants I knew from my college days—probably the Annex, with its red-and-white checkered tablecloths and knotty-pine walls. She's smoking cigarettes, eating nothing, crying in the restroom and muttering to herself a prayer culled from a nineteenth-century Russian text. The perfect combination of self-indulgent torpor and collegiate angst.

Several years later I was looking for help in my prayer life. I wanted to find someone I could check in regularly with, someone who would keep me honest and ask me questions. Someone to whom I could say, "Do you really think God is telling me what I think he's telling me?"

I kept putting off the search. It would be one big bother, I told myself. I didn't have time for one more person in my life. There weren't enough hours in the day to see the friends I had. My colleague Peola Hicks calls this "prayer paralysis." You know you should do something but you don't move. You get stuck. But then if you hold that need long enough you'll meet it.

Sitting on the subway one morning, eyes closed, train rumbling, I said, "I know there's someone out there who can teach me more about prayer, someone I can meet with regularly, someone I can pray with and ask any stupid question I have." I got bolder with my request. "I've got friends my age I already meet with. We unload about all sorts of stuff, about the economy, our jobs, our families. But I'd like someone a little older, more experienced, wiser.

"It shouldn't be someone from work," I went on, "or someone from our church. It should be someone outside of my day-to-day world who will challenge me more and give me a different perspective. And it should be someone who lives in New York City or close enough so it's easy to meet."

The name came to me as clear as day: Arthur Caliandro.

Naturally there was more prayer paralysis. How could I ask Arthur? As the senior pastor at Marble Collegiate Church, he had a congregation of thousands and a TV congregation of thousands more. He was way too busy. He'd followed in Norman Vincent Peale's footsteps and led a dynamic ministry. I'd met him through the magazine and admired him, but this would be a huge imposition.

As soon as I said, "That won't work," the thought came back to me: *Isn't he exactly what you said you wanted, wise and knowledgeable, and not a member of your church? He works only a couple of blocks from your office. It wouldn't be hard to get together.*

I made plenty of excuses, postponing the call. Finally I got fed up with myself for procrastinating. I picked up the phone, left a message with his assistant, and hoped that was that. He called back within an hour. I blurted out: "Arthur, I know this is an outrageous request, but I've been looking for someone to meet with regularly and talk about our prayer lives. Your name keeps coming back to me. You've got a million things on your plate..."

"Let's have lunch next week," he said.

"Really?" I asked. "You have time for this?"

"Of course."

We kept it up for eighteen years.

At that first lunch at a dimly lit place filled with businessmen in dark suits and loud ties, he brought up the Jesus Prayer. "Do you pray regularly?" I asked him.

"First thing in the morning I sit by myself in the den," he said. "I have a long list of people who've asked for prayers, but even before I mention them, I start out with the Jesus Prayer. Are you familiar with it?"

"Maybe," I said. "How does it go?" I reached for more butter for my roll.

"This is the version I use." He gazed from our table in the back corner of the restaurant to the bar and the few windows in the front. "Jesus Christ, have mercy on me. Make haste to help me. Rescue me and save me. Let thy will be done in my life."

He said it again and I repeated it to myself.

"Those aren't the exact words of the traditional prayer," he said. "I've expanded the end because I'm always looking for guidance and I need to be rescued. Am I doing what Jesus has called me to do? Am I following God? Am I doing what he's asked of me? Am I becoming his follower? I say it a lot."

"How often?"

"Dozens of times a day. Whenever I need it. It keeps me focused. You might try it."

Indeed I would. I muttered it to myself as I headed back to the office. I used it on the subway after I said my psalms. I looked for it in my old copy of *Franny and Zooey*. I've turned to it when anxiety and worry threatened to undo me. I've said it in doctors' offices and hospital waiting rooms when worst-case scenarios were all I could think of. And like I said, I've used it in the middle of meetings when I feared I was going to blow a gasket. I even made it the centerpiece of a romance novel I wrote a few years ago (*Reading Between the Lines*, if you must know, and yes, to my amazement, it's still in print).

The prayer has been a welcome companion, a reaffirmation of faith in a few words, a quick reminder of my priorities. Jacob Astley, during the English Civil War, proclaimed famously before the Battle of Edgehill in 1642, "O Lord, thou knowest how busy I must be this day. If I forget thee, do not thou forget me." Then he said, "Boys, march." The Jesus Prayer is that in-the-trenches prayer I say so I *won't* forget him. Its meditative power lies in its distillation of the essentials.

Just from the opening, "Jesus Christ, have mercy on me…" comes the reminder of *whose* we are. You can pledge your life to Jesus, have an on-the-road-to-Damascus experience, but you still need to keep connecting. The Lord's Prayer is the prayer Jesus taught us. The Jesus Prayer is one directed *to* him. As my colleague Lemuel Beckett in the prayer division at Guideposts said to me, "What an honor that we get to pray directly to Jesus. It makes me feel like a king." It's a relationship prayer: This is who I am, Lord, and this is who you are to me. But to remember who Jesus is I need to delve back into the Scriptures, which is a sort of prayer, and I look to how others have followed Jesus.

Richard Stearns is the president of World Vision, the multibillion-dollar humanitarian organization. By any standard he would have been considered a serious Christian long before he took the job. It wasn't always so.

In business school he was a hard-headed atheist. All he wanted to do was get his degree, become the CEO of some Fortune 500 company and get rich. His girlfriend Reneé broke up with him when he told her he'd never follow her in faith. Then he started reading the Bible and other books on religion and philosophy. Gradually he became convinced that Jesus Christ was God's son and one day he fell to the floor and cried out, "My Lord and my God!" He committed himself to following Jesus for the rest of his life.

For twenty-five years the fruits of that decision seemed apparent. He and Reneé got married, had five children, lived in a ten-bedroom farmhouse. He became the CEO of Lenox, one of the world's largest makers of fine china. He had a luxurious office at Lenox headquarters, a cherry-wood desk, oil paintings on the walls, a private bathroom, a Jaguar in the CEO's reserved spot. He and Reneé attended church regularly. They tithed, participated in Bible studies, supported missions. God had blessed them and they gave back.

One day Richard got a call from Bill Bryce, an old friend from church who had moved away to take a job raising money for World Vision. "Hi, Rich," Bill said. There was something funny in his voice.

"Everything okay?" Richard asked.

"Sure," Bill said. "It's just that our president is leaving World Vision." Then came the weird part. "I've been praying, Rich, and the thing is, God told me you're going to be the next president of World Vision. I know it sounds crazy, but I'm certain God spoke to me."

Richard was just as certain that he was totally unqualified for the job. He had no experience leading a charity. He didn't know anything about the challenges of international relief. He had a good job that paid well, one he liked. "No," he said. "I'm not interested." That would be that, he figured. Occasionally he heard a bit more from Bill about how the job search was going but that was it.

Then he got a call from a job recruiter. "Rich, I'm Rob Stevenson, a recruiter for World Vision. They're looking for a new president."

"Did Bill Bryce put you up to this?" Richard asked suspiciously.

"Bill who? No, I got your name from a list of World Vision donors." Did Richard know of any possible candidates for the job?

"You'd have to be part CEO, part Mother Teresa, part Indiana Jones," he said. "I don't know anyone like that."

"What about you? You interested?"

"Me? I run a luxury-goods company. I don't know anything about international relief." Again Richard insisted he wasn't qualified.

The recruiter persisted and then he too said an odd thing. "You're not going to believe this, but while we've been talking I've sensed the Holy Spirit telling me that we ought to meet. I've talked to two hundred people so far and you're the first I've had this feeling about."

Needless to say, Richard was getting very uncomfortable.

Rob asked another question. "Are you willing to be open to God's will for your life?"

Richard wanted to drop the phone. "Of course," he stammered, "but I'm pretty sure this isn't it..."

"Let's find out. Have dinner with me."

The conversations continued. To his chagrin Richard Stearns ended up on the shortlist for the World Vision job. In interview after interview he tried to explain why he was a terrible fit. To no avail. Finally he got a congratulatory phone call: He got the job!

How had this happened? He'd done all he could to discourage the search committee. The position fit no definition of God's plan that he understood. He hadn't gone to business school to run a nonprofit. What about the kids' college tuition bills? Reneé was no help. "You never know what God might have in store," she said. "We need to be open to his leading."

On the day he was to fly out to World Vision headquarters in Seattle and see if this offer was something he wanted to pursue, he got another call and another offer altogether, one far more lucrative. Keith, a successful tableware executive, was buying an English china company and planning to merge it with his own. He wanted Richard to be the CEO of the new merged company. He'd even get a ten percent stake in the business.

Richard explained that he had another offer he needed to check out first, one with a charity. He didn't mention the name of the organization.

"That's admirable," Keith said. Out of the blue Keith launched into a story about a girl he and his wife had sponsored in India through a relief organization. They did it after their own daughter had died. That simple act of helping another child had eased their grief. "The charity that put me in touch with her was absolutely wonderful," he said. "They're called World Vision."

Richard was stunned. By the time Keith finished speaking Richard seemed to hear another voice. He realized that he and Reneé were witnessing something profound, God working directly in their lives, showing them that his plan involved something more amazing than they could have imagined.

"My corporate career, my comfortable life, my safe and tidy church involvement," Richard wrote, "all of it was just prologue, maybe even a distraction from serving the Jesus I had committed my life to twenty-five years earlier. I knew then that if I truly wanted to follow that Jesus, I would have to follow the one who gave himself for the poor and dispossessed."

Following Jesus can take you right out of your comfort zone. Had Richard Stearns missed his calling? Did it take him twenty-five years to understand where Jesus really wanted him to be or were those years meant as preparation for where he was supposed to go? In the end his prayer life led him to do something that he never would have guessed, the exact opposite of following the path of least resistance. "Jesus Christ, have mercy on me, a miserable sinner...Let thy will be done in my life." That's not something you say once and have done with it. You say it over and over, searching for the way, like Richard.

Another Jesus follower whose journey amazed and touched me was Scott Morris, a doctor and ordained minister. Even as a boy in Sunday school, Scott was struck with how often Jesus was healing people, how much he cared about the sick. One Sunday, sitting in the pews of his big Atlanta church, he went through the Gospels and started adding it up. "Do you know that over a third of the gospels are about health?" he told his mother that day at dinner. "And in the book of Acts I found nineteen examples of healing by Christ's followers."

Why didn't they do more at his Methodist church for the sick? They put people on the prayer lists or the pastor would visit them in the hospital. Maybe his mom or some of the ladies would make a casserole. That was it. They helped but they didn't heal like Jesus.

If Scott was going to be like Jesus, he figured he should become a doctor. He was a good student and he assumed he was up to the challenge. But one semester of organic chemistry at the University of Virginia did him in. He was miserable. It wasn't the subject matter, which fascinated him. It was the competitiveness of the other pre-med students. "They hardly cared about what they were learning," he wrote. "All they wanted was to get top grades."

Scott decided to go to seminary instead. He would become a minister.

Two things happened there. In a seminar on counseling the chronically ill he was assigned a patient named Sidney Tillery at the VA hospital. Scott arrived with a slew of questions. Even though he was headed for the ministry, he was still interested in health. Where did Sidney feel the pain? How bad was it? What was it like, eating, sitting, sleeping? At the end of the interview Sidney asked, "Want to play cribbage?"

"I've never played before," Scott said.

"I'll teach you," Sidney said.

That was the beginning of their friendship. Week after week they played cribbage. Scott gave up his list of questions. He learned how to listen. He saw how a chronic illness did its most crippling damage to the spirit. "Your patients will become your teachers," his professor had said. Sidney Tillery taught him how to reach beyond someone's physical aches and pains to minister to their soul. In essence, Jesus' healing mission came alive to him over the cribbage board.

The second thing that changed Scott's trajectory was a pamphlet he saw in the chaplain's office: "How to Start a Church-Based Clinic." He called the writer, did some research and discovered others who'd started church-based clinics for the poor. A light bulb went off in his head: *This is what I want to do with my life.* This was exactly what he'd been looking for. He'd start a church-based clinic for the poor. They'd use the best that modern medicine had to offer and the spiritual tools Christ gave. He'd be both minister and doctor.

With the seminary's support he went back and took the premed classes he needed, then enrolled in med school. With both an MD and an MDiv, he joined the staff of St. John's United Methodist Church in Memphis as an associate pastor and laid out his vision. In a year they opened the Church Health Center in an old house across the street from the church. There was only one nurse and Scott. They saw twelve patients that first day.

Today, over twenty-five years later, they have a staff of 220 and some 55,000 patients. Scott is a busy man but he's never forgotten the lesson of the cribbage board. He still sees patients one-on-one and listens to them.

Most of them are the poorest of the poor. They have worked hard their whole lives, tough manual labor. Often their families have broken up and they've seen their lot of sorrow—drugs, violence, poverty. But when he asks them how they are, they will say, "I'm blessed."

Some of them bless him quite literally. They lay their hands on him and pray over him. They remind him that he is not the healer. God is, and it is the duty of the church to participate in that work. This was the calling Scott discovered when he was a kid thumbing through a Bible in the pew. Jesus cared about the sick. And Scott has made it his life's work to follow Jesus in that passion.

Perhaps it will sound like a wild exaggeration if I tell you that in praying the Jesus Prayer I feel like I'm taking part in the journey that Richard Stearns and Scott Morris have taken. I don't think my meandering footsteps have come close to the paths they have forged or the extraordinary work they have done, but they are models. Something to bump up against and stretch myself around. I look to see if God's moving in my life like he moved in theirs.

"Jesus Christ, have mercy on me, a miserable sinner," I pray in the middle of a very busy life. "Make haste to help me. Rescue me and save me. Let thy will be done in my life." There are a thousand and one distractions to put me off track. The worst is when I congratulate myself, as Richard Stearns used to, and say, "I go to church regularly. I give generously. I sing in the choir. I read the Bible. I'm doing okay, right?" Not with a self-righteous, pharisaical attitude like that.

Not long ago I edited a story by Bear Grylls. Before I worked with him I knew nothing about his faith. I just knew him as the British adventurer on the TV show *Man vs. Wild* who ventured into some of the most dangerous places on earth—remote jungles, stinking swamps, forbidding mountain ranges, searing deserts. He was always seen getting out of tight spots, dodging a huge croc, avoiding a vicious snake, surviving whitewater rapids and describing what was happening in his bloke-next-door accent. But then I learned about an off-camera turnaround from his boyhood.

Like others in his distinguished military family he went off to boarding school at a young age. As a boy, faith had come very naturally to him. Life was full of outdoor adventures that his father devised and Bear relished, like climbing up a sheer cliff and pretending that they were lobbing grenades at the enemy. God seemed present in every challenge and he talked easily and openly to Jesus. But in school he was forced to sit through long chapel services with prayers in Latin and people droning on. "I thought that I had got the whole faith deal wrong," he wrote. "Maybe God wasn't intimate and personal but was tedious, judgmental, boring and irrelevant." The instinctive faith he had known evaporated.

Then he learned that his godfather Stephen had died. Stephen had been his father's best friend and was like a second father to Bear. "He came on all our family holidays and spent almost every weekend with us in the summer, sailing with Dad and me," Bear wrote. "He died very suddenly of a heart attack."

The day he got word of his godfather's death, he went out to the school grounds and climbed a tree. Sitting there in the branches he prayed the simplest, most heartfelt prayer of his life. "God, if you're like you were when I used to know you, will you be that again? Comfort me."

"Blow me down if he didn't do just that!" Bear Grylls told me in that inimitable British accent.

"It is a sign of great strength to need Jesus," he wrote in his story. "My faith is about being held, comforted, forgiven, strengthened and loved. Faith in Christ has been the great empowering presence in my life."

Strength comes from showing your need, exposing your vulnerabilities, especially in prayer. The people Jesus helped in his ministry were the ones who approached him in absolute humility—Nicodemus coming to him in the middle of the night, the paralytic who was dropped down on his pallet through a hole in the roof, the woman who'd been hemorrhaging and only needed to touch his cloak to be healed. The centurion who came to him asking for his servant to be healed said, "Lord, I am not worthy to have you come under my roof, but only speak the word and my servant will be healed" (Matthew 8:8).

That's the attitude I find in the words, "Jesus Christ, have mercy upon me."

◆ ◆ ◆

So why the "miserable sinner" part? Why would I call myself a sinner in the middle of a prayer? Arthur Caliandro doesn't usually include that part of the prayer, as you might have noticed when I quoted him. For Arthur, who grew up the son of a Methodist minister, calling himself a sinner in the middle of prayer sends his imagination down the wrong path. It conjures up a stern, judgmental God, not the loving one he is praying to. I'm reminded of another friend who avoids the first verse of "Amazing Grace" because he hates singing "a wretch like me." "I'm not a wretch," he says, and he's not. He's a saintly man who washes pots at his church soup kitchen and visits patients in hospice care. I won't argue with him.

But I can tell you what I find helpful about those words. I'll give you two examples of people who have prayed them.

A man I'll call Joe made his living as a pickpocket. He'd worked with the best of the "light-fingered fraternity," and was proud of his skills. No pocket was safe, no safety clasp secure. He could remove a man's suspenders without the man feeling anything but a loss of support. His eyes were alert and busy, ferreting out marks, always on guard for police officers and plainclothes detectives.

Joe spent a few terms in prison and tried to go straight, working as a bellhop for a time, then a salesman, but he always returned to pickpocketing. With its lure of fast and easy money and its covert excitement, it was a sort of disease, an addiction. He'd notice a man patting his pocket, making sure the contents were safe—"fanning" it, in the pickpocket's lexicon—and the temptation would be too much for him. In a split second he'd have the wallet. Then he'd step back and watch the reaction. "I don't know whether I'd do this sort of thing because I was devilish or whether I wanted to satisfy my ego, but I did it," he wrote.

Life caught up with Joe. He rushed home to be at his dying father's bedside. A few years later it was his mother's bedside and funeral. Standing in the cemetery, he could see himself clearly. He was a thief, a sneak and felon. How could he have wandered so far from his mother's values? What a disappointment he must have been to her even if she never knew the full truth about him. The third time he rushed home was to be with his dangerously ill sister. Would he lose her too?

She recovered from emergency surgery but in her hospital bed she asked him to pray for her. He promised he would, and he did pray, but he reserved for himself the right to make a living the only way he knew how. He made a compromise with God, giving a percentage of his profits to the needy. "I was too much a con man to know that you don't make deals with God," he wrote.

Then Joe started to lose his touch. A large roll of money would slip from his grip. A wallet would be empty. Or he'd find himself surrounded by plainclothesmen. One day he lifted a fat wallet, opened it up and was stunned to find the most beautiful picture of Christ he had ever seen. Jesus' arms were outstretched on the cross and his expression was full of mercy and compassion. Joe looked at it in disbelief. He started to mumble over and over, "Jesus, have mercy on me, a sinner."

In the quiet of his room he knelt down and prayed, "O God, let thy will be done, not mine. Make me a better man. Give me strength to follow thy guidance. Let me be thy humble servant and serve thee well." The first thing he did when he got up was mail the wallet back to its owner.

He never stole again. Going straight was a constant struggle. That he did he saw as a credit to the power of prayer. He also prayed to be forgiven. "I know this is possible," he wrote, "because Jesus forgave Dismas, the thief on the cross."

The actor and songwriter Clifton Davis, author of the Jackson 5 hit "Never Can Say Good-bye" and star of the 1980s TV show *Amen* offers a different sort of example. He'd grown up a P.K.—a preacher's kid—was baptized and accepted Jesus into his life in a perfunctory way, but spiritually he was empty. Eventually he gave up on organized religion. He became an actor and moved to Hollywood. He was in a successful series and told himself he had made it, but inside he was deeply insecure. He took refuge in alcohol, then cocaine. By the late 1970s he was a habitual user.

His career went downhill. He sold his house in the Hollywood Hills and spent half the money on drugs. He sent his girlfriend packing because, in one of his few lucid moments, he realized he was actually a danger to her. She kept calling him, five or six times a day, pleading, "Don't snort those drugs. Talk to me." He'd slam down the phone. Finally he stopped answering it altogether.

By December 1980 he was drinking a quart of vodka a day and was down to skin and bones. At Christmas he decided he'd end his life. There was nothing left to live for. With his last thousand dollars he bought enough drugs to take an overdose.

While others in his apartment building were hanging wreaths and decorating trees, he got a hammer and nailed his apartment door shut. He didn't want anyone coming in and stopping him. He scrawled his will on a napkin and left it on a table.

All through Christmas Day he hunched on his bed, arms locked around his knees, preparing to take that final dose. The faint strains of carols like "Hark, the Herald Angels Sing" and "We Wish You a Merry Christmas" drifted in. The room darkened. Clifton's hurt grew unbearable. The phone rang. For a long time he wasn't even aware of it. Then something compelled him to pick up the receiver. It was his brother Carlyle. "Clifton?"

Clifton grunted.

"We're all worried about you," his brother went on. "Mama dreamed last night that you were dying."

Clifton started to hang up. His brother was a pastor and he didn't want to hear any preaching.

"The whole family is here," Carlyle said, "all your brothers and sisters. We are all so worried about you that none of us have opened our presents. We're having an all-night prayer meeting for you instead."

"Leave me alone," Clifton said.

"The Lord has given us the strong impression that we should keep on trying to let you know that God still loves you, that he wants you to live."

"What does God want with me anyway? There's nothing for me. I've seen it all, done it all. Why are you calling?"

"Brother, will you kneel down and pray with me?"

Steadying himself, Clifton knelt shakily on the floor. The only thing he could say was, "Lord, have mercy on me, a sinner."

Then he broke down and wept uncontrollably. He prayed in moans and groans. He felt unburdened of all those years of running away from God. He sensed Jesus standing right beside him and he knew without a doubt that Jesus had been standing by his side all along, just waiting for him.

"All right, Lord," he cried. "I surrender my life to you. Do with it what you will." As he lay on the cold floor, a gentle hand seemed to touch his head, and a warm peace filled him. He put the phone in the cradle. He felt no need for the cocaine. Somehow that night he left the apartment, got himself to the airport and caught a plane for Jacksonville, North Carolina, to be with his family.

With their support he freed himself from his drug dependency and recommitted himself to Christ. He went back to college, studied for the ministry and became ordained. He married the girlfriend who hadn't given up on him and they had a family. He took on the role in *Amen*, his life turned around.

Jesus Christ, have mercy on me, a miserable sinner... I'm not a pickpocket. I'm not a thief. I'm not a criminal. I've never been arrested. I'm not a drug abuser or a drunk. I've never felt such loss that I'm ready to close out the world and commit suicide. So what do I have in common with a pickpocket or an addict?

Nothing and everything. I can be arrogant, boastful, hardhearted, mean, stingy, unkind, cruel and selfish. Just because my sins seem subtler to the outside world doesn't mean they don't exist or aren't in some ways more pernicious because of their very murkiness. I would say that my worst sin, the sort of moral flaw that Jesus comes down hardest on, is my self-righteousness, the tape that plays inside my head telling me I'm better than others.

"Two men went up to the temple to pray," Jesus said, "one a Pharisee and the other a tax collector. The Pharisee, standing by himself, was praying thus: 'God, I thank you that I am not like other people: thieves, rogues, adulterers, or even like this tax collector. I fast twice a week. I give a tenth of all my income.' But the tax collector, standing far off, would not even look up to heaven, but was beating his breast and saying, 'God, be merciful to me, a sinner!' I tell you, this man went down to his home justified rather than the other; for all who exalt themselves will be humbled, but all who humble themselves will be exalted" (Luke 18:10–14).

Seems pretty clear to me where the most helpful attitude in prayer is. Bragging about being a sinner is not being humble. In fact, it can be downright tiresome. But praying with a sense of your sinfulness and failings is liberating. Reformed pickpockets and recovering addicts have a lot to offer people like me. The father loves the prodigal son's older brother, the one who stayed behind and did the right thing, just as much as he loves the wayward son. We're all God's children.

◆ ◆ ◆

One more thing about the Jesus Prayer: It's the easiest means I've ever found of satisfying that command of Paul's to pray without ceasing. There are times you need to think quite consciously about what you're praying. You need to do a moral inventory, an emotional self-exam. You need to come clean. There are other times when you just need to connect. God knows what's wrong, you don't, but if you could just get in touch you'd feel a lot better.

I'm not kidding when I say that I've prayed this one at work tons of times. I've prayed it often enough over the years that I don't have to concentrate on the words. I can simply flick the on switch and the prayer will be there. There is a lot of talk these days about multitasking. Quite frankly multitasking for me means doing several things at once and none of them well. I am best off if I'm one hundred percent present with the task at hand and that could mean sitting in a meeting and offering some insight, if I have an insight. But it means silencing the inner monologue. It means listening, paying attention, understanding.

To pray "Jesus Christ, have mercy on me, a miserable sinner. Make haste to help me, rescue me and save me, let thy will be done in my life" isn't adding a task to a multitasking day. It's taking away the needless tasks and distractions. It's asking God to be very present where we are. To use Kierkegaard's phrase, it is "to will one thing." To become a creature of hope and love, not fear. To encourage and not condemn, to trust and not flee.

A couple years ago I was in the back of an ambulance being whisked off to an ER, the EMTs hovering over me. I wasn't sure what was wrong with me, but the dark possibilities were endless: a stroke? A brain tumor? A seizure? An aneurysm? I'd been in the middle of a meeting with my colleagues when I realized I had no idea what anyone was saying. "Something's not right with my brain," I remember saying.

"We'll call Carol," they said. "What's your home number?"

I couldn't remember it.

They called 911 and they called Carol to meet me at the hospital. I was conscious of what was happening but couldn't understand what exactly was wrong. Stress would have been the best explanation, but I wasn't feeling especially stressed at the time. It was all very eerie.

As the ambulance sped through the streets of New York, I started praying the Jesus Prayer, the words circulating through my head. My racing pulse slowed down immediately. My fears were instantly allayed. My biggest concern was putting Carol through a harried trip to the ER. "You will be fine," came the message. Not that I was certain whether I would live or die, but I would be fine.

I was put on a gurney in the ER and got an MRI. Those machines make a racket, even through headphones, and to someone given to claustrophobia, as I am, they are no picnic. But my calm remained, and as I listened to the rattle of the machine I thought, "This has something to do with your dad dying." Somehow my body or my brain was reacting to a loss that it was still trying to process. As I write about it now, I feel myself wishing I could downplay the whole thing. What I don't want to do is diminish the comfort the Jesus Prayer gave me.

Five hours and a battery of tests later, I was released. I was fine. No seizure, no brain tumor, no stroke. All normal cognition returned. A follow-up trip to a neurologist revealed that, yes, I was fine. Did the prayer save me? Of course not. Did it reverse some dark scenario that was about to play itself out? I don't believe so. The medical explanation was something called Transient Global Amnesia, a brief episode of memory loss. Or at least that was the best diagnosis I could get out of any doctor and the usual poking around on the web.

The prayer had ministered to my fears. At a moment when I couldn't remember my own phone number I had no problem pulling up that prayer. It was right there ready to be used when I needed it most. Of course God was ready to help me. As I've said before, the words of a prayer aren't there for him as much as they are there for us. He hears us no matter what. But those words focused me on my relationship with God, my lifeline. "Jesus Christ, have mercy on me, a miserable sinner. Make haste to help me. Rescue me and save me. Let thy will be done in my life." With that I could trust.

CHAPTER NINE

Pray in Thanksgiving
at All Times

———————→✦←———————

"Thanks."

Mary Neal takes you by surprise. She's a doctor, an orthopedic surgeon, passionate and intense but very careful with her words, a rigorous thinker. She never exaggerates or embroiders a story. On the contrary, she works through the details with the care of an accountant going over a tax form. You know she's telling the truth, which makes it all the more compelling when she discusses something as numinous and insubstantial as the world beyond this one.

Her self-published memoir *To Heaven and Back* was an unexpected bestseller. And yet it was a book she put off writing for over ten years. She knew she had to tell her story but she had to mull over what to say, wanting to make sure she got it right. When she came by my office shortly after the book was published, I was impressed by her humility. She's fit and outdoorsy, with piercing blue eyes and a quiet voice. I can be wary of people who have had near-death experiences. I wonder how helpful their stories can be to those of us who haven't been so blessed. But Mary is a pragmatic person, and there was a message of thankfulness in her experience, thankfulness at the worst of times, that immediately spoke to me.

She and her husband, Bill, are experienced kayakers. When their four children were old enough to be left with a babysitter, they went on a vacation to the Chilean Andes to experience white-water kayaking in a remote corner of the globe, snow-fed rivers tumbling down volcanic slopes in subtropical terrain. Their guides were good friends, expert boaters.

That day in Chile towards the end of their week, Bill chose not to go out on the river. Mary started having second thoughts about going. There would be newer, less experienced kayakers joining the group and that made her uneasy, but Bill encouraged her to go. After all, this was the trip of a lifetime. She kissed her husband good-bye and headed off.

On the water, she hit trouble at the first drop. One of the novice kayakers got her boat lodged backwards going down the channel in front of Mary, and Mary had to navigate a more treacherous route. She took a deep breath and plunged fifteen, twenty feet down the falls. Her kayak dropped straight down. The paddle was ripped from her hands and the kayak smashed into some submerged rocks. Then it stopped.

She was trapped underwater, pinned by the sheer force of the waterfall above her, pushing her down. She couldn't move, couldn't release herself from the boat. Her body flopped in the vicious current like a rag doll. Fresh air was only a couple of feet above her but she couldn't reach it. She was stuck, unable to breathe, her kayak her coffin. As a doctor she assessed her situation and knew there was no hope. All she could do was pray. For a moment she fought mentally against her fate. She was terrified. Then she let go. God, she said, *thy will be done.*

Something in her shifted. The fear was gone and a great calm took over. No matter what happened, even if she died, even if she had to leave her husband and children, she knew everything would be okay. She was at peace, a sort of unexplainable heavenly peace, cosmic thankfulness beyond reason.

The current grabbed at her and jerked her body out of the kayak. Mary the orthopedic surgeon took notice as though she were her own patient: "Your knee bones just broke...You just tore your ligaments..."

At the same moment, with a *pop*, her soul rose from her body. She shot up above the river into another realm. Fifteen or twenty spirits rushed forward to welcome her. They hugged her and danced with her. Though their outlines were blurry, she knew that she knew them and that they were sent by God. "I couldn't identify each by name as, for instance, my dead grandfather or my old babysitter," she said, "but I knew each of them well."

With the spirits she began to glide along a path. She was going home, heading to her eternal home. Her companions could barely contain their joy, joy at her death. A feeling of absolute love pierced her, a feeling greater than anything she'd ever known. Below her, Mary could see her body on the riverbank, the shell of an old friend.

On the riverbank, Mary's earthly friends were giving her CPR, desperately trying to bring her back to life. "Breathe, Mary, breathe," they cried. She loved them and didn't want them to be sad so she flew back to take a breath, then continued on her heavenly journey with her spiritual companions.

They headed to a great hall with an immense dome and a central arch built with shimmering gold blocks. She was flooded with a longing to be reunited with God. Still, her friends on earth beckoned, and she returned to take another breath, and another, before continuing her journey.

At the gate of heaven her companions revealed to her that it wasn't her time to enter. "You have more to do on earth," she was told. Sorrow filled her but she knew she had to go back, back to life. She opened her eyes on the riverbank to see the stunned faces of her friends, thankful that she was alive.

She and Bill had a long, exhausting trip flying back to their home in Jackson Hole, Wyoming. She almost died a second time en route and was perilously close to death when she was finally hospitalized.

She woke up to see two deacons from church. They brought her some outdoor magazines to read and she remembered thinking that as nice as it was to see her friends, she really wanted to read the magazines. She had no pain and her mind was clear.

But as soon as her friends left and Mary picked up the magazines, the pages became too blurry to read. She put them down and turned on the TV. It was too blurry to watch. Even the face of the nurse who came in later was a blur. After a nap Mary asked for a Bible and picked it up, looking for verses to guide her. Maybe she could find one of her favorite psalms for reassurance. But those words were a blur. She couldn't grasp the meaning of any sentences.

Mary was about to give up in frustration and put the book aside, when she turned to 1 Thessalonians. One verse became clear: "Rejoice always." What a reminder that joy was a choice, not something based on circumstances but what came from a willingness to focus on hope and the promises of God.

Then another verse became visible: "Pray without ceasing." Prayer was the way to communicate directly with God, listening for his guidance. She'd just had an extraordinary experience of prayer, praying at the moment of death, "Thy will be done" and through prayer she saw where her soul would take her when her body was gone. Paul's advice to pray without ceasing landed on very willing ears. Prayer was the only way to understand what had happened to her.

Finally a third verse became clear: "Give thanks in all circumstances, for this is the will of God in Christ Jesus for you."

Give thanks in all things, in all circumstances, even in this. Give thanks for this life even when the next life promised indescribable joy. Give thanks through the pain of recovery and all that she was still meant to do on earth.

For the next several days the rest of the Bible remained blurry, magazines proved impossible to read, people's faces—even her loved ones'—were unrecognizable. But these three verses were crystal clear. Three verses that summarize what God asks of us and what we can do.

◆ ◆ ◆

Of all the means of prayer, gratitude is one of the easiest. Even people who are not particularly faithful can choose gratitude. At Thanksgiving at our house we usually go around the dinner table and each person mentions something they're grateful for: good health, great kids, a winning soccer team, the food on our plates, the presidential election, a passing grade in chemistry. Other virtues can be so much harder to acquire. Tell yourself to be hopeful and if you're worried sick and biting your fingernails it's not going to change your thinking. Tell yourself to be patient and after ten minutes at baggage claim at the airport, looking for your green suitcase among all the black ones, you will be fuming. But "let gratitude be your attitude" is one of those pithy sayings you can actually make happen. It doesn't take much to train your mind to be grateful. A pen and paper will do.

Several years ago I worked with newscaster Deborah Norville on an article about gratitude. In her three decades as a TV reporter, she observed, "I've always marveled that certain people, even in the face of heart-stopping obstacles and the most difficult circumstances, are able to go forward with smiles on their faces and optimism in their outlooks. How is that possible? In each instance, it comes down to the same answer: They were grateful."

Deborah believes in actually writing down what you are grateful for, keeping track of your blessings in a journal the way you keep track of your checks in your checkbook. She insists it's good for your career, your family life, your marriage, your well-being, and she offered scientific research to prove it. Studies have shown a measurable increase in health, resilience, cognitive skills and the ability to undo stress through gratitude. She pointed out the work of two professors in particular, Robert Emmons and Michael McCullough.

In one experiment they took three groups of volunteers and randomly assigned them to focus on one of three things for a week: hassles, things for which they were grateful, or ordinary life events. The people who focused on gratitude were happier. They reported fewer negative physical symptoms and were active in healthy ways. They spent almost an hour and a half more per week exercising than the people who focused on their hassles.

Deborah told me about how she used gratitude to combat a health problem. "For years I've suffered migraines," she said. "I've done everything every doctor recommended, but after my investigation into gratitude I tried something new. I made a daily habit of writing down the things that made me grateful. And I started seeing the benefits. My migraines have all but disappeared, my energy has increased and I've experienced joy by 'being there' for others."

She called it "Thank You Power" and wrote a book with the same name. Her prescription: Write down three things every day that you're thankful for. Three things was all, duly noted and recorded. "You need to work on it consciously to make a difference," she said.

Her advice made sense though I was certain it wasn't anything I needed to follow. I'm a natural optimist. Why did I need to write down what I was thankful for? If I just felt grateful, wasn't that enough? I had plenty of ways to pray. I could sing or talk to God or use the Jesus Prayer. To have to write things down seemed so artificial. Couldn't I be like Mary Neal and just read Paul's advice to the Thessalonians?

To give thanks in all circumstances would be just like going around the Thanksgiving table (note I hadn't really taken in the "in all circumstances" part). To thank the cook who made the meal and then the grocer who supplied the ingredients would lead back to God who gave the sun and the rain and the soil that made the food grow.

Oh, writer beware.

Yes, thankfulness is something you can put into practice even when you're not feeling it. Doing so offers all sorts of lifestyle benefits, but sometimes thankfulness is the only way you can pray and to do it at the worst of times is to acquire an invaluable tool of faith, startling because it seems so counterintuitive. Prayers like *"Nooooooooo!"* and "Help me, God" and "My heart's breaking" or "I feel like shouting for joy" are just what comes out of us at the moment. "Thanks" can take work but the work is everything.

Before I share my own story of thankfulness, let me tell you two others.

◆ ◆ ◆

For two years after her divorce Sheryl Smith-Rodgers's teenage son, Patrick, didn't speak to her. He chose to stay with his father and didn't even say good-bye when she moved out of the house. He barely spoke when she called. He blocked her e-mails. He ignored her invitations to come over for sloppy joes, his favorite. Occasionally she'd catch a glimpse of him driving his pickup around their small Texas town or she'd see him at the feed store where he worked.

One afternoon, fed up with the blocked e-mails and ignored calls, Sheryl drove to the feed store and climbed into the passenger seat of Patrick's unlocked pickup truck to wait for him. When Patrick came out and saw her his expression turned sour. He slid behind the wheel and said, "Can you get out, please?"

"Can't we talk?" she pleaded.

"I'm going to say it once more—please get out, Mother." She shook her head.

"Then do me a favor," Patrick said, "and lock both doors before you leave." He slid back out and slammed the door.

The pain of it was unbearable. She and Patrick had been so close when he was young. She missed him so much, hated being locked out of his life. On the Sunday before Thanksgiving her pastor had preached on the text from 1Thessalonians, the same one that inspired Mary Neal—"In everything give thanks"—but Sheryl didn't know how she could do it. How could she be grateful if her son wouldn't be joining her for the holiday?

"Instead of asking God for things you want," the minister had said, "try thanking him for what he's given you."

Thanksgiving morning Sheryl forced herself to do just that. She'd focus on the good things she'd been given. She was thankful that Patrick was doing well in school. That he worked hard and had close friends. That he was healthy and that she'd had so much time with him when he was young. Before she even got out of bed, she thanked God for her house, for another day, for her daughter, for her parents, with whom they would be spending Thanksgiving. And she thanked God for her son.

Later that morning she found a stack of greeting cards and wrote in a blank one: "I love you more than you can ever imagine. Always. Happy Thanksgiving!" Then on her way to dinner with her parents, she dropped by the feed store.

Patrick looked tired, stressed, stacking some feed bags. She kept it low-key. "Here," she said, handing him the card. "Happy Thanksgiving!" He opened it up and read. Was there a hint of a smile on his face? Did he open up just a little? "Tell Grandma and Grandpa hello for me," he said. Sheryl nodded and waved and got back in the car.

She stuck with her morning prayers of gratitude and thanked God for little things throughout the day. She opened up a new e-mail account and wrote Patrick chatty little notes. She ended each with "I love you, Mom." Was he reading them? She had no clue. At least he wasn't blocking them.

A few weeks later he showed up at her door. "Can I come in?" he asked.

"Of course," she said. They talked about school, his girlfriend, work. He even agreed to come over for sloppy joes. Then he started showing up for dinner once a week. On his eighteenth birthday she hosted a birthday party for him (sloppy joes were on the menu, of course). Her son was back in her life.

I generally avoid using the phrase "prayer works." In the Bible the operative word is more often that God "answers" prayer or God "hears" our prayers, different from the quid-pro-quo notion that "prayer works." The prayer that works best for you might not be the one you expect, the way God hears you might not be how you think.

Sheryl's greatest hopes were realized when she expressed gratitude for what she already had, not for what she fervently wished for. God answered her prayer "Please bring Patrick back to me" when she took a leap of faith. Maybe it was all a matter of time. Perhaps Patrick would have resumed talking to her anyway. But I suspect the change in her attitude was what made their reunion possible. Her prayerful response to a painful situation changed the situation. It changed her, changed her expectations. Give thanks for everything? Well, yes. Everything.

◆ ◆ ◆

The second story is far more dramatic and doesn't offer the happy ending that Sheryl's does, but perhaps it's worth remembering that the author of 1 Thessalonians was frequently writing from prison and by his own account, in his second letter to the Corinthians, was beaten, stoned, shipwrecked, adrift at sea, threatened by bandits, hungry, thirsty, cold, exhausted. If the Apostle Paul could be thankful in all circumstances, he knew just how difficult that could be. And how necessary.

Chet Bitterman Jr. was in the middle of an Amazon jungle at the graveside of his twenty-eight-year-old son and clinging to thankfulness as his very lifeline. He told himself to be thankful that it wasn't raining that day, that the location was beautiful, that his wife was with him, that his son's short life had been lived for a larger purpose.

His son, also named Chet, had gone to Colombia to work with Wycliffe Bible Translators, an organization that has translated the Bible into hundreds of languages that had never been written down before. Young Chet would be in a tribal area working with the native people. His wife had flown to Bogotá for a week for a medical check when the Wycliffe house where they were staying was invaded by armed guerrillas. They took one hostage, Chet III. The price for his return: the withdrawal of all Wycliffe workers in Colombia.

Back in Pennsylvania Chet the father raged. He paced the house, up to the kitchen, back to the basement. He was a man of action, the head of a small business. While his wife called endless organizations, asking for prayers, Chet wanted to do something. He'd get some guns and with his buddies, fly to Bogotá and take the place apart, brick by brick, until they found his son.

Of course it was a fantasy, but he needed some outlet for his rage. "Lord," he prayed, "there's got to be something I can do."

There is. Give thanks.

The thought came out of nowhere and it wouldn't go away. *Give thanks.* Unlike his missionary son, Chet hadn't learned hundreds of Bible verses by heart, but this one he knew: "In every thing give thanks: for this is the will of God . . ."

He argued and protested. Give thanks for his son's kidnapping? The pointlessness of it, the stupidity made him want to throw something. He felt shocked, angry, frustrated—anything but thankful. Then he noticed that the verse didn't say anything about how you felt. "Give thanks" was the command, not "feel thankful." Thanksgiving was a matter not of the emotions but of the will.

He wanted justice, he wanted revenge, but as he paced, he forced himself to do what seemed utterly unnatural. He would be honest. Where could he start?

Well, he would be thankful for all those Bible verses his son could recite. They must have been helpful. And thankful that Chet III was young and strong and in such good shape. He took out a piece of paper and began writing things down. Thank God that his son spoke fluent Spanish. Thank God that he made friends easily. Thank God that he had called only two days earlier and had such a good talk with his mother.

As he wrote, the tension and rage and anguish drained away. He felt light, free...thankful. Feelings that he could never have drummed up by straining for them had come through an act of obedience.

The kidnappers' deadline was one month away. Then it got extended two weeks. Chet and his wife, Mary, grew hopeful. Surely their son would be released. At no point did they suggest that Wycliffe capitulate to the kidnappers' demands. That could endanger Wycliffe workers all over the world. Rumors flared, but he had to believe that his son was still alive. They had to trust.

Less than two months after the kidnapping, the terrible news came: Chet Bitterman III was dead, his body found in an abandoned bus on a side street in Bogotá.

The next few days passed in a blur. Sympathy from friends at church. A letter from the president. More news from Colombia and then the burial in a jungle clearing near the Wycliffe base.

When life came back into focus for Chet, it was from a different angle, a new one for him, "the view from forever," as he called it. He would still struggle with his tragedy, still object to the senselessness of his son's death, but he had a tool to cling to. The key to seeing as God does is to give thanks in everything. He could stand by his son's grave with love, not anger. He could forgive the horror that had been done. He could look forward. Prayer had given him a new perspective, giving thanks when he felt anything but thankful.

◆ ◆ ◆

Am I thankful that I had open-heart surgery? Of course. I am thankful to the doctors, thankful that someone figured out I had an aneurysm before it ruptured, thankful to the nurses who took such good care of me. Without surgery I would not be alive. But here's something a little harder to explain: I'm thankful for the compassion it's given me for anyone else who goes through the trials of major surgery. Especially the recovery.

Four weeks out of surgery, I crashed. I felt rotten. I would lie in bed shivering under a mountain of quilts, close my eyes in the hope of sleep, and what came to me was a small dark block in my head. Imagine all your deepest fears pressed down and packed together into a domino that's lodged in your head. You can't step around it, you can't ignore it, you can feel its brooding presence and you wonder if it will explode or suck you into endless night. I could almost locate it near my forehead. I started calling it the black domino, all dark blankness and not a single dot of light.

I had asked my cardiologist about my chances of sinking into depression. It's a well-known side effect of open-heart surgery. Some call it pump head, blaming it on the heart-lung machine that takes over for your heart during surgery. Others suggest it's the result of confronting mortality.

"I don't think depression will be a problem for you," Dr. Ravalli said cautiously. "You're in good shape. You'll be recovering at home with your family. Depression isn't as much a problem as it used to be. Do you normally get depressed?"

"No," I said confidently. I'm more prone to anxiety than depression. Depressives tend to look backward at their lives, shaking their heads with regret, remembering all the "could have beens" and "would have beens," the "if I only." My head doesn't fly that way. I'm more likely to be looking forward, worrying, wondering, "Can I?" or "Will I" or "What if I don't?"

I lay in bed, watching the black domino warily, monitoring it like the enemy. It *was* the enemy. Was I going to plunge into a bottomless pit of gloom? Was I going off the deep end? I could count on one hand the few times in my life when I'd brushed against something that felt like depression, nothing close to the paralyzing depression I've seen others suffer.

I remembered an August day before my junior year of college. I had spent the summer backpacking around Europe on a fifteen-dollar-a-day budget. It was near the end of my trip and I was sitting on a hill in an Edinburgh park on a languid afternoon, incapable of moving. I'd either traveled too much or seen too many old paintings or believed too little that I didn't want to do anything for weeks on end. I couldn't bear to visit another museum or castle or church or town square or sleep in another youth hostel or bed and breakfast. It all seemed purposeless and I figured if I stayed on that patch of Scottish grass all night, no one would really care. I could die there and it wouldn't matter. I was overcome with a kind of lassitude that only the young, with their boundless energy, can ever know.

I slept for hours and when I awoke saw only my failures, which appeared as numberless as the stars in the sky. What an insignificant person I was, what a terrible fake. In the dark I finally shook off my torpor, got up and got something to eat, returning to the dreary dorm room I had rented. For a long while that was my benchmark for depression. I could tell myself, "I don't want to go there," and managed through some combination of exercise, prayer, optimism and genetic good fortune to stay away.

Till now with this black domino lodged in my brain, this black hole that threatened to absorb everything.

Was it claustrophobia? I hate being in closed spaces. In my editorial career there is only one story that gave me the creeps so much I couldn't work on it. It was about a man who went scuba diving through Caribbean coral caves and came to a spot that got narrower and narrower until he couldn't get out. He couldn't turn around and he couldn't figure out the route that would take him back. His air was running out. Through the murky water and the coral he could see sunlight above but couldn't reach it.

Fortunately for him, he was able to escape, but that remains my worst nightmare. To be trapped. Maybe my body was still objecting to being strapped down on a hospital bed for hours of surgery, a machine doing the work of my heart and lungs.

"But you're doing all the right things," I told myself. I walked around the small park near our house three times a day. I took naps. I ate carefully, filling myself up with protein and iron. I had oatmeal for breakfast and lentil soup for lunch. I took prescription painkillers when I had to. Otherwise two Advil at bedtime and another two in the middle of the night.

"I'm not getting better," I told Carol.

"Give it some time," she said. "It's not going to be a straightforward trajectory. You'll have good days and some bad days—a few steps forward, a few steps back—but you'll feel better over the long term."

No reason why that shouldn't happen. But I couldn't believe it and I felt myself unalterably changed. The novelty of being a patient had worn off. The adrenaline of surgery was long gone. I was in the deep slough of recovery and I hated it. Like that scuba diver in the Caribbean trapped in his coral cave, I could see the light of day but it was agonizingly out of reach. And when I closed my eyes I could still see the black domino.

I couldn't pray. I couldn't reach God. He was that light above me. I could accept that he was there but I couldn't get to him. This time it wasn't enough to tell myself that others were praying for me and doing it on my behalf. Not anymore.

"You should keep a positive attitude," I told myself. I'd read about how positive thinking could help you bounce back from surgery and help in your recovery. But I couldn't force myself to be positive and that made me feel even more like a failure. If you're not positive, you're not going to get better. "Thanks a lot," I wanted to say. Couldn't I be angry that I felt awful? Why couldn't I express my anger to God?

I picked up my battered volume of the New Testament and Psalms and complained, "I'm mad at you, God." I read from a psalm (3:7) that was full of rage: "Arise, O Lord; save me, O my God, for thou has smitten all mine enemies upon the cheek bone; thou hast broken the teeth of the ungodly." I thought it could get me in touch with my anger. But it didn't make me feel any better.

I turned to the cheery brochure that was supposed to guide us in our recovery. If my temperature shot up to 102, then I was supposed to take myself to the ER. If the dull pain in my chest became a dagger, call 911. If my incision began to puff up and ooze, I should call my surgeon. Otherwise I was to keep up the walking, the stretching, eating three meals a day, sleeping at regular hours. No lifting groceries. No driving. Light dusting was okay and vacuuming but no pushing heavy furniture around or reaching up to wash the windows. There was nothing in there about the black domino.

Maybe I had PTSD. The surgery itself is traumatic. Your sternum has been sawed open—"stretched," in my surgeon's euphemistic words. Your body has been chilled in surgery. You had all that anesthesia. You were strapped down and put out, then cut open and wired shut. Is it any wonder that some part of you reacts by declaring, "Don't do that again!"? My head was trying to defend against anything so violent happening to my body again. The shell-shocked soldier who comes back from war, who hits the deck at the backfiring of a car, requires countless hours of therapy to feel right with the world again.

I searched the brochure for some evidence that that's what I was going through. No mention of this nightmare.

"Do you have a fever?" Carol asked, watching me shiver.

"I don't know. I haven't taken my temperature."

"Are you hot?"

"I'm cold."

"You could call the doctor."

"The brochure says you don't need to call the doctor unless you have a fever of 102. Mine's not that high."

"How do you know?"

I got out the old gray thermometer that we used for the kids and stuck it in my mouth until it bleeped. I showed Carol the evidence just to prove that I wasn't that sick: 100.4. High enough to feel bad but not so alarming as to rush to the hospital or call the doctor. I was tired of being a patient, weary of finding myself in a narrative that had no clear middle or end. Open-heart surgery was a story, something to write home about. Surgery was a crisis moment when everyone could pray and send me e-mails. There was nothing to say about the muddle of recovery. What do you say about a fever that was only 100.4?

"You've talked about wanting to have a sabbatical someday," Carol said, looking for the upside. "Maybe you can think of this time as your sabbatical."

A nice thought, but not one I could put into practice. On the ideal sabbatical my head would be clear enough so that I could read through Proust and Tolstoy and Dante, savoring the greats with the greatest mental agility. I wasn't up to that. I watched old videos and thumbed my way through the books friends had sent me.

I was a dead weight. I couldn't clean the house or give a dinner party or even do the laundry. About the only challenge I was up for was writing a thank-you note. That I could try. "Just the kind of thing Deborah Norville would have you do," I thought. I'd e-mailed her shortly after surgery, just to tell her what I was going through. She'd responded with a generous prayer. But her "thank-you power" advice? That was still on file somewhere in my head.

I sat on the side of my bed and took out a note card. I looked over at the gifts people had sent. There was a bowl my coworker Celeste had given me for my oatmeal, the perfect thing. But why write her? I would see her soon enough back at the office. I could say something then. She wouldn't be expecting anything from me.

No, I needed to write it down now, all my gratitude. I would forget it in a couple of days. I scrawled a few sentences. At once there was an inner *ping*, as sure as the clanging of a bell: "Yes, that's right. That's you, Rick. That's who you are. That's where you want to be." I was hungry to be grateful, desperate like a starving man seeking food or a thirsty one crawling across the desert for water. It was almost physical, holding a pen in my hand and opening a blank card, my mind looking for words to describe a kindness. Thankfulness was the one thing that would keep the black domino from sucking me up and absorbing me. Thankfulness expressed in very specific terms.

I wrote another note and another. Thank you for the card, thanks for the roses, thanks for the burritos from FreshDirect, thanks for the bottle of wine, thanks for the friendship, thanks for the postcard that made me laugh, thanks for the CD, thanks for the phone call, thanks for the prayers, thanks for the visit, thanks for the e-mail.

I could hear myself as I wrote. I could feel stirrings of faith even if I was writing nothing about my faith because I was participating again in the goodness of the world. Sitting on the side of my bed and writing was my therapy. Later at church someone said, "I can't believe you sent me a note thanking me for my note." How could I say that the note I sent her was vital to my recovery?

Prayer *is* communication and this was essential communication. Our friend F. Paul had sent me a slew of witty postcards over the last month, every one of them a gem. One day I picked out a dozen of them and made a silly collage of the images to send to him as thanks. Back at ya. I couldn't pray the way I was accustomed to, but writing thank-you notes—something so mundane and yet so profound—was my prayer. I could connect to my spiritual core. I could do battle against the inner darkness pulling me down. I could linger in the light.

In a matter of weeks I sent seventy-five thank-you notes and postcards. I hope I never have to read them. I'm sure they were inane or over-the-top or even illegible. But they were a godsend to me. I could wait, pen in hand, and tell myself, "I don't really have anything to say," but once I started writing, all sorts of things came out. Gratitude wasn't far beneath the surface. It was just waiting to be expressed. I'm amazed that I actually had seventy-five different people to write, seventy-five people who did nice things for me. But once you start looking for things to be grateful for, you end up feeling grateful in the most cosmic way.

For me it was a way to reclaim the turf I longed to inhabit and it kept me from sinking into godless despair. It was many months before the black domino disappeared—I can still conjure it up like a phantom in a Stephen King novel. But I had found the tool to banish it, one I still use.

Be thankful in all things. Write them down. Even if you don't feel grateful, even if you can't pray. What you write will be your prayer. Feelings you can't force, faith is not something you can necessarily talk yourself into, but thankfulness you can. All it takes is a pen or a pencil and a scrap of paper. You can write to yourself, you can write to a friend, you can write to God. Put your gratitude down, even at the worst of times. Especially then. What you say will lift you back up.

CHAPTER TEN

Pray Yes

"Yes, and . . . "

For Tim's graduation from high school, some intrepid parent, who happened to be a TV producer, talked comedian Tina Fey into being the guest speaker. She was short even in heels, pretty, gracious, funny and visibly nervous at the prospect of delivering an inspiring talk to a bunch of teens.

Her comedic background had been in improvisational theater and she used the rules of improv as a jumping-off point to explain how to get the most out of life. One of those rules was "Yes, and…"

Her point was that when you're doing improv and someone says something like, "What a fine horse you were riding this morning," you don't say, "That wasn't a horse! It was an elephant, you idiot." You go with whatever they said and build on it. "Yes, and did you know that I'm using it to train for the Olympics this summer to win another gold medal in dressage?" or "Yes, and we just came from a cowboy breakfast on the ranch" or "Yes, and it's the horse my grandfather gave me for my twenty-first birthday." "Yes, and..." instead of "No, but..."

She wanted the graduates to be open to life's possibilities, to make the most of the opportunities that God had presented them and *would* present to them. "Yes, and..." means seeing people in a positive, generous light, listening closely to what they were saying and loving them. "Yes, and..." would require chipping away at the walls of cynicism and defensiveness. "Yes, and..." would be a worldview of imagination and creativity. Instead of saying "I couldn't possibly do that," you might find you can do more than you ever thought possible when you say "Yes, and..."

Sitting under the sycamores in dappled shade, listening to Tina Fey, I felt like she was speaking to me as much as to the graduates in their caps and gowns. What was my knee-jerk response to the internal nudges of charity, generosity, adventure? "No, God, I couldn't do that" or "Yes, and what else did you have in mind and how can you help me accomplish it?" Couldn't I live a little more dangerously? The Bible is full of occasions when Jesus seemed to be looking for a "Yes, and..." and got a No instead.

Take the rich young man who came to Jesus and asked what good deed he should do to earn eternal life. What if he hadn't walked away at the answer? Jesus' first response was to tell him to keep the commandments. "Which ones?" the young man asked. Jesus went through the familiar litany (in case the fellow was clueless): you shall not murder, you shall not commit adultery, you shall not steal, you shall not bear false witness, honor your father and mother.

Smugly—you can hear the self-satisfaction—the young man said, "I have kept all these. What do I still lack?" Jesus answered: "Go, sell your possessions and give to the poor and you will have treasure in heaven. Then, come follow me" (Matthew 19:16).

What if the young man had said "Yes, and...?" What if his answer were even as equivocal as "Yes, Lord, I want to follow you but it's a big step for me and I need your help"? Instead he walked away, "grieving," in the Bible's damning phrase, "for he had many possessions."

We Americans, by any reckoning of the world's resources, have many possessions. What would we have said? If that guy had stuck around just a little bit longer he might have heard Jesus give a more hopeful prognosis. No, the rich didn't have a chance. After all, it is easier for a camel to go through the eye of a needle than for a rich man to enter the kingdom of heaven. Yet "for mortals it is impossible, but for God all things are possible."

"Yes, and..."

Not too many years ago Elizabeth Sherrill was writing at her computer at home, struggling to meet a deadline, when she heard a rustling in the woods outside. At the edge of the trees she caught sight of a skunk zigzagging across the lawn. What was that on his head? A bizarre-looking helmet: a yellow plastic yogurt container. Like a drunk he whirled in one direction and then another, bumping against the picnic table in the backyard, shaking his head frantically. But the container was wedged tight.

Tibby wasn't about to go out there and take the yogurt container off. How would she ever catch the skunk? It would take too long.

What if she got sprayed? The odor was impossible to get rid of. But she couldn't get the skunk out of her mind.

She called the SPCA and was told to call the Department of Wildlife. There the man listened to her story. He put her on hold, talked to someone else in the office, let her know that if the skunk couldn't see her, he wouldn't spray. She could take off the carton and then throw a blanket over the skunk just in case, letting it amble out when she was at a safe distance.

Tibby glanced outside. No more skunk. She was off the hook. Surely the animal was long gone by now. Someone else would find it. They'd get a conservation officer who could handle the problem.

Still, as soon as she hung up the phone she went outside. No blanket, no special strategy. "My feet never slowed," she wrote. "I turned left and dashed down the street as though rushing to a long-ordained appointment." She'd gotten a hundred yards down the road when a black-and-white streak emerged from the bushes and ran straight at her, the yellow helmet on his head.

She stooped and grabbed hold of the yogurt container. The animal tugged and twisted. She had to grab it with both of her hands and tug—until a small black head popped free. "A sharp quivering nose, two small round ears and alert black eyes stared straight into mine," she wrote.

For a full ten seconds they held each other's gaze. Then the skunk turned and vanished into a culvert.

She hadn't wanted to get involved. She was busy after all. Why bother? She could have justified not going outside, leaving this problem in the capable hands of some professional. Instead she tried and it worked, and for years afterward she kept that plastic yogurt container on her desk as a reminder that "every now and then God's answer to a need is me." Something had to be done and that something involved her.

Prayer might seem like a quiet, contemplative thing. It is, but it is also an action to take. Jesus spent forty days in the wilderness, praying and fasting, before he launched his ministry. Even then he was frequently leaving the crowd and going off by himself to be alone to pray, but the narrative of the Gospels is an account of exhausting activity. He healed the sick, raised the dead, fed the hungry with loaves and fishes, made the lame walk and the blind see, preached, exhorted, taught and blessed. In John's phrase, there were so many "other things that Jesus did; if every one of them were written down, I suppose that the world itself could not contain the books that would be written" John 21:25. To pray and to act. A prayer can inspire an act but the act can be the prayer itself.

Kevin Felts is a freelance cameraman who was hired to film a famous Oregon author for a documentary. Part of the shoot involved going back to the house the author had lived in before his unexpected fame, when times were tough for him. The father of six, he was working three jobs and barely making ends meet back then.

The house looked very familiar to Kevin. It reminded him of a Christmas not long before when he wanted to make a gift to someone in his community. He'd come through some tough times and knew what it was like to face the holidays in diminished circumstances.

Now that things were going well he wanted to pass along his good fortune. He'd heard of a family that needed help. He didn't know their name and didn't want to. He put a hundred dollars in an envelope and slipped it in under their door. Not that it would solve all their problems, but it might give them hope. He'd had this urge to give and had acted on it.

And now Kevin was looking at the same house.

Kevin told the famous author the story about the cash in the envelope, what he'd heard about the family of eight needing help, how he'd done the whole thing anonymously and put the money under the door.

The author was amazed. Yes, he said, he was the one who'd picked up the envelope. In fact, the gift of a hundred dollars had come at just the right time. He'd been working on a book, something he'd written just for his family, the amazing story of a man finding faith at the hardest, saddest, toughest point of his life. He'd finished a draft of the novel, but didn't have any money to make copies of it. Then came the unexpected hundred.

"I had fifteen copies of it printed up at Office Depot," the author said, "and gave the book away. If I hadn't had that money I probably would never have shared it." He might never have been urged to pass it along, might never have decided to publish it.

That book, *The Shack*, went on to sell some fifteen million copies and became an international phenomenon for the author, Paul Young. Of course, it is entirely possible that some other form of good fortune would have come Paul's way. *The Shack* might have found its way to the public through some other means. Or maybe Paul would have gotten a lucrative full-time job and put the manuscript into a drawer to be forgotten for years. But look at what an anonymous gift did when it came at just the right time. Kevin said, "Yes, and…" Moreover he got to find out what actually happened when he acted.

For years I've saved a prayer that was a favorite of Eleanor Roosevelt's. According to her son Elliott, she said it every night before she went to bed:

Our Father, who has set a restlessness in our hearts and made us all seekers after that which we can never fully find, forbid us to be satisfied with what we make of life. Draw us from base content and set our eyes on far-off goals. Keep us at tasks too hard for us that we may be driven to thee for strength. Deliver us from fretfulness and self-pitying; make us sure of the good we cannot see and of the hidden good in the world. Open our eyes to simple beauty all around us and our hearts to the loveliness men hide from us because we do not try to understand them. Save us from ourselves and show us a vision of a world made new.

I am especially fond of the phrase "keep us at tasks too hard for us that we may be driven to thee for strength." If there was ever someone who took on difficult tasks, it was Eleanor Roosevelt, especially when you consider some of the emotional challenges she had to overcome.

Shy, awkward, ungainly, bookish, she was born to wealth and status, the niece of a president, but what a tragic childhood. Her mother, a great beauty, died when Eleanor was eight; her father, a terrible alcoholic, died two years later. I remember one story from her girlhood when she was accompanying her father to his club. He left her in a downstairs room, "the dogs' room" as it was called, to get a quick drink. Hours later, Eleanor waiting all the while, he was carried back down, passed out. As a friend pointed out, "No wonder she couldn't bear being with anyone who drank." She was so serious a child her society mother called her Granny, which must have only confirmed her low self-worth; then when she married the handsome, charismatic Franklin, she spent years sharing the same house with his doting, demanding mother. Later she had to cope with the heartbreaking evidence of his infidelity.

And yet her passion for the oppressed and the poor drove her beyond her insecurities, fueling her. By the time she was First Lady she led an exhausting schedule of speeches, newspaper columns, press conferences, dinners, lunches, trips to the front lines, meetings with the unemployed. She was an advocate for civil rights, famously inviting the black contralto Marian Anderson to sing at the Lincoln Memorial when she had been blocked from performing at Constitution Hall. After the war, she was America's delegate to the UN, chairing the committee that created the Universal Declaration of Human Rights.

Historian Mary Ann Glendon took those last words from the prayer—"a world made new"—as the title of her book on Eleanor Roosevelt's key role in the human rights movement. It is the nature of the inner life that it leaves fewer documents behind of its workings, especially compared to the clamor of political wrangling and daily news. Only God knows exactly what petitions Eleanor added to her bedside prayer, but her actions show evidence of her prayer at work.

"Courage is fear that has said its prayers," goes an old saying. It is not that the courageous have fewer fears than the rest of us but that they move beyond them. They say, "Yes, and..." despite their insecurity and fears.

Bob Macauley founded the relief organization AmeriCares, distributing medicine and medical supplies to the world's poor at times of disaster. They've given billions of dollars of aid to more than 135 countries in thirty years. Bob himself was a terrific fundraiser, going hat in hand to the CEOs of some of the biggest corporations but as he said, he learned how to beg from the very best.

Back in the early days of AmeriCares, when Bob was still trying to grow the organization and wondering how on earth he could get the means to fund his vision, he was on a trip visiting orphanages in Guatemala with the diminutive and tireless Mother Teresa. Bob was tall and strapping and Mother Teresa less than five feet. He showed me a picture of the two of them walking on the tarmac at some airport, his hand at her back.

"You seem to be giving Mother Teresa a hand," people would say when they saw the photo.

"Not at all," Bob insisted. "I've got my hand on her back to slow her down. I couldn't keep up!"

The two of them were on a Taca Airlines flight from Guatemala to Mexico City. The flight attendant brought them their lunches.

"Excuse me," Mother Teresa said, "how much does this meal cost?" A question Bob was pretty sure no passenger had ever asked.

The flight attendant shrugged. "I don't know. About one dollar in US currency."

"If I give it back to you," Mother Teresa said, "would you give me that dollar to give to the poor?"

The flight attendant looked startled. "I don't know," she stammered. "It's not something we normally do." She left her cart, went to the front of the plane to consult the pilot, then returned. "Yes, Mother," she said. "You may have the money for the poor."

"Here then," Mother Teresa handed back the tray. No matter how hungry he might have been, Bob did the same. No way was he going to be able to eat in peace with Mother Teresa seated next to him. As it turned out, the rest of the passengers on the plane followed suit. The flight attendant got on the speaker and announced, "If anyone gives up their meal, the airline will give one dollar to Mother Teresa for the poor." It seemed no one wanted to eat their lunch. Bob got up and counted: 129 people gave up their lunches, including the crew.

"Pretty good," he said to Mother Teresa, "now you've got one hundred and twenty-nine dollars for the poor."

But she wasn't finished. "Bub," she said—with her thick Albanian accent she called him "Bub"—"get me the food."

"What?" he asked. "What are you going to do with one hundred and twenty-nine airline lunches?"

"They can't use them. We can give them to the poor."

The flight landed and with some reluctance Bob went to the airline officials who were gathered on the tarmac to greet Mother Teresa. They shook hands and he finally asked, "Mother would like to know if she could have the lunches too?" The officials responded, "Of course...anything Mother Teresa wants."

Bob returned to Mother Teresa with the good news. She hardly paused for breath: "Bub, get me the truck."

A few minutes later lanky Bob Macauley was sitting in the passenger seat of a Taca Airlines truck being driven by a nun who was so short that she had to peer between the steering wheel and the dashboard to see. Where were they going? To the poor. She was a terrible driver and he figured it was only by the grace of God that she didn't get in an accident. In half an hour they were in one of Mexico City's desperately poor neighborhoods, handing out airline meals. "Just ask" was the message Bob took from the experience. "It's easy to ask when you're doing it for the poor," Mother Teresa told him. God could give the power to do anything when you were doing it for the people who needed it most.

But it means taking a risk, sticking your neck out and trying something that no one else has tried yet. "No, that's not going to work" or "No, I could never do that" get bumped out of place with a "Yes, and…"

I've mentioned those yellow Post-it notes that I use for scribbling the names of people I've promised to pray for (would that I could remember their names without writing them down but maybe the writing down is part of the prayer process). Did you know they were the project of a 3M inventor who came up with the idea when he was singing in his church choir at North Presbyterian in St. Paul and lost his place in the hymnal for the introit? He had a slip of paper marking the spot but it fell out and fluttered to the floor when he rose to sing. How frustrating. Which page were they on? Which line? Couldn't someone come up with some better way to mark a spot than a loose scrap of paper?

What if that someone were him?

Arthur Fry started by thinking he'd make some sort of self-sticking, removable, hymnal page marker. He had a colleague who'd developed an adhesive that nobody could find any use for because it wouldn't grip permanently. It would hold two pieces of paper together but anybody could easily peel the papers apart. What good was that?

He applied the adhesive to a piece of paper and it stuck in the hymnal all right but it left a residue on the page. (Some of those hymnal pages at North Presbyterian were stuck together for years.) With some experimenting in the lab at 3M Arthur found a way of getting a residue-free glue into the narrow "low tack" range—not too sticky but sticky enough. In due time he had a pad of nice little peel-off bookmarks that he could use in his hymnal.

Then it hit him. Who else would want these things? Had he spent his time developing a failure of a product (at 3M research scientists like Arthur were given the privilege of spending fifteen percent of their time on pet projects)? When he stuck one of them on a report that he had to send to his boss and it came back with an answer scrawled on the same sticky note, it finally occurred to him that this could be more than just a bookmark. You could put the notes on anything—a phone, a refrigerator, a magazine. Stick 'em on and peel 'em off.

It was only when they passed sample pads of the peel-off notes around the office that Arthur had his first indication that he might have a success on his hands. Everybody started coming back for more.

And later, when 3M marketed them to office supply stores, it was only by giving samples for people to use that Post-It notes took off. They were hooked. People didn't know they needed them till they had them in hand. My prayer list sits next to my phone or by my computer or on my desk or gets folded up in my pocket. Until I fill up another Post-it note. Thanks to a choir singer who lost his place in a hymnal — and was convinced there was a better way.

Arthur Fry was lucky to be able to see the success of his creation but that's not always the case. There are times you say "Yes, and..." and then don't know for years — if at all — what God meant when he was moving in your life, when he gave you that nudge and you responded in such good faith. "If they had been thinking of the land they left behind," says the author of the letter of the Hebrews, referring to the faithful of past and present, "they would have had opportunity to return. But as it is, they desire a better country, that is, a heavenly one. Therefore God is not ashamed to be called their God; indeed, he has prepared a city for them" (Hebrews 11:15-16). Hope carries all of us on. It gives us that heavenly city to work for and dream of, that better country. Hope is one of those great gifts we can give each other.

Betty McFarlane remembered the day her mother declared that she was going to be a writer. It was what she felt the Lord was telling her to do. Her great dream. She bought stationery and business cards with her name, address and the words "Writer and Lecturer" confidently printed on them. She cleared a corner in the basement, made a desk by putting a door across two file cabinets and borrowed a typewriter. Most importantly — what Betty couldn't forget — was the box her mother put on the desk. Covered in cream-colored cotton printed with tiny forget-me-nots, it had a pale blue ribbon tied around it and the words "Acceptance Letters."

Betty said, "It must have never occurred to Mama that she might get some rejections."

But before she had the chance to probe too deeply into *Writer's Market* or even finish an article and send it off, her husband left her and Betty's mother was suddenly the sole provider for her children. There was no time for crafting stories for publication. Her writing was limited to the encouraging notes she slipped into lunch boxes and left on dressers for her children.

Betty doesn't remember when her mother put the stationery or the box with its hopeful blue ribbon away. Whenever she'd see her mom sitting down to write, it was more likely a letter to one of her brothers in the service or a card to a friend or a note cheering up a relative. Even after the kids moved out, her mom was busy: caring for her son after a serious car accident, helping her daughter with a baby, taking in Grandpa when he got sick, lending a hand with a neighbor who had no one else to turn to.

After her mother died Betty found the old box with its forget-me-not cover in a cedar chest. To Betty's surprise it was heavy when she lifted it out, the blue ribbon frayed from tying and untying. What would her mom have put inside? Betty opened the box and began to read the "acceptance letters" her mom had saved over the years:

"Thank you, Mom, for your letters," her brother wrote. "I could never have made it through boot camp without them."

"Just a note to tell you how much I appreciated your support…"

"Thank you for writing during those months I was pregnant…"

"Thank you for taking the time to send me the pretty note cards…"

"Your letter came when I was at my lowest point."

"Mama, thank you for your constant support, prayers and love…"

Betty's mother's dream *had* come true in an unexpected way. She had a writing career that was successful beyond her wildest imaginings. The accolades in the box proved it.

I must confess that I have a file in my desk drawer with letters I've collected over the years from friends, strangers, loved ones who have written incredibly kind things I don't want to forget. When I'm feeling rotten or discouraged or wonder if I have done much with my life, I open the file and read. It's like getting a premature eulogy or sitting down at some impossible-to-arrange dinner party with guests from across the years and across the continent, and watching them stand up to say, "Rick, you did all right." I slip the letters back into the file and feel like writing a note myself to someone else, surprising them— I hope—with an unexpected, well-deserved good word.

I remember one Christmas as a kid thumbing through the pile of cards we received, stacks of family photos taken on exotic vacations or pictures of families dressed in red and green and posed in front of a mantel decorated with holly and ivy, everyone smiling and wishing Merry Christmas. But then there'd be a Hallmark card from some person I didn't know, the signature scrawled in a fragile hand with a message saying, "So glad to receive your note. You're so nice to remember me. Merry Christmas to you all!"

"Mom, who's this?" I asked.

"Oh," she said, "she was our house mother in college. I haven't seen her in years but I always send her a card." Or it would be a long-ago babysitter or the woman who retired from the cleaner's or some distant teacher. "I remember visiting her at Christmas once and seeing just a few cards on her bedside table. I thought she should have some more."

The people that need our help are many. Like the young rich man with so many possessions he simply walked away grieving, we can feel so overwhelmed by their needs we want to give up. We do nothing, say nothing. But "Yes, and..." can start with just one small response. A card, a word, a letter, an e-mail, a note, a hospital visit. You'll feel the prompting in your heart and even though you won't know what to say, the words will come. Sometimes just your presence will be enough.

The *Guideposts* story I'm most likely to retell if someone asks me, "What do you do?" or "Where do you work?" and "What kind of stories do you publish?" is one called "Mrs. Lake's Eyes," by an author who asked to remain anonymous. Mrs. Lake was the sixth grade teacher she could never forget, the one who changed her life.

It happened the day of the parent-teacher conferences. Mrs. Lake had set up chairs in the back of the room and as each set of parents came in, she met with them and talked over their child's progress. The girl knew her parents wouldn't show up. They never had. She'd asked them before to come to parent-teacher conferences. She'd brought home notices. Other teachers had made phone calls. Her mother would say, "Yes, we'll try," but didn't come. Some excuse was always made or, worse, nothing was ever said.

How could she explain that to Mrs. Lake? How could she tell this beloved teacher that the reason her parents didn't come to back-to-school night or chaperone field trips or even come by school at the end of the day to pick her up was that they both drank? It was too humiliating. And somehow she feared it was all her fault.

One by one the other students sat with their parents and Mrs. Lake and then returned to their desks. At last it was her turn. With a sinking feeling, she went to face Mrs. Lake. "I'm sorry," she wanted to say, "I told my parents...."

Mrs. Lake took the words out of her mouth. She stood up, folded up the two chairs parents usually sat in, and gestured to the girl to sit in the one chair left. "I know why your parents aren't here," she said. "But I just wanted to tell you all the good things I would have said to them." She went on to give the girl a glowing report.

It was a watershed moment. There would be years before she fully understood and years before she worked it out, but that moment that Mrs. Lake looked her in the eye and said, "I know why your parents aren't here..." was the beginning of healing for her. It was the first time an adult had ever acknowledged that she was not her parents and their problems were not her fault. It was the first glimpse she had of God's love for her. She saw it in Mrs. Lake's eyes.

What would have happened if Mrs. Lake hadn't spoken up? What prompted her to say just the right words? When the story was published, did she see it? (This must be the editor in me talking.) Did she get to find out—as Kevin Felts did—what an influence she'd had? "When you give alms, do not let your left hand know what your right hand is doing, so that your alms may be done in secret; and your Father who sees in secret will reward you," Jesus said (Matthew 6:3-4). When we act nobly it is all the nobler if we don't expect thanks or rewards for it. The same is true for our prayer life; the best part of it is done in secret. As Jesus says a few verses later: "Whenever you pray, go into your room and shut the door and pray to your Father who is in secret; and your Father who sees in secret will reward you" (Matthew 6:6).

Carol Burnett has often told a story about the man who helped her launch her career. She was a stage-struck drama student at UCLA and performed at a party with some friends at a professor's house in San Diego. Afterward a stranger came up to her, introduced himself, asked her what she hoped to do with her life. Go to New York and be an actress, Carol said. He wondered what was stopping her. She had to admit that she had barely enough money to get home, let alone cross the country. She grew up in a family where, at times, her mother, her grandmother and her sister had all been on welfare. The man said he would be happy to lend her the money to go to New York. A thousand dollars.

"Well, in those days I was pretty innocent," Carol admitted, "but not *that* innocent." She politely refused.

The man was insistent, and just to make clear that he meant well, he introduced Carol to his wife and made the offer again. He had only three conditions: If she were successful, that she repay the loan without interest in five years. That she never reveal his identity. And finally, if she accepted his offer, she was to pass the kindness along, to help some other person in similar circumstances when she was able to.

He told her to think it over and call him. He made the same offer to one of her fellow performers.

The next day, afraid she'd dreamed the whole thing, she called the number he had given, said she had decided to accept the conditions. Both her mother and grandmother had discouraged her, told her to have nothing to do with the man. But she was convinced he was sincere and that this was just the push she needed. She was being guided. If she didn't accept the offer and go to New York, she would regret it for the rest of her life.

She and a friend drove down to the man's office in San Diego, waited for half an hour, were ushered in, received their checks, cashed one of them so they would have enough money to pay for gas to get back to Los Angeles (after a banker's phone call to make sure the check wasn't a forgery), then drove home. Carol used a portion of the funds to get two teeth filled and one extracted—she hadn't been able to afford a dentist. Then she headed for New York.

It was a tough slog, hard to get work, hard to get noticed by agents, hard to get experience, but slowly, surely, she made her way. She let her secret benefactor know how she was doing, but heard very little from him. He continued to insist upon his anonymity and showed no desire to share the spotlight or take any credit.

Five years to the day that she had accepted the loan, Carol Burnett paid the man back. She has kept her pledge never to reveal his identity, throughout a career that went from Broadway to TV to films. As for his provision that she pass the kindness along to others—well, that's been her secret.

"Yes, and..." is what we say. God can be as quick to say it back to us: "Yes, and..." The answers become secrets we're meant to treasure, like Carol Burnett's. Or they become secrets we're meant to give away. "I find it just too hard to get silent and sit and pray," said a musician friend recently, someone who gives generously as a teacher and coach and choir director. "But don't you realize," I said impatiently, "you're praying all the time with all those kind deeds you do." "I'm never sure if it's God speaking or not when I think I get his guidance," another friend said, "and I'm tempted not to do anything." "But, but, but," I sputtered, "how can you know until you act on the guidance?" If you make some terrible mistake, God can help, but if you do nothing, he can do nothing.

We can hesitate, we can back up, we can look the other way, we can postpone, we can be locked in prayer paralysis, but why not take a chance and make a leap of faith? "Yes, and..." What a great way to live.

Epilogue

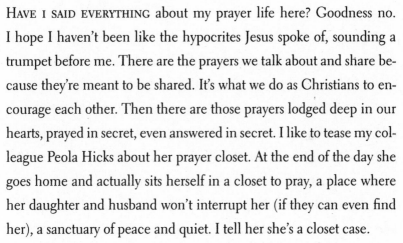

HAVE I SAID EVERYTHING about my prayer life here? Goodness no. I hope I haven't been like the hypocrites Jesus spoke of, sounding a trumpet before me. There are the prayers we talk about and share because they're meant to be shared. It's what we do as Christians to encourage each other. Then there are those prayers lodged deep in our hearts, prayed in secret, even answered in secret. I like to tease my colleague Peola Hicks about her prayer closet. At the end of the day she goes home and actually sits herself in a closet to pray, a place where her daughter and husband won't interrupt her (if they can even find her), a sanctuary of peace and quiet. I tell her she's a closet case.

But Peola has the right idea. I once heard of an alcoholic who would sneak her booze in the closet where she thought no one would notice (she was only fooling herself). When she got sober she went back to that same closet and made it her praying place. And her giving place. It was as though she were rewriting the story of her life, transforming a place of pain through prayer.

Are there really just ten prayers you can't live without? Aren't there more? I believe there are as many prayers as there are people in the world. God has made us all different, each of us unique. The sound I make when I cry out for help is going to be very different from the sound you make. Voices are so unique that on the phone most of us can identify a caller in a word or two, especially when it's someone we love. As a performer on stage I've always been struck by how just a cough or a clearing of the throat from someone I know and love is immediately identifiable. An actor friend said he could tell if his mother was in the audience by the jangle of the charm bracelet she always wore.

Our sounds, our being, our requests, our presence, our needs, our petitions, our exclamations of thanks and praise must be just as identifiable to God and as often anticipated.

Can you live without prayer? You can, but why would you? It's like asking why you would live without love and kindness and hope and faith and good friends and family members who spur you on. Why would you not take advantage of what's freely offered and extravagantly given? Be bold, be playful, be quick, be patient, be thoughtful and then forget all words and thoughts. Just be. Complain all you want about how hard it is but don't say, "I don't know how to pray." Of course you know how. You were made to pray.

Acknowledgments

NOT LONG AGO, David Morris and I took a long drive to visit John and Elizabeth Sherrill in Massachusetts and we talked a lot about what makes a book work. Would that this were such a book. David, pal, thanks for shepherding this tome through its genesis, creation and any afterlife it has.

My colleagues here at *Guideposts* magazine have to take credit—or blame—for what writer I've become. Edward Grinnan, master editor, has been not only a brilliant teacher over the years but a dear friend. Colleen Hughes reminds me again and again of the tenets of good storytelling. Amy Wong continues to coax me into writing clearly and economically. She also always makes me laugh. I'm especially grateful, Amy, for your eagle eye on this project.

Rebecca Maker offered much help in the generation of this project; Jon Woodhams sent me a crucial help-me-rethink-this-book memo; Marcus Silverman has been an important cheerleader and valued friend. Anne Adriance and Kelly Coyne, thanks for your research and your reminders of the daily place prayer has in people's lives. Kristine Cunningham and Lu Broas, thanks for your marketing genius and getting this book out the door. Anne Simpkinson and Nina Hammerling, you have helped me hone my thoughts again and again as editors of my blog, asking me the crucial question, "What exactly *do* you mean here?" Celeste McCauley, you have often saved me from myself. Mary Lou Carney, you are a great encourager; Nancy Galya, your chocolates and friendship give me fuel.

To our wonderful OurPrayer bunch and Outreach team, you guys really wrote the book on prayer and rewrite it day after day, helping millions. Some of you appear by name here (hi, Peola Hicks; hi, Lemuel Blackett); others of you appear anonymously. Thanks for your good work, Pablo Diaz, Mary Ann Gillespie, Angela Adams, Sandy Wisor, Kelly Mangold, Sabra Ciancanelli, Kathleen Ryan, Donna Marino. I'm with you every Monday morning along with those of us at the table in New York City, particularly our dear Sharon Azar whose experience of prayer is probably more various than anybody's — "with timbrel and dance" as the psalmist says. Rocco Martino, thanks for having confidence in me. May it not be misplaced. My agent, Emma Sweeney, has put my mind at ease too many times. Stacy and Brenda, you saw portions of this in an earlier draft and may you know that your appreciation gave me much courage.

My church, St. Michael's Episcopal, has prayed us through the ups and downs of life for thirty years, God bless you. To the vestry and staff, amen! My men's group buddies Scott, David and Jim, you've been incredible prayer companions over the years. And to the choir, forgive me for all those wrong notes in praise and chant.

My immediate family has endured patiently and heroically their inclusion in my storytelling, particularly my wife, Carol, who politely doesn't challenge my version of things, at least in print. To the boys, Will and Tim, you can do no wrong in my book. To the rest of our large clan, you are constant reiteration of Dad's many blessings.

Rick Thyne and Neil Warren, dear mentors, I hear your voices when I read Paul's passionate words of prayer. Arthur Caliandro, who died just as this book was going to press, Godspeed, you good and faithful servant and prayer friend. Finally, I would like to thank all those people who have told their stories in *Guideposts* and the editors who have made those stories happen. I couldn't improve upon your words.

Discover More Prayer Resources

To read more from Rick Hamlin, visit his blog guideposts.org/blogs/on-the-journey and on Facebook: Facebook.com/RickHamlinPray.

Visit OurPrayer.org, a community of faith seekers, to submit a prayer request or to sign up for OurPrayer Daily newsletter as well as find free e-books on prayer.

To learn more about other Guideposts publications, including the best-selling devotional *Daily Guideposts*, go to Guideposts.org.

Questions for Reflection

As you read *10 Prayers You Can't Live Without* by Rick Hamlin, you may find yourself thinking about how you might strengthen your prayers in your walk with God. The following questions can help you put your thinking into action. Consider writing in a journal, or perhaps you'll find these questions helpful for a group discussion about prayer. As you reflect, ask God to help you articulate your answers with clarity and in a way that will bring the greatest impact.

Chapter One: Pray at Mealtime

1. Was there a special prayer you recited before meals when you were a child? Write down or share a special memory associated with this prayer or with another grace you remember from your youth.

2. What does it mean to bless someone or something? Who has the ability to bless? Why do we refer to the good things in our lives as blessings?

3. How can we use prayer to combat the negative influences in our lives (bad news, critical colleagues, gloomy family members)? Can mealtime graces be about more than food?

4. C. S. Lewis said, "God likes food; he invented hunger." Why do you suppose that is? How are we to honor our God-given need to eat?

Chapter Two: Prayer as Conversation

1. If you could use only ten words to describe prayer, what would those words be? Has your idea of prayer changed as you matured in your faith?

2. Do you have a special designated place where you pray? Do you think this is important? Why or why not?

3. How do you incorporate prayer into your daily routine? What would you say to those who say they do not have time to pray?

Chapter Three: Pray for Others

1. How important do you think it is to pray for other people? Do you believe our prayers have any real impact on their lives?

2. Do you have a prayer list or other aid (such as candles, beads, etc.) that you use to help you remember the ones you want to pray for? When you pray for your loved ones, what do you ask God for? How do you know God is listening to your requests?

3. Have you ever prayed for a stranger? What prompted your action? How did you feel afterward?

4. What happens when you don't get what you asked for? What are the benefits of praying for other people?

Chapter Four: Pray the Lord's Prayer

1. What is your earliest memory of praying the Lord's Prayer? How often do you pray it? Do you think it is important to pray it every day? Why or why not?

2. Do you think Jesus' disciples were surprised by this simple prayer? How did it differ from the way the Pharisees and other religious leaders of the day offered up their prayers? Can a short prayer be as effective as a long one?

3. Why is this prayer of Jesus spoken in the plural (give *us*, forgive *us*, lead *us*)? Are Christians alone in their efforts to live for God? How

can you be a support to other Christians? How does the Lord's Prayer bind us together?

Chapter Five: Praying for Forgiveness

1. Write down or share a time when someone hurt your feelings or made you angry. How did you feel? What did you do? What do you think Jesus would have done in that same situation?

2. Why do we find it so hard to forgive each other? How do you feel when you pray, "Forgive us our trespasses as we forgive those who trespass against us"?

3. Can you forgive but not forget? What dangers—spiritual, emotional, physical—are involved with holding on to old hurts?

4. Recall a time when you had to ask someone to forgive you. Is it easier to forgive or to ask for forgiveness?

Chapter Six: Pray through a Crisis

1. Has there ever been a time in your life when something so terrible happened to you that all you wanted to do was shout "No!"? How do you think God feels when we are too distraught even to pray? How does the Holy Spirit help us in times such as these?

2. How would you explain the nature of God to someone who had had no exposure to religious thought of any kind? Do you believe God gets angry? At what? What is God's most distinguishing, consistent character trait?

3. Why do bad things happen to good people? Is God able to identify with our pain? Why or why not?

4. Is it ever okay to be angry with God? Have you ever been angry with God? Is there a way to constructively use that anger? How do

we resolve feelings of anger or abandonment by God? How can Scripture help us in this?

Chapter Seven: Sing Your Prayer

1. What role has music played in your faith journey? Write down or share a favorite music-related memory from your past.

2. Look up the words *song* and *sing* in a Bible concordance. Read out loud Scripture related to singing.

3. Do you have a favorite hymn? What about it speaks to your heart and mind? Sing it or read it out loud.

4. Can songs serve as prayers? How? What does it mean to praise God? How do songs help us do this?

Chapter Eight: A Classic Prayer to Focus Your Thoughts

1. Have you used the "Jesus Prayer" as part of your devotional life? If so, share your experience with it. How could this prayer keep you focused on God throughout the day?

2. Why do you think so many people find this prayer to be powerful and effective? What is the prayer asking? Why is it important to pray this often?

3. Write down or share a time when God asked you to step out of your comfort zone in order to serve God. What gave you the courage to follow through? What feelings surface when you think about surrendering your life completely to God's will?

Chapter Nine: Pray in Thanksgiving at All Times

1. Gratitude is one of the easiest means of prayer. Why is that? On a scale of one to ten (ten being the highest), how grateful are you on a daily basis? What could you do to improve this score?

2. Have you ever kept a gratitude journal? For the next week, try writing down three things every day for which you're grateful. Then discuss the process with your study group. Was this exercise easy? Difficult? Were you surprised at any of the things you wrote down? Did keeping this journal make you more aware of God's blessings? Is it something you would consider continuing to do?

3. Do you spend more time asking God for things you want or thanking God for things God has given you? How do you think God feels about your answer?

4. The Bible commands us to "give thanks in all circumstances" (1 Thessalonians 5:18). How is this possible? Do you know anyone who continually displays an "attitude of gratitude"?

Chapter Ten: Pray Yes

1. When you are faced with a new opportunity or challenge, are you more apt to respond with "yes" or "no"? Why?

2. Write down or share a time when you believe God was using you as an answer to someone's prayer, a time when your "yes" helped build God's kingdom on earth. How do you feel looking back on those events? How has that experience impacted your own spiritual walk?

3. Do you think of prayer as active or passive? Why?

4. Hope is one of the greatest gifts we can give each other. Recall a time when someone helped move you out of despair and hopelessness. What are some practical, specific ways you can help bring hope into your home, your church, your community, your world?